UPPER INTERMEDIATE

Language
LEADER
TEACHER'S BOOK
and Test Master CD-ROM

David Albery

CONTENTS

INTRODUCTION

To the teacher: introduction by the authors

We are pleased to welcome you to this new course: *Language Leader*. In this introduction we outline some of our ideas about the course. We have done our very best to write a series of books that teachers (and students!) will enjoy using, and we very much hope that, although we may be physically far apart, we share with you – as teachers – a common set of beliefs and practices, and a common sense of purpose.

Approach

Language Leader is an international course with a global focus, and is aimed at citizens of the 21st century world – people who cross (and communicate across) national borders. We believe that students are curious about the modern world, and that this course engages with it. *Language Leader* enables students to be better informed and helps them understand and express their ideas and feelings about the world.

We believe it is important to offer students stimulating topics that engage their interest and increase their motivation for learning. We have made use of our diverse backgrounds, personalities and interests as authors, in the hope of providing students with a rich variety of different topics. Each unit contains an 'umbrella topic' with a different subtopic in each lesson, allowing us to explore a range of issues within a single topic and also to recycle vocabulary. We think that the approach to the topics in the course will challenge students and allow them to develop their powers of expression and analysis and their critical thinking skills. *Language Leader* reflects our belief that language learning is not merely a form of training, but should be situated in a broader educational context. We hope that students who use the series will not only learn English, but – through English – will also learn interesting things about the world and about themselves. Perhaps, sometimes, they may not even be aware that they are actually learning English!

Language Leader is not based on one particular teaching 'philosophy' or methodology, but is informed by sound pedagogical principles, plus an intuitive sense – the result of many years' experience – of what works in the classroom. Having said this, we use a broadly communicative methodology and a text and task-based approach. Pair and group work is an important part of the learning process. The Common European Framework has informed many of the speaking activities.

Language development

Throughout the units, there is careful development and logical staging of new language, as well as substantial recycling of previous language, enabling students to move forward rapidly. The Review, Language Reference and Extra Practice sections consolidate and extend students' learning.

The texts in *Language Leader* not only provide context for grammar and vocabulary but systematically develop students' reading and listening skills. The reading texts are authentic or semi-authentic, or at lower levels based on real sources, and are taken from a variety of genres (for example, newspapers, magazines, literature and publicity materials). Listening skills are also developed throughout the course. Each unit has a number of listening activities and there is a wide variety of different listening texts (for example, radio programmes, conversations, interviews, talks and lectures), as well as a varied range of activity types.

There is considerable variety in the length of these reading and listening texts: some are relatively short, but *Language Leader* also offers students an opportunity to deal – in a supported way – with some longer texts. Students who suddenly find themselves in an English-speaking environment – whether in their home country or abroad – often have difficulty with the large quantities of spoken and written English that they are exposed to. This course helps them to build up their confidence in handling extended amounts of English. In addition, many of the reading and listening exercises are based on exam-type questions.

There are constant opportunities throughout the course for students to improve their speaking skills, with speaking exercises in every unit. Students can comment on the topics and discuss the issues that arise, as well as talk about more personal experiences and knowledge, through a variety of exercises, such as information gaps, personalised question and answer activities, role plays and debates.

The Scenario lessons are, we believe, an important communicative feature of *Language Leader*. Every unit includes a Scenario lesson, devoted to extended speaking practice in a real-life situation. Information has to be processed – and decisions made – leading to a specific outcome. Students are given language support to carry out the task.

The course covers all the key grammar points. These points are all contextualised and students are generally encouraged to analyse and understand grammar through an inductive approach with reference to examples in the texts. The grammar is practised in motivating and interesting activities. The Language reference and Extra practice section at the back of the book extends students' knowledge of grammar and provides essential further practice. It can be used in the class or for independent study at home.

Lack of vocabulary is one of the main problems many students face. Consequently, students struggle to make sense of texts and express themselves. They need more words. To address this, *Language Leader* has a wide range of vocabulary, and students are able to acquire and use this vocabulary through contextualisation and recycling.

Writing skills and study skills

Writing in English has become increasingly important, but is often students' weakest skill and something that they don't really enjoy. Even with very able students, it often drags down their scores in examinations in which they would otherwise do well. We consider, however, that writing is also a skill in which – with a little help – students can make significant progress. *Language*

Leader has a page in every unit that is devoted to the development of writing skills, and there are also further writing activities throughout the course. Because of the systematic approach to the development of writing skills in the course, students should be able to make real progress in their writing, and derive great satisfaction from this. Again, there is wide variety in the length and type of tasks. We place considerable emphasis, even at the lower levels, on discourse features of written English, with frequent analysis of text models and plenty of writing practice at both paragraph and text level. In addition, we have included activities designed to encourage students to be rigorous in checking their own writing.

Each unit also includes a Study skills page, which aims to encourage students to be independent learners with a high level of self-awareness. The skills that we cover in this section are not just for students who are on educational courses in schools, colleges and universities; they are also transferable skills which will be useful to students in many different contexts, including their careers and personal lives.

Flexibility

Of course, we hope that you will use every page in the book! But the *Language Leader* format deliberately lends itself to different teaching situations and can be adapted easily depending on the length and type of course you are teaching.

To conclude, we trust that you and your students will find *Language Leader* interesting, motivating and enjoyable. We also hope that it will meet your students' needs as well as providing something new. We welcome your comments on the course and hope to have the pleasure of meeting you in the future!

David Cotton, David Falvey, Simon Kent (Intermediate and Upper Intermediate)
Gareth Rees, Ian Lebeau (Elementary and Pre-intermediate)

Language Leader: course description

Language Leader is a general English series for adults and young adults. The course has a topic-based multi-strand syllabus which includes comprehensive work on grammar, vocabulary, pronunciation and integrated skills, where strong emphasis is placed on reading, writing and study skills as well as speaking and listening. With its purposeful approach *Language Leader* is particularly suitable for general English students working towards exams, and those learners who may go on to, or are already in, further education.

Language Leader has four levels and takes learners from Elementary to Upper Intermediate; each level offers 90–120 hours of work.

Coursebook

The twelve Coursebook units are divided into double-page lessons, each with a clear aim, which are designed to make the course flexible and easy-to-use.

- **Introductory lesson:** in *Language Leader Upper Intermediate* the first spread is where the unit topic is presented with core vocabulary and lexis through reading and listening texts, and where students discuss some of the themes of the unit and activate any previous knowledge and vocabulary.

- **Input lessons:** there are two input lessons in each unit. Here, new language is presented through informative texts with a balanced mix of grammar, vocabulary, pronunciation and skills work.

- **Scenario:** in the fourth lesson, learners integrate and practise the language presented in the previous lessons through a communicative task. This major speaking activity is carefully staged; the Key language section gives extra support by developing functional exponents and the Other useful phrases boxes provide helpful fixed phrases.

- **Study and Writing Skills:** the fifth lesson consists of a Study skills section, followed by Writing skills, which helps students to write a particular text type.

Language Leader Coursebook also features the following:

- **Review:** the Review spreads occur after every three units; these provide mixed practice for ongoing revision. The Language check section is a quick self-edit exercise and Look back encourages reflection on the previous units.

- **Language reference/ Extra practice:** this section consists of one cross-referenced spread for each unit. The left-hand page includes a grammar summary for the unit, plus reference lists for Key language and Vocabulary. The right-hand page provides extra practice for consolidation.

CD-ROM

- This component is attached to the back of the Coursebook.

- It provides extra practice and self-assessment for the learners with a variety of exercises, including listening. With the help of the Language Reference and the Dictionary, the CD-ROM helps learners develop their learning skills. The unique Writing section includes models for different writing tasks from everyday notes to academic essays.

Class CDs

- These provide all the recorded material from the Coursebook.

Workbook

- This contains further practice of areas covered in the corresponding units of the Coursebook and introduces Extra vocabulary to build lexis in the topic area.

- To help the development of language skills, useful strategies are introduced through Read better and Listen better boxes.

- In each unit there is a Translation exercise for students to compare English with their L1, and Dictation exercises provide more listening and writing.

INTRODUCTION

Workbook CD

- Attached to the back of the Workbook, the CD contains all the recorded material for extra practice.

Teacher's Book

- This provides all the support teachers need from detailed teaching notes to extra photocopiable activities.
- There are **warning points** to alert teachers about possible problem areas as well as **teaching tips** to help them. Taking into account teachers' busy schedules, the Teacher's Book notes are designed as lesson plans, with ideas for **extension** and **adjustment,** which are especially useful for mixed ability groups.

 warning points   extension

teaching tips   adjustment

Test Master CD-ROM

- Attached to the back of the Teacher's Book, the Test Master CD-ROM is an invaluable resource to accompany *Language Leader*. The tests are based strictly on the content of the Coursebooks, providing a fair measure of students' progress.
- The audio files for the listening tests are conveniently located on the same CD-ROM.
- The tests can be printed out and used as they are, or can be adapted using Microsoft® Word to edit them to suit different teaching situations.
- The Test Master CD-ROM contains the following:
  - Unit Tests (one 'A' and one 'B' test for each unit)
  - Progress Tests (one 'A' and one 'B' test for every three units plus additional optional speaking and writing tests)
  - Final Test (one 'A' and one 'B' version)

Syllabus areas

- **Topics:** to motivate learners the units are based on up-to-date topics of international interest or new angles on familiar subjects. Themes have been carefully chosen to engage the learners and to provide a springboard for their own ideas and communicative needs.
- **Grammar:** *Language Leader* follows an established syllabus progression and learners are actively involved in developing their knowledge of grammar. The Grammar sections in the input lessons focus on the main language points presented through the texts and learners are encouraged to work out the rules for themselves. They are supported by the Grammar tip boxes and cross-referred to the corresponding Language reference and Extra practice pages at the back of the book for reinforcement.
- **Vocabulary:** vocabulary input is derived from the unit topics and texts, allowing the teacher to build on words and phrases the students already know to create lexical sets. Additional attention is paid to word building and lexical patterns. The vocabulary is recycled through the speaking activities in each unit, revised in the Review lesson and Extra practice and practised further in the Workbook.

- **Pronunciation:** regular pronunciation sections are integrated with the presentation of new language or included on the Scenario spread as part of the communicative task. The pronunciation syllabus covers word and sentence stress, difficult sounds, contractions and intonation.
- **Reading:** there is a wide range of reading material in *Language Leader* and a variety of exercise types developing the reading skills. The informative texts have been chosen for their interest and to provide a context for the grammar and vocabulary items being studied. The texts are based on real-life sources (magazines, websites, etc) and related activities include comprehension, vocabulary and reading sub-skills work.
- **Listening:** students are given many opportunities to develop a wide range of listening skills in *Language Leader,* both in terms of text types and activity types (e.g. checking predictions, table and note-completion). There is more listening practice in the Workbooks and CD-ROMs to further build the learners' confidence.
- **Speaking:** opportunities for oral practice of language and freer discussion appear regularly in every lesson. There is at least one explicit speaking activity per lesson and a major communicative task in the Scenario lesson.
- **Writing:** the writing syllabus introduces students to different genres and develops students' writing through analysis of models and practice in producing different text styles.
- **Study skills:** a systematic approach to developing study skills fosters independent dictionary use, encourages students to take notes effectively and gives them help in approaching exams and learning outside the classroom.

External organisations and link to examinations

- **Common European Framework of Reference:** the ethos of the CEFR is reflected throughout *Language Leader* in a variety of ways. For example, the outcomes of the Scenario lessons reflect the 'Can do' descriptors and help students use the language they have learnt effectively. Also, great emphasis is placed on the development of independent learning across the course including the extensive work on study skills, good study habits and self-assessment. For more information on *Language Leader* and the CEFR see the website www.pearsonlongman.com/languageleader.
- **Bologna Process:** as part of this initiative to harmonise tertiary education, many institutions now offer credit-bearing English language programmes. *Language Leader* reflects the values of the Bologna Process with its emphasis on individual responsibility for learning.
- **Link to examinations:** ELT examination exercise-types occur regularly throughout *Language Leader* to help prepare students for a range of common exams (IELTS in particular). The website provides grids correlating *Language Leader* to international ELT exams.

INTRODUCTION

How a unit works (Upper Intermediate)

Introductory lesson

The contents of each unit are clearly labelled at the top of the opening page.

Stimulating topic-related quotation to engage learners.

Listening exercises guide students through audio texts and encourage different styles of listening.

Speaking exercises get students talking about the topic.

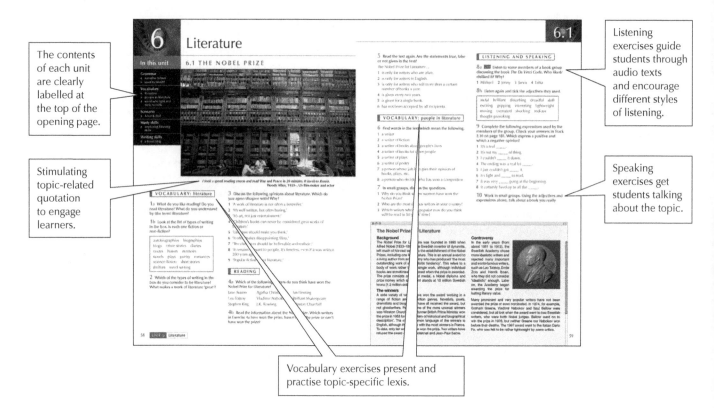

Vocabulary exercises present and practise topic-specific lexis.

Input lesson (1)

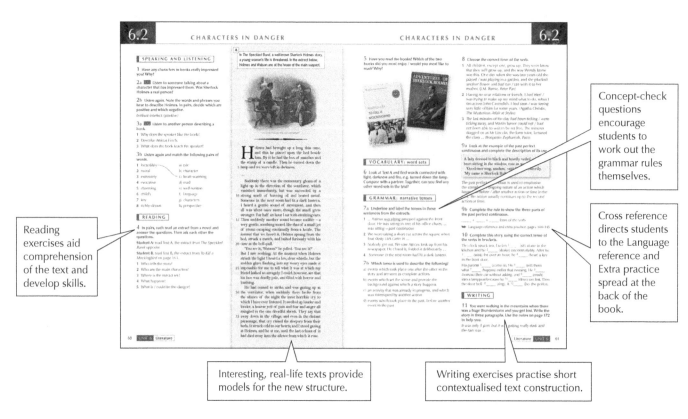

Concept-check questions encourage students to work out the grammar rules themselves.

Cross reference directs students to the Language reference and Extra practice spread at the back of the book.

Reading exercises aid comprehension of the text and develop skills.

Interesting, real-life texts provide models for the new structure.

Writing exercises practise short contextualised text construction.

INTRODUCTION

Input lesson (2)

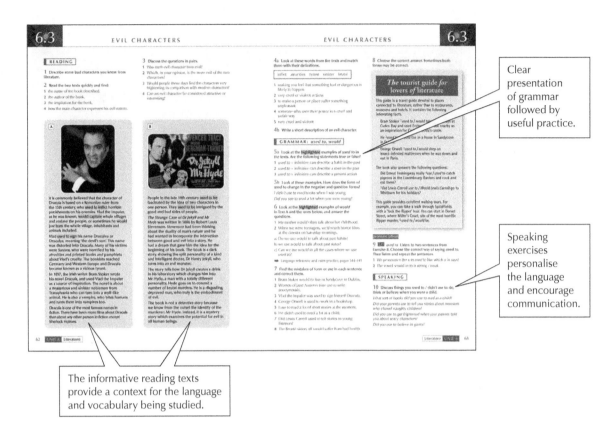

Clear presentation of grammar followed by useful practice.

Speaking exercises personalise the language and encourage communication.

The informative reading texts provide a context for the language and vocabulary being studied.

Scenario

Scenario lessons practise Key language from the unit through a meaningful final task.

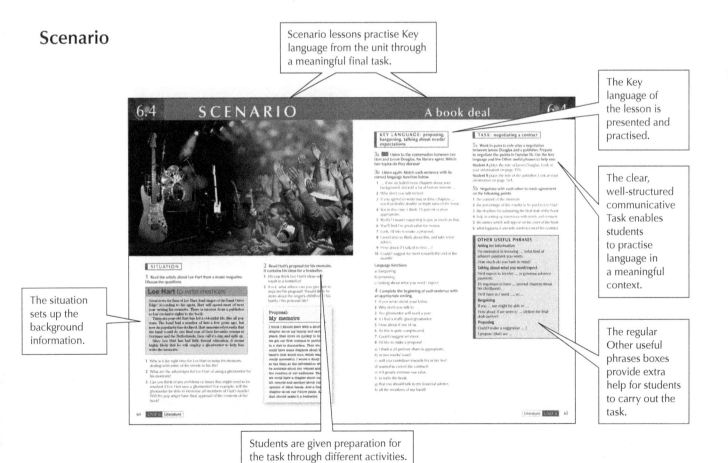

The Key language of the lesson is presented and practised.

The clear, well-structured communicative Task enables students to practise language in a meaningful context.

The situation sets up the background information.

The regular Other useful phrases boxes provide extra help for students to carry out the task.

Students are given preparation for the task through different activities.

Study and writing skills

Writing Skills focus on a different genre of writing in each unit.

The Study skills section develops students' ability to work on their own and in the classroom environment.

Students are given real life tasks.

Students are given model texts to follow and analyse.

Students are given a guided writing task

Other sections
Review

Review lessons occur after every three units; they revise and consolidate the Grammar, Vocabulary and Key language from the previous units.

Students are encouraged to check and comment on their own learning, and reflect on what they have learned.

Language reference / Extra practice

There is one Language reference and Extra practice spread for each unit at the back of the book.

Grammar is cross-referenced to separate grammar points in each unit.

Extra practice exercises for the Grammar, Key language and Vocabulary studied in the unit.

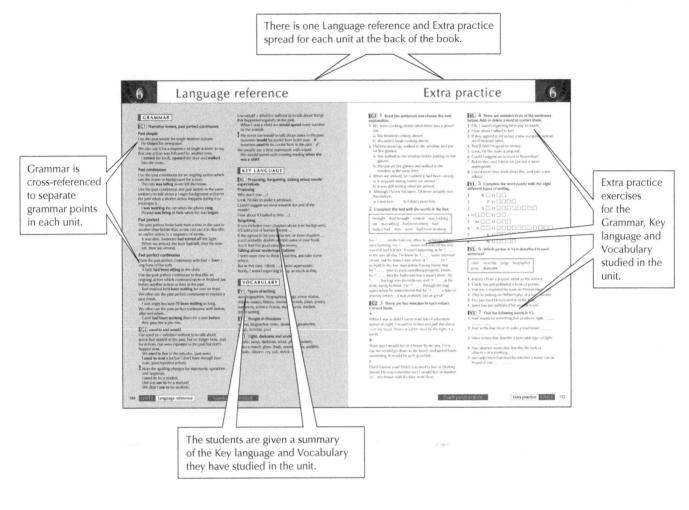

The students are given a summary of the Key language and Vocabulary they have studied in the unit.

Workbook spread

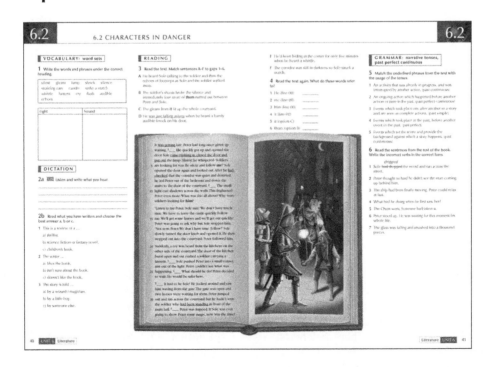

Communication

1.1 GREAT COMMUNICATORS

Lesson topic and staging

This lesson looks at what makes a good communicator. Students discuss when and who they communicate with and then focus on vocabulary to describe a good communicator. Next, students listen to people talking about what makes a good communicator. They then read and listen to speeches by three famous people and decide the topic, the function and various features of the speeches before practising one themselves. Finally, students write the beginning to a speech of their own.

Objectives

By the end of the lesson, students should have:

- expanded their vocabulary related to good communicators
- read and listened to three speeches to extract the function, specific information and different features of effective speech making
- written the beginning to a speech of their own
- practised giving part of a speech with a focus on where speakers pause and what words they emphasise.

Timings

If short of time, you could drop exercise 4 on page 6. Alternatively, set writing exercise 10 on page 7 for homework and ask students to give their speech in the next lesson. A possible lesson break would be after exercise 4 on page 6.

WARM-UP

This activity introduces the topic of communication by looking at different non-verbal ways of expressing meaning.

- Lead in by asking students to look at the photo on page 6. Elicit that this shows a whale and that many species of whales communicate by 'singing'.
- Then write the following words on the board: *shout, sigh, mutter, wave, yawn, nod, clap, laugh*.
- Focus students on *laugh* and elicit a situation in which people do this and what they are generally communicating (i.e. what kind of message they are trying to send to other people) when they do it. For example, they are showing others they find something funny, they are showing they are nervous, they are encouraging someone to say more, etc.

- Then put students into pairs or small groups and tell them to think of a situation for all the other words. Students can also include how close the speakers are (both emotionally and physically) in each situation they describe. The first group to finish wins.
- Ask different groups for a situation for each word.

Peter Drucker quote:
This quote means that the most important skill of a good communicator is to be aware of and interpret signals other than the actual words someone uses in order to understand their meaning. These signals might include body language, facial expressions, pauses, changes in voice tone, etc.

SPEAKING AND VOCABULARY

1 Explain to students that they are going to discuss communication in their everyday lives and ask two or three to try to remember how many people they have communicated with today.

- Give students a short time to read the questions and then put them in small groups (maximum four students) for the discussion.
- While they are speaking, listen to find out if students use any of the vocabulary in exercise 2a.
- For feedback, ask a few students to give one or two answers in open class.

> Answers will depend on students' opinions.

2a If students used any of the vocabulary in the box during their discussion in exercise 1, ask those students to repeat what was said earlier and show the class that this word is in the box.

- Students work individually to complete the gaps in sentences 1–12, using their dictionaries if necessary.
- Ask students to compare with a partner before you check answers with the class. Point out collocations such as *suffer from nerves*, *a good sense of humour*, and *maintain eye contact*.
- Finally, ask students if they think any of this vocabulary applies to the communicator they talked about in exercise 1, question 2.

> 1 listener; 2 language; 3 rambler; 4 nerves;
> 5 cultures; 6 vocabulary; 7 humour; 8 appearance;
> 9 eye; 10 pace; 11 charisma; 12 digressions

For further practice, ask students to do exercise V1 5 on page 135 in the Language reference.

2b Give students two minutes to read the sentences again and decide if they would like to add other ideas.

- Then put them into small groups to discuss if they agree or disagree with each sentence in 2a. For continuity, keep students in the same groups as exercise 1. Tell them to give reasons for their opinions and to disagree with each other if necessary.

- Finally, ask each group if there were any sentences they all agreed or disagreed with.

> Answers will depend on students' opinions.

Put students in small groups and tell them to decide which four sentences are most important and which four are least important for a good communicator. Then ask them to present their ideas to the rest of the class and justify their answers. Encourage other groups to ask questions and disagree if necessary.

LISTENING

3 Read through the instructions with the class and check students understand *digress*, *ramble* (the verbs of *digression* and *rambler*, from exercise 2), and *clarify* (make something clearer).

- Pause the track after each speaker to give students time to think and note their answer.

- Ask students to compare with a partner and monitor to check how many they have got right. If necessary, play the track again before you check answers with the class.

- To follow up, ask students if they agree or disagree with the speakers' opinions.

> **1** b); **2** g); **3** c); **4** e); **5** d); **6** a); **7** f) (Note: students may answer **4** f) and **7** e). Both answers are acceptable.)

Track 1.2
1 The most important thing for me is that someone doesn't talk in a confused and boring way. I can't stand people who go on and on for ages without saying anything at all. Good communicators stick to the point and don't lose their train of thought.
2 I hate it when people stop me speaking all the time when I'm trying to tell them something. You know – just let me finish!
3 I think good communicators anticipate when a listener doesn't understand something – you know, if they use an unfamiliar word or phrase, or some kind of jargon, they give an example of what they mean.
4 Well, for me, good communicators don't make things complicated or difficult to understand for their listener. They talk in a logical way, you know, so what they say is easy to follow.

---

5 I don't like it when people get off the point and start talking about an unrelated subject, and don't tell you that's what they're doing. I find it really annoying when someone starts doing it and you don't know what they are talking about. Some people do it all the time.
6 The key point for me is simple – do they actually pay attention to what someone else is saying or, are they already thinking about what they want to say?
7 I think the best communicators are people who make things easy to understand by giving reasons – they don't assume too much knowledge. I hate people who think you know what they are talking about all the time.

4 Use the follow-up discussion from exercise 3 as a lead in to this activity.

- Give students three minutes to think about their answers to the questions (1–5) and then put them in pairs or small groups to discuss their ideas.

- For feedback, ask one or two groups for their ideas.

To help prepare students for writing part of a speech of their own later in the lesson, focus the class on question 4 and elicit as many ideas as possible. Ask students to note these down and use some of them when they do exercise 10 on page 7.

READING

5a Explain that students are going to read and listen to three famous speeches.

- Do the first question as a whole class and elicit as many great public speakers as possible.

- Then focus students on the photos on page 7 and put them in pairs or small groups to discuss the second question.

- In feedback, elicit the name of each person and write a few facts about each one on the board. Use the background information below if necessary.

> **A** Margaret Thatcher; **B** John F. Kennedy; **C** Martin Luther King Jnr

5b Give students a maximum of four minutes to read the texts and decide who gave each speech.

- In feedback, use the background information below to provide more information about each speech.

> **1** John F. Kennedy; **2** Martin Luther King Jnr; **3** Margaret Thatcher

John F. (Fitzgerald) Kennedy (1917–1963) was the 35th President of the United States, serving from 1961 until his assassination in 1963. This is an extract from Kennedy's inaugural address on becoming US President in 1961.

Martin Luther King Jnr (1929–1968) was one of the main leaders of the American civil rights movement which demanded equal rights for Afro-Americans in the US. This speech was delivered during the 1963 March on Washington and the quote he used is from the American Declaration of Independence. In 1964, King became the youngest person to receive the Nobel Peace Prize. He was assassinated in 1968.

Margaret Thatcher (born 1925) was the first, and to date the only, woman to hold the post of British Prime Minister. This speech was delivered when she first took office in 1979. No. 10 refers to number 10 Downing Street, the official residence of the British Prime Minister.

6 Tell students to choose a topic for each speech without reading the texts again. Check answers with the class.

> 1 b); 2 c); 3 g)

7a Tell students to try to do this activity without reading the texts again. If they find this difficult, tell students to skim the texts quickly.

- Ask students to compare with a partner before you check answers with the class.

> 1 c); 2 b); 3 d)

7b As an example, use speech 2 to elicit an example of repetition (I have a dream).

- Allow five minutes for students to do this activity individually, then compare their answers with a partner before you check with the class.

- ☀ If possible reproduce the texts so that the whole class can see them (perhaps on the Interactive Whiteboard or an OHP). When you check answers with the class, mark each text to show where the examples are.

> a) Text 1: my fellow … ask not what … (final two paragraphs); Text 2: I have a dream (beginning of each paragraph); Text 3: where there is …, may we bring (final 4 lines). b) Text 1: the energy, the faith, the devotion (paragraph one). c) Text 1: shrink from/welcome (paragraph one); Text 2: former slaves/former slave owners (paragraph two), injustice/justice, oppression/freedom (paragraph three), color of their skin/content of their character (paragraph four); Text 3: discord/harmony, error/truth, doubt/faith, despair/hope (final 4 lines). d) Text 2: We hold these truths to be self-evident, that all men are created equal (paragraph one); Text 3: Where there is discord … may we bring hope (final 4 lines).

8 Put students in pairs or small groups to briefly discuss this question and then elicit ideas from the class.

> Answers depend on students' own opinions.

9a Before students listen, elicit why a speech might be impressive and write ideas on the board.

- Play the track, pausing briefly after each speech to give students time to write notes. Students can refer to the ideas on the board if necessary.

- Ask students to compare with a partner before you elicit ideas from the class.

9b Tell students to write // to show the pauses and to underline the emphasised words in the text on page 7.

- Pause the track after each speech and ask students to compare with a partner before playing the next.

- Check answers with the whole class before you ask students to practise saying one of the speeches.

- Put students in pairs to practise saying the speech because they may find it intimidating in open class.

- ☀ If possible reproduce the texts so that the whole class can see them (perhaps on the Interactive Whiteboard or an OHP). When you check answers with the class, mark each text to show where pauses and emphases are.

WRITING

10 Emphasise that students should only write the beginning of the speech (about 150 words). Go through the situations with the class – or ask them to suggest situations.

- Re-elicit the features of a good speech from exercise 7b (repetition, contrast, etc.).

- Allow 20 minutes for students to write. Monitor to help with vocabulary and make suggestions.

- Put students in pairs to deliver their speech to each other, or if they are confident, ask them to deliver their speeches to the whole class.

- While they are speaking, note any improvements they could make in delivery (e.g. pauses, emphasis) and go through these when all the speeches are finished.

- Take the speeches in for marking, paying particular attention to the features covered in exercise 7b.

HOMEWORK OPTIONS

Students do the exercises on page 4 of the Workbook.

Students use the Internet to research one of the great speakers from this lesson (or choose a different great speaker) and then write the beginning of a speech about this person.

Students do exercise V1 5 on page 135 in the Language reference.

1.2 IMPROVING COMMUNICATION

Lesson topic and staging

This lesson looks at ways of improving how you communicate in different situations. Students read a leaflet about a course on how to communicate better and then learn a set of idioms related to communication. Next, students focus on and practise using grammar contextualised in the leaflet: the continuous aspect. Finally, students use the continuous aspect to talk about current trends in communication.

Objectives

By the end of the lesson, students should have:

- read a leaflet and extracted specific information
- expanded their range of idioms related to communication
- revised and extended their understanding of the continuous aspect
- used the continuous aspect in a group speaking activity.

Timings

If short of time, you could drop exercise 5a on page 9 and set it for homework, and then discuss the questions in exercise 5b in the following lesson. A possible lesson break would be after exercise 4b or 5b on page 9.

This activity introduces the topic of communicating in different situations and how students feel about it.

- Ask students if they generally find it easy to speak to other people and elicit that it depends on the situation.
- Write the following situations on the board: *to an individual stranger at a party, to an individual student in class, to a teacher, to a police officer, to a stranger on the phone, to ask a stranger to do something for you, to ask someone you know if you could borrow a large sum of money, to a doctor when you're feeling ill.*
- Ask students to rank the situations from most to least stressful and then put them in pairs to compare.
- Finally, ask students if they agreed on the most and least stressful situations and, if possible, get the class to agree on the most stressful situation.

1a If you used the Warm-up activity, use this as a lead in to the three situations in this exercise.

- Put students in groups to discuss the situations and tell them to say why they feel the way they do.
- In feedback, ask two or three groups how they feel about each situation and elicit reasons.

1b Do this activity as a whole class and elicit advice to the board.

> Answers depend on students' own opinions.

2 Give students one minute to read the leaflet and refer them to ideas from exercise 1b on the board.

- Tell students not to worry about unknown vocabulary at this stage.
- Ask students to briefly compare with a partner before you check answers with the class.

> Answers depends on students' ideas in exercise 1b.

3 Tell students to read the five extracts before they read the leaflet again and to use their dictionaries for unknown vocabulary, but not to worry about *get a word in edgeways* because this will be covered in exercise 5a.

- Ask students to briefly compare with a partner before you check answers with the class.

> Extract A = Week 3; Extract B = Week 11; Extract C = Week 5; Extract D = Week 1; Extract E = Week 2

4a Ask students to read the statements and check they understand *speech impediment* (a problem when speaking, e.g. a *stammer* – demonstrate a stammer, but be careful not to offend anyone in your class), *interact* (communicate with and respond to other people), and *be yourself* (behave naturally).

- Ask students to try to decide if the statements are true or false before they read the leaflet again.
- Then give students four minutes to re-read the leaflet to check their ideas and answer any statements they couldn't do in the previous stage.
- Ask students to compare with a partner before you check answers with the class.

> **1** False; **2** False; **3** False; **4** True; **5** True; **6** False (the word 'not' makes this false); **7** True

4b Give students two minutes to think about these questions and then put them into pairs or small groups to discuss. Encourage them to say why they think they're good at or need to develop some skills.

- To follow up, ask students if this is a course they'd be interested in doing and why.

5a Elicit/tell students that idioms may often have a meaning that is not conveyed by individual words.

- If students have good English/English dictionaries, you could ask them to use these to check their answers. Tell them to decide which are the key words in the idioms to help them find the entry.

- Students work individually before comparing their answers with a partner. If they don't know an idiom and aren't using dictionaries, tell them to guess.
- Go through the answers with the class.

> **1** f); **2** g); **3** d); **4** c); **5** b); **6** a); **7** e)

5b Give students a minute to think about their answers before putting them in pairs to discuss.

- Encourage them to ask each other questions to find out as much information as possible.
- For feedback, ask students for the most interesting thing they heard in question 4, if they agreed on question 1, and if they had similar experiences in questions 2 and 3.

For further practice, ask students to do exercise V2,3 6 on page 135 in the Language reference.

GRAMMAR: the continuous aspect

6a Elicit how the continuous aspect is formed (*be* + verb *-ing*) and any uses the students already know.

- Tell students to find the four examples and underline them in the texts. (Note: the fourth example is in the handout extracts [extract E].)
- Put students in pairs to try to decide the time frame for each example (e.g. in progress, changing, etc.) before they look at exercise 6b.

6b Students do this activity individually and then compare their answers with their partner from exercise 6a.

- If necessary, refer students to the Language reference on page 134.
- Go through answers with the class and if necessary elicit/give another example of the continuous aspect for each use.
- Finally, ask students to read the sentence on the simple aspect and elicit/give an example for each use.

> The following words/phrases should be ticked: temporary; unfinished; in progress; changing.

(!) Students may be confused by *complete*. In a sense, the continuous aspect can be used for complete actions, e.g. 'I was living in Paris up until 1985'. In this case, the action was *in progress* up the point it was *completed*.

7 Keep students in the same pairs as for exercise 6a and 6b. Students will benefit from having to think through their answers with another student so don't interrupt or prompt too much while they're working. Tell students to refer to exercises 6a and 6b, and the Language reference on page 134 if they need help.

- Check answers with the class and finally read through the Grammar Tip, eliciting the term *state verbs*.

> **1 a)** present continuous: in progress; **b)** present simple: habitual; **2 a)** present simple: permanent; **b)** present continuous: temporary/in progress; **3 a)** past simple: complete; **b)** past continuous: unfinished and in progress (during the flight)

8 Keep students in the same pairs, following the same procedure as in exercise 7.

- Check answers with the class and elicit why the sentences are wrong.

> **1** Wrong: *agree* is a state verb; **2** Correct; **3** Correct; **4** Wrong: the action is temporary; **5** Wrong: *know* is a state verb; **6** Wrong: the word *look* shows this action is happening now, in progress; **7** Correct; **8** Wrong: *these days* shows that the situation is changing, the trend is in progress.

For further practice, ask students to do exercises G1 1 and G2 2 on page 135 in the Language reference.

SPEAKING

9 To lead in, remind students of sentence 8 in exercise 8 which shows a changing situation, a trend in progress.

- Give students individually a few minutes to think about their ideas for some or all of the current trends in the list.
- Put students in groups (maximum of four students) to discuss the trends, saying how and why they are in progress and/or changing. If necessary, refer students to the example to start with.
- For feedback, ask two or three groups to tell the class what they discussed for one of the items.
- To follow up, ask students which item they think is changing most quickly and why.

> Answers depend on students' own ideas.

HOMEWORK OPTIONS

Students do the exercises on pages 5–6 of the Workbook.

Students choose a trend in progress other than those in exercise 9, research it and write a short presentation (about 150 words) on how and why it is changing. They can give their presentations in the following lesson. Take the presentations in for marking, paying particular attention to the present continuous and present simple.

Students do exercises V2,3 6, G1 1 and G2 2 on page 135 in the Language reference.

1.3 WHO DOES THE TALKING?

IN THIS LESSON

Lesson topic and staging

This lesson looks at the differences between men's and women's communication. Students listen to a radio programme about a socio-linguist (Deborah Tannen) which contextualises the grammar for this lesson: the perfect aspect. Students do activities focusing on the meaning and practise using the grammar. Next, students read two extracts from Deborah Tannen's book and then focus on idioms related to communication. Finally, students do a speaking activity to practise using the perfect aspect.

Objectives

By the end of the lesson, students should have:

- extracted specific information and language items from listening and reading texts
- revised and extended their understanding of the perfect aspect and contrasted this with the past simple
- extended their range of idioms in the context of communication
- engaged in an extended speaking activity.

Timings

If short of time, you could drop exercise 9a on page 10 and set if for homework. A possible lesson break would be after exercise 5 or 8b on page 10.

WARM-UP

This activity introduces the topic of differences between men's and women's communication.

- Write the following two sentences on the board: 'Men are good communicators because ..., Women are good communicators because ...'.
- Divide the class into two groups. Tell one to think of three reasons why men are good communicators and the other to do the same for women. You can either divide the class into groups of men and women, or keep the sexes mixed, depending on the number of each sex in your class. It may be more challenging for students to think of three reasons for the opposite sex's good communication skills.
- Put the students together in pairs or groups of four with equal numbers from each of the original groups and give them a maximum of ten minutes to give their reasons. Encourage them to disagree with each other.
- Finally, ask the class to vote on which sex they think communicates better.

LISTENING

1 Elicit answers to this question to the board.
- Ask if anyone in the class has read the book or knows anything about it and/or Deborah Tannen.

2a Play the track without pausing and tell students to use the ideas on the board as a reminder.

2b Read through the instructions with the class and tell students to answer as many questions as possible before you play the track again.
- Play the track without pausing and then ask students to compare with a partner before you check answers with the class.

> 1 1990; 2 1994; 3 not given; 4 1979

[i] Georgetown University is a private research university in Washington DC, US. It was founded in 1789.

GRAMMAR: the perfect aspect

3 First, elicit the form of the present perfect (have + past participle), past perfect (had + past participle), and a few examples of the past simple (started, wrote, etc.).
- Then ask students to underline examples in the audioscript on page 175 and compare with a partner before you check with the class. Don't focus on the meaning of these forms at this stage because students will consider this in exercise 4 below.

[☼] If possible reproduce the audioscript so that the whole class can see it (perhaps on the Interactive Whiteboard or an OHP). When you check answers with the class, mark the text to show where the examples are so that they can use the examples and the context in exercise 4.

[!] Students may list was published as a perfect aspect because it uses the past participle. This is not a perfect aspect, it is the past simple in a passive voice (was + past participle).

> Present perfect: has become famous, has written (x 2), has published, She's also become, has appeared, has been, has lectured. Past perfect: had already written, had published, had written. Past simple: was published (past simple passive), spent, contained, decided, was, wrote

> **Audioscript and answers to exercises 2&3:**
> **Track 1.4**
> We're starting today by discussing the work of Deborah Tannen. Many of you will have heard of Deborah – she **has become famous** through her research into male and female communication and **has written** several books on interpersonal relations and communication. Her most famous book, *You Just Don't Understand*, **was published** in 1990 and it **spent** nearly four years on the New York Times bestseller list. *continued...*

Deborah **had already written** a book on conversational styles, which **contained** just one chapter on gender differences. But after receiving a huge popular response to that chapter she **decided** to focus more of her research on the subject – and the result **was** *You Just Don't Understand*. In 1994 she **wrote** the highly successful *Talking from 9 to 5*. Deborah **has written** for most major newspapers and magazines. In addition to her academic research and writing, she **has published** poetry, short stories and essays. In fact by 2006, she **had published** 20 books and **had written** over 100 articles. **She's also become** a bit of a celebrity and **has appeared** on the Larry King show, and on Oprah. Deborah **has been** in the Linguistics Faculty at Georgetown University since 1979 and **has lectured** all over the world. … Let's start with one of Deborah's most interesting quotes: 'Saying that men talk about baseball in order to avoid talking about their feelings is the same as saying that women talk about their feelings in order to avoid talking about baseball'. Jeremy, can I ask you first, what's your interpretation … *[fade]*

4   Put students in pairs for this activity and refer them to the context of the audioscript and the Language reference on page 134 if they need help.

•   When you check answers with the class, refer back to the context of the audioscript and the examples.

> The present perfect looks back from now to a time before now. The past perfect looks back from a time in the past to another time before that. The past simple refers to a completed event at a definite time in the past.

5   Set the context and tell students that some of the verbs (e.g. *rise, go up*) can go in more than one gap. Tell students they will need to change the form of the verbs.

•   Students work individually and then compare answers with a partner. Refer students to exercise 4 and the Language reference on page 134 if they need help.

•   Go through answers with the class and highlight the gaps where more than one possible answer could be given (see brackets in the answers).

> **1** started; **2** 've (have) built; **3** 've (have) just had; **4** employed (had); **5** had risen (gone up); **6** moved; **7** 've (have) taken on (employed); **8** 's (has) grown (risen, gone up); **9** have gone up (risen, grown); **10** had reached; **11** has ('s) contributed

(!) Students may ask when we should use a contraction of *have/has*. The contraction is common after a subject pronoun (*I, you, he, she*, etc.) and after the relative pronoun *who*. It is not as common after a proper noun (e.g. *costs*) in the written form. Generally, the contracted *have/has* is more common in speaking than writing.

For further practice, ask students to do exercise G3 3 on page 135 in the Language reference.

READING

6   Explain to students that they are going to read extracts from Deborah Tannen's book. Re-elicit what the book is about.

•   Put students in small groups to discuss the statements. Encourage them to give reasons for their opinions.

•   In feedback, ask two or three students their opinion on each statement and ask others if they agree.

7   Tell students not to worry about unknown vocabulary at this stage.

•   Allow four minutes for students to read and highlight the parts of the text that give the answers.

•   Ask them to compare with a partner before you check answers with the class.

•   To follow up, ask students if their experience of men and women talking supports the author's ideas.

> **1** Women are believed to talk more than men but the evidence shows the opposite. Men talk more outside the home and in public, women may talk more in the home and in private situations. **2** The extracts don't specifically mention sports or feelings. However, they say that women use conversation to establish connections and negotiate relationships (which may be connected to feelings). Men use conversation to negotiate status and talk about knowledge and skill (which may be connected to sports). **3** The author claims that this is true. See the examples given in 1 and 2 above.

8a Ask students to read the statements and try to answer before they read the texts again.

•   Then allow about five minutes for students to read the texts and use their dictionaries if necessary.

•   Don't check answers with the class at this stage.

> **1** M; **2** W; **3** M; **4** M; **5** W; **6** W

8b Give students two minutes to underline sections of the text and then about three minutes to compare with their partner before you check answers with the class.

VOCABULARY: idioms

9a Tell students to read the idioms (a–d) and guess the meaning before they match them to the ideas (1–4).

•   Ask students to briefly compare with a partner before you check answers with the class.

> **a)** 3; **b)** 4; **c)** 2; **d)** 1

9b Tell students they will need to change the form of some idioms when they use them in the gaps.

•   Students work individually and then compare with a partner before you check answers with the class.

- To follow up, ask students if any of the idioms are true of them.

> **1** runs out of; **2** hold centre stage; **3** the life of the party; **4** burst into laughter

SPEAKING

10 Give students a few minutes to think about their experiences before you put them into groups of three or four for the discussion.

- Encourage students to give as much information as possible and to ask each other questions.

- While students are speaking, monitor to note mistakes when using the perfect aspect, the past simple and the idioms from exercise 9a.

- When they have finished, ask each group to tell the class the most serious problem they discussed.

- Finally, correct some of the mistakes you noted earlier.

HOMEWORK OPTIONS

Students do the exercises on pages 7–8 of the Workbook.

Students listen to conversations at home, in school, while out with friends. They note who speaks more (men or women) and what they speak about. They then write a short letter or email to the producers of the radio programme, either supporting or disagreeing with Deborah Tannen's claims.

Students do exercise G3 3 on page 135 in the Language reference.

1.4 SCENARIO: FLAT SHARING

IN THIS LESSON

Lesson topic and staging

This lesson focuses on the language of outlining problems and offering solutions. Students are introduced to the scenario of a Student Advice Centre and the service it provides, and then to a student needing help with paying his rent. Then, they listen to counsellors from an Advice Centre discussing the problem and focus on the KEY LANGUAGE. Next, students read about four students sharing a flat and discuss their problems before listening to them having a similar discussion. Finally, students do the main part of the TASK where they play counsellors discussing the flatmates' problems and suggesting solutions.

Objectives

By the end of the lesson, students should have:

- learned useful phrases for outlining problems and offering solutions

- used this language in a 'real-life' situation to discuss problems faced by students living together

- extracted specific information and language items from reading and listening texts

- participated effectively in extended speaking practice.

Common European Framework

Students can use language effectively to make their opinions/reactions clear as regards finding solutions to problems.

Timings

If short of time, you could drop exercise 7 on page 13 as students will already have discussed solutions to problems in exercise 6c. A possible lesson break would be after exercise 3b or exercise 5b on page 12.

WARM-UP

This activity introduces the topic of problems that students may have and finding solutions to such problems.

- Ask the class what kind of problems students often have. (This can be students at university and/or school.)

- Write their ideas on the board and, if necessary, add some of the following: *can't afford to eat properly, can't finish an essay, can't find the book you want, late handing in your work, failed an exam, stressed out by exams.* Check students understand *stressed out* (very worried).

- Then write a second column containing the following words: *your parents, your best friend, your teacher, a student counsellor.*

- Tell students they must decide which person would be best to talk to about which problem. Emphasise that there are no 'right' answers, but that students must justify their ideas.

- Put students in pairs for the discussion and when they have finished, ask each pair what they decided and why.

SITUATION

1 Focus students on the poster and remind them that one source of help suggested in the Warm-up activity was a *student counsellor.*

- Put students in pairs to briefly discuss the questions. If you think your students will find the first part of question 2 too personal, change it to *Do you know anyone who has used a service like this?*

- If you used the Warm-up activity, students will already have listed different problems, so make this exercise and the feedback brief.

2a Read through the introduction with the class and emphasise they only need to identify the general problem.

- Play the track without pausing and then elicit the answer from the class.

He has a financial problem (he can't pay the rent).

2b Ask students to read the questions to see if they can answer any before you play the track again.

- Pre-teach *a tricky situation* as students need this to answer question 2. Warn students that there are two parts of the track that have the answer to question 2.

- Then play the track and, if necessary, pause at the points indicated in the audioscript opposite to give students time to make short notes.

- Ask student to compare with a partner before you check answers with the class. Don't ask personalised questions to follow up as students may feel uncomfortable about the topic.

1 He's been spending too much.; 2 They've broken an expensive lamp and have to pay the owner / Marco comes from a poor family and works part-time to pay for his studies.; 3 Give him advice about managing his money. (Answers are bold in the audioscript opposite.)

Audioscript and answers to exercises 2&3: Track 1.5

C: I saw Marco in your office again this morning, Jean. What did he want this time?

J: He needs money. He shares a flat with a couple of other students, as you know. 1 *The problem is* that **1 he's been spending too much recently** and he can't pay this month's rent. The others aren't happy as they'll have to pay more than usual.

C: Well, 2 *we can sort it out*, can't we? The best way 3 *to deal with it* is to tell him to get a loan from the student union.

J: Yeah, it's the obvious solution, but 4 *the trouble with that* is that it's the third time he's run out of money. There's a pattern: he spends too much money, he can't pay the rent, and then he gets a loan from friends or the student union. It's 5 *a vicious circle* – he can't escape from it.

C: Mmm, I see what you mean.

J: It's a 6 *very tricky situation* because **2 it's not just about the rent. They have a lot of parties in the flat and once again they've broken something. A really expensive lamp. And the owner wants to charge them a lot of money to replace it.** Marco just doesn't have any money to pay his share of the cost. [PAUSE]

C: Mmm, he's really got problems, hasn't he? It's 7 *a rather difficult situation*, isn't it? If I remember, **2 Marco comes from a poor family and he has to work part-time to pay for his studies.** He's really struggling. I must say, I feel a bit of sympathy for him. [PAUSE]

J: Me too. I think we should both have a chat with him. **3 Give him some advice about managing his money.** That might 8 *well solve the problem* – at least in the future.

C: Yes, that seems 9 *to be the way forward*, but will he listen to us?

J: He has to. It's his last chance. Let's do that. And now we need to think about how we can get some money for him to pay this month's rent? Oh, and for the lamp they broke, of course.

KEY LANGUAGE: outlining problems, offering solutions

3a Give students a few minutes to try to complete the gaps before you play the track again. Tell them that each gap needs more than one word.

- Play the track, pausing at the points indicated in the audioscript to give students time to write.

- When you go through answers with the class, check students understand *vicious circle* (the context should make this clear) and *the way forward* (a good plan for solving a problem).

1 **problem is**; 2 **we can sort it out**; 3 **to deal with it**; 4 **the trouble with that**; 5 **a vicious circle**; 6 **very tricky situation**; 7 **a rather difficult situation**; 8 **well solve the problem**; 9 **to be the way forward** (Answers are italicised in the audioscript above.)

3b Give students two minutes for this activity and then ask them to compare with a partner before checking answers with the class.

a) the problem is that, a vicious circle, it's a very tricky situation, it's a rather difficult situation;
b) we can sort it out; the best way to deal with it;
c) the trouble with that is, that might well solve the problem, that seems to be the way forward.

For further practice, ask students to do exercise KL 4 on page 135 in the Language reference.

TASK: solving the communication problems

4 Read through the introduction with the class and allow five minutes for students to read the descriptions and discuss the possible problems. If possible, students do this activity in groups of four.

- In feedback, elicit a few ideas from two or three of the groups.

5a Read the instructions with the class and then play the track without pausing.

- Ask students to compare in their groups before you check answers with the class. Answers are under exercise 5b below and in bold in the audioscript.

- In feedback, check students understand *rota* (a schedule saying when each person in a team/group should do particular tasks).

5b Play the track again, pausing at the points indicated in the audioscript to give students time to write.

- Ask them to compare in their groups before you check answers with the class.

- Ask students what Paul finally suggests and use this to lead in to exercise 6a.

Rules:	What Martin says:
1 Buy food in larger quantities	It's cheaper (the others don't agree).
2 Share the washing up	He usually does it, he puts up notices about it, he wants to make out a rota (the others don't agree).
3 Cleaning more often	He wants to make out a rota (the others don't agree).
4 Other people shouldn't stay for a long time	Stewart's friend Tom has been there for days, just sitting in the living room, bothering everyone else (Paul agrees, Stewart and Carlos do not).

Audioscript and answers to exercise 5:
Track 1.6
M: OK, guys. I wanted us to meet because there are a few issues with the flat. The problem is, we don't have any rules.
C: Rules? What do you mean, we're all adults Martin, we're not at school any more. We don't need any rules. What do you think, Paul?
P: Well … I don't know. What have you got in mind, Martin?
M: OK, **1 we need a rule about buying food, don't we? It'd be much cheaper for us if we bought in larger quantities** – that's why we need a rule.
C: I don't think so, Martin, it's much better if we each buy the food we want, and just put it in the fridge or on the shelves. It's simpler that way.
P: Yeah, I think Carlos is right, Martin. Anyway I don't eat much food, and Stewart eats hardly any food at all.
S: Yeah, it's true, Paul, I'm not a big eater. I'm trying to save money, so I don't spend much on food. Personally, I think we should just carry on buying our own food. [PAUSE]
M: *(sighs heavily).* OK, forget about food, but what about **2 and 3 washing up and cleaning? I come down each morning for breakfast and there's always a load of dirty dishes to wash up. And it's me who usually does it. I put up notices about it, but no one pays any attention. It's the same thing with the cleaning. The place is a dump, we need to clean it much more often.**
C: Martin, really, you're exaggerating, it's not as bad as that.
M: Exaggerating? I don't think so. **2 and 3 Look, why don't I make out a rota, with set times when we do the washing up and cleaning?** Paul, what's wrong?
P: I don't know, Martin. I don't like rotas, and, actually, I'm getting fed up with your little notes and messages everywhere. What do you think, Stewart?
S: Er…no, no, a rota isn't necessary. [PAUSE]
M: Well… OK, we'll leave things as they are. But there's one thing I do feel strongly about and I want us to have a rule about it. It's **4 people staying for long periods. Stewart, your friend Tom's been staying here for days now. He just sits around in the living room, bothering the rest of us.** I want him to leave. Right away.
S: Oh? I thought you liked him. Actually, he's just staying until he finds a job. What's wrong with that? I pay the rent, surely I can have friends to stay if I want to.
M: Sorry, I don't agree. What do you think, Paul?
P: Well, to be honest I'm not keen on people staying. I need to study during the day, not chat to Tom. How about you, Carlos?
C: Well, I love having friends in our flat. We don't want to study all the time. We want to have some fun as well. We don't need a rule about that, Martin.
M: Actually, Carlos, we do. Paul and I are here to study. You should respect our opinion. The best way to deal with this is to have a rule, it's quite simple, 'no long-term visitors'.
P: You know, you may think this is stupid, but I think the way to sort out our problems might be to go and see the university counselling service – they deal with all sorts of things …

6a If possible, keep students in the same groups of four as the previous exercises. If you have an odd number in your class, form groups of three and omit the Stewart text as most information was introduced in exercise 5.

- Give students three minutes to read their information and note the key points.

6b Allow five minutes in total for students to present their information.

6c Ask students to read the questions and then remind them of the KEY LANGUAGE on page 12 and go through the OTHER USEFUL PHRASES box on page 13.

- Allow at least 15 minutes for the discussion and monitor to note errors with students' use of the KEY LANGUAGE and USEFUL PHRASES.

- When they have finished, correct some of the mistakes you noted earlier. Don't elicit solutions to the problems they discussed as this is done in exercise 7 below.

7 This activity gives students an opportunity to use the KEY LANGUAGE and USEFUL PHRASES again.

- If you have a large class, divide students into two groups to discuss the solutions they thought of in exercise 6c.

- Allow about ten minutes for this activity and when they have finished, ask the class to vote on the best solution.

HOMEWORK OPTIONS

Students do the exercises on page 9 of the Workbook.

Students use the problems and solutions they discussed in exercises 6c and 7 to write an advice sheet from the Student Advice Centre for students sharing a flat. The advice sheet should give tips for a harmonious life.

Students do exercise KL 4 on page 135 in the Language reference.

1.5 STUDY AND WRITING SKILLS

IN THIS LESSON

Lesson topic and staging

This lesson focuses on note-taking, writing and checking emails. Students read a radio guide entry about a series of talks. They then focus on the structure of talks before listening and taking notes on part of a talk. Next, students consider techniques for note-taking and practise by listening to another part of the talk. Students then reconstruct the talk from the notes they have made. Next, students focus on the formal and informal register of emails before writing an email themselves. Finally, students look at criteria for judging writing and then check their partner's email.

Objectives

By the end of the lesson, students should have:

- extracted specific information and language items from reading and listening texts

- learned (more) about techniques for note-taking and practised taking notes while listening

- extended their knowledge of formal and informal register in emails and practised writing one

- learned criteria for checking written work and practised using these by checking another student's work

Common European Framework

Students can write notes conveying simple information, write connected texts describing an event and convey short simple factual information, note mistakes and consciously monitor written work.

Timings

If short of time, you could drop exercise 10 on page 15 and set it for homework. Students can then check their partner's work in the following lesson. A possible lesson break would be after exercise 5 on page 14.

WARM-UP

To lead in to the activities on note-taking, ask students if they find taking notes while listening difficult (the answer will be 'yes'!).

- Put students into pairs and ask them to list as many reasons as possible why they find this difficult.

- Explain that students are going to look at ways of taking notes. After exercise 4, ask students if the techniques they have used help them with the difficulties they listed.

STUDY SKILLS: note-taking

1a Introduce the context, ask students to quickly read the text and then elicit suggestions.

1b Put students in pairs to discuss the questions and then elicit their ideas to the board. This will be referred to in exercise 3a below.

2a Structure of talks

- Read through the introduction with the class and tell them that the examples (a–e) are 'signposts'.

- Check students understand *exemplifying* (giving an example) in number 5.

- Give students one minute to match the headings and examples (signposts) and then check answers with the class.

> 1 b); 2 e); 3 d); 4 c); 5 a)

2b Put students into pairs or small groups for this activity.

- Get suggestions for the class and write these on the board so that all students can copy them.

> Answers depend on students' suggestions. Some suggestions are: **1** I'm going to talk about, This talk will look at …; **2** Second, then, next, after that …; **3** The crux, the main point is …; **4** To put it another way; **5** For example, To give an example …

3a Note-taking

- First, ask students for a few suggestions for good note-taking.

- Tell students not to worry if they find this activity difficult. They will compare their notes with another student.

- Refer students to the ideas on the board from exercise 1b as this will help them predict the content.

- Play the track, pausing at appropriate points for students to take notes. (The audioscript is on page 176 of the Coursebook.)

- Check answers with the class after exercise 3b.

3b Ask students to compare the main points and then focus them on the questions in this exercise.

- Go through answers and elicit useful note-taking techniques to the board for use in exercise 3c below.

> **1** main points are: public speaking is the worst phobia (much more than just nerves) for many people; people react with a 'fight or flight' response; making a speech is an opportunity to impress/show what you can do; people worry about making mistakes, not being liked or understood; **2** Answers depend on students' own ideas; **3** in other words, for instance, First(ly)

3c Refer students to the other techniques listed on the board (from exercise 3b) and ask which of these they would find useful.

4a Emphasise that this is an opportunity for students to try some new note-taking techniques.

- Play the track and, if necessary, pause it two or three times to allow students writing time. (The audioscript is on page 176 of the Coursebook.)

> Main points are: rehearsal is essential, practise your speech, know your introduction by heart (i.e. from memory), begin with some kind of interest hook (i.e. to get people's attention), take some deep breaths before you start, try and look confident, focus on something other than yourself, use plenty of eye contact, change the pace of your delivery, change the volume of your voice, and perhaps move around a bit. Don't worry too much about mistakes, use humour, there are no rules, find what works for you.

4b Ask students to tell a partner if their notes are clearer than the first attempt and why.

- If you used the Warm-up activity, ask students if the techniques have helped them with the difficulties they listed at the beginning of the lesson.

5 Tell students not to read the audioscript while they do this activity, but to compare their version with the audioscript when they have finished. Ask the class if their versions are similar to the audioscript.

WRITING SKILLS: writing and checking emails

6 Put students in pairs to discuss these questions.

> Top of email: who it's from, who it's to and/ or copied to, the date sent, the subject line. Differences: We don't write our address top right in an email, the date refers to when it was written and not when it was sent, people it is copied to are included after the name at the bottom of a letter, you don't use a subject line but may use a reference after the salutation in a letter.

7a Register

- Give students one minute to read the emails and then elicit answers from the class.

> **1** They don't know each other (formal register); **2** They know each other (informal register).

7b Give students five minutes to complete the chart and then compare with a partner before you check answers with the class.

	Formal / neutral	Informal
Greeting	Dear Mr Hammond	Hi James
Request	I would like to invite you to speak ...	Fancy giving a talk ...
Mention of attachment	Please find attached a document ...	See attached for the ...
Additional information	Should you have any further questions, please do not hesitate to contact me.	Any problems or queries, just let me know.
Future contact	I look forward to hearing from you.	Hope to hear from you soon.
Ending	Your sincerely + full name	Best + first name

8a Give students five minutes to do this activity and then compare with a partner before you check answers.

	1	2	3	4	5	6	7
Email 1	a	i	d	k	c	m	g
Email 2	h	l	b	e	f	j	n

8b Give students five minutes to complete the chart and then compare with a partner before you check answers with the class.

	Formal / neutral	Informal
Thanking	Thank you for your ... inviting me to...	Thanks for the invite to ....
Giving bad news	I am afraid that I will be unable to ...	Sorry, but I won't be able to ...
Offering help	If you wish, I could ...	If you want, I can see if ...
Apologising	Once again, I would like to apologise ...	Anyway, sorry again for ...
Future contact	Please do not hesitate to contact me ...	Please let me know about ...

9 Give students a few minutes to think about this question and then discuss it with a partner.

> Informal language: more contractions; shortened words (e.g. *invite* for *invitation*) and abbreviations (e.g. Mon for Monday), more colloquial (*let me know*), informal form of words (e.g. *want* not *wish*, *can* not *could*), more similar to spoken language; short expressions and sentences; vague language (e.g. *stuff*, *things*), little use of passive voice. (Note: the opposite is true of formal language.)

10a Peer checking

- Tell students they cannot both choose the same email.
- Give them 20–30 minutes to write the email and monitor to help with vocabulary, if necessary.

10b First, elicit the advantages of checking each other's writing (e.g. it's easier to see others' mistakes).

- Then, read through the introduction and GRASP and tell students that the same procedure can be used when they check their own work.

- Give students five minutes to read each other's emails and note the corrections that are necessary.
- Ask them to return the email to the student who wrote it, who then makes the necessary changes.
- Students then give their corrected emails back to their partner to use in exercise 11.

11 Give students 20 minutes to write the reply, paying attention to the type of mistakes they made in exercise 10, and then give it to their partner.

Students could repeat the procedure in exercise 10, using the replies they write in exercise 11.

HOMEWORK OPTIONS

Students do the exercises on page 10 of the Workbook.

Students write an email to find out more information about a topic they are interested in. The topic may be something they heard on the radio, saw on the TV or read on the Internet. They need to decide how formal or informal to make the email.

Environment

2.1 LOCAL ENVIRONMENT

Lesson topic and staging

This lesson looks at local environmental issues. Students listen to three people talking about their local area, learn a set of urban/rural-related vocabulary and focus on the pronunciation of these. Next, students discuss what they like about their area and compare with a published survey. Students then read an article about the survey. Finally, they discuss two surveys on local environmental issues and write a report.

Objectives

By the end of the lesson, students should have:

- extracted specific information and language items from listening and reading texts
- extended their range of urban/rural-related word combinations and practised the pronunciation of these
- participated in pair/group discussions on urban and local environmental issues
- written a report describing the findings of surveys on local environmental issues.

Timings

If short of time, you could drop exercise 6 on page 17 but make sure you introduce the two surveys before beginning exercise 7a. A possible lesson break would be after exercise 5b on page 17.

This activity introduces the topic of urban versus rural environments.

- Divide the class into two groups and tell Group A they support urban environments and Group B rural environments.
- Then tell students in Group A to list three advantages of living in an urban environment and three disadvantages of living in a rural environment. Group B do the opposite.
- When they have their lists, put students into A/B pairs and give them five minutes to persuade each other that their environment is better.
- Finally, ask the class to vote on which environment they prefer to live in. Ask one or two students why.

Bob Dylan quote:

This quote is not really connected in meaning to the environment. It is a play on words with *weatherman* and *wind blows*. The meaning of *to know which way the wind blows* is to be able to predict/see what is going to happen based on what you know about current events and situations. The quote means, you don't need someone to tell you what's going to happen because you can guess from current evidence.

i Bob Dylan (born 1941) is a famous US singer and songwriter in the folk genre. He was particularly popular during the 1960s and early 1970s when his protest songs represented the feelings of many liberals to the perceived threat from imperialism and US policies. He was very active in the anti-Vietnam War movement.

1a Use the Warm-up activity as a lead in. Students will have considered the advantages and disadvantages of both environments and you can quickly elicit what specific likes/dislikes they have.

1b Introduce the context and ask students to look at the chart.

- Play the track, pausing after each extract to give students time to fill in the chart.
- Tell students not to worry about vocabulary at this stage as it is covered in exercise 2. They should be able to guess most vocabulary from the context.
- Ask students to compare with a partner before you check answers with the class. (Sections giving the information are bold in the audioscript below.)
- Finally, ask students if any of the points made by the different speakers were similar to their own likes/dislikes.

	Person 1	Person 2	Person 3
Type of building	Detached house	Farm cottage	Apartment block
Where they live	Suburb of a major city	Countryside, edge of a very small village	City centre
What they like	Access to cultural events and shops, local area is green, good public transport connections	Peace and quiet, fresh air, no traffic congestion, little noise and light pollution, pace of life is slower, stunning views	Cosmopolitan atmosphere, plenty to do, wide range of shops, get whatever I want any time, liveliness, surrounded by people all the time, loads of police so feel very safe
Problem	Mindless vandalism	Abandoned cars	Litter

ENVIRONMENT

Audioscript and answers to exercise 1b:
Track 1.9
1
Well, **I live in a detached house in a suburb of a major city**. What do I like about it? Mmm, well, **I like the access to all the cultural events and shops, but I also like the fact that my local area is very green** – you know, lots of parks and open spaces for the kids. The **public transport connections are very good too**, so I can be in the city centre in a very short time if I avoid the rush hour, so I guess you could say I have the best of both worlds! **The only real problem I think is the mindless vandalism** that goes on, you know damage to cars and bus stops, which we all have to pay for in the end. It's bored young people with nothing to do. I suppose it's the price you pay for living in a city.
2
I live in a **farm cottage on the edge of a very small village**, almost a hamlet really, in the **countryside**. It really is very rural – about 25 kilometres to the nearest town. **It's the peace and quiet I like really, and the fresh air.** There's not many vehicles on the roads – **so no traffic congestion** … the air is very clean, and there's **very little noise and light pollution**. The whole **pace of life is much slower** – no one rushes anywhere. Oh yes, and the **stunning views**, I'm surrounded by **magnificent scenery**. One **problem we are having at the moment is abandoned cars**. People are dumping old cars they don't want any more in the village at night. We then have to wait for ages before they're taken away.
3
I live in an **apartment block in the city centre**. It's the **cosmopolitan atmosphere I like**. There's always **plenty to do, and such a wide range of shops**. I can go out at **any time of the day or night and get whatever I want**, either food and drink or entertainment. I love the **liveliness of the city and being surrounded by people all the time** – you know, that constant buzz of activity. People talk about the crime rate in the city, but where I live there always seem to be **loads of police so I feel very safe**. The one thing that **gets me down is the amount of litter** people drop on the streets. It's so unnecessary and just makes me feel depressed. I sometimes feel like saying to them 'I have to live here with all your rubbish'. The council could do more to keep the streets clean as well I suppose, but we all have to pay for it in higher taxes.

2a Give students three minutes to make as many combinations as they can and then ask them to compare with a partner.
- Tell students to try to guess meaning from the context and then play the track again.
- Go through answers with the class and provide the meaning of unknown words if necessary.

> **1** spaces; **2** pollution; **3** atmosphere; **4** rate; **5** house; **6** hour; **7** stunning; **8** apartment; **9** abandoned; **10** transport; **11** mindless; **12** traffic

For further practice, ask students to do exercise V1 6 on page 137 in the Language reference.

pronunciation

2b Word combinations
- Do the first example with the class so they know your system for marking stress. Then put them in pairs to mark the others.
- When they have finished, play the track, pausing after each item to allow students to check the stress.
- Write the combinations on the board and mark the stress as you go through answers with the class.

> **Track 1.10**
> 1 open spaces   2 noise pollution
> 3 cosmopolitan atmosphere   4 crime rate
> 5 detached house   6 rush hour   7 stunning views
> 8 apartment block   9 abandoned cars
> 10 transport connections   11 mindless vandalism
> 12 traffic congestion

You could elicit/tell students that in compound nouns (e.g. *noise pollution, crime rate, apartment block*) the stress is most commonly on the first word or the first part if it is written as one word (e.g. *whiteboard*). If the phrase is adjective + noun (e.g. *detached house, abandoned cars, mindless vandalism*), the stress is typically on the second word (i.e. the noun). However, this is dependent on context.

READING

3a Do the first question quickly as a whole class (students have discussed this in previous exercises).
- Then put students into small groups to discuss the list and add other examples. Monitor to help with vocabulary if necessary.
- Elicit answers from the class and write useful additions on the board so all students can copy them.

3b Students work individually to order the problems (including any additions you wrote on the board).
- When students have compared with their partner, ask them how much of their list was in a similar order.

4 Focus students on the photo and the title of the article and elicit what they think it is about.
- Tell students to read the questions before they read the article and not to worry about vocabulary as this will be covered in exercise 5a below.
- Ask them to compare with a partner before you check answers with the class.
- Finally, ask students how many of the ideas they discussed in exercise 3 were mentioned in the article.

> **1** more than 2,000; **2** residents who were already dissatisfied with their home, residents in medium- or high-rise flats; **3 a)** two in five, **b)** one in four; **4** because people are able to develop 'immunity' to it, they consider it part of the environment

5a Give students five minutes to find the vocabulary and then compare their answers with a partner.

- Go through answers with the class.

> **1** findings; **2** poll; **3** issues; **4** scale; **5** develop 'immunity' (Note: 'immunity' is in inverted commas because it is normally associated with disease.); **6** synonymous; **7** lack of consideration; **8** priority

5b Students work individually and then compare with a partner before you check answers with the class.

- Tell students they will need to use these phrases and the vocabulary from exercise 5a later in the lesson.

> **1** The government-commissioned survey, The study – carried out for; **2** designed to measure; **3** was a problem of similar scale, ranked much more highly; **4** according to a new survey, the survey also established, the survey finds

SPEAKING AND WRITING

6 Briefly do question 1 as a whole class as many of their ideas will have been discussed earlier.

- Put students into small groups to discuss questions 2 and 3, then elicit a few ideas from the class.

> Answers depend on students' own opinions and ideas.

7a Divide the class into As and Bs to discuss the results of two other surveys.

- Give students three minutes to look at their survey and answer the questions.

- Don't go through answers with the class as this is done after exercise 7b.

7b Put students into A/B pairs to tell each other the information from their surveys.

- Tell them to ask questions for more information. To make this activity easier, tell students they can show each other the surveys.

- Check answers with the class.

> **A: 1** Mercer HR consulting; **2** the changes in cost of living between 2006–2007 in eight cities; **3** the main trend is that cost of living has risen, the main change is that London has moved from fifth to second most expensive city, the cost of living in Hong Kong and Moscow has risen quite a lot; **4** London has changed ranking so much, Moscow is the most expensive city.

> **B: 1** Mercer HR consulting; **2** The relative quality of life in different cities in 2006–2007; **3** The main trend is that the quality of life has remained the same, the main change is that Vienna and Dusseldorf have risen one place in the ranking; **4** that most of the cities in the top eight are in Switzerland or Germany.

8 Read through the instructions with the class and allow 30 minutes for students to write their reports.

- Monitor to help with vocabulary or ask students to use their dictionaries.

- They can use the article on page 17 as a model, but should aim for a formal register.

- Take the reports in for marking, paying particular attention to the use of vocabulary from exercise 5.

🔧 When students have finished writing, remind them of the work they did on correcting work in Lesson 1.5 (GRASP). Tell students to swap reports and try to correct using only G, R, A, S and P to show where a mistake is. Students then try to correct their own work, based on the notes made by their partner.

HOMEWORK OPTIONS

Students do the exercises on page 11 of the Workbook.

Students design a survey of people in their school, university, their friends, or their family on any topic they choose. They then write a report similar to that in exercise 8.

Students do exercise V1 6 on page 137 in the Language reference.

2.2 CHANGING ENVIRONMENT

IN THIS LESSON

Lesson topic and staging

This lesson looks at how the environment is changing. Students read an article on the problems facing polar bears in the Arctic and work on vocabulary from the text. Next, students learn a set of word combinations related to environmental change. Students then look at the use of present perfect simple and continuous in the article and practise using these tenses. Finally, students discuss environmental changes in their local environment.

Objectives

By the end of the lesson, students should have:

- extracted specific information and language items from the reading text
- extended their range of vocabulary in the context of environmental change
- revised/extended their understanding of the present perfect simple and continuous
- participated in extended speaking practice to discuss changes in their own environments.

Timings

If short of time, you could drop exercises 2 and 3 on page 18, but make sure you introduce the article before students do exercise 4. A possible lesson break would be after exercise 5 or 6b on page 19.

WARM-UP

This activity introduces the topic of environmental change and what we can do about it.

- Focus students on the photo on page 18 and elicit that the Arctic is melting, probably due to global warming.
- Write the following on the board: *recycle, use public transport, fly less, become vegetarian, insulate your house, buy food grown locally,* and check students understand each term.
- Put students into groups of three or four to discuss which things they have already started doing, which they think they should do, and which they think are a waste of time.
- Finally, ask students to vote who is the 'greenest' person in their group.

READING

1 Focus students on the photo and headline on page 18 and ask if they know what problems the bears are having. Elicit/give the meaning of *extinction* (to die and completely disappear), and *in the wake of retreating sea ice* (as the sea ice disappears).

- Then put students into groups to discuss the questions before you get some ideas from the class.

> Answers depend on students' own knowledge.

2a Students do this activity individually and underline the words they have chosen.

> Answers depend on students' own knowledge and existing vocabulary.

2b Students work individually and then compare with a partner before you check answers with the class.

- Students can then use their dictionaries to find any other unknown words if they need to.

> 1 fast; 2 species; 3 prey; 4 cubs; 5 mammals;
> 6 marine

3 Elicit/tell students the meaning of *scan* (to find specific items in a text).

- Tell them to look at the words they underlined in exercise 2a and then quickly read the text to find them.
- Ask students how many of their words were mentioned in the text.

4 Tell students to read the questions and check they understand *shrinking* (becoming smaller) before they read the introduction to the text.

- Ask them to briefly compare with a partner before you check answers with the class.

> 1 for 20 years and they're still rising (more rapidly);
> 2 for 30 years and it's still shrinking; 3 They've had no significant success.

5 Allow about five minutes for students to read the article carefully and complete the sentences. Tell students they need to use information from the article, but may need to use their own words in the gaps.

- Ask them to compare with a partner before you go through answers with the class and check students understand *susceptible to disease* (more likely to get a disease).
- To follow up, ask students if this issue is known about in their countries and what people think.

> 1 climate change; 2 find food; 3 spotting/seeing a polar bear; 4 Canadian Wildlife Service (CWS); 5 more susceptible to disease; 6 sea ice

VOCABULARY: word combinations

6a Tell students that these combinations all come from the article they have just read.

- Ask them to try to match as many as possible before they read the article to check.

- Go through answers with the class.

> **1** b); **2** e); **3** c); **4** f); **5** a); **6** d)

6b Ask students to complete the gaps individually and then compare with a partner before you check answers with the class.

> **1** scientific journal; **2** climate change; **3** satellite images; **4** global warming; **5** significant effects; **6** false impression

For further practice, ask students to do exercise V2 7 on page 137 in the Language reference.

GRAMMAR: present perfect simple and continuous

7 Focus students on the two sentences and elicit the name of each tense (1 = present perfect continuous, 2 = present perfect simple). Elicit the form of each.

- Then put students into pairs to discuss the questions, referring them to the Language reference on page 136 if they need help.

- Check answers with the class and then read though the Grammar Tip with the class, giving another example if necessary.

> **a)** 1 present perfect continuous; **b)** 2 present perfect simple; **c)** present perfect simple

8 Give students five minutes to complete the activity and then ask them to compare with a partner.

- To encourage them to think about their answers, ask them to use the Language reference on page 136 rather then provide help yourself.

> **1** has been disappearing; **2** has been shrinking; **3** has already vanished; **4** We've been waiting; **5** has sent; **6** has been trying

For further practice, ask students to do exercises G1 1 and 2 on page 137 in the Language reference.

i Al Gore is a former Vice President of the US who lost the election for President in 2000. His film about the causes and effects of global warming *An Inconvenient Truth* won as Oscar (American film award) for best documentary in 2006. He was joint winner of the Nobel Peace Prize in 2007.

The Maldives are a group of low-lying islands in the Indian under significant threat from rising sea levels.

SPEAKING

9 Explain that students are going to practise the present perfect simple and continuous by talking about changes in their local environment.

- First, give students a few minutes to think about changes in their environments, and tell them to refer to the Language reference on page 136 if they need help and use their dictionaries for unknown vocabulary.

- Then, elicit the pronunciation for contracted 'have' ('ve) and tell students to try to use this in their discussion.

- Put students into small groups for the discussion and monitor to note mistakes using the present perfect or continuous.

- For feedback, ask students if any of the changes they discussed were similar to other students' ideas.

- Finally, correct some of the mistakes you noted earlier.

HOMEWORK OPTIONS

Students do the exercises on pages 12–13 of the Workbook.

Students write a letter to their local newspaper describing the changes they have noticed in their local environments, saying either how concerned they are, or if they think the changes aren't a problem. They can use the ideas they discussed in exercise 9.

Students do exercises G1 1 and 2, and V2 7 on page 137 in the Language reference.

2.3 EXTREME ENVIRONMENT

Lesson topic and staging

This lesson looks at volcanoes and volcanic regions. Students test their knowledge of volcanoes, then listen to a talk about these to check their answers. Next, students look at indirect questions in the listening text and practise using the grammar themselves. Students then read about Yellowstone Park in the US and focus on adverbs contained in the text. Finally, students discuss facts about volcanoes before writing a fact sheet.

Objectives

By the end of the lesson, students should have:

- extracted specific information and language items from a listening and a reading text
- revised/learned about indirect questions and practised using these
- revised and/or extended their range of adverbs
- used the language focus of the lesson to participate in a speaking practice activity
- used the language focus of the lesson to write a fact sheet about volcanoes.

Timings

If short of time and your students are confident using indirect questions, you could drop exercise 6b on page 20. A possible lesson break would be after exercise 6b on page 20.

WARM-UP

This activity introduces the topic of extreme environments and pre-teaches *lava* and *eruption* for later activities.

- Write the following on the board:
  - o Volcanoes   lava
  - o Sea/water   flood
  - o Land   hurricane
  - o Air   blaze
  - o Forest   earthquake
                         tsunami
                         eruption
                         tornado
- Put students in pairs and tell them to match the words on the left with those on the right. Tell students that some words on the left may match with more than one on the right, e.g. an earthquake can happen under the sea.

- When they have finished, check answers and vocabulary and finally, ask the class if anyone has experienced one of these.

> Volcanoes: lava; eruption. Sea/water: flood, hurricane, tsunami. Land: earthquake. Air: tornado, hurricane. Forest: blaze.

LISTENING

1 Focus students on the title of the quiz and ask them to give you three or four things they know about volcanoes (e.g. the name of a famous volcano, what happens when they erupt). If possible, elicit the vocabulary *volcanic activity*, *volcano*, *lava* and *erupt(ion)* as you get ideas from the class.

- Allow students three minutes to guess the answers to the T/F questions and then compare with a partner.

- Answers will be checked in exercise 2a.

2a Play the track without pausing and then ask students how many they answered correctly.

- Go through answers and ask the class if they found any of this information surprising.

> 1 T; 2 T; 3 F (Pacific Ocean); 4 T; 5 F; 6 T; 7 T; 8 F; 9 T; 10 T

(!) The quiz says that Mauna Loa is the biggest volcano in the world, but the Bill Bryson extract in exercise 7 say that Yellowstone Park is. This is because there are different ways of measuring volcanoes. Both are correct depending on the measure being used.

2b Ask students to discuss these questions in pairs before you play the track again.

- Check answers with the class.

> Situation: The end of a lecture when students ask the professor questions. Relationship: professor/ students – therefore quite formal.

GRAMMAR: indirect questions

3 Remind students about the relationship discussed in exercise 2b (this will also help students in exercise 4).

- Before students read the audioscript, ask them to discuss with a partner how they think the questions in the table were asked.

- Then give them four minutes to check the audioscript and fill in the table.

- Check answers with the class.

> 1 Can I ask what the biggest volcano in the world is?; 2 Do you know whether people can go inside volcanoes?; 3 Could you tell me if Vesuvius is an active volcano?; 4 I'd like to know why volcanoes stop erupting.

4 Students discuss this question in pairs before you elicit ideas from the class.

> Because of the relationship between the professor and the students. Direct questions are less formal and therefore show the professor is in a 'powerful' position. Indirect questions are more formal/polite and show the students are in a less powerful position. Indirect questions are more tentative than direct questions.

5 Students work individually using the examples in exercise 3 to help them.

- Ask students to compare with a partner and use the Language reference on page 136 if they need extra help.

- Check answers with the class and elicit the relevant examples from exercise 3.

> **1** True; **2** True; **3** False (we only use a question word if the introductory phrase itself is a question e.g. *Do you know …?*); **4** False (except where the indirect question begins with *Do you know …*); **5** False (we use a question mark only when the introductory sentence itself is a question (e.g. *Do you know …?*).

For further information, ask students to read the Language reference on page 136.

6a Re-elicit the introductory phrases from exercise 3 (*Can I ask …, Do you know ..., Could you tell me …, I'd like to know …*) and then do the first example with the class, if necessary writing the direct and indirect forms on the board to demonstrate the changes.

- Students work individually and then compare with a partner. Encourage them to use the examples in exercise 3, the information in exercise 5 and the Language reference if they need help. If possible, don't correct students yourself.

- While they are working, write the direct questions on the board and when you check answers, write the indirect versions to clearly show the changes. (Note: students will probably have used different forms in their indirect questions; accept any correct and meaningful answers.)

> Example answers: **2** Can you tell me how many volcanoes erupt each year?; **3** Do you know how many eruptions were reported between 1975 and 1985?; **4** Id like to know if you can go inside an erupting volcano.; **5** Could you tell me what causes a volcano to erupt?; **6** Can you tell me which the biggest volcano in the USA is?; **7** Do you know which volcano has been showing a lot of activity recently?; **8** I'd like to know when Vesuvius destroyed Pompeii.; **9** Could you tell me when Vesuvius last erupted?; **10** Can you tell me whether a lot of people live near Vesuvius?

6b Put students in pairs to ask/answer the questions, referring to the audioscript on page 176 if they don't know the answer.

🔧 To make this activity more challenging, ask students to read the audioscript on page 176 and then close their books. Put students in pairs to take it in turns to ask each other a question. They should try to answer it from memory and if they're not sure, guess. Each student notes the other's answers. When they have finished, students look again at the audioscript and count how many questions they answered correctly.

For further practice, ask students to do exercises G2 3 and 4 on page 137 in the Language reference.

READING

7 Focus students on the photo and title on page 21 and ask if any of them have been to Yellowstone Park or if they know anything about it. (See background information below.)

- Tell students to read the instructions and ask if they have heard of Bill Bryson or read any of his books. (See background information below.)

- Ask students to read the questions and check they understand *cataclysm* (huge and terrible disaster).

- Then tell students to read the text and emphasise they should answer in their own words.

- Ask students to compare with a partner before you check answer with the class.

- Finally, ask students if they're interested in visiting the park and why/not.

ⓘ Yellowstone Park is located mostly in the USA state of Wyoming and was the world's first national park (1872).

Bill Bryson (born in the USA in 1951) is a best-selling writer of humorous travel and language books. He lived in the UK for more than 20 years, then moved back to the USA before recently returning to the UK. His books include *Notes from a Small Island*, *Neither Here Nor There*, and *Mother Tongue*. In 2003, he published the bestseller *A Short History of Nearly Everything* which explains areas of science in everyday language.

> **1** It means that Yellowstone Park is a beautiful place, but is also very dangerous because of the volcanic activity.; **2** It's about 72 kilometres across, i.e. from one side to the other and about 13 kilometres thick.; **3** Because the explosion would be enormous but nobody can predict exactly how bad it would be.; **4** No, because nobody was there the previous time it exploded, so they don't know what the warning signs are.; **5** Because there are already all the usual warning signs (earthquakes, etc.) but nothing has happened yet.; **6** Because more than three million people visit it each year, the roads are narrow which slows traffic down, and it can take half a day to drive across the park.

8 Give students one minute to find the adverbs.

• Then, give students three minutes to do the activity. They can use their dictionaries if necessary.

• Ask them to compare with a partner before you check answers with the class.

> deliberately = intentionally; relatively = comparatively; normally = generally; perhaps = possibly; mainly = mostly; slowly and pensively = thoughtfully

For further practice, ask students to do exercise V3 8 on page 137 in the Language reference.

SPEAKING AND WRITING

9a Give students a few minutes to think about the facts they have learned about volcanoes in this lesson.

• Put them in pairs to discuss the list and emphasise that the facts they choose are for schoolchildren.

• They can only choose five or six facts between them and should justify why they have chosen these.

When pairs have chosen their list, put them with another pair to make groups of four and tell them to compare their lists. They need to say why they chose each fact and challenge each others' decisions if appropriate. Students can then change their list if they want to.

9b Elicit what a fact sheet might look like from the class (e.g. a title, a very short introduction and then bulleted facts).

• Keep students in the same pairs as exercise 9a and give them 20–30 minutes to write their fact sheets. Remind them to use the vocabulary they have learned in this lesson. Tell them that indirect questions are not appropriate to a fact sheet, but they can use direct questions as headings.

• Monitor to point out mistakes and to help with vocabulary if necessary.

• When they have finished, put the pairs into groups of four to compare their fact sheets.

When they have finished writing, ask students to post their fact sheets around the walls. Then ask the class to read each of the sheets and finally vote on the best.

HOMEWORK OPTIONS

Students do the exercises on pages 14–15 of the Workbook.

Students use the Internet to research another kind of extreme environment (see the Warm-up activity for ideas) and then write a fact sheet for the others in the class. These can be posted around the room for everyone to read.

Students do exercises G2 3 and 4, and V3 8 on page 137 in the Language reference.

2.4 SCENARIO: SPARROW HILL WIND FARM

IN THIS LESSON

Lesson topic and staging

This lesson focuses on the language of agreeing/ disagreeing politely and asking polite questions. Students are introduced to the scenario of a company who wants to build a wind farm. They then listen to a government official and a company representative talking about the farm, which leads to a focus on the KEY LANGUAGE. Finally, students do the main TASK where they take part in a meeting to discuss the proposal.

Objectives

By the end of the lesson, students should have:

• learned useful phrases for agreeing and disagreeing politely and asking questions politely

• used this language in a 'real-life' situation to discuss a proposal to build a wind farm

• extracted specific information and language items from a reading and a listening text

• participated effectively in extended speaking practice.

Common European Framework

Students can use language effectively to agree and disagree politely, express their opinions and give reasons for these.

Timings

If short of time, you could drop exercise 4 on page 23, but make sure you model pronunciation and monitor its use during exercise 5. A possible lesson break would be after exercise 2 on page 22 or exercise 4 on page 23.

WARM-UP

This activity introduces the topic of renewable resources and agreeing/disagreeing.

• Write the following on the board: *fossil fuels* (*gas*, *oil*, *coal*), *wind energy*, *solar energy* (*sun*), *wave energy* (*the sea*), and *nuclear energy*.

• Put students into pairs and give one resource to each pair.

• Tell students to think of as many advantages of their resource as possible and one disadvantage for each of the other resources.

• Then put students into groups of three to six so that each student in a group represents a different resource. Tell them to argue why their resource is better than the others and to disagree with other students.

- Monitor while they are speaking and note the language they use for disagreeing.
- Finally, ask students which resource had the most advantages in their group and then write some of the phrases students used for disagreeing. Tell students they will be looking at other phrases for disagreeing (as well as agreeing) in this lesson.

SITUATION

1 Focus students on the photo on pages 22–23 and elicit that this is a wind farm. Take this opportunity to pre-teach *turbine* (refer to the photo).

- Then ask students to name some other kinds of alternative power (e.g. *wave*, *solar*). Students will have discussed some kinds of alternative power if you used the Warm-up activity.
- Use this opportunity to elicit *renewable sources* from *wave* and *solar*.
- Explain that students are going to discuss building a wind farm later in the lesson.
- Ask students to read the questions before they read the text. They can use their dictionaries if necessary.
- Put students into pairs to compare answers and then check with the class.
- Finally, ask the class if wind farms are common in their country and/or what kind of renewable sources of power are used or could be used.

> **1** Facts and figures: 80 turbines, 60 metres tall, turbine of 35m diameter, an area of several kilometres (students may also say that the fact it will take five years to complete is evidence that it will be large. Accept if suggested but don't give this as an answer yourself.); **2** commercially viable; **3** Sources of energy and advantages (+) and disadvantages (–) mentioned: fossil fuels (+ none mentioned, – being used up, emit carbon dioxide); nuclear power (+ none mentioned, – doubts about safety); solar (+ renewable, – none given); wave (+ renewable, – none given); wind power (+ renewable, – spoil the landscape, not reliable)

2 Read the introduction and questions with the class. Tell students that Deborah is the government official and John is the power company representative.

- Play the track without pausing and then give students two minutes to compare with a partner before you check answers with the class. (Parts of the text giving the answers are bold and numbered in the audioscript below exercise 3b.)

> **1** John is initially against the idea but changes his mind. Deborah supports the idea.; **2** He thinks it's too early and that it'll cause trouble; it could get out of hand.; **3** They decide to call a public meeting in July.

KEY LANGUAGE: agreeing and disagreeing politely, polite questions

3a Tell students if they don't know the order to guess. They will hear the track again in exercise 3b.

- Students work individually and then compare with a partner. Monitor to make sure students have used contractions when possible. Answers are checked after exercise 3b.

3b Play the track without pausing and then ask students to compare their answers. If necessary, play the track again.

- When you check answers, write the sentences on the board so that students can see the order, or refer to the Tip below.
- Finally, ask students to decide if the phrases are used for agreeing, disagreeing or asking polite questions.

> **1** that's one way of looking at it, but (disagreeing); **2** You're absolutely right, because (agreeing); **3** I'd like to know (polite question); **4** You have a point, but don't you think (disagreeing); **5** I'm interested in knowing (polite question); **6** That's very true, because (agreeing); **7** I'd go along with you there because (agreeing).

If possible, reproduce the audioscript so that the whole class can see it (perhaps on an Interactive Whiteboard or an overhead projector). When you check answers, underline the correct sentences in the audioscript. (These are underlined in the audioscript below.)

For further practice, ask students to do exercise KL 5 on page 137 in the Language reference.

Audioscript and answers to exercise 2:
Track 1.12
Switchboard; Deborah Rydell; John Reynolds
s: Good morning, Power Gas and Electricity, how can I help you?
DR: Good morning. Can I speak to John Reynolds, please?
s: Certainly. Who's calling please?
DR: It's Deborah Rydell, from the Department of Energy.
s: Putting you through now.
DR: Hello, is that John?
JR: Speaking.
DR: Hi John, it's Deborah from the energy department. I wanted to have a chat with you about the wind farm proposal, you know, the one at Sparrow Hill.
JR: OK, Deborah. You're still in favour of it, I hope. You're not going to cancel it, are you?
DR: Well, it's not really my decision, John. Personally, there's no doubt in my mind that wind farms are the future, although some of my colleagues seem to think we should be doing more with nuclear power. It's much more cost effective at the moment, they say.
continued…

JR: Well, <u>that's one way of looking at it, but</u> we need to think long term. We just can't go on in the same old way.

DR: <u>You're absolutely right, because</u> oil and gas will run out eventually. Well, really my reason for calling, John, is that <u>I'd like to know</u> if you think we should have a public meeting about Sparrow Hill. You know, to stop any rumours.

JR: **2 No, it's much too early.** I'm totally convinced that we should wait until we get the approval, as **2 there's likely to be a lot of trouble about this.**

DR: <u>You have a point, but 1 don't you think</u> we should **have a meeting and put our case?** I mean, I'm sure we'll be able to get some supporters to attend.

JR: Mmm, **2 I'm just worried that it could get out of hand** – you know a lot of people feel strongly about this sort of thing. **1 Though thinking about it,** <u>I'm interested in knowing</u> **what sort of local support we're likely to get, and perhaps it could be a chance to see how people who live in the area really feel.**

DR: Yes, exactly. I just think if we want it to get public approval, we need to persuade people it's right for the area, and this would be a good opportunity.

JR: <u>That's very true, because</u> without local support we're probably not going to get much further.

DR: OK, **3 I'll sort out a venue for some time in July** and organise some publicity and security. I think that's important in case things get out of hand.

JR: <u>I'd go along with you there, because</u> some of these environmental groups can get quite violent. But, don't worry, I'm sure it will be OK. Remember, all the really great ideas are unpopular at first.

DR: Yes, OK, John. Goodbye.

JR: Goodbye.

4   First, ask one or two students to say the sentences or model them yourself so that the class can hear them.

•   Then put students into pairs to practise saying the sentences while you monitor to correct pronunciation.

TASK: attending a public meeting

5   Divide the class into five groups, As, Bs, Cs, Ds and Es.

•   Tell all the As to look at their role card on page 158, all the Bs to look at page 161 and so on.

•   In their groups, ask students to prepare what they want to say at the meeting and to brainstorm any other ideas they have. Monitor to help with vocabulary and prompt with ideas if necessary.

6   Put the students into five new groups so that there is one of each student (A–E) in each group.

•   Ask students to look again at the KEY LANGUAGE in exercise 3 and go through the OTHER USEFUL PHRASES box with the class, checking pronunciation of each phrase.

•   Then give the groups 20–30 minutes to have their meeting, emphasising that they must ask questions, give opinions and persuade others in their group that their opinion is right.

•   While they are speaking, monitor and note mistakes when using the KEY LANGUAGE or OTHER USEFUL PHRASES. These will be corrected in exercise 7 below.

7   Give the groups about five minutes to decide how to summarise the results of their meeting and elect a spokesperson.

•   Give each group's spokesperson two minutes to report to the rest of the class.

•   Then ask the class to vote on whether they think the wind farm should be built or not.

•   Finally, correct some of the more common or important mistakes you noted in exercise 6 above.

8   Put students into small groups, if possible with representatives of different countries in each group.

•   Give them five minutes to discuss the question. Encourage them to ask questions and give reasons for their answers.

•   Ask two or three students to say what would happen in their country.

HOMEWORK OPTIONS

Students do the exercises on page 16 of the Workbook.

Tell students that they are a journalist who attended the meeting in exercise 6. Ask them to write a short article on the different opinions at the meeting and what was decided.

Students do exercise KL 5 on page 137 in the Language reference.

2.5 STUDY AND WRITING SKILLS

Lesson topic and staging

This lesson focuses on designing and writing a questionnaire. Students discuss questionnaires they have answered and which organisations use them. They then listen to a lecturer giving advice on designing a questionnaire before looking in more detail at the advantages of different types of questions. Next, students read about and listen to members of an environmental organisation who want to design a questionnaire. Finally, students choose questions and design the questionnaire for the organisation to use.

Objectives

By the end of the lesson, students should have:

- extracted specific information from reading and listening texts
- learned about techniques for designing questionnaires and the types of question to use
- designed and written a questionnaire for use by an environmental organisation

Common European Framework

Students can convey short simple factual information to friends/colleagues or ask for information. They can note mistakes and consciously monitor written work.

Timings

If short of time, you could drop exercise 8b on page 25 and set it for homework. A possible lesson break would be after exercise 3c page 25.

WARM-UP

This activity introduces the idea of asking productive questions.

- Tell students they are going to ask each other one question. It must get the most interesting answers possible. If necessary, give an example of a dull question (e.g. 'How old are you? Where do you live?').
- Give students two minutes to think of their question. If students have no ideas, put them into pairs to discuss possible topic areas or provide some yourself (e.g. life, favourite things, why people would/ wouldn't do something, etc.).
- Then ask students to move around the room, asking their question to as many others as possible.
- When they have finished, ask three or four students to tell the class what they found out.
- Finally, ask the class to vote on the most interesting/ the best question.

STUDY SKILLS: designing a questionnaire

1   Write the word *questionnaire* on the board and ask students what it is and what it does.

- Ask students to read the introduction to this activity to check their answer.
- Then put students in pairs to discuss the two questions before eliciting ideas from two or three students.
- Use this opportunity to elicit/point out that students at university often have to design questionnaires as part of their research and pre-teach *data* (the information you get) and *analyse* (study and think about the significance of data) – this will lead in to exercise 2a.

> Answers depend on students' own ideas and experiences.

2a Set the context and ask students to read the questions before playing the track without pausing.

- Ask students to compare with a partner before you check answers with the class. Students' answers do not need to be too specific because they will listen again and answer more questions in exercise 2b.

> 1 Ask the right questions to get the information you want, get enough data to analyse.; 2 open and closed questions; 3 Think about how you're going to analyse the data.

2b Tell students to read the questions before you play the track again, pausing at the points indicated in the audioscript to give students time to write if necessary.

- Ask students to compare with a partner before you check answers with the class. (Answers are bold in the audioscript below.)

> 1 Some people won't bother to answer them, and other people won't understand them if they're long.; 2 Open questions allow people to answer as they wish, closed questions give the answers in a list of choices.; 3 It takes a lot longer to analyse all the answers, ask for only one piece of information at a time.; 4 Respondents should be able to see the point of the question, they shouldn't think 'what does it mean?'; 5 Fairly simple questions which people can answer easily.

Audioscript and answers to exercise 2:
Track 1.13
Lecturer, Student
L: It's not easy to design a good questionnaire, Paula. I'm not surprised you're having problems. How can I help?
S: Well, a few tips would be useful. I mean, what are the key points?

L: Erm, OK, when you design your questionnaire, remember two things: Firstly, you need to ask the right questions so you get the information you're looking for. And secondly, you want to make sure you get enough data to analyse, you need as many questionnaires as possible to be completed and returned to you. OK?

S: OK, so I have to choose good questions and get as many responses as possible.

L: Exactly. Now would you like me to give you a few tips about the wording of questions? Of course, the type of question depends on what the aims of the questionnaire are, but there are certain rules, I'd say …

S: Oh, yes?

L: Mmm, first of all, use simple, short sentences. And avoid questions which are too long. **1 Some people just won't bother to answer them if they're long, and other people just won't understand them.**

S: OK, short and snappy questions, I've got it. [PAUSE]

L: Another thing, Paula. Try to use open and closed questions in your questionnaire. Mix them if possible.

S: Hold on, can you explain, erm, open and closed questions?

L: Sure. **2 Open questions, well, they allow people to answer as they wish, for example, if you ask people, 'How do you feel about the quality of the teaching you received?' it's an open question. You'll probably get a variety of answers. But closed questions are questions to which the answers are given, so the person answering has a limited choice. For example, a question like, 'How satisfied are you with your course? a) satisfied b) not satisfied c) don't know. Circle the appropriate answer.'** Well, that's a closed question; the choices are given to you. OK? [PAUSE]

S: Right. I suppose you get more information with open questions.

L: Yes, you do, but **3 it takes a lot longer to analyse all the answers!**

S: Yeah, I can see that.

L: A word of warning about open questions. **3 Ask for only one piece of information at a time.** For example, if you ask, 'What is your opinion of the course materials and teaching method', that's not really a good question. It's really two questions, and it would be better to use two separate questions, not one, to get your information.

S: I see, OK. [PAUSE]

L: Another thing about questions. All questions should be clear and well structured. **4 In other words, respondents should be able to see the point of the question, they shouldn't be thinking 'what on earth does it mean?'** Also, it's good to **5 start with fairly simple questions which people can answer easily.** This encourages them to complete the questionnaire.

S: Yes, I see! OK, I've got all that.

L: One final piece of advice. Before designing your questionnaire, you need to look ahead and think carefully about how you're going to analyse the data you get. People often forget to do this when they design a questionnaire, and they find out they can't analyse the data very easily. It's too late then!

2c Elicit brief answers from the class as most points have already been covered in exercise 2b.

- To follow up, ask students which type of questions were included on questionnaires they've designed or completed in the past.

> Open questions: Advantages = people can answer as they wish, you get a variety of answers, you get more information. Disadvantages = it takes a long time to analyse the data. Closed questions: Advantages = they're easier to analyse. Disadvantages = they limit the responses.

3a Question types

- Read through the introduction with the class and then give students three minutes to do the activity.

- Ask students to compare with a partner before you check answers with the class.

> **1 C; 2 G; 3 B; 4 F; 5 A; 6 E; 7 D**

3b Give students a few minutes to decide if they think the questions are good or poor. Some questions may have good and poor elements.

- Then put them into pairs to compare answers, before checking answers with the class.

  (Note: the answers below are the ideal ones. However, some students may argue that other questions are poor [as we don't know the function of the questionnaire]. Accept reasonable answers and suggestions.)

> **1** Good because it's easy to tick and put respondents into an age category. Poor because the categories are uneven and respondents to this questionnaire are more likely to be over 20. Suggestion = 20–30, 30–40, 40–50, 50–60, 60–70, over 70; **2** Good question (Students from some cultures may say this question is too obvious because the accepted answer in their culture is 'yes'.); **3** Poor question because there are two questions. First part is fine, but 'is it new and fuel-efficient' may lead to a lot of 'don't knows'. **4** A good simple question (but perhaps too limited – although we don't know the intention of the designer here); **5** A good question

3c Put students in small groups for this activity. Give them five minutes to discuss why they labelled some questions as 'poor' and to suggest alternatives.

- Elicit ideas and one alternative for each question labelled as 'poor' in exercise 3b.

WRITING SKILLS: writing a questionnaire

4 Set the context and read through the introduction with the class. Then give them a few minutes to note their ideas and compare with a partner.

• Elicit ideas to the board so that students can refer to them in exercise 5a.

> Answers depend on students' own ideas.

5a Ask students to try to complete the gaps before you play the track.

• Play the track without pausing.

• Ask students to compare with a partner before you check answers with the class (underlined in the audioscript below).

> Marital status; Educational qualifications; Work or student status

5b Play the track again. Ask the class to compare their notes with the ideas written on the board in exercise 4.

• Check answers with the class (bold in the audioscript below).

> nuclear power; climate change; air pollution; real food (i.e. not genetically engineered)

Audioscript and answers to exercise 5:
Track 1.14
Donna, Eduardo, Sophie

PART 1

D: OK, let's talk about the questions we'll put in our questionnaire. Eduardo, you've done some work on this, what have you come up with?

E: OK, well, I think we all agree that we need to get some basic data about the respondents in our sample. You know, we'll need to know their age, sex, <u>marital status</u>, that sort of thing. And their <u>educational qualifications</u>, of course.

D: Yes, and also get something about their current employment situation. Are they <u>employed or still students</u>?

E: Exactly. And I'd add a question about their nationality – that could be very useful for us to know.

D: True, let's get that as well. OK, the next thing is …what issues do we want to include? Sophie, I think you've got some ideas about that.

S: Yeah, I've done a bit of research, the key issues are … let's see … in no particular order: **nuclear power; climate change; air pollution; real food, in other words, there's a lot of concern about genetic engineering of food products – GMOs.** Those are the four key issues. OK?

D: It's a good list. How about protecting rainforests?

S: It's an important issue, I agree, but I think four issues are enough.

D: OK, we'll go with those. Now, what other questions … [*fade out*]

6 Tell students to read the questions and then play the track without pausing.

• Go through answers with the class or ask students to check the audioscript on page 178.

> The following should be ticked: 1; 2; 4; 6

7a Put students into their groups of four and make sure each student chooses a different issue.

• Give students 15–20 minutes to write their questions and refer them to exercises 2 and 3 to remind them of features of good questions. Monitor to point out mistakes and help with vocabulary.

• Students can remind themselves of the discussion in exercise 6 by looking at the audioscript on page 178.

7b Give students a maximum of five minutes to correct each others' mistakes.

8 Give students five minutes to add suggestions to each others' questionnaires.

8b Tell students to elect one member of their group to write the questionnaire while everyone else gives ideas and suggestions.

• When they have finished, ask them to show their questionnaire to others in the class.

• Finally, vote on the best questionnaire based on how good the questions are.

If possible, ask students to prepare their questionnaire in a Word (or similar) document so that it can be displayed on the Interactive Whiteboard later. Alternatively, give students an overhead transparency or a large sheet of paper which can be posted on the walls of the classroom.

HOMEWORK OPTIONS

Students do the exercises on page 17 of the Workbook.

Students use their questionnaires on groups of respondents they select themselves (e.g. family, friends, another class in the school). They then write a report for the class analysing the results.

3 Sport

3.1 FAIR PLAY

Lesson topic and staging

This lesson looks at sports with a specific focus on football (soccer). Students do a quiz to name as many different sports as possible and then discuss different aspects of these. Next, students read an article about football and extract vocabulary. Students then learn a set of idioms related to sport. Finally, students discuss their opinions on various aspects of sport.

Objectives

By the end of the lesson, students should have:

- extracted specific information and language items from a reading text
- extended their range of vocabulary and idioms related to sport
- participated in group discussions to express their opinions on different aspects of sport.

Timings

If short of time, you could drop exercise 6a and 6b on page 27 and set it for homework. A possible lesson break would be after exercise 5 on page 27.

WARM-UP

This activity introduces the topic of sport and some of the vocabulary students may need for exercise 1.

- Focus students on the photo on page 26. Elicit *cycling* and ask how many students like cycling.
- Explain that students are going to find out what other people in the class think about sports.
- Write the following on the board and check students understand the vocabulary:

  Find someone who:

  1 Prefers rugby to football (soccer)
  2 Doesn't like tennis at all
  3 Likes watching football but can't play
  4 Understands the rules of baseball
  5 Used to play basketball at school

- Tell them to ask questions to find a student in the class who answers 'yes' to one of the items.
- Encourage students to ask further questions (e.g. 'Why do you prefer rugby? Did you play in a team at school?') to get as much information as possible.

- Finally, ask students for the name of one student who said 'yes' to question 1, another who said 'yes' to question 2 and so on. Ask them to tell you any other information they found out.

George Orwell quote:

This quote refers to the (stereotypically British) concept of *fair play*; the idea that being fair to others is more important than winning or being good at something. It is a concept that British people often pride themselves on in sport. But Orwell negates this by saying that in *serious sport* there are more important issues (perhaps, money, winning, etc.) and, essentially, people who say otherwise are hypocritical.

i George Orwell (1903–1950) was a British writer and journalist. His two most famous novels are *Animal Farm* (1945) and *Nineteen Eighty-Four* (1949).

SPEAKING

1a Sports quiz
If you used the Warm-up activity, tell students they are going to do a quiz to name more sports.

- Read through the instructions and list of prompts and then focus students on the photo as an example of a sport (*cycling*) in which people wear *special clothes* (number 2). Check students understand *injured* (mime being in pain) and *against the clock* (you have to finish the game or turn within a specific time).
- Put students into pairs and set the time limit. Give students a time check after one minute.

1b Group the pairs with another pair and ask them to compare their ideas.

- If students don't know the name of the sport in English, tell them to draw a picture, or say how and where the sport is played.
- Then elicit students' ideas to the board so that the class can copy the vocabulary they want to keep.

Answers depend on students' own ideas.

2 Check students understand *complicated* (a lot of rules, difficult to understand how to play) and *take up* (start doing).

- Put students back into their pairs from exercise 1a and give them five minutes to discuss the questions.
- Elicit one answer from six different pairs. For question 3, elicit/give *cricket* as this appears in the article in exercise 3.

Answers depend on students' own ideas.

Take this opportunity to revise which verb (*play, do* or *go*) collocates with each sport (e.g. *play football, do judo, go swimming*). Ask students to label each of the sports on the board with one of the verbs and then check answers with the class.

READING

3 Focus students on the title and photo on page 27 and ask who they think the photo is of (Charles Miller) and if they've heard of him. Then ask students if they know what *the beautiful game* is and if they can guess from the photo (football). Students find out why it's called *the beautiful game* when they read the article.

• Ask students to read the titles (a–h) and then give them two minutes to read and match.

• Ask them to compare with a partner before you check answers with the class.

> **1** f); **2** d); **3** c); **4** a); **5** h); **6** e)

4 Give students five to eight minutes to read the article again and answer the questions. They can use their dictionaries if necessary.

• Ask them to compare with a partner before you check answers with the class.

> **1** False (he was amateur); **2** True; **3** Not given;
> **4** False (they played against Argentina); **5** Not given; **6** Not given (although they've won more times that any other country); **7** True (the *chaleira*); **8** False (the club already existed but played mainly cricket, Miller persuaded them to take up football)

i Pelé (full name: Edson Arantes do Nascimento) (born 1940) was given the title *Athlete of the Century* by the International Olympic Committee and jointly received a FIFA (Federation Internationale de Football Association) award for the greatest player in the history of the game.

5 Give students a maximum of two minutes to underline all the sportspeople words they can find.

• Then put them into pairs to match the words to the categories (1–5), using dictionaries if necessary.

• Go through answers with the class and check students' pronunciation of *amateur*.

• As a follow up, ask students if they agree with Miller that sportspeople should be amateur.

> **1** spectator; **2** fan; **3** coach; **4** referee; **5** amateur

VOCABULARY: idioms

6a Focus students on the example (number 1) and elicit/tell them that this is an *idiom* (a phrase that has a meaning not necessarily given by the individual words in the phrase).

• Check students understand *goalposts* (draw this on the board), *field* (a flat area of grass), *level* (flat) and *score* (get a point, in football – kick the ball through the goalposts).

• Give students two minutes to complete the gaps and tell them to guess if they don't know.

• Ask students to compare with a partner before you check answers with the class.

• Finally, ask students if they know the meaning of any of the idioms, but don't give the answers as these are checked in exercise 6b.

> **1** ball; **2** goalposts; **3** eye; **4** field; **5** game; **6** goal;
> **7** ball

6b Students do this activity in pairs before you check answers with the class.

• Tell students that these idioms are used in many situations (not just sport) and give examples to reinforce the meaning.

> **a)** 5; **b)** 1; **c)** 7; **d)** 2; **e)** 3; **f)** 6; **g)** 4

For further practice, ask students to do exercise V1 5 on page 139 in the Language reference.

SPEAKING

7 Ask students to read the questions and check students understand *the beautiful game* (the most wonderful, the best game).

• Give students one minute to think about their answers to the questions and then put them in groups of three or four for the discussion.

• Tell students to give reasons for their opinions and to disagree with each other if necessary.

• If you revised collocations with *play, do* and *go* in exercise 2, monitor to check that students are using these correctly.

• Finally, get answers and opinions from three or four students from different groups in the class and encourage further whole-class discussion.

HOMEWORK OPTIONS

Students do the exercises on page 18 of the Workbook.

Students use the Internet to research a famous person in sport and write an article similar to the one in this lesson.

Students do exercise V1 5 on page 139 in the Language reference.

3.2 MARTIAL ARTS

Lesson topic and staging

This lesson looks at the martial art of karate. Students listen to a karate teacher talking about his experiences and then read a leaflet for a karate club. Next, students focus on vocabulary contained in the leaflet; combinations with *self-* and abstract nouns. Students then study the grammar focus (quantifiers) and practise using these before using quantifiers to discuss true statements about themselves.

Objectives

By the end of the lesson, students should have:

- extracted specific information and language items from a listening and a reading text

- extended their range of word combination beginning with *self-* and abstract nouns

- revised/extended their understanding of the use of different quantifiers (*none*, *almost none*, etc.)

- participated in personalised speaking practice using different quantifiers.

Timings

If short of time, you could drop exercises 9 and/or 10 on page 29 and set them for homework. A possible lesson break would be after exercise 4 or 6b on page 29.

WARM-UP

This topic introduces different martial arts (along with other sports/exercises).

- Write the following on the board:

○ Tai Chi	Japan
○ Karate	Thailand
○ Kick boxing	China
○ Cricket	Scotland
○ Boules	England
○ Curling	France
○ Snooker	Canada/the USA
○ Lacrosse	India

- Put students in pairs and tell them to match the sport/exercise to the country it's strongly associated with now or in the past. Some answers may seem obvious but tell students they can use each country only once. (Note: students cannot count Canada/the USA as two countries in this activity.)

- Students can use their dictionaries if necessary and the first pair to finish wins.

- Go through answers with the class and use *karate* as a lead in to exercise 1.

- To follow up, see Homework options at the end of this lesson.

> Tai Chi – China; karate – Japan; kick boxing – Thailand; cricket – India (Note: it was invented in England but it's the most popular sport in India.); boules – France; curling – Scotland; snooker – England; lacrosse – Canada/the USA (Note: this was invented by Native North Americans.)

LISTENING

1 Focus students on the photos on page 28 and elicit *karate* and *martial arts*.

- Then put students into pairs to think of other martial arts (e.g. Tai Chi, judo) and reasons for doing them.

- Get a few ideas from the class.

> Answers depend on students' own ideas and opinions.

2a Introduce the context and ask students if any of them do karate or would like to.

- Ask students to read the questions and check they understand *belts* (show the black belt in the photo).

- Play the track, if necessary pausing at the points indicated in the audioscript below.

- Ask students to compare answers with a partner.

- Go through answers with the class and check they understand *impact* (influence) and *joy* (happiness). (Answers are bold in the audioscript below.)

> 1 just over 25 years, two to five times a week;
> 2 having an impact on people; 3 you can measure students' progress; 4 it makes him extremely happy

Audioscript and answers to exercise 2a:
Track 1.16
Interviewer, Mr Coles
I: How long have you been doing karate?
C: OK. My time in karate is 1 **just over 25 years** now. I started back in 1981 in my final year at university down in Bath and I've been 1 **training ever since** on the basis of something like between two and five times a week. So, 25 years in karate. Like, we say it takes about five to six years to get to black belt – that's what we say is the beginning of karate. So I achieved my black belt in 1987 and since then I've been working my way as a black belt through the various levels and I'm now at the fifth level of black belt. [PAUSE]
I: What gives you most satisfaction in teaching karate?
C: Well, I think I'm going to sum it up with one word. 2 **Impact ... having an impact on people** – our students – students who now these days range from four to ... I was going to say 64, but we've had someone of 73 in one of our clubs. [PAUSE]

continued...

3 We can measure progress through different belts something which was introduced in the West. These days people need to measure their achievement and that's good. It's a way to distinguish different levels. [PAUSE] And when students achieve their new belt .... **4 I take tremendous joy in seeing their reaction,** you get smiling faces, you get some children coming up and saying 'Wow, it's the best day of my life'. I mean, for the adults it may be simply an expression of relief – the fact they've got through an exam 20 years after having left school and not taking anything of this like before.

But I'd like to take that a step further. I take greatest satisfaction from witnessing the change in a student's approach and attitude. When I see students who cross a barrier from just doing movements to feeling or living their karate, then I feel great – we've made a change somewhere, and I can think of a number of incidences where I've had, say, children who are floppy and not really with it, and after a certain level something snaps – all of a sudden they are down in their stances, they're breathing, they're concentrating, they're looking, things are working, and for me that's a case of ... well, between us, them and me, we've made a change.

2b Ask students to read the questions and then play the track without pausing.

- Ask students to compare with a partner before you check answers with the class. (Answers are bold in the audioscript below.)
- Follow up by asking the class which of the reasons in question 2 they think are good reasons to do karate.

> 1 a hobby; 2 attracted by glamour and excitement, they see it on TV or on Playstation, parents encourage them to do it, they believe it gives discipline and control, child can learn things that help them protect themselves physically.

Audioscript and answers to exercise 2b:
Track 1.17
Interviewer, Mr Coles
I: Is it a hobby or is it more of a way of life?
C: Yeah, this is a classic question, really. I mean, **1 for most people who do it these days it's undoubtedly a hobby.** Mmm, for some, lessons learnt in karate can be part of their life, it can become part of their life if they do it for longer and longer.
But for me, you see, I mean, it took like I said, it took six years to get to black belt. So, after the six years we say it takes to start karate, to some extent when you get to black belt, you kind of come down from a high of training a good number of times during the week, you've had extreme effort and concentration, and it's a case of 'Can you survive to the next level?' as we say, ... and really after black belt, we say you just have to keep training, which is very hard for some people to accept. So, for them it's not a way of life, it's become more than a hobby, it's become a goal in their life to achieve black belt and a very admirable one, and we've had people who've achieved black belt and said 'That's my lot', and that's fair enough, as long as they admit that to me and to themselves. But for others it's a case of, they've become disillusioned, it's black belt and where do I go now? and it almost just stops, and sometimes that's a bit of a shame if they can't accept that.

continued...

I: Why do people start karate?
C: The majority of the new starters these days are children and either they **2 are attracted themselves by the glamour and excitement of karate,** the martial arts, they've **seen it on TV,** they've enacted it **on their Playstation games,** they see the noise, the excitement, they see the fast flowing kicks and so on. Or it may be because **their mum or dad has encouraged them to attend.** And there could be the twin attractions there of karate **installing discipline and control** in their children. As is increasingly the case these days, maybe things don't work at home, parents are out at work more often. Maybe the school doesn't instil discipline. Very often these days teachers are restricted in terms of what they can say and can do and parents bring their children and say 'sort them out'. And the kid can also, from a parent's perspective, their child can also **learn stuff which enables them to look after themselves,** and that's an admirable aim in itself because everyone's fearful of their child being out of their sight.

READING

3a Lead in by asking students if they think people would be interested in doing karate having heard what Mr Coles said about it.

- Then explain they are going to read a leaflet about doing karate classes and check students understand *championships* (competitions to give an important award, e.g. world champion = the best in the world).
- Give students one minute to tick the options they think will be mentioned. Answers are checked in exercise 3b.

3b Give students one minute to read the leaflet and check their answers to 3a above.

- Go through answers with the class.

> The following are mentioned in the leaflet: 2; 3; 4; 5; 7

4 Read the instructions with the class. Emphasise that students should cross out the options that are *not* correct. Tell students that if an item is *not mentioned,* they should cross it out.

- Don't pre-teach vocabulary because students will study it in exercises 5 and 6a.
- Give students five minutes to read the text.
- Ask students to compare with a partner before you check answers with the class.

> The following should be crossed out: 1 d); 2 a); 3 d); 4 c)

VOCABULARY: *self-*, abstract nouns

5a Students do this activity individually and then compare answers with a partner.

- As you go through answers with the class, write each word on the board and mark the main stress (bold in the answers below). Tell students that in compound nouns, both words are stressed.

> 1 self-respect; 2 self-confidence; 3 self-control; 4 self-defence; 5 self-discipline; 6 self-development

5b Students do this activity individually, referring to the meanings discussed in exercise 5a if necessary.

- As you elicit answers from the class, correct their pronunciation if necessary.

> 1 self-defence; 2 self-control; 3 self-respect; 4 self-confidence; 5 self-discipline

For further practice, ask students to do exercise V2 6 on page 139 in the Language reference.

6a Students do this activity individually and then compare answers with a partner.

- Go through answers with the class and model the pronunciation, asking students to repeat.

> courtesy; tolerance; coordination; flexibility; agility; calm

6b Students can use their dictionaries to do this activity.

- Check answers with the class.

> Body: coordination, flexibility, agility; polite behaviour: courtesy, tolerance

GRAMMAR: quantifiers

7a Ask students what a *quantifier* is (tells you the amount/quantity of something) and get one or two examples from the class.

- Give students 30 seconds to find the quantifiers in the text and then three minutes to complete the scale.

- Ask students to compare with a partner before you check answers with the class. Answers are below exercise 7b.

(!) The use of these quantifiers will depend on context for meaning. For example, A: 'I've got a few problems', B: 'Not many, then.' A: 'Actually, far too many.'

7b Elicit examples of countable (e.g. *cars*, *people*) and uncountable (e.g. *money*, *sugar*) nouns and elicit/tell students that 'many' can go with 'cars/people', but not with 'money/sugar'.

- Put students in pairs to divide the other quantifiers into groups and refer them to the Language reference on page 138 if necessary. Tell them to write 'U' (uncountable), 'C' (countable) or 'B' (both) next to each quantifier.

- Check answers and then read through the Grammar Tip with the class.

(!) 'None' is used as a pronoun and cannot be used with either an uncountable or a countable noun (e.g. None cars **x**). We have to use 'no' before a noun (e.g. No people). We have to use the phrases 'None of the ___' if we want to use it with a noun (e.g. None of the people).

> 1 hardly any; 2 (a) little/few; 3 a few; 4 some; 5/6 a lot of/many/much; 7 far too much/far too many; 8 all

8 If students find this activity very difficult, do the first example with the class and show them that we can use *some* when the sentence has *a few* or *a little* (normally a positive meaning).

- Go though the answers and notes below with the class.

> 1 *a few* means *some* (positive meaning – I'm pleased to say); 2 can replace *few* with *not many* (negative meaning – unfortunately); 3 can replace *little* with *not much* and it can also mean *some* (Note: if you use *some* in this context, the meaning becomes more positive.); 4 *a little* means *some*

(!) *Some* can have a positive or a negative meaning. In the sentences above where it replaces *a few, a little* or *little* it has a positive meaning.

9 Students do this activity individually and refer to the Language reference on page 138 for help.

- Ask students to compare with a partner before you check answers with the class.

- In feedback, ask students to tell you why the sentences they corrected are wrong.

> Corrections: **1** Several ~~of~~ my friends; **2** Far too ~~much~~ many; **3** ... give me a little; **4** ~~A little~~ Few/A few of the parents; **5** Hardly any ~~of~~; **6** ... get a few tickets; **7** ... have ~~a~~ little information

10 Do the first sentence with the class, using yourself as an example. Tell students why you used the quantifier you did and encourage them to ask follow-up questions.

- Give students three minutes to make the sentences true for themselves and then put them in pairs to compare and ask follow-up questions.

- In feedback, get two or three students to tell the class a few of their sentences and encourage more follow-up questions.

HOMEWORK OPTIONS

Students do the exercises on pages 19–20 of the Workbook.

Students use the Internet to research one of the sports/ exercises from the Warm-up and write a factsheet about it.

Students do exercises V2 6 and G1 1 on page 139 in the Language reference.

3.3 BABE

Lesson topic and staging

This lesson looks at women in sport. Students read an article about Babe Didrikson (an American sportswoman) and then focus on adjectives taken from the text. Next, students study definite and zero articles in the text and use these in a series of practice activities. Students then focus on the pronunciation of articles. Finally, students discuss and then write about whether the sexes should compete equally in sports.

Objectives

By the end of the lesson, students should have:

- extracted specific information and language items from a reading text
- revised/learned about the use of definite and zero articles and practised using these
- revised and/or extended their range of adjectives related to women in sport
- discussed and written about equality of the sexes in sport.

Timings

If short of time, and your students are confident using definite and zero articles, you could drop exercise 6 on page 31. A possible lesson break would be after exercise 3 on page 30 or exercise 5 on page 31.

This activity introduces the topic of famous and successful women.

- Write the following on the board:

○ Marie Curie	art
○ Indira Gandhi	medicine
○ Martina Navratilova	writing
○ Doris Lessing	sport
○ Sarah Bernhardt	politics
○ Rachel Whiteread	acting

- Put students in pairs to match the woman to her field. If they don't know, they can guess.
- Give students one point for each correct answer.
- Students can use these women for the topic of an article in the Homework options.

1a Focus students on the photo on the top left of page 31 and ask if they know who this woman is (Babe Didrikson – American sportswoman) and/or what she is doing.

- Give students two minutes to think of a famous sportswoman or women and make notes about why they admire her/them.
- Put students in pairs to briefly compare their ideas.

1b Explain that students are going to compare the achievements of the woman/women they chose in exercise 1a with Babe Didrikson.

- Give students one minute to read the article and tell them not to worry about vocabulary at this stage.
- Then put students into pairs to discuss how their famous woman/women compare to Babe Didrikson.

i The word 'babe' in the title refers to Babe Didrikson's name, but also the colloquial meaning of 'young, attractive woman'. The title is ironic because Didrikson is not a woman who would normally be referred to as 'babe'. Didrikson was named 'Babe' after Babe Ruth (1895–1948), an exceptionally talented and iconic American baseball player.

! Tell students that calling a woman 'babe' can often be impolite and sexist.

2 Check students understand *chronological* (in order of date, earliest date first) and ask students to try to number the information before they read the text again.

- Then give them four minutes to read, check their answers and order the events they couldn't do above.
- Tell them not to worry about vocabulary at this stage because exercise 3 focuses on some of this.
- Ask students to compare with a partner before you check answers with the class. Students may be confused about the order of e) and f) so refer to the notes in the answers below.
- Finally, ask students what they think is the most impressive thing about Babe Didrikson.

> **1** d); **2** c); **3** e); **4** f) (in the Olympics *that followed* the Amateur Athletic Union event and five world records); **5** b); **6** a)

3 Give students four minutes to do this activity individually before comparing answers with a partner.

- Go through answers with the class and check pronunciation.

> **1** expert; **2** disgusted; **3** phenomenal; **4** illegal; **5** aggressive; **6** dramatic; **7** professional (abbreviation = pro)

GRAMMAR: definite and zero articles

4a Ask the class what the definite and zero articles are (*the* and *no article used*).

- Tell students to underline the phrases in the text before they match them to uses (a–d).

- Tell students to look at the sentence around the definite article in each example (1–4) to help them decide its use. If necessary, students can refer to the Language reference on page 138.

- Ask students to compare with a partner before you check answers with the class.

> **1** b); **2** a); **3** c); **4** d)

4b Students work individually to match the phrases to uses and then compare their answers with a partner.

- Go through the answers and with the class and, if necessary, refer to the text to give reasons.

> the province: a) (of the male); the amazing life of Babe Didrikson: a); The marriage notice: c) (substitute noun for the phrase *how Time magazine reported his wedding*) or b); the sixth child of seven born to Ole: d); the team award (b); the train: b); the title: c) (substitute noun for *equal first*) or b); the tour: b)

5 Tell students to look at the sentence around the zero article in each example (1–3) to help decide its use.

- Ask students to compare with a partner before you check answers with the class.

- Finally, read through the Grammar Tip with the class and contrast this with use a) in exercise 5.

> **1** c); **2** a); **3** b)

6 Focus students on the photo in the article on page 31 and ask students if they know who this is (Mia Hamm) and what sport she plays (football/soccer).

- Orient students to the text by doing the following: 1 students brainstorm what information they expect to find in the text; 2 students read the text quickly to compare their ideas; 3 ask students for the most interesting piece of information they read.

- Then set the task and give students a maximum of ten minutes to edit the text.

- Ask students to compare with a partner and give reasons for making the corrections. Students can refer to exercises 4, 5 and the Language reference on page 138 if they need help.

- Go through answers with the class and elicit the reasons for the corrections.

> At the age of 15, Mia Hamm became *the* youngest player ever to play for *the* national soccer team of the United States. She was the first international star of *the* women's game and eventually became one of *the* most famous women athletes in the world, giving ~~the~~ hope to ~~the~~ young sportswomen.
>
> She was born in 1972 and went to ~~the~~ high school in Northern Virginia. In 1989 she entered North Carolina University, where Michael Jordan had also studied.
>
> She became *the* youngest American woman to win **a** World Cup championship at the age of 19. As part of the US women's soccer team, she won *the* World Cup in 1991 and 1999, and also Olympic gold medals in 1996 and 2004. In addition to winning four major championships, the US women finished third in the 1995 and 2003 World Cup tournaments.
>
> Mia devotes much of her free time to ~~the~~ charities, and in 1999, she began the Mia Foundation to help with bone marrow research and to develop sports programmes for women with ~~the~~ sporting ability. Her book, *Go for the Goal*, was published in 1999. *The* book, aimed at young female athletes, has proved inspirational for a generation of young women.

7 Tell students that the definite article is often difficult to hear because it is weak (not stressed). However, we can often use the context of a sentence to decide if there is a definite article or not.

- Ask students to read the nouns in 1–5 and check they understand *captain* (leader of the team) and *wrist* (point to your wrist).

- Play the track, pausing after each sentence and tell students to tick the noun if there is a definite article and put a cross if not.

- Ask students to compare with a partner before you check answers with the class.

- Finally, play sentences 1 and 2 again and highlight that the article in 2 is weak. Ask students to repeat the sentence to practise saying the weak form.

> **1** university: no article; **2** university: article; **3** game: article, captain: article; **4** tennis players: no article, wrist injuries: no article; **5** tennis players: article, courts: article

SPEAKING AND WRITING

8a Remind students of Babe Didrikson and Mia Hamm and ask if these women played against men or only other women (probably only other women). Elicit that this is the most usual situation.

- Read through the instructions with the class and then put students into groups for the discussion. If possible, make sure there is a mix of sexes in each group. Tell students to give reasons for their opinions and disagree with each other if necessary.

- Finally, ask students if they agreed that men and women should compete equally and why/why not.

8b Give students 20–30 minutes to write their paragraph and then take them in for marking, paying particular attention to the use of definite and zero articles.

HOMEWORK OPTIONS

Students do the exercises on pages 21–22 of the Workbook.

Students use the Internet to research another famous woman (their own choice or one of the women mentioned in the Warm-up activity) and write a short article about her. Post the articles around the room and ask the class to decide which woman they think is the most impressive/most interesting.

Students do exercises G2 2 and 3, and V3,4 7 on page 139 in the Language reference. (Note: V3,4 7 includes vocabulary from exercise 6 in Lesson 3.2.)

3.4 SCENARIO: WHO WAS THE GREATEST?

IN THIS LESSON

Lesson topic and staging

This lesson focuses on the language of emphasis and comparison. Students are introduced to the scenario of a TV sports channel competition to decide the greatest modern sportsperson. Students discuss criteria for choosing this person and then listen to a woman talking about her choice. This leads to a focus on the KEY LANGUAGE and students then practise using the language. Finally, the main TASK asks students to give a talk about their choice for the greatest sportsperson.

Objectives

By the end of the lesson, students should have:
- learned useful phrases for emphasising and comparing information
- used this language in a 'real-life' situation to give a talk on the most outstanding modern sportsperson
- extracted specific information and language items from a reading and a listening text
- participated effectively in extended speaking practice.

Common European Framework

Students can use language effectively to express beliefs, views and opinions in discussing topics of interest.

Timings

If short of time, you could cut the number of options for discussion in exercise 3a on page 32. A possible lesson break would be after exercise 7 on page 33.

WARM-UP

This activity focuses on different sports and the people who do them:
- Focus students on the photos on pages 32 and 33 and ask them to discuss the following questions in pairs:
  - What's the name of these sports?
  - Have you tried any of them?
  - Which would you like to try?
  - Which are popular in your country (as a sport to watch, a sport to play/do)?
  - Which do you think is the most dangerous?
  - Can you name a famous sportsperson in one of these sports?
- Put the pairs into groups of four to compare their answers.
- Get a few ideas for each question from the class.

1a Read through the instructions with the class and tell students the famous sportspeople they think of do not need to be currently doing the sport.

• If they can think of none or only one name in a sport, they should move on the next as quickly as possible.

• Give students a time check after one minute and stop them at exactly two minutes.

1b Put pairs together to compare, then elicit answers from the class and write them on the board (students can use these in exercises 8 and 9).

• Award one point for each sportsperson named. The pair with most points wins.

> Answers depend on students' own ideas.

2 Tell students to read the questions and check they understand *channel* (i.e. a TV channel).

• Give students three minutes to read the situation and answer the questions, then elicit answers from the class.

> **1** to attract viewers' interest – it's a new channel; **2** in the last 20 years; **3** viewers write an email/letter about a sportsperson, selected writers take part in a TV debate, the audience will vote on the greatest sportsperson

3a Read through the instructions and criteria and check students understand *competitors* (people in a competition), *status* (how others think/feel about you), *role model* (an example for others to follow), *fame* (being famous), *overcome* (find solutions to) and *fair play* (always fair to other competitors, never lying or cheating in their sport).

• Introduce the collocation *break a record* (go faster, etc. than the current record) as students need this in exercise 4.

• Put students into groups of three or four and tell them they must agree on which five criteria to choose.

3b Elicit answers for exercise 3a, then ask the whole class to discuss and agree on which five should be finally chosen.

4 Focus students on the photos on page 33 and elicit/tell them this is Ellen MacArthur, a British *yachtswoman* (refer to the second photo). Model the pronunciation of *yacht*.

• Read the introduction and tell students that *Maria* is one of the viewers Global Sports has invited to the TV debate.

• Ask them to read the questions and then play the track without pausing.

• Ask students to compare with a partner before you check answers with the class. (Answers are bold in the audioscript below exercise 5b.)

> **1** a famous round-the-world solo yachting race; **2** She came second and was the fastest woman competitor.; **3** In 2005 she broke the record for sailing non-stop around the world, it was a very hard and dangerous race.

| KEY LANGUAGE: emphasis and comparison |

5a Read through the instructions and examples with students, then play the track pausing at the points indicated in the audioscript below to give students time to note their answers.

5b Ask students to compare answers to 5a with a partner before they check the audioscript on page 178.

• Go through answers to 5a with the class (italicised in the audioscript below), modelling and highlighting the use of an emphatic stress on the adjectives and adverbs (e.g. *aMAzing*). Ask students to repeat.

☀ If possible, reproduce the audioscript so that the whole class can see it (perhaps on an Interactive Whiteboard or an overhead projector). When you elicit answers, underline comparison words/phrases on the text.

> **Audioscript and answers to exercises 4 and 5: Track 1.19**
>
> Ellen MacArthur was born in England in 1976. She's a *truly* remarkable person. In my opinion, she's *definitely* <u>the greatest</u> modern sportsperson. Let me tell you why.
>
> She first came to people's attention when she took part in a **1 famous yachting race, the Vendée Globe. It's a round-the-world solo yacht race**, which takes place every four years, and the competitors are top class yachtsmen and women. Ellen MacArthur **2 came second in the race, and was <u>the fastest</u> woman competitor.** It was an *amazing* achievement, and the French were *particularly* impressed with her performance. In fact, she became a heroine in France, they just love her there. [PAUSE]
>
> But, *most of all*, she's famous because **3 in 2005, she broke the record for sailing non-stop around the world.** Her voyage took 71 days. The record was previously held by a Frenchman, Francis Joyon. It was an *incredible* achievement, **especially as the seas were very rough in the South Atlantic area**, and in other parts of the world, she was sailing in *extremely* hot weather. The journey back was '*incredibly* hard', she said, and she was *totally* exhausted at the end of the trip. [PAUSE]
>
> She's a great competitor, *there's no doubt about that*, but *above all*, she's a great person, a *really* fine human being. And that's why people admire her so much. For example, during the Vendee Globe race, she stopped sailing at one point to help another yachtsman who was in difficulties. It was a marvellous, unselfish act.
>
> *continued...*

What's extraordinary, also, about her is that she's a small woman, without obvious physical advantages, but you need to be very strong to take part in round-the-world races. Like many other top sportspeople, she's got *tremendous* determination and courage. [PAUSE] But <u>compared to people like</u> Tiger Woods, the golfer, she doesn't attract a great deal of financial support, you know, endorsements from businesses, that sort of thing. Some sportspeople make a fortune that way. Another thing, sailing around the world is actually very dangerous. If Ellen fell overboard, she could easily drown. And <u>unlike other top sports people</u>, erm, footballers, golfers, tennis players and so on, she doesn't make a lot of money from her sailing. She just loves the sport. Oh, I forgot to mention, she often beats male competitors – <u>not many women can do that!</u> *It's really impressive*, don't you think?

I'd like to stress that she's both a fantastic competitor and a wonderful human being. She's a role model for all sportspeople. She's *undoubtedly the greatest sportsperson* of the modern era. Please vote for me and my choice, Ellen MacArthur.

6   Students do this activity individually, then compare with a partner.

* Go through the answers with the class and write them on the board so all students can see the order.

* Ask students if they've heard of any of these people and, if possible, elicit a few facts about each. Students may want to talk about one of these sportspeople in exercises 8 and 9 later.

> 1 Pele was a truly fantastic Brazilian footballer.;
> 2 Tiger Woods is definitely the best golfer in the world.; 3 Andre Agassi was a particularly charismatic tennis player.; 4 What's extraordinary about Serena Williams is her determination.;
> 5 I'd like to stress that Ellen MacArthur is incredibly courageous.; 6 Mohammed Ali will be remembered most of all for his match against George Foreman.

7   Ask students to underline the words/phrases for comparison in the audioscript on page 178 and compare their answers with a partner.

* Elicit the words/phrases for comparison from the class (underlined in the audioscript above).

For further practice, ask students to do exercise KL 4 on page 139 in the Language reference.

TASK: choosing the greatest modern sportsperson

8a Remind students of the Global Sports situation outlined earlier in this lesson and give them four minutes to decide which sportsperson they want to talk about.

* If they want to choose a sportsperson of their own, students can look at previous exercises in this lesson or previous lessons in this unit to help them decide.

8b Tell students to think about the structure of their presentation, how to make it interesting, how to engage their listeners, the variety of language they use, how to introduce and conclude what they want to say, and most of all how they will make their presentations persuasive.

* Give students 20–30 minutes to make their notes and monitor to help with any of the features of presentations mentioned above.

9a Remind students of the KEY LANGUAGE and go through the OTHER USEFUL PHRASES.

* Then put students into groups (maximum of five in a group) and tell them they have two to three minutes each to give their presentations. Emphasise they can ask each other questions at the end of the presentation.

* While they are speaking, monitor to note mistakes using the KEY LANGUAGE and OTHER PHRASES.

9b When they have voted, ask each group to tell the class which sportsperson won and why.

* Encourage other students in the class to say if they think this is a good choice or if they're surprised.

HOMEWORK OPTIONS

Students do the exercises on page 23 of the Workbook.

Students use their notes from exercise 8b to write a fact sheet about the sportsperson.

Students do exercise KL 4 on page 139 in the Language reference.

3.5 STUDY AND WRITING SKILLS

Lesson topic and staging

This lesson focuses on understanding essay questions and writing 'for and against' essays. Students discuss what makes a good essay and then analyse the language used in some essay questions. Next, students listen to a lecturer giving advice about essays and analyse an essay question. Students then read an essay and focus on the content, organisation and the language used before finally writing an essay of their own.

Objectives

By the end of the lesson, students should have:

- extracted specific information and language items from a listening and a reading text
- learned (more) about the language used in essay questions, how to write an essay and the structure and language of a 'for and against' essay
- written a 'for and against' essay.

Common European Framework

Students can write simple connected texts on a range of topics, express personal view/opinions and link a series of discrete items into a connected linear sequence of points.

Timings

If short of time, you could ask students to plan their essay together in exercise 11b, but then write it individually for homework. A possible lesson break would be after exercise 4 on page 34.

WARM-UP

This activity introduces the topic of how much sportspeople should be paid and vocabulary for exercise 6.

- Write the following on the board: *tennis player, surfer, motor racing driver, mountaineer, boxer.*
- Check students understand the terms and then tell them to rank the people on the board according to who they think should be paid the most (1) to who should be paid the least (5).
- Put students into pairs to compare and give reasons for their lists.
- Finally, elicit a list from two or three students and ask the class if they agree.

STUDY SKILLS: understanding essay questions

1 Explain that students are going to write an essay later in the lesson.

- Set the question, focus students on the examples and then put them into pairs to make a list.
- Elicit a few ideas from two or three pairs and ask the class if they agree.

2a Understanding key words.

- Put students into pairs or small groups and tell them to underline the key words in each question as they discuss it.
- Elicit the key words from the class, but not what each question means as this is checked in exercise 2b.

> 1 Analyse; 2 Compare, contrast; 3 To what extent; 4 Account for; 5 Outline; 6 Discuss; 7 Describe

2b Students do this activity and then compare with a partner before you check answers with the class.

- In feedback, check students understand *to what extent* and *how far* by explaining question 3 in exercise 2a (e.g. is winning the most important thing, the least important thing, or is it somewhere between?).

> 1 c); 2 g); 3 d); 4 a); 5 f); 6 e); 7 b)

3a Essay writing

- Read through the introduction and instructions and then play the track without pausing.
- Elicit answers from the class and ask if this point is similar to any of their ideas in exercise 1.

> An essay is a question which needs an answer, not an opportunity to write everything you know.

3b Give students one minute to read the notes, then play the track pausing at appropriate points for students to complete the notes. (The audioscript is on page 179 of the Coursebook.)

- Ask students to compare with a partner and, if necessary, play the track again.
- Go through answers with the class and check they understand *brainstorm* (note ideas quickly in no particular order), *restate* (say/write again) and *abbreviations* (shortened words).

> 1 Analyse; 2 underline; 3 Decide; 4 Make; 5 Brainstorm; 6 Ask; 7 Organise; 8 middle; 9 end; 10 restate the question in your own words and introduce the topic; 11 refer back to the question and offer your own opinion, if appropriate; 12 neutral; 13 yourself; 14 Passive; 15 abbreviations

4 Give students five minutes for this activity. Remind them that exercise 2b will help them analyse the question they choose.

- If necessary, give students a few ideas of the kind of thing they might include in an essay (e.g. examples, arguments for and against, your opinion, others' opinions, etc.).

- For feedback ask students how many of them chose each of the questions in exercise 2a. Then ask for a few ideas of what might be included in each.

WRITING SKILLS: for and against essays

5   Explain that students are going to read an essay about how much sportspeople earn.

- Ask students who the people in the photos are (Lewis Hamilton, a famous motor racing driver, and Anna Kournikova, a famous tennis player). Then ask why Hamilton has logos on his clothes and why Kournikova is holding a shoe. Take this opportunity to pre-teach *sponsorship*.

- Give students a few minutes to discuss this question and then elicit some ideas from the class.

6   Tell students to read the questions and then give them three minutes to read the essay and answer the questions.

- Ask students to compare with a partner before you check answers with the class.

   1 football, golf, tennis, boxing, motor racing; 2 salaries; prize money; sponsorship deals, advertising contracts; 3 She/he thinks that sportspeople should be paid what they are, they're worth it.

7   Students work individually and then compare with a partner before you check answers with the class.

   a) 4; b) 5; c) 1; d) 3; e) 2

8a Introductions

- Put students in pairs to discuss this question. Answers are checked in exercise 8b.

8b Give students a maximum of one minute to read and check, then elicit answers from the class.

   2; 3; 4

9a Ask students to read the introduction and then give them three minutes to answer the questions.

- Ask students to compare with a partner before you check answers with the class.

   Changes: 1 (present perfect); 3 (present perfect); 4 (present perfect); 6 (present perfect).
   Generalise: 2 (present); 5 (present); 7 (present). (Note: the tenses for all items can be simple or continuous.)

(!) All the expressions under 'changes' can also be used to introduce generalisations: it depends on the noun phrase that follows, e.g. 'In the past decade, most people have …').

9b Give students ten minutes to write three or four opening sentences while you monitor to correct.

- Elicit two or three good examples to the board as a model for the class.

10 Formal expressions

- Tell students to underline the expressions in the essay. They may find two for number 3.

- Ask students to compare with a partner and then elicit answers from the class.

- Then, ask students why this is a good essay and refer them to the ideas they had in exercise 1.

- Finally, ask students if they agree with the writer's opinion and why/why not.

   1 The objective of this essay is to decide; 2 for instance; 3 Many people argue, It can also be argued that; 4 In simple terms; 5 In contrast; 6 It is also clear that; 7 In conclusion; 8 On balance

11a Tell students to spend four minutes discussing each question and give regular time checks.

11b Ask students to decide which title they found most interesting or which generated most discussion in exercise 11a. Advise them to choose this title for their essay.

- Give the pairs 15–20 minutes to plan their essay and emphasise they should only make notes on content and structure, not write full sentences at this stage. Both students need a copy of the notes.

- Monitor to help with vocabulary or provide prompts if necessary.

- Then allow 30–40 minutes for students to write their essays.

- Take essays in for marking, paying attention to structure and use of expressions from this lesson. Alternatively, ask students to edit each other's work and then re-write with corrections before you take them in for marking.

HOMEWORK OPTIONS

Students do the exercises on page 24 of the Workbook.

Refer students to the Warm-up activity in which they decided which kind of sportsperson should be paid more than others. Write the following on the board: *X should be paid more than all other sportspeople. Discuss.* Students then write a 'for and against' essay for homework.

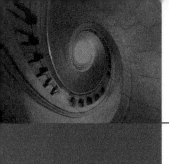

REVIEW

UNITS 1–3

GRAMMAR

1a Tell students to discuss the possible answers before they read the text. Students will read the text and answer the questions in exercise 1b.

1b Give students three minutes to read the text and answer the questions in exercise 1a.

- Check answers with the class and ask students how many they knew/had already guessed in exercise 1a.

> **1** Mount Everest; **2** Sir Edmund Hillary and Tenzing Norgay; **3** over 40 (on some days); **4** oxygen tanks, tents, sleeping bags, food, water, Frisbees, baseball bats, cans

2 Tell students they will need to look at the sentences surrounding the gaps to decide which answer is best.

- Give students five minutes to complete the gaps.
- Ask them to compare with a partner before you check answers with the class.
- In feedback, ask students to say why the answer is correct and if necessary refer students to the relevant sections of the Language reference on page 138.

> **1** b); **2** a); **3** a); **4** c); **5** c) **6** c); **7** b); **8** a); **9** b); **10** a); **11** c); **12** c); **13** c); **14** a); **15** c); **16** b)

3a Give students ten minutes to write as many questions as possible.

- Monitor to correct students' questions if necessary as a correct version is essential in exercise 3b.
- Elicit one or two questions from the class and write them on the board.

> Answers depend on students' own ideas.

3b Use the questions you wrote on the board in exercise 3a as examples and elicit/make the changes necessary to turn these into indirect questions.

- Then put students into the same pairs as exercise 3a and give them ten minutes to re-write five of their questions in an indirect form.
- Monitor to point out mistakes but encourage students to self-correct using the Language reference on page 138 if necessary.
- In feedback, get three or four direct and then indirect questions from the class.

> Answers depend on students' questions in exercise 3a.

VOCABULARY

4 Give students five minutes to complete the gaps.

- Put them in pairs to compare before you check answers with the class.

> **1** intentionally; **2** culture; **3** sense; **4** transport; **5** Global; **6** aggressive; **7** block; **8** congestion; **9** rush; **10** self-discipline

5 Students do this activity individually and then compare with a partner.

- Check answers with the class.

> **1** ~~sideways~~ edgeways; **2** ~~did~~ scored; **3** ~~say~~ speak; **4** ~~topic~~ ball; **5** ~~see~~ hear; **6** ~~modern~~ new; **7** ~~in~~ on; **8** ~~put~~ take

KEY LANGUAGE

6 Introduce the context and read through the names and a–f with the class.

- Play the track without pausing and ask students to compare answers in pairs.
- Play the track again if necessary and then check answers with the class.

> **1** d); **2** c); **3** f); **4** a); **5** e); **6** b)

7 Tell students to try and complete the gaps before you play the track again.

- Then play the track for students to check and complete their answers.
- Go through answers with the class.

> **1** definitely; **2** situation; **3** trouble; **4** have; **5** solve; **6** Compared

---

Track 1.21

Kenny, Chloe, Vince

K: Right, I think we need to talk about the line-up for next week's match. Chloe, what's the situation with injuries?

C: Not too bad, but Marek definitely isn't going to be fit by Saturday.

V: What about Steve?

C: Well, it's a very tricky situation, Vince. He's still suffering from that knee injury. I just don't know if he'll be well enough to play on Saturday.

V: Let's get Patrice in to replace him.

continued…

> K: The trouble with that is we'll be very weak in defence. Patrice is really more of a striker.
>
> C: That's very true.
>
> V: OK. You have a point. We could try out Sinan. I know he hasn't played for the first team before, but he did incredibly well in the trials last month.
>
> C: Yes. That could solve the problem.
>
> K: I'm not so sure. Perhaps we should give Giancarlo a chance. I've been watching him recently. Compared to Sinan, I think he's got a lot more potential.
>
> V: OK Kenny. You're the manager. It's your decision.

LANGUAGE CHECK

8 Tell students to try all the sentences before they look at the page in the Coursebook to check.

> 1 people <u>are</u> studying; 2 louder <u>than</u> words; 3 she <u>had</u> written; 4 have <u>been</u> going up; 5 long <u>has</u> the sea; 6 false <u>impression</u> that; 7 we <u>would</u> like; 8 his <u>self</u>-control; 9 that <u>a</u> few; 10 entered <u>the</u> Royal College

LOOK BACK

9 The aim of this activity is to remind students of areas they looked at in Units 1–3. This will help reinforce any language or skills they had difficulties with or were particularly good at.

> read a speech by Martin Luther King: 1.1, exercise 5; learn about verbs we rarely use with the continuous aspect: 1.2, Grammar Tip; check your partner's email for mistakes: 1.5, exercise 10b; discuss the results of two surveys: 2.1, exercise 7; learn about using *since* and *for* with the present perfect simple and continuous: 2.2, Grammar Tip; design a questionnaire: 2.5, exercises 7 and 8; read about the father of Brazilian football: 3.1, exercise 4; learn seven idioms connected with sport: 3.1, exercise 6; prepare a talk about the greatest sportsperson: 3.4, exercise 8

☀ If students have problems remembering these exercises, you could put them into small groups to remind each other (as appropriate) of the vocabulary learned, the content of the text, the topic they talked about.

✎ To extend the activity, ask students to choose one of the exercises and write a test for other students. This could be a list of questions, a true/false, a gapfill, etc.

4 Medicine

4.1 MEDICAL BREAKTHROUGHS

Lesson topic and staging

This lesson looks at important advances in medical science. Students discuss what makes a good doctor and then look at the meaning and pronunciation of a set of medical terms. Next, students read different texts about medical advances and swap information with a partner. Finally, students discuss a set of important issues about medicine and the medical profession.

Objectives

By the end of the lesson, students should have:

- extracted specific information from a reading text
- extended their range of vocabulary related to medicine and the medical profession
- participated in group discussions to express their opinions on different aspects of medicine.

Timings

If short of time, you could cut the number of statements they discuss in exercise 1 on page 38 or drop exercise 6 on page 39. A possible lesson break would be after exercise 3 on page 39.

WARM-UP

This activity introduces the topic of medicine and medical advances.

- Ask students to read the quote on page 38 and discuss what it means before you give them the information under 'Jackie Mason quote' opposite.
- Elicit reasons why people in wealthy cultures may think they have a sickness when they don't and write these on the board. If students can't think of any, write the following: *there are more sicknesses that we know about today, pharmaceutical companies 'advertise' different sicknesses to encourage us to buy pills, clinics advertise sicknesses to make us go, people have nothing else to worry about, people can get information more easily via the Internet and so diagnose themselves more, it makes people feel different from others if they have a sickness.*
- Put students in pairs to rank the options on the board from most to least probable in their opinion.
- Ask students to compare with another pair and give reasons for their choices.
- Finally, elicit the most and least likely reasons from two or three different groups.

Jackie Mason quote:

This is a humorous quote referring to the idea that in wealthy cultures there is a tendency for people to diagnose themselves or want to be diagnosed with medical conditions, even if there's not much wrong with them. In the past, in contrast, people wanted to be told they had no medical conditions at all. It implies that a lot of people who believe they are ill are actually fine.

i Jackie Mason (born 1931) is a US comedian controversially known for his 'politically incorrect' humour. His jokes include references to Jewish people (Mason himself is Jewish) and the American way of life which many may find offensive.

SPEAKING

1 Write *A good doctor …* on the board and elicit a few ideas from the class to finish the sentence.

- Then ask students to read the statements and use their dictionaries for vocabulary they don't know.
- Put students into pairs and give them five to ten minutes to discuss and rank the statements. They can include those on the board if they are different from those in the list.
- Finally, ask two or three pairs which they thought were the most important and why.

Answers depend on students' own opinions.

VOCABULARY: medical terms

2a Ask students to do this activity in pairs and to help each other with vocabulary if necessary or use their dictionaries.

- Check answers with the class and check the pronunciation of any difficult sounds (stressed syllables are focused on in exercise 3).
- Tell students that *Alzheimer's* has a capital letter because it is someone's name.

1 anaesthetist, midwife, pharmacist, psychiatrist, radiologist, surgeon; 2 antibiotic, injection, morphine, painkiller, physiotherapy, transplant; 3 Alzheimer's, arthritis, cancer, chest infection, diabetes, heart disease

2b Students do this activity individually and use their dictionaries to check unknown vocabulary (e.g. *insulin*).

- Ask students to compare with a partner before you check answers with the class.
- As you go through answers, model the words so that students can hear them again. This is useful for exercise 3.

> 1 pharmacist; 2 physiotherapy; 3 transplant;
> 4 diabetes; 5 psychiatrist; 6 injection;
> 7 heart disease

Don't ask students to do exercise V1,2 5 on page 141 in the Language reference as this also contains vocabulary from Lesson 4.2.

pronunciation

3 Stressed syllables

- Tell students they should have heard most of the words a few times in previous exercises.
- Read the instructions and do one example (**anaest**hetist) with the class, eliciting the main stress and the pronunciation of the stressed syllable. ə'niːsθətɪst
- Give students a few minutes to mark the stress and think about the pronunciation individually.
- While students are working, write the words on the board for use in feedback later.
- Then put them into pairs to compare their answers, saying the words for each other to provide a model.
- Play the track and pause after each item to give students time to check and correct their work.
- Play the track again, pausing after each item, and elicit answers from the class. Mark the stress on the board, model the stressed vowel sound and ask students to repeat.

> **Track 2.2**
> Alzheimer's   anaesthetist   antibiotic   arthritis
> cancer   chest infection   diabetes   heart disease
> injection   midwife   morphine   painkiller
> pharmacist   physiotherapy   psychiatrist
> radiologist   surgeon   transplant

READING

4 Focus students on the photos on page 39 and ask if they know what they show (*penicillin mould* and *an X-ray image*).

- Then elicit *breakthrough* (important medical improvement/advance) and use the photos as examples.
- Put students in pairs to brainstorm other medical breakthroughs and elicit some ideas to the board. Students can use these in exercise 6.

5a Keep students in the same pairs as exercise 4 and make sure they only look at their own text.

- Read through the instructions with the class and give them five minutes to read the texts and answer the questions.

- Don't go through answers as a whole class until the end of exercise 5b.

5b Ask students to take it in turns to tell their partner about the breakthroughs (i.e. Student A talks about X-rays and penicillin, then Student B talks about aspirin and anaesthesia, and so on).

- Tell students to ask each other questions to get as much information as possible.
- Monitor while students are speaking to identify any problems that students had understanding the information.
- When students have finished, don't go through all the answers with the class, but focus specifically on any points you identified while monitoring.

6 Keep students in the same pairs as exercise 5.

- Ask students to read the questions and check they understand *thermometer* (mime using this), *scalpel* (a surgeon uses it for cutting skin, etc.) and *stethoscope* (used for listening to your heart, mime using this).
- Give students five minutes to discuss the questions and tell them to use the items you wrote on the board in exercise 4 as more examples. Tell students to give reasons for their answers.
- Monitor while students are speaking and note mistakes when pronouncing the words introduced in this lesson.
- When students have finished, elicit answers from three or four pairs and ask for the reasons. Ask the rest of the class if they agree and why/why not.
- Finally, go through pronunciation mistakes you noted earlier.

When students have discussed the questions in their pairs, put them with another pair to compare answers and give reasons. Students should try to persuade each other that their ideas are better.

SPEAKING

7 Put students in groups of three or four for this activity.

- Allow ten minutes for the discussion and give students a time check every two minutes to remind them to move on to the next question.
- In feedback, ask two or three groups to give their ideas for one or two of the questions.

HOMEWORK OPTIONS

Students do the exercises on page 25 of the Workbook.

Students use the Internet to research one of the medical advances they discussed in exercise 6, question 2. They then produce a fact sheet for other students in the class to read.

4.2 MALARIA

Possible answers: *blood*: HIV/AIDS, hepatitis; *coughing and sneezing*: TB (tuberculosis), flu, colds; *water*: cholera, typhoid, hepatitis, diarrhoea; *food*: diarrhoea, hepatitis, salmonella; *insects*: malaria, lime disease

IN THIS LESSON

Lesson topic and staging

This lesson looks at the global killer disease, malaria. Students listen to a talk by a medical professor about why some people don't get treatment. Then they read four short texts about malaria and focus on vocabulary taken from the texts. Next, students study the future continuous, the present continuous and *going to,* and practise using these forms. Finally, students plan an illness awareness-raising day.

Objectives

By the end of the lesson, students should have:

- extracted specific information and language items from a listening and reading texts
- extended their range of vocabulary related to illness and medicine
- revised/extended their understanding of the use of the future and present continuous, and *going to*
- discussed and planned an awareness-raising day for an illness of their choice.

Timings

If short of time and your class is fairly confident using the grammar from this lesson, you could drop exercise 8 and set it for homework. A possible lesson break would be after exercise 6 on page 41.

WARM-UP

This activity introduces the topic of transmitting diseases and provides vocabulary for the Listening and exercise 10.

- Focus students on the photo on page 40 and elicit *mosquito* and that these insects are responsible for transmitting malaria.
- Write the following on the board: *blood, coughing and sneezing, water, food, insects.*
- Put students in pairs and give them two minutes to think of illnesses that are transmitted in these ways.
- Elicit answers from the class and give one point for each illness correctly identified. The pair with the most points wins.
- Take this opportunity to elicit/pre-teach *malaria* (a disease carried by mosquitoes and a serious problem in Africa, Asia and South America).
- If students don't know the diseases you elicit from the class, write them on the board and ask others to explain or tell students to use their dictionaries.

LISTENING

1   Students discuss the questions in pairs or small groups before you elicit answers from the class.

- If you didn't use the Warm-up activity, take this opportunity to elicit *malaria*.

2a Read through the introduction with the class and check students understand *drugs* = medicine.

- Play the track without pausing and ask students to briefly compare answers with a partner.
- Go through answers with the class and check students understand *pharmaceutical companies* (companies that develop and sell drugs).

> Because the drugs are often expensive and some people/countries cannot afford them.

2b Ask students to read the three questions before you play the track again.

- If necessary, pause the track at the points indicated in the audioscript below.
- Ask students to compare with a partner before you check answers with the class. (Answers are bold in the audioscript.)

> **1** because many of the existing drugs have become less effective as the malaria parasite has become resistant to them; **2** because the drugs will probably not be very profitable for them (the countries in most need of these drugs are generally poor); **3** work in partnership with universities to produce and develop drugs to a stage where pharmaceutical companies would be interested in bringing them to the market.

Audioscript and answers to exercise 2:
Track 2.3
The pharmaceutical industry has a problem at the present time because the very common diseases throughout the world such as high blood pressure, asthma, diabetes and so on have huge markets with potentially very large profits for successful drugs, but the people who are paying for the drug, such as insurance companies and state health services, do not wish to pay more than they have to for an effective treatment. That is why so much money goes into marketing as well as into development and testing of drugs.

continued...

There are still very large areas of medicine where new drugs are desperately needed. For example, it would be wonderful if we had more anti-malarial drugs **1 because many of the existing preparations have become less effective as time has gone on and the malaria parasite has become resistant to them.** Ideally, we need a vaccine against malaria so that all the people in a particular malarial country can be immunised and thereby protected. This of course needs to be combined with measures to reduce mosquitoes and so on. [PAUSE] But these countries where there are huge needs for effective new treatment are generally poor and can't afford the huge cost of new drugs. So **2 the pharmaceutical companies are less keen to develop new treatments which will not be very profitable.** [PAUSE] This type of development really depends upon support from international agencies such as the World Health Organisation, the World Bank, the European Union and similar organisations. **3 Working in partnerships with university departments the agencies can try to produce treatments and develop them to a stage where a pharmaceutical company would be interested in bringing them to the market.**

READING

3 Students discuss these questions in pairs or small groups.

- Elicit answers and write them on the board for students to refer to in exercise 4a.
- Take this opportunity to pre-teach *parasite* (the small creature that causes malaria, carried by the mosquito) which students need for exercise 4b.

4a Elicit/tell students what *scan* means (finding specific words, information in a text).

- Remind students of the ideas written on the board in exercise 3: can they find these in the texts?
- Ask students to compare with a partner before you check answers with the class.

> Answers depend on students' own ideas.

4b Give students four minutes to scan the texts again.

- Ask students to compare with a partner before you check answers with the class.

> two famous people: Alexander the Great, Genghis Khan (see background information); three continents: Asia, Africa, [Central and South] America; a university: John Hopkins in Baltimore; a North American swimming club: the Carleton Place Water Dragons (Canada); the name of the parasite: *plasmodium*; the animal infected in tests: mice; Africa Malaria Day: 25 April

i Alexander the Great lived over 2000 years ago and was one of the most successful military leaders in history. He initially controlled Macedonia, Greece and parts of western Europe before going on to conquer huge areas of eastern Europe, western Asia and northern Africa.

Genghis Khan (c1162–1227) founded the Mongol Empire in central Asia and created a vast empire from China to Russia.

5 Tell students they can read more efficiently by deciding first which text will contain the information.

- Give students two minutes to read the texts again.
- Ask them to compare with a partner before you check answers with the class.

> **1** False; **2** True; **3** False; **4** True

VOCABULARY: illness and medicine

6 Students do this activity individually and then compare answers with a partner.

- Go through answers with the class and check students can pronounce *symptoms, fever, contract* (verb) and *vaccine*.
- To follow up, ask a few students for one new thing they've learned about malaria.

> **1** infection; **2** parasite; **3** symptoms; **4** fever; **5** contract; **6** vaccine

For further practice, ask students to do exercise V1,2 5 on page 141 in the Language reference. (Note: this exercise also contains vocabulary from exercise 2 in lesson 4.1.)

GRAMMAR: future continuous, *going to*, present continuous

7a Ask students to read the two example sentences and then elicit the name of the tense (future continuous).

- Ask students to underline the future continuous form in the examples (*will be organising, will be asking*).
- Then give students two minutes to complete the gaps in the rules and compare with a partner.
- If students are not sure, ask them to look at the Language reference on page 140.
- Write one of the example sentences on the board and then go through answers with the class, highlighting the form.

> We use the future continuous to talk about an action in *progress* at a particular *time* in the *future*. It is formed with *will* + *be* + the *-ing* form of the verb.

7b Ask students to read the sentences (1–3) first and tell them that they don't need to focus on *I won't be here* in number 3 when matching them to the meanings.

- Give students one minute to match the sentences and meanings and then compare with a partner.
- If students find this difficult, encourage them to use the Language reference on page 140 rather than help them too much yourself. (See also Warning! below.)

- Go through answers with the class and tell students that sentence 3 is also an action in progress at a particular time (as they saw in exercise 7a).

    1 c); **2** a); **3** b)

(!) These tenses have subtle differences in meaning/use. Tell students that the meaning/use of this grammar (like so much grammar in English) is not necessarily to do with the action itself, but with the speaker's intention when using a particular form. For example, in number 1 the speaker wants us to know it's a plan that can't be changed, in 3 they're explaining why they won't be here, in 2 they're implying that this activity might change. Always advise students to decide what *message* they want to convey *before* they choose the grammar.

8 Put students into pairs for this activity to encourage them to think through and justify their answers.

- Tell them to look at exercises 7a and 7b, and the Language reference on page 140 if they need help. This will encourage them to think for themselves.

- Monitor to point out any mistakes they make and ask them to think again.

- Finally, go through answers with the class and ask students to give reasons for the choices they made (see notes in brackets).

    1 I'm studying medicine (this is probably not a fixed arrangement because they don't know where yet. It's an intention); **2** Are you passing (they are asking someone about a plan because they want them to do something); **3** I'm going to start (stating a fact about an action in progress at a time in the future); **4** Both forms are correct (the context doesn't tell us if this is a plan or an intention); **5** I'm going to operate (an action in progress at a particular time in the future); **6** I'm going to start (this is a fixed arrangement because job start-times are fixed); **7** we are landing (a fact about an action happening in the future); **8** I'm recovering (a fact about an action happening in the future)

(☼) As you go through answers, model the pronunciation of the future continuous form (contractions: *I'll*, *he'll*, *she'll*, etc., the weak form of *be* and the stress on the -ing verb). Ask students to repeat the present continuous sentences in exercise 8, then write one example on the board and highlight elements of pronunciation. This will help students with exercise 9.

For further practice, ask students to do exercise G1 1 on page 141 in the Language reference.

9 Focus students on the question *What will you be doing ....* and model the pronunciation of *what'll* and the weak form of *be*. Ask students to repeat and correct them if necessary.

- Give students a minute to think about their answers but tell them not to write these down.

- Then put students into pairs to ask/answer the questions. Encourage them to ask follow-up questions to get as much information as possible (e.g. 'Do you do that every summer?').

- Monitor while students are speaking to note mistakes with form and pronunciation.

- In feedback, ask students to tell you the most interesting/surprising thing they heard.

- Finally, correct some of the mistakes you noted earlier.

SPEAKING AND WRITING

10 Remind students of Africa Malaria Day in the texts on page 40.

- Read through the instructions and put students into groups of four to brainstorm ideas for possible events on an Awareness Day.

- Elicit ideas from the class and write these on the board to give students a pool of ideas to use.

- Put students into pairs and give them one minute to choose an illness for their Day. Students can use the illnesses in the Warm-up or any other illness they want.

- Then allow ten minutes for students to plan their Day. They should think about events, locations, times, people attending, the media and other relevant areas.

- Monitor to help with ideas and vocabulary if necessary.

- When students have finished, ask two or three pairs to tell the class about a few of their events.

HOMEWORK OPTIONS

Students do the exercises on pages 26–27 of the Workbook.

Students use the Internet to research the illness they chose in exercise 10a and write a fact sheet, using the Facts about malaria text on page 40 as a model.

Students do exercises G1 1 and V1,2 5 on page 141 in the Language reference.

4.3 A NEW FACE

Lesson topic and staging

This lesson looks at the medical field of transplants. Students read an article about the world's first partial face transplant and then focus on verbs with dependent prepositions in the text. Next, students study the meaning/use and form of the future perfect and *will* before doing a series of activities to practise these. Finally, students discuss a list of ethical questions related to medicine.

Objectives

By the end of the lesson, students should have:

- extracted specific information and language items from a reading text
- revised and/or extended their range of verbs and dependent prepositions
- revised/learned about the future perfect and *will*, and practised using these
- discussed in groups a selection of ethical issues related to medicine.

Timings

If short of time, you could drop exercise 4 on page 42 and set it for homework. A possible lesson break would be after exercise 4 on page 42.

WARM-UP

This activity introduces the topic of medical transplants and vocabulary that students may need for the lesson.

- Focus students on the title of the article on page 42 and check they understand *transplant* (using part of one person's body to help/repair another person's body) and *organ* (e.g. eye, heart). Tell students that transplants of fluids (e.g. blood) are normally called *transfusions*.
- Write the following on the board: *tareh, gnlu, viler, yenidk, nobe rrmowa, ksin ftarg, doolb*, and tell students that these are all types of transplant or transfusion with the letters mixed up.
- Do the first example (*tareh*) with the class (*heart*) and then put students into pairs to do the others.
- Students can use a bilingual dictionary to help by looking for transplants in their own language, finding the English equivalent and then seeing if the word is in the list on the board.
- Give students five minutes to do as many as possible, then check answers with the class.

> heart; lung; liver; kidney; bone marrow; skin graft; blood (transfusion)

READING

1 If you didn't use the Warm-up activity, focus students on the title of the article and check they understand *transplant*, *organ* (see definition above) and *partial* (adjective of *part*).

- Then put students into pairs to discuss the questions before you elicit answers from the class.
- Check students understand each organ you elicit by pointing to the relevant part or your body. In question 2, teach *reject/rejection* (your body doesn't want the new organ).
- Finally, ask students if they know anything about this case and to tell the class a few facts.

> **Possible answers: 1** heart, liver, kidney, lung;
> **2** rejection by the body

2 Tell students to read the questions and then give them three minutes to read the article.

- Ask students to compare with a partner before you go through answers with the class.
- Check students understand *disfigure* (change, alter the appearance in a negative way), *facial* (adjective of *face*), *donor* (the person whose organ/blood is used in the transplant) and *reconstructing* (rebuilding, re-making so that it's similar to the original).

> **1** because her dog disfigured her face when it tried to wake her after she'd taken sleeping pills;
> **2** yes, because she is making a good recovery;
> **3** yes, surgeons in other countries have received permission to do this operation

3 Read through the instructions and questions and check students understand *pros and cons* (advantages and disadvantages).

- Give students five minutes for this activity and ask them to underline the actual predictions in the text (these will be useful later in exercise 7).
- Ask students to compare answers with a partner before you check with the class.
- Take this opportunity to teach *ethical* (moral reasons for and against something).

> **The following will probably happen: 1** She will have to take drugs for many years.; **2** She will probably also need psychological counselling.;
> **3** In a few years' time, surgeons in such countries as the United States, Britain and China will probably have carried out many such transplants.
> **The following will probably not happen: 4** The debate about the ethical and moral issues relating to face transplants will undoubtedly continue.;
> **5** Some scientists predict it will have become legal for people to buy and sell organs for transplant on the Internet.

VOCABULARY: dependent prepositions

4 Give students 30 seconds to write the prepositions or guess if they don't know.

- Then ask students to scan the article to check their answers and, if necessary, guess the meaning of unknown verbs (1–6) or use their dictionaries.

- Go through answers and notes in brackets below with the class.

> **1** in; **2** to; **3** in; **4** of; **5** to; **6** to (All the verbs can be followed by a noun or the *-ing* form.)

GRAMMAR: future perfect, *will*

5a If possible, elicit an example of the future perfect from the class but don't analyse form at this stage.

- Students work individually and then compare with a partner.

- Check answers with the class and tell students that the examples mean the action will happen some time between now and the point in time referred to (i.e. *In a few years' time, by the end of the decade*).

> We use the future perfect for an action completed before a point in time in the future.

5b Students work individually and then compare with a partner.

- Check answers with the class and elicit that *won't* = *will not*, and a few more example past participles.

- Elicit the contractions of *will* (e.g. *I'll, he'll, you'll*) and then model the pronunciation of these contractions and *won't*. Then elicit/model the pronunciation of *I'll've* and *I won't've*. Ask students to repeat. Tell students you can't use these contractions in writing.

> The future perfect = <u>will</u>/won't + <u>have</u> + past participle.

6 Students work individually and then compare with a partner.

- Go through answers with the class, writing them on the board so all students can see the word order.

- Point out the use of a comma after the time clause (e.g. *By the year 2050, …*) if this comes at the beginning of the sentence, and the position of *yet* at the end of the sentence.

> *(Note: by the year, by the time you get here* and *in three weeks* can go at the beginning or end of the sentence.) **1** I'm afraid I won't have finished by then.; **2** By the year 2050, we'll have made progress in the field of transplants.; **3** I'll have had the operation by the time you get here.; **4** They won't have come out of the hospital yet.; **5** In three weeks, the term will have finished.

7a Remind students that in exercise 3 they underlined examples in the article of *will* and modals of certainty.

- Elicit/tell students what *prediction* means (something you believe will/won't happen in the future).

- Students work individually and then compare with a partner.

- Go through the answers and notes in brackets with the class. Adverbs of certainty are italicised.

- Finally, elicit that the modal *will* is followed by the infinitive without *to*.

> **1 & 2** she will have to take drugs; No one really knows what the effects of these drugs will be on her health in the long term; she will *probably* also need psychological counselling; will *probably* have carried out (Note: this is the future perfect form, but it is also being used to express a prediction.); the debate … will *undoubtedly* continue; will be a subject for ethical debate for some time; the need … *definitely* won't decrease in the future; it will have become legal for people (Note: this is the future perfect form but it is also being used to express a prediction.) The adverbs of certainty come after *will* but before *won't*. This is the most common pattern with these adverbs.

⚠ Adverbs of certainty *may* sometimes be placed before (instead of after) *will*. This is normally to add emphasis to the adverb, e.g. 'He definitely will arrive before I do'. There are other adverbs in the text (*exactly, completely*). These are not adverbs of certainty and the sentence structure *won't* + adverb is used. These adverbs come after *won't* (and after *will*).

💡 If possible, reproduce the article so that all the students can see it (perhaps on an Interactive Whiteboard or an overhead projector). When you go through answers, underline the examples to clearly show the position of *will* and the adverbs of certainty.

7b Give students five minutes to complete the sentences.

- Monitor to point out mistakes but don't correct these. Instead, refer students to exercises 5b, 7a and the Language reference on page 140.

- Ask students to compare with a partner and then elicit ideas from two or three students in the class.

> Answers depend on students' own ideas but you should check that the form *will* (+ adverb*)* or (adverb) + *won't* + infinitive or have + past participle is correct in each example.

8 First, write *Anderson Bio-Sciences* on the board and orient students to the text by asking them to predict what the company does and then quickly reading to check.

- Then ask students to underline three words they don't know in the text, use their dictionaries to find the meaning, and then put students into pairs to teach each other the words.

- Read through the instructions for this activity with the class and give them ten minutes to fill the gaps.

- Students can refer to the Language reference on page 140 if they need help.
- Ask students to compare with a partner before you check answers with the class.

> 1 will form; 2 will have expanded; 3 will have become; 4 will publish; 5 will revolutionise; 6 will give; 7 will include; 8 will permit; 9 will have made

9 Read through the instructions and examples with the class and then give students five to ten minutes to make some notes on their ideas.

- Monitor to help with vocabulary if necessary.
- Remind students of the pronunciation of *I'll, won't, I'll've* and *I won't've*.
- Put students into pairs to discuss the predictions and encourage them to ask follow-up questions (e.g. 'Why do you think you'll have done that?').
- While they are speaking, monitor and note mistakes with the future perfect, *will* or adverbs of certainty.
- For feedback, ask three or four students the most interesting/surprising thing they hear.
- Finally, correct some of the more common or important mistakes you noted earlier.

SPEAKING

10 Ask students to read through the question and check they understand *financial incentives* (money to encourage someone to do something) and *donate* (give something without payment).

- If short of time, choose only two or three of the questions for discussion or ask students to choose.
- Give students a few minutes to think about their answers, then put them into groups of three or four for the discussion.
- Encourage students to ask each other questions and disagree if necessary.
- Monitor to note mistakes using the vocabulary from this lesson.
- For feedback, ask two or three groups to tell the class what they decided for one of the questions and ask the other students if they agree.
- Finally, correct some of the more common or important mistakes you noted earlier.

HOMEWORK OPTIONS

Students do the exercises on pages 28–29 of the Workbook.

Students write a short letter to a newspaper outlining their reasons for or against one of the issues they discussed in exercise 10.

Students do exercises G2 2 and 3 on page 141 in the Language reference.

4.4 SCENARIO: THE DOWLING HOSPITAL

IN THIS LESSON

Lesson topic and staging

This lesson focuses on the language of predicting. Students read two texts which introduce the scenario of a charitably funded hospital with money problems receiving $1,000,000 grant. Next, students listen to senior staff discussing the money and then focus on the KEY LANGUAGE. Finally, the main TASK asks students to discuss and then make a difficult choice about how the money should be spent.

Objectives

By the end of the lesson, students should have:

- learned useful phrases for predicting, discussing options, considering implications, and making a choice
- used this language in a 'real-life' situation to discuss how a charitable hospital should spend a grant
- extracted specific information and language items from a reading and a listening text
- participated effectively in extended speaking practice.

Common European Framework

Students can use language effectively to make their opinions clear as regards finding solutions to problems and express beliefs, views and opinions.

Timings

If short of time, you could cut the number of options in exercise 4, but make sure you have enough for students to choose the best three and rank them. A possible lesson break would be after exercise 3b on page 45.

WARM-UP

This activity introduces the topic of charitable donations and the kinds of things they can be spent on.

- Tell students they have $1,000,000 to donate to a charity and give them two minutes to think about what charity (or type of charity) they would like to give this money to and what they'd like it spent on.
- Then put students into small groups to discuss their ideas, giving reasons for their choice and asking one another questions.
- Ask three or four students to tell the class their ideas and reasons.

SITUATION

1 Focus students on the photos on page 44 and tell them this is the Dowling Hospital in St Lucia and the man is Edgar Dowling, the founder.

- To orient students to the text, ask them to read it quickly and decide if it's a private or a state hospital (private/fee paying, but fees are kept low).

- Then put students into pairs to discuss the question in the rubric.

- Get a few ideas from the class and check they understand *fees* (money charged for a service) and *benefactor* (the person who gives money as a gift to an organisation, normally a charitable organisation).

> Answers depend on students' own ideas.

2 Focus students on the title of the article and check they understand *grant* (money given to a person/institution for a specific purpose. The person/institution does not have to pay the money back).

- Ask why this is good news for the hospital (they rely on donations and they have financial problems).

- Then tell students to read the questions and give them three minutes to read the text and answer.

- Ask students to compare with a partner before you check answers with the class.

- To follow up, ask students if they have this kind of hospital in their country or if the health system is funded completely by the government.

> 1 the Goldwater Foundation; 2 the hospital is known to be experiencing financial difficulties, there are a number of projects that need funding; 3 helped provide high-quality treatments, maintain fees at an affordable level

KEY LANGUAGE: predicting

3a Tell students they are going to decide later what to spend the $1,000,000 on. Two ideas are the gardens and a full-time gardener.

- Read through the introduction and instructions with the class and then play the track without pausing.

- Ask students to compare with a partner before you check answers with the class.

- Finally, ask students if these are good reasons for not spending the money on the gardens.

> The following should be ticked: 2, 3, 4, 5. (Answers are bold in the audioscript after exercise 3b.)

3b Tell students to read the sentences (1–8) before you play the track again.

- If necessary, pause at the points indicated in the audioscript to give students time to write.

- Ask students to compare with a partner each time you pause the track as some sentences are grouped very closely.

- Check answers (underlined in the audioscript below) with the class. If necessary, ask students to read the audioscript on page 174.

> 1 'll probably cost; 2 'd probably use up (Note: 'd = *would*.); 3 spend the money on; 4 'll want us; 5 'll greatly improve; 6 that it could have; 7 might have; 8 'll be talking

Audioscript and answers to exercise 3:
Track 2.4
Medical Director, Nursing Director

MD: Let's talk about the Goldwater grant, Jenny. Everyone seems to have different ideas about how to spend the money. What's your opinion?

ND: Well ... I'd like to do something about the gardens. They're in a terrible mess at the moment – a real eyesore. And they're the first thing people see when they visit the hospital. It doesn't make a very good impression. We need to get an expert to landscape the gardens, then employ full-time gardeners to look after them.

MD: You're right, of course, the gardens are in a dreadful state. But 1 <u>it'll probably cost</u> quite a lot to have them landscaped and then employ gardeners. I don't have precise figures, but I'd say it 2 <u>'d probably use up</u> over half of the grant.

ND: Maybe, but the gardens are very important for patients. It's where they go to recuperate from operations, and where they take their friends and relatives for a chat. It's important to have beautiful, well cared for gardens. When you're sick, you appreciate that sort of thing, and when you're getting better, you spend a lot of time in them. [PAUSE]

MD: I think we need to look at the implications of that choice, Jenny. If we 3 <u>spend the money on</u> the gardens, **2 I don't think the Boston Medical Foundation will be very pleased.** They 4 <u>'ll want us</u> to **3 spend the grant on up-to-date equipment.** They're very keen for us to get a new scanner, they think it 5 <u>'ll greatly improve</u> our treatments.

ND: Mmm, I see what you mean. [PAUSE]

MD: Another thing to think about, if we spend the money on the gardens, is, 6 <u>that it could have</u> an effect on other projects ...

ND: Ah, you're thinking of research, I imagine.

MD: Exactly. It 7 <u>might have</u> a big **4 impact on research. We wouldn't have enough money to hire a new research assistant** – and that's something we've wanted to do for a long time.

ND: That's a thought, I must say. What angle do you think the local newspaper would have, if we spent some money on the gardens?

MD: My guess is that they wouldn't like it. They'd say we were betraying the principles of the hospital, you know, that **5 money should be spent on low-income patients.** [PAUSE]

ND: Well, we have to make a choice, that's for sure. Talking of principles, I wonder what Edgar Dowling would have done with the money.

continued...

MD: Somehow, I don't think he'd have spent it on the gardens. He preferred to spend money on medical care and the latest equipment! You know, Jenny, I think we need to think this through. We need to listen to people, get their opinions, then make up our minds. Our decision must be in the interests of patients and the hospital.

ND: Absolutely. That's the best way forward.

MD: I 8'll be talking to Diana Marsden some time this weekend, she's chief surgeon at Boston State. I'll see what she has to say. I respect her opinions a lot.

ND: Good idea.

MD: And next week, say Wednesday or Thursday, we can meet, look at the options and make a decision.

🔧 If you have a very large class, instead of a whole-class discussion, divide students into two large groups.

HOMEWORK OPTIONS

Students do the exercises on page 30 of the Workbook.

Students write an article of about 100 words for the local newspaper (see the article in exercise 2) reporting what the $1,000,000 will be spent on and what the benefits of this will be to the hospital and the community.

Students do exercise KL 4 on page 141 in the Language reference.

TASK: making a difficult decision

4 Ask students to read the instructions, the criteria and the options, and to use their dictionaries for any unknown vocabulary.

• Give them three minutes to think about their opinions on each option using the criteria.

• Remind students of the KEY LANGUAGE and go through the OTHER USEFUL PHRASES box with the class, checking pronunciation of any difficult phrases.

• Then, put students into groups of three or four and give them 15–20 minutes to discuss the advantages and disadvantages of each option.

• Monitor while students are speaking and note mistakes with the KEY LANGUAGE and OTHER PHRASES language.

• Don't elicit ideas from the class at this stage.

• Correct some of the mistakes you noted earlier and tell students they have another chance to use the KEY LANGUAGE and OTHER PHRASES in exercise 5.

5a Tell students that the three options are separate. They are deciding to spend the money on just one of them.

• They should say what they would do with any remaining money in each case, and what they could do with any extra money generated by an option.

• Give students 15 minutes to choose their three options and rank them.

• Monitor while students are speaking and note mistakes with, and improvements to, their use of KEY LANGUAGE and OTHER PHRASES.

5b Elicit the three options from each group and write them in separate areas on the board.

• Ask each group to present their options to the rest of the class and to give reasons for their choices.

• Tell the rest of the class to ask questions and give their comments at the end of each presentation.

• When all the presentations are finished, ask the class to discuss and vote on which option(s) to spend the money on.

4.5 STUDY AND WRITING SKILLS

IN THIS LESSON

Lesson topic and staging

This lesson focuses on evaluating resources on the Internet and writing short reports. Students discuss a list of suggestions for evaluating research websites. They then listen to a lecture on evaluating websites before using the suggestions they have considered to evaluate three websites themselves. Next, students read and analyse a website report on homeopathy and finally write a report of their own.

Objectives

By the end of the lesson, students should have:

- extracted specific information and language items from a listening and a reading text
- extended their range of techniques for evaluating a website
- learned (more) about the organisation and language used in report writing
- written a short report on herbal remedies for a website.

Common European Framework

Students can write a brief report to a standard conventionalised format and link a series of discrete items into a connected linear sequence of points.

Timings

If short of time, you could ask students to plan their report in exercise 8a but then write it for homework. A possible lesson break would be after exercise 4 on page 46.

WARM-UP

This activity introduces the topic of evaluating websites.

- Give students three minutes to think about their favourite website and make notes on why they like it.
- Put students into pairs or small groups to say which website they chose and why.
- Encourage students to ask each other questions to get as much information as possible.
- If any students have chosen the same website, ask them to compare why they like it and see how many of their reasons are the same.
- Finally, ask students if they are interested in looking at any of the websites they heard about.

STUDY SKILLS: evaluating resources on the Internet

1   Ask students if they use the Internet for research and what kind of things they research (e.g. topics for school, college, work, holidays, music).

- Tell students it's necessary to evaluate the websites they look at to decide if they can be trusted, are accurate, etc.
- Elicit any techniques students have for evaluating the websites they look at and then explain that they are going to discuss some suggestions.
- Read through the instructions with the class, give students a few minutes to read the suggestions and check any unknown vocabulary in their dictionaries.
- Put students into pairs to discuss the suggestions and give reasons why they agree or disagree with each.
- Ask two or three pairs for suggestions they *agreed* with and ask the class if they chose the same ones.

When students have decided which suggestions they agree with, ask them to rank them from most to least useful. Ask pairs to compare their lists with another pair. Elicit the most useful suggestions from the class.

2 Ask the class to read the instructions and questions before you play the track without pausing.

- Ask students to briefly compare with a partner before you check answers with the class. (Answers are bold in the audioscript below.)

> 1 Find out who's responsible for the site and its information, find out the purpose of the site (e.g. trying to inform, educate, persuade or sell?); 2 If it's a commercial site, you need to be careful because the information may be misleading or inaccurate.

Audioscript and answers to exercise 2:
Track 2.5
PART 1
When you're looking at websites for research, you must trust the source of your information and get the very best quality of information you're searching for. Now, there are two points which I consider to be very important. Firstly, **1 it's essential to know who's responsible for the site and its information.** A good site will tell you that, usually at the bottom of each page, or you can generally find it out in the 'About Us' section. Government websites are usually excellent sources of information.
Secondly, **1 you must know the purpose of the site.** It should be clear what the purpose is, and when you know that, it should help you to evaluate the site. For example, you need to ask yourself, if the aim of the website is to inform or educate you, or if it is trying to persuade you or sell you something.
2 If the site is trying to get you to buy something, either directly or indirectly, you need to be careful. Commercial sites may not give you objective information; the sites are often biased in some way and give you misleading or inaccurate information. They're there to sell things and often exaggerate the qualities of their products.

3 Read through the instructions with the class and tell students to read the list of points (1–7).

- Check students understand *reliable* (you can trust the information) and *link* (connections to other sites).

- Then play the track without pausing.

- Ask students to compare their answers with a partner and, if necessary, play the track again.

- Go through answers with the class. (Answers are bold in the audioscript below.) Check students understand *trustworthy* (you can trust this).

- Write *.gov, .ac, .edu,* and *.com* on the board, and elicit which kind of website uses each ending (see audioscript below). Students will find this useful in exercise 4 later.

- Finally, ask the class which suggestions for evaluating a website they found particularly useful.

> The following should be ticked: **1, 3, 4, 6** (Note: students might tick **5**: use the audioscript to show that a website can contain opinions but it should be clear which are facts and which opinions.)

Audioscript and answers to exercise 3:
Track 2.6
PART 2
What are the websites you can rely on? Well, of course, **1 government-sponsored sites, educational sites run by universities or medical schools,** and websites of well known professional organisations, they're usually non-profit making and **1 should be trustworthy,** you can rely on them. By the way, government agencies in the UK usually have the suffix *.gov* in the address, and educational bodies have *.ac,* though in the United States *.edu* is more commonly used for academic sites. Professional organisations and charities sometimes have *.org* and commercial organisations often finish with *.com.* A word about health and medical information you find on the net. Any statement or evidence should be supported by well established research or medical institutions. Or, **3 if the material you find has been reviewed by an expert, that's a good sign. We call that 'peer reviews'. If the material has not been reviewed, then be careful. Check other sources,** other websites, to see if they support the statement or evidence you have found. **4 The material should be up to date** – medical sites should really be updated weekly or monthly – well that's the ideal. I think one other point is worth mentioning. It's important the website separates opinion from research results. Research results are based on evidence, and you need to know what the evidence is. It's OK for opinions to be included in the website, as long as it's clear they are opinions, and not scientific facts. Oh yes, and by the way, **6 a good website will provide links with other sources of information so you can check if these back up the findings or research results.**
Well, I hope these tips will help you to evaluate information you get from Internet websites. You're lucky to have this source of information. When I was studying medicine, the library was the main source of information for me. Nowadays, I use the Internet a lot in my research, but I'm very careful what websites I use, I'm sure you will be too.

4 Write *hypnotherapy* on the board and ask students to check the meaning in their dictionaries.

- Ask students if they know anyone who has tried hypnotherapy, what for and why?

- Then ask students to read the instructions for this activity.

- If you have computers and an Internet connection in the school, ask students to use this to find their three websites. If not, ask students to use the connection they have at home or in an Internet café.

- Tell students to use the suggestions from exercises 1, 2 and 3 to help them evaluate the sites.

- Students should note the reasons why they have chosen each site.

- When students have chosen, ask them to compare their findings with two or three others in the class.

- Finally, ask the class which websites seem to be the best for researching hypnotherapy. (Note: students can use this information for the second homework option at the end of this lesson.)

WRITING SKILLS: writing short reports

5 Focus students on the report and the photos on page 47 and ask what they think the report is about. Students don't need to be specific.

- Ask them to read the introduction to this activity (not the introduction to the report) and check they understand *alternative therapies* (alternative medicine and treatments, not common/standard medicine).

- Then put students into pairs or small groups to discuss the three questions.

- If students have never tried any alternative therapies, they can talk about someone they know who has.

- Students can use their dictionaries if necessary.

- Get a few answers to each question from the class and check that students understand the alternative remedies listed in the rubric by asking for the definitions they found in their dictionaries.

> Answers depend on students' own experiences.

6 Re-elicit the name of the website from exercise 5.

- Give students four minutes to read the report and identify each section.

- Ask students to compare with a partner before you check answers with the class.

- To follow up, ask students if they would be interested in trying homeopathy.

> **1** Conclusion; **2** Facts and findings;
> **3** Recommendations; **4** Introduction

7a Making recommendations

- Elicit the introductory words for recommendation 1 from the class and write them on the board (*You should consult* (infinitive without *to*).

- Then ask students to underline the introductory words in the other recommendations (i.e. question 1 only) and compare with a partner.

- Students can use their dictionaries to check *vital* and *essential*.

- Check answers to question 1 with the class before you ask them to do the other questions (2–4) and elicit the form of the final verb in each case (see brackets in the answers below).

- Put students into pairs to answer questions 2–4 and then check answers with the class.

> **1** You should consult (infinitive without *to*), It is vital to consult (= infinitive), The instructions on homeopathic products must be read (= past participle), It is essential to understand that symptoms (= noun), Homeopathic products should be bought (= past participle), Homeopathic remedies may alleviate (= infinitive without *to*);
> **2** Strongest: recommendations 2 (*vital*), 3 (*must*) and 4 (*essential*), the language in brackets make these recommendations strong. Weakest: 1 (*should*), 5 (*should*), 6 (*may*), the language in brackets make these recommendations weak and 6 is the weakest recommendation of all. **3** 3 (*must be read*), 5 (*should be bought*); 4 Because it makes the tone of the writing more formal and therefore it sounds important (recommendations often include important information).

- ☀ If possible, reproduce the report so that all the students can see it (perhaps on an Interactive Whiteboard or an overhead projector). As you go through answers to question 1, underline the relevant part of the recommendations.

7b Read through the instructions and alternative grammatical structures with the class.

- Elicit the passive uses *be* + past participle (see examples in exercise 7a above) and that if *to* is used, it is followed by the infinitive (see example in exercise 7a above).

- Elicit which alternative grammatical structures are strong or weak (Strong: *must* + verb/passive verb), *It is vital that*. Weak: *It is advisable to*, *might/could* + verb/passive verb, *It is a good idea to*).

- Then focus students on recommendation 4 in the report and ask students if it's strong or weak (strong).

- Read through the example in the rubric with the class and elicit that *must understand* has been used because the recommendation is strong and *must* + verb is a strong alternative grammatical structure. Point out that *Members* has been used because the structure needs a subject noun.

- Then give students ten minutes to re-write the other recommendations from the report, making any necessary adjustments to the original sentence.

- Monitor to check that students are using a weak/strong alternative structure to re-write a weak/strong recommendation and make sure the grammatical form is used correctly.

- Ask students to compare with a partner before you check answers with the class.

- As you go through answers, write them on the board so all students can see the structure.

> Answers depend on the grammatical structure students use to re-write the recommendations. However, check that each structure is used correctly.

8a Read through the instructions with the class and ask them if they have tried herbal remedies.

- Elicit any facts students know about herbal remedies and then ask them to read the notes on page 170 to compare their ideas.

- Remind students of the organisation of the report in exercises 5 and 6 and the structures used for weak/strong recommendations.

- Then give students 20–30 minutes to write their reports.

- Monitor to prompt with ideas and correct grammatical structures if necessary.

8b When students have finished, ask them to swap reports with a partner and give them five minutes to note any suggestions for improvements (e.g. grammar, vocabulary, organisation).

- Then ask students to explain the suggestions to their partner, before giving the report back for any necessary changes.

- When students have finished, take the reports in for marking, paying particular attention to the organisation and use of structures for weak/strong recommendations.

- 🔧 Alternatively, post the reports around the room so that all students can read them and decide which is the most useful, most complete report.

HOMEWORK OPTIONS

Students do the exercises on page 31 of the Workbook.

Students write a short report on two of the websites they looked at in exercise 4, evaluating how useful these are.

Transcript

5.1 GETTING FROM A TO B

Lesson topic and staging

This lesson looks at transport and road safety. Students discuss transport they use and then brainstorm different kinds of transport. Students then study vocabulary for kinds of transport and their associated problems. Next, students read an article about road accidents and focus on safety-related vocabulary in the text. Finally, students discuss ways to make roads safer before writing recommendations.

Objectives

By the end of the lesson, students should have:

- extracted specific information and language items from a reading text
- extended their range of vocabulary related to transport, transport problems and road safety
- participated in a group discussion to express their opinions on road safety
- written a set of recommendations for a report on improving road safety.

Timings

If short of time, you could drop exercise 3 on page 48 and/or set exercise 10 for homework. A possible lesson break would be after exercise 7 on page 49.

WARM-UP

This activity introduces the topic of different means of transport and provides vocabulary for exercise 1 and 2a.

- Write the word *transport* on the board and then the following items: *nairt, cra, alnep, pish, ceylbci, ahcco, ramt, rootibkme*.
- Tell students that the items are kinds of transport with the letters mixed up.
- Put students in pairs and tell them to write the words in the correct order as quickly as possible.
- Go through answers with the class.

> train, car, plane, ship, bicycle, coach, tram, motorbike

Steven Wright quote:

This is a humorous quote referring to the idea that people judge how far away a place is by asking *Is it walking distance?* The quote means, logically, it's really a matter of time not distance. The humour lies in us imagining the situation of saying to someone

It depends how much time you have? and the reaction we'd get. This idea of experiencing the unexpected in a familiar situation is often called *surreal*. The quote is also implying that people in modern society rush too much.

i Steven Wright (born 1955) is an American comedian known particularly for his surreal humour.

VOCABULARY: transport

1 Focus students on the photo of the plane at the top of page 48 and ask students if and how often they fly.

- Put students in pairs to discuss the questions.
- If you used the Warm-up activity, students can refer to some of this vocabulary in their discussion.
- Then elicit three or four students' preferred method of transport and the reasons they like it.
- Ask the rest of the class if they agree.

> Answers depend on students' own experiences.

i KLM is the national airline of The Netherlands.

2a Give students three minutes to write as many words on the mind map as possible.

- Draw the mind map on the board and elicit ideas from the class.
- Ask students to add any additional vocabulary to the mind map in the Coursebook.

2b Students can use their dictionaries to do this activity.

- Give students five minutes to add the methods of transport to the mind map and then compare answers with a partner.
- Students may not find *Maglev train* (a very fast train travelling on magnetic currents) or *quad bike* (a small four-wheeled motorised vehicle for use off-road) in their dictionaries.
- Go through answers with the class checking the pronunciation of any difficult words (e.g. *hydrofoil*). (Note: *cable car, hovercraft, tram* and *Maglev train* may cause some disagreement about whether the first is land or air, the second is sea or air, the third is rail or road and the fourth is rail or air.)

> Rail: Maglev train, tram; Road: coach, lorry/truck, motorbike, quad bike, scooter, tram, van; Land: (possibly) cable car, quad bike; Air: balloon, cable car, glider, helicopter, (possibly) hovercraft; Sea/water: barge, ferry, hovercraft, hydrofoil, submarine

For further practice, ask students to do exercise V1 5 on page 143 in the Language reference.

2c Focus students on the photo of the plane and ask them what kind of problems there might be when you fly.

- Then give students five minutes to match the problems to types of transport, using their dictionaries if necessary.

- Ask students to compare with a partner before you check answers with the class.

- In feedback, ask students for the meaning of each problem and check pronunciation (e.g. *puncture*). Explain that *lane* here means the separate sections of a wide road (e.g. a motorway/freeway) that has more than one *lane* for travelling in one direction.

- To follow up, ask students if they've experienced any of the problems in the list and what happened.

> fogbound runway = air; lane closure = road; low tide = sea; platform alteration = rail; puncture = road; rough weather = sea (Note: we don't use *rough weather* for air transport, we normally say *bad weather*.); signalling problems = rail; tailback = road; turbulence = air (Note: *turbulence* can also refer to water, though this is less common.)

For further practice, ask students to do exercise V2 6 on page 143 in the Language reference.

3 Put students into pairs to discuss these questions

- For question 4, provide the prompts *punctuality, safety, convenience, the environment, comfort, cost* and *speed* if students need them.

- Monitor to note mistakes in pronouncing the types of transport and the problems associated with them.

- When students have finished, put the pairs with other pairs to form groups of four and ask them to compare their answers to question 4.

- Finally, get a few answers to question 4 from the class.

> Answers depend on students' own experience and ideas.

READING

4 Focus students on the three photos and ask them which car they would prefer to buy.

- Set the activity and give students a minute to think about their answers to the questions. Then put students in pairs to discuss.

- Get answers from two or three pairs.

> Answers depend on students' own ideas and opinions.

☀ *Do not* at any point in exercises 5, 6 or 7 below try to personalise the topic by asking students about their own experiences of road safety or accidents.

5a Explain that students are going to read an article about road safety.

- Read through the instructions with the class and check they understand *crash* (vehicles hitting each other or an object).

- Put students in pairs to discuss the list and tell them to put the causes into three groups (1 very important, 2 not sure, 3 not very important).

- Get ideas for causes in each of the groupings (1–3) and ask the rest of the class if they agree.

> Answers depend on students' own ideas.

5b Give students one minute to read the article.

- Tell them not to worry about vocabulary at this stage.

- Ask students to briefly compare with a partner before you check answers with the class.

> The writer feels the biggest cause *is the psychology of drivers* (see paragraph 4).

6 Give students one minute to read the methods listed and try to remember if any were mentioned in the text.

- Then give them five minutes to re-read the article and tick the methods mentioned.

- Ask students to compare with a partner before you check answers with the class.

- In feedback, check students understand *traffic signals* (draw on the board), *speed cameras* (a camera that takes your picture if you're driving too fast), *anti-lock brakes* (when you use the brakes, they make the wheel slow down gradually and evenly, not suddenly). Don't write these items on the board because this will help students too much in exercise 7 below.

> The following methods are mentioned (examples in brackets): restricting the speed at which people can drive (The Locomotive and Highways Act of 1865 introduced the idea of speed limits – paragraph 2); introducing technological innovations to make people slow down (traffic signals, speed cameras – paragraph 2); improving safety features in cars (seat belts, anti-lock brakes, air bags – paragraph 3); having tough penalties for drivers who break the law (fines for breaking motoring laws – paragraph 2); assessing drivers' abilities and issuing of documents (compulsory driver testing and licensing – paragraph 2)

VOCABULARY: safety features

7 If you wrote any of these words on the board in exercise 6, make sure you clear it and emphasise that students cannot look at the article again.

- Give them one minute to complete as many of the safety features as they can remember

- Ask them to compare with a partner and then read the article again to check their answers.

- Students can use their dictionaries to check meaning if necessary.

- Go through answers with the class and (re)elicit the meaning of each item.

> **1** speed limits; **2** anti-lock brakes; **3** traffic signals; **4** airbags; **5** speed cameras; **6** seat belts; **7** one-way streets

For further practice, ask students to do exercise V3 7 on page 143 in the Language reference.

SPEAKING AND WRITING

8a First, divide the class into three groups (As, Bs and Cs) and ask students to read the information given.

- Tell students to summarise the main points in their information and help each other with vocabulary, if necessary.

8b Put students into groups of three with an A, a B and a C student in each group. If you have too many As, for example, put two As into the same group.

- Give students about 15 minutes to swap their information and decide the most effective method.

8c Ask a student in each group to report their decision and the reasons for it. Write the decisions on the board. Don't encourage other groups to disagree or argue at this stage.

9 If you have a very large class, divide students into two groups.

- Ask the class to discuss the decisions on the board, decide which recommendations they should make and how strong these should be.

10 Remind students of the structures for writing recommendations in lesson 4.5.

- Give them 15 minutes to write their recommendations.
- Monitor to help with ideas and language if asked.
- Ask students to compare recommendations with a partner and correct each other's work if necessary.

HOMEWORK OPTIONS

Students do the exercises on page 32 of the Workbook.

Students write a short newspaper article reporting the recommendations they decided on in exercise 10. They need to give information on where the recommendations come from, why they are useful and any disadvantages there might be.

Students do exercises V1 5, V2 6 and V3 7 on page 143 in the Language reference.

5.2 TRANSPORT IN THE FUTURE

IN THIS LESSON

Lesson topic and staging

This lesson looks at how transport might change in the future. Students listen to a report on a development in urban transport. Next, they read the introduction to an article on changes in transport, then read three extracts from the article and swap information. Students then study vocabulary taken from the text. Next, students study future modal verbs from the text and focus on the meaning and form. Finally, students discuss their opinions on how transport might change in the future.

Objectives

By the end of the lesson, students should have:

- extracted specific information and language items from a listening and reading texts
- extended their range of vocabulary related to transport
- revised/extended their understanding of the use of future modal verbs
- discussed their opinions on changes to transport in the future.

Timings

If short of time, you could drop exercise 6b and set it for homework. A possible lesson break would be after exercise 5 on page 50 or 6b on page 51.

WARM-UP

This activity focuses students on current problems with urban transport in preparation for exercise 1.

- Ask students how they travel to school/college/work and if there are any problems with this form of transport. If your class is in a rural area, ask students how they travel in the city.
- Write the following on the board: *pollution, overcrowding, too slow, too hot, dangerous, expensive*.
- Put students in pairs and ask them to talk about the transport in your town/city (i.e. the town/city where the class is being held) and rank the problems above from most to least serious.
- Ask pairs to compare their lists with other pairs and to give reasons.
- Finally, ask two or three pairs for their lists and ask the class if they agree with the order.

LISTENING

1a Ask students to read the introduction and elicit/tell them the BBC is a British TV and radio company.

- Play the track without pausing and then elicit the answer from the class.

- Ask students if they've heard of a transport system like this before and focus them on the photo of the pod on page 50.

> The Ultra is an (electrical) battery powered, computerised pod (small 'box') which can carry a small number of people at up to 25 miles per hour.

1b Play the track again without pausing and give students two minutes to make some notes before they compare with a partner.

- Go through answers with the class and ask students if they think the Ultra is a good idea and why.

> Advantages: no fumes, no driver, private space, low cost, cheap as a bus ride, you can share with your friends, goes straight to your destination

2 Put students in pairs or small groups for this activity and emphasise they must give reasons for their ideas.

- Elicit possible developments and reasons for these from the class and write them on the board.

READING

3 Focus students on the photo on pages 50–51 and tell them that it shows a new form of transport that they will read about later. Ask students if they can guess what it might be.

- Give students one minute to read the introduction and remind them their ideas from exercise 2 are on the board.

- Elicit the reasons from the class and write on the board for students to refer to in exercise 4a.

- Ask if their ideas from exercise 2 were similar.

- Check students understand *pander to* (provide someone with anything they want) and *thrill-seeking* (looking for excitement).

> Three reasons: we will need to depend less on fossil fuels (e.g. oil), society is getting faster, some people want more excitement.

4a Divide the class into three groups (A, B and C) and make sure they read only the text for their group.

- Remind students that the three reasons are on the board and give them one minute to read the text and answer the question.

- Tell them not to worry about vocabulary at this stage.

- Ask students to compare with others in their group and then elicit answers from the class.

> Text A: excitement, thrill-seeking; Text B: we will need to depend less on fossil fuels; Text C: society is getting faster.

You need a minimum of three students in your class for exercises 4a, 4b and 5 to work well. If you have fewer than three students, ask the class to read all the texts. If you have four or five students in your class, don't divide them into As, Bs and Cs for exercises 4a and 4b, but make one group with at least one A, one B and one C student. Follow the rest of the procedure as normal.

4b Give students five minutes to read their text again and make *short* notes. Tell students not to worry about unknown vocabulary at this stage because they will look at this in exercise 6 later.

- Keep students in their groups from exercise 4a and ask them to compare notes.

- Then put students into three new groups so that there are A, B and C students in each group.

- Give them five to ten minutes to swap information about their texts and ask each other questions to get as much information as possible.

5 Tell students that statements 1–3 are for Text A, 4–6 for Text B and 7–9 for Text C.

- Tell students to answer as many questions as possible before they read the text to check.

- Make sure students are in groups with an A, B and C student in each and ask them to swap information.

- Go through answers with the class and follow up by asking students which development they think is most interesting/exciting.

> Text A: **1** False (it's owned by Sir Richard Branson); **2** False (Burt Rutan was the first person to send a private spaceship into space, SpaceShipOne in 2004); **3** False (they will need about a week's initial training). Text B: **4** False (hydrogen could replace petrol, diesel or gas); **5** False (experts believe if it is handled properly, it will not be any more dangerous as a fuel); **6** True (but not only fuel cell design, there are other recent technological advances that have made hydrogen a possible alternative fuel); **Text C: 7** True (they are driven by magnetic power); **8** False (the only commercially run Maglev train is in Shanghai, China; Maglev trains are currently being developed in Germany and Japan); **9** True (it was probably the result of human error)

If you want the whole class to read all three texts at this stage, tell them to do so and decide if all nine statements are true or false.

VOCABULARY

6a Tell students find the words in the text(s) they read in the previous exercises.

- Monitor to give extra help with the meaning of these words if necessary.
- Ask them to swap information about their words with students who read the other two texts.
- Make sure all students write down the words and definitions for all three texts as a record.
- Go through answers with the class and check pronunciation of any difficult words (e.g. *freight*).

> **Text A: 1** tycoon; **2** fleet; **3** masses. **Text B: 4** emit;
> **5** fumes; **6** feasible; **Text C: 7** elevated; **8** freight;
> **9** shuttle

6b Make sure students are in groups with an A, a B and a C student in each.
- Ask students to work together to complete the gaps.
- Go through answers with the class.

> **1** emit; **2** fumes; **3** feasible; **4** freight; **5** fleet;
> **6** masses; **7** shuttles

For further practice, ask students to do exercise V4 8 on page 143 in the Language reference.

GRAMMAR: modal verbs (future)

7 Tell students they may not be able to find examples for all categories in their text.
- Ask students to underline the examples in their text and then complete the chart with students who read the other texts.
- Go through the answers and notes below with the class and elicit the negative forms of each (*won't be able to, won't have to, won't need to, might not, could not*).

	ability	possibility	obligation
Text A	will be able to	might /could	will need to (necessary)
Text B	*xxxxx*	might / could	will have to (obliged)
Text C	will be able to	could	*xxxxx*

(!) *Be able to* and *have to* are modal in meaning but not in form, e.g. they have a past form (*was able to*) and are inflected in the third person (*he has to*) unlike pure modals which do not (*musted, he mights* are wrong). *Need* can be used as a modal (e.g. *he needn't go*) or as a main verb (*he needs to go*). In the example above, it is a main verb, not a modal. *Enable* in Text A expresses ability but it is not a modal verb.

8 Before students do this activity, ask them to read the Language reference on page 142 for information on form.
- Give pairs five to ten minutes to find and correct the grammar errors in six of the sentences.

- Monitor to point out mistakes but encourage students to refer to the Language reference and self-correct if necessary.
- Go through answers with the class.

> **1** Security ~~will~~ must improve; **2** Correct; **3** We ~~might~~ have to/will have to work faster; **4** we will all ~~have to~~ be able to travel in space; **5** many of us ~~can~~ will be able to travel on; **6** So I'll *have to* drive him; **7** We will need <u>to</u> find feasible; **8** Correct

9 Tell students to complete the sentences so that they are true for themselves.
- Monitor to help with vocabulary or ask students to use their dictionaries.
- Then put students into pairs to discuss their sentences and ask each other follow-up questions (e.g. 'Why do you think that might happen?').
- Monitor to note mistakes when using the form of modals.
- In feedback, ask students the most interesting/ surprising thing they heard.
- Finally, correct some of the more common or important mistakes you noted earlier.

For further practice, ask students to do exercise G1 1 on page 143 in the Language reference.

SPEAKING

10 Give students five minutes to discuss the statements and complete them in a way that they both agree on.
- Put students into groups of four (i.e. two pairs in each group) and ask them to compare.
- Tell students to give reasons for the modal they have used and to disagree with each other if necessary.
- Finally, elicit one idea for each statement from the class and ask other students if they agree and why/ why not.

HOMEWORK OPTIONS

Students do the exercises on pages 33–34 of the Workbook.

Students write a letter to a local newspaper complaining about transport in their city and making suggestions/ recommendations for improvements. They can use their ideas from the Warm-up and information from exercise 1 and Texts B and/or C in the Reading exercises.

Students do exercises V4 8 and G1 1 on page 143 in the Language reference.

5.3 GREAT RAILWAY JOURNEYS

Lesson topic and staging

This lesson looks at famous and interesting railway journeys. Students read an article about three famous railway journeys and then focus on vocabulary from the text. Next, students look at past modal verbs in the text and study the form and meaning of these before practising them. Finally, students use the grammar to describe a journey they made to another student in the class.

Objectives

By the end of the lesson, students should have:

- extracted specific information and language items from a reading text
- revised and/or extended their range of vocabulary using the reading text as a source
- revised/learned about how modals are used in the past and practised using these themselves
- talked to another student about a journey they made in the past.

Timings

If short of time, you could drop exercise 4 on page 52 and set it for homework. A possible lesson break would be after exercise 5 on page 52.

This activity focuses on the advantages/disadvantages of travelling by train on holiday.

- Focus students on the three photos on pages 52–53 and ask them if they have ever travelled by train to go on holiday.
- Put students into pairs and ask them to list the advantages/disadvantages of travelling by train rather than by plane.
- Put the pairs together in groups of four and ask them to compare their ideas.
- Finally, elicit ideas from the class and ask students to vote on whether they prefer trains or planes when they travel on holiday.

1a Focus students on the photos on pages 52–53 and tell them that these are all famous railway journeys.

- Elicit guesses from the class about where/what these journeys are.

- Then set the question in the rubric and elicit any other famous railway journeys they know.

1b Give students a maximum of one minute to read the article quickly and find the journeys mentioned.

- Tell students not to worry about vocabulary at this stage as this will be looked at in exercise 4.
- Elicit answers from the class and ask them if they've heard of any of these journeys, but don't ask for further information at this stage

> The Quinghai–Tibet line; The Trans-Siberian Express; The Orient Express

2 Elicit/remind students what *scan* means (looking for specific words/information).

- Read through the list (1–8) and check students understand *capital city* (the place where a county's government is situated), *ruler* (e.g. a king or queen) and *luxurious* (very comfortable and expensive).
- Give students three minutes to find the items in the list and underline them in the text. (Note: five capital cities are mentioned but students only need to find four.)
- Ask students to compare with a partner before you check answers with the class and go through the notes in brackets.

> **1** Beijing, Lhasa (the capital of Tibet), Moscow, Paris, Ulaanbaatar (Note: Ankara, not Istanbul, is the capital of Turkey.); **2** Agatha Christie (a British crime/thriller writer), Graham Greene (a British writer of fiction); **3** Tsar Alexander the Third (he ruled 1881–1909); **4** Lake Baikal; **5** The Orient Express; **6** The Trans-Siberian Express, 9,198km; **7** Quinghai–Tibet line, 5,072m above sea level; **8** the Fenghuosha tunnel, 4,905m above sea level

3 Give students five to eight minutes to read the text again and note their answers.

- Tell students to use their dictionaries to help them answer number 5 if necessary.
- Ask students to compare with a partner before you check answers with the class.

> **1** in order to do research for a Great Railways travel guide; **2** to prevent it freezing; **3** the views of the Himalaya mountains, the scenic Lake Baikal; **4** only the richest people, famous people, royalty; **5** unmatched luxuriousness, extravagantly elegant, opulence, fine cuisine, sleeping, restaurant and salon cars, ladies' drawing rooms

4 Give students one minute to scan the text to find and underline the words in the box.

- Then give them three minutes to complete the gaps.
- Encourage them to use the context of the article to help with meaning, and then use their dictionaries if necessary.

- Ask students to compare with a partner before you check answers with the class.

- In feedback, check students' pronunciation of any difficult words (e.g. *gruelling*).

> **1** gruelling; **2** impeccable; **3** era; **4** opulence; **5** altitude; **6** nomads; **7** icon; **8** nostalgia

5 Put students into pairs or small groups to discuss this question and give reasons.

- Get answers and reasons from three or four students and then ask the class to vote on the most popular choice.

GRAMMAR: modal verbs (past)

6a Tell students to find *all* the ways of talking about ability, possibility and obligation in the past, not just the modal verbs.

- Give students three minutes to find and underline the examples.

- Ask students to compare with a partner and say if each one expresses ability, possibility or obligation.

- Go through answers with the class and write each example on the board for analysis in exercise 6b and c.

- Check students understand *managed to* (it was difficult but we succeeded).

> was able to find (ability); managed to persuade (ability); had to take (obligation); couldn't get (ability OR possibility) (Note: see the Warning! under Grammar Tip opposite.); had to get (obligation); had to be heated (obligation); succeeded in getting (ability); were able to eat (ability); could afford (ability)

If possible, reproduce the article so that all students can see it (perhaps on an Interactive Whiteboard or an overhead projector). When you check answers to exercises 6a and 6b, underline the examples in the text.

(!) *Was able to* and *had to* are modal in meaning but not in form (i.e. they have a past form). *Can* is a pure modal but is the only one which has its own past form (*could*).

6b Tell students to use the examples they underlined in the text to help them with this activity.

- Ask students to compare with a partner but don't check answers with the class at this stage. Answers with be checked in exercise 6c.

6c Give students a few minutes to decide their answers and then ask them to compare with a partner, discussing reasons for each.

- Refer students to exercises 6a, 6b and the Language reference on page 142 if they need help.

- Go through answers and the notes in brackets with the class.

- Underline the relevant parts of the examples you wrote on the board in exercise 6a to further highlight the form for the class.

- Finally, read through the Grammar tip with the class and the Warning! below.

For further information, ask students to read the Language reference on page 142.

> **1** We use ~~can~~/could to talk about general abilities in the past. (Note the form, *could/couldn't* + infinitive [without *to*.]); **2** We use ~~must~~/had to to talk about obligation in the past. (Note the form, *had to* + infinitive [without *to*]; *had to be heated* in the text is a passive structure, i.e. *have to* + infinitive *be* + past participle.); **3** The past of *can* is *could/was able to*. (Note the form, *be able to* + infinitive [without *to*].); **4** We use *managed to/* ~~could~~ to suggest that we had difficulty in achieving the action.; **5** The verb *manage to* is similar to ~~must~~/succeed in.; **6** We use the *-ing* form of the verb after ~~manage to~~/succeed in. (Note the form, *manage to* + infinitive [without *to*].)

(!) Grammar tip: we can use *couldn't* to talk about a single action that we did in the past (i.e. the example in line 14 of the article).

7 Tell students that the text is about a journey on the Quinghai–Tibet line.

- To orient students to the text, ask them to read it quickly and list the problems the author had in organising the journey.

- Ask students to compare with a partner and then elicit answers from the class (didn't organise the train journey before they left London, didn't get much access to the Internet in China so didn't get much information).

- Students then work individually to choose the most appropriate alternative forms in the text.

- Ask students to compare with a partner before you go through answers and the notes in brackets with the class.

> **1** had to (this is a personally felt obligation); **2** manage; **3** weren't able to; **4** managed to; **5** managed to OR were able to; **6** were able to; **7** succeeded in; **8** could OR were able to; **9** couldn't; **10** had to (because there was no alternative)

For further practice, ask students to do exercise G2 2 and 3 on page 143 in the Language reference.

8   Re-elicit the problems students found in the text in exercise 7 as a lead in to this activity.

• Read through the instructions with the class and tell them to imagine a complicated journey if they have never experienced one themselves.

• Give students a maximum of ten minutes to make notes using the prompts.

• Monitor to help students with vocabulary if necessary.

• Then put students into pairs to describe their journeys and ask each other questions to get as much information as possible.

• Monitor to note mistakes with verbs to express possibility, ability and obligation.

• When they have finished, ask each pair who had the more difficult or organisationally complicated journey and why.

• Finally, correct some of the more common or important mistakes you noted earlier.

Students do the exercises on pages 35–36 of the Workbook.

Students use the journey they discussed in exercise 8 to write an email to a friend describing the problems they had and what was good about the journey. They can use the text in exercise 7 as a model.

Students do exercises G2 2 and 3 on page 143 in the Language reference.

5.4 SCENARIO: TRANSPORT: A NEW PLAN

Lesson topic and staging

This lesson focuses on the language of persuading and recommending action. Students are introduced to the scenario of a city that has asked consultants to help improve the transport system. Next, students listen to a radio programme talking about the transport problems and brainstorm some possible solutions before discussing the consultants' suggestions. Students then listen to the consultants discussing some of the suggestions and focus on the KEY LANGUAGE. Finally, the main TASK asks students to discuss suggestions and choose the best ideas.

Objectives

By the end of the lesson, students should have:

• learned useful phrases for persuading, and for recommending action

• used this language in a 'real-life' situation to discuss suggestions for improving a transport system

• extracted specific information and language items from a reading and listening texts

• participated effectively in extended speaking practice.

Common European Framework

Students can use language effectively to make their opinions clear as regards finding solutions to problems and express beliefs, views and opinions.

Timings

If short of time, you could drop exercise 3b on page 54. A possible lesson break would be after exercise 4b on page 54.

This activity revises vocabulary for describing transport problems.

• Focus students on the photos on pages 54–55 and ask the class if they think these places have transport problems (yes, they do).

• Put students into pairs and tell them to use the photos to identify as many problems as possible in one minute. (Note: some problems cannot be physically seen but can be guessed from the situation in the photos.)

- Elicit ideas from the class, write them on the board and check students understand each one by referring to the photos.

> **Possible answers:** traffic congestion, nowhere to park, cars getting blocked in, exhaust fumes/pollution, noise pollution, dangerous because too many vehicles on the road

SITUATION

1 If you used the Warm-up activity, students can use some of the vocabulary in this discussion.

- If you didn't use the Warm-up, focus students on the photo on page 55 and ask the class if they think this city has transport problems and then discuss the questions in exercise 1 in pairs.

- Elicit a few ideas from two or three pairs and check all students understand the vocabulary used.

- You can refer to the photos to help with the meaning of vocabulary.

> Answers depend on students' own ideas.

2 Introduce the text and tell students to read it quickly and look at the map on page 54.

- Tell students that the photos on pages 54 and 55 are of the city in the description and then put students in pairs to discuss the question using the photos and the map for information.

> **Possible answers:** traffic congestion, nowhere to park, cars getting blocked in, exhaust fumes/pollution, noise pollution, dangerous because too many vehicles on the road

3a Set the context and tell students that the city in the listening is the one they read about in exercise 2.

- Ask student to read the list of problems and check students understand *traffic jams* (see the photo on page 55) and *peak times* (rush hour, the busiest times of the day).

- Play the track without pausing and then ask students to compare with a partner.

- If necessary, play the track again.

- Go through answers with the class. (Answers are bold in the audioscript after exercise 3b.)

- Finally, ask students if the city's problems are similar to the ones they discuss in exercise 2 earlier.

> The following should be ticked: too many cars; traffic jams at peak times; not enough car parks; too much noise; unreliable bus services; on-street parking

3b Check students understand *percentage* (e.g. write 80% on the board) and tell them to write each number next to the ticked items in exercise 3a.

- Warn students that the percentages do not occur in the same order as the list in exercise 3a.

- Play the track without pausing and ask students to compare with a partner

- Go through answers with the class and check students have the correct stress on *percent* (*perCENT*).

- Finally, elicit the meaning of *roughly 60%* (*about 60%*).

> too many cars: over 75%; traffic jams at peak times: over 80%; not enough car parks: about 70%; too much noise: roughly 60%; unreliable bus services: 40%; on-street parking: just over 45%

Audioscript and answers to exercise 3:
Track 2.8

… And now some news for all you tourists who are planning to go to the beautiful city of Beauciel for a vacation. The results of a survey about the transport system in the city have just been published by the newspaper, *Echo de France*. It reveals some interesting information.
As many people know, Beauciel has serious problems concerning transport. The main problems, according to the survey are **too many cars in the city**, huge **traffic jams at peak times, not enough car parks, too much noise** and slow, **unreliable buses.**
The residents also mentioned **on-street parking** and the fact that the city had no underground, unlike some major European cities.
For most people in the survey, **over 80%**, traffic congestion was the biggest problem. At peak times, 8-10 in the morning and 4-6 in the evening, there are usually serious **traffic jams when people enter and leave the city.** It's a nightmare for drivers at these times.
Over 75% of the residents in the survey considered that there were just **too many cars** in the city. According to them, it was vital to reduce the number of cars.
Many residents, **about 70%** of those surveyed, felt that the city needed **more car parks.** There's only one car park in the centre of the city, and that's always full, according to them. The other car parks, dotted around the city, are generally small and inadequate for the number of cars.
Many residents, **roughly 60%** in the survey, spoke of the unacceptable **noise levels**, especially in the morning and evening, and not just from cars but also from motorcycles. According to them, this has a bad effect on their quality of life.
Just over 45% drew attention to the problem of **on-street parking.** According to them, there are too many private cars parked on the road. This caused problems for people who had an essential need to park on the road, such as ambulance drivers, taxis, school buses, and so on.
Other problems mentioned were the **unreliable bus services**, criticised by **40%** in the survey. And the length of time it took to travel by bus from the centre of the city in the West to the old town and port in the East. The bus journey was usually over an hour – far too long, according to the residents.
The survey results have come at the right time. They'll no doubt be studied carefully by the group of international consultants who are at this very moment trying to sort out the city's transport problems. That's all from me. I'll be back again tomorrow morning at 11 o'clock.

4a Give the groups three minutes to brainstorm their ideas.

- Elicit ideas to the board so that all students can note them down.

4b Keep students in the same groups as exercise 4a.

- Read through the instructions with the class and give students eight minutes to discuss the suggestions.

- Get a few ideas from two or three groups for question 1.

- Go through the possible answers for question 2 with the class, but accept any reasonable alternatives.

> **1** Answers depend on students' own opinions;
> **2** Possible answers: cheap = 2, 8; reasonable = 1, 4, 6; expensive: 3, 5, 7

KEY LANGUAGE: persuading, recommending action

5a Set the context and tell students they don't need to note problems, just solutions.

- Play the track, if necessary pausing at the points indicated in the audioscript below exercise 5c.

- Ask students to compare with a partner before you check answers with the class. (Answers are bold in the audioscript below exercise 5c.)

- Check students understand *pedestrian mall* (a shopping area just for people on foot), and *permits* (a piece of paper allowing you to do something).

> pedestrian mall (close the area to cars); persuade people to use smaller cars; more car parks; sell permits to people who want to use cars; good, cheap bus system; building a tram system; building more bicycle lanes

⁘ If possible, reproduce the audioscript so that all the students can see it (perhaps on an Interactive Whiteboard or an overhead projector). As you go through answers to exercises 5a, b and c, highlight them in the text.

5b Ask students to read the sentences (1–7) and try to complete as many as possible before you play the track again.

- Pause the track at the points indicated in the audioscript below exercise 5c.

- Ask students to compare with a partner and, if necessary, play the track again without pausing.

- Go through answers with the class. (The full phrases are *italicised* in the audioscript below exercise 5c.)

- Check students are stressing the words *really, must, essential, no doubt, sure* and *can't* as you elicit answers from the class.

> **1** really think; **2** you must agree that; **3** it's essential; **4** Don't you think that; **5** no doubt; **6** you can see; **7** you can't argue

For further practice, ask students to do exercise KL 4 on page 143 in the Language reference.

5c Set the activity, emphasising that students should only look for expressions that recommend action.

- Tell students there are more than five expressions in the text.

- Give students three minutes to underline five expressions and then ask them to compare with a partner.

- Elicit answers from the class and write them on the board so students can see them all. (Answers are underlined in the audioscript below.)

> Expressions to recommend action: the best solution would be to ...; that'd be a good idea; it's the way forward for us; the answer is to ...; I'm also very much in favour of; that's the best way to ...; we need action now to ...; I recommend ...; we need to ...; It would be very useful to ...

Audioscript and answers to exercise 5:
Track 2.9
Jim, Melanie, Luc

L: So, what do you think can be done about our transport problems? You know, it took me over an hour to get to the centre, and another twenty minutes to park. I was tired out before I even started work.

M: The first thing, Luc, is that I'm convinced there are too many cars in the centre. I think <u>the best solution would be to</u> **have a pedestrian mall there. Close the area to cars completely** – <u>that'd be a good idea</u>.

L: Maybe you're right, Melanie. That would be good for shoppers, but what about people who would still have to come into the centre – business people, traders, you know?

J: OK, Luc, but, 1 *I really think* we've got to do something about the number of cars in the city. 2 *Surely you must agree that* there are just too many cars – that's the heart of the problem. We've got to reduce the number somehow. [PAUSE]

L: Well, I suppose you're right, Jim. But there are other issues. 3 *I think it's essential to* **persuade people to use smaller cars;** there just isn't the space here for big cars. It makes me angry when I see a huge four-wheel drive with just one person in it.

M: I'm not too sure about that. A lot of people have families, they need big cars. [PAUSE]

J: OK, but I strongly believe we need to sort out the main problem first, I mean, too many cars in the city.

L: I agree, but we also need to think about other things. 4 *Don't you think that* **more car parks** are necessary? I mean, parking is one of our issues.

J: No, I disagree. It's not the answer to build loads of car parks. That'll just bring more cars into the centre and increase the traffic jams. No, I heard of a good idea recently, <u>it's the way forward for us</u>, in my opinion. The Council should **sell permits to people who want to use cars here.** Maybe 10,000 euros for a large car and 5,000 euros for a small car. The money could go to improving the roads and bus service. [PAUSE]

continued...

M: No, I don't think that'd work, Jim. People would be very upset if that was proposed. 5 *There's no doubt in my mind that* the answer is to offer people a really **good, cheap bus system**, and get some of the cars off the roads. I'm also very much in favour of **building a tram system**. 6 *I'm sure you can* see that's the best way to get people round the city quickly and efficiently – and we can build on the old system that closed down years ago. [PAUSE]

L: Maybe you're right, Melanie. But 7 *you can't argue that* it's the best solution for us right now. It would be very expensive, take years to finish and be very disruptive for businesses. It's a very long-term solution. We need action now to improve things. I recommend some simple solutions, like, erm, **building more bicycle lanes**. Now that wouldn't be too expensive and it would be something we can put in place quite quickly. We need to think in terms of both short- and long-term solutions. OK, can you do a report on where we are for my next council meeting? It would be very useful to have some costings ... *[fade]*

- Give students regular time checks to ensure they finish within the time limit.
- Then ask each group to present their six choices to the class and give the reasons for these.
- Students can ask questions at the end of each presentation.
- Finally, ask the class to vote on the best six suggestions from all those made in the previous stage.

HOMEWORK OPTIONS

Students do the exercises on page 37 of the Workbook.

Students write an email to the radio station in exercise 3a outlining how they intend to solve the city's transport problems. They should also try to persuade the radio station to use this information in a programme.

Students do exercise KL 4 on page 143 in the Language reference.

TASK: making an action plan

6a Go through the OTHER USEFUL PHRASES box with the class and ask students to re-read KEY LANGUAGE exercise 5b and the expressions to recommend actions in 5c.

- Give students a few minutes to think about the best suggestions in exercises 4 and 5.
- Then put students into groups of three or four and give them 15 minutes to discuss the suggestions, giving reasons for the six they choose.
- Students should keep a note of the group decisions they make.
- Monitor to note mistakes with the KEY LANGUAGE and OTHER PHRASES.
- When they have finished, don't elicit answers from the class but correct some of the mistakes you noted earlier. Tell students they have another chance to use the language in exercise 6b.

6b Allow the groups 15 minutes for this activity.

- Students should keep a note of the group decisions they make.
- Monitor to note improvements in students' use of the KEY LANGUAGE and OTHER PHRASES.
- When they have finished, don't elicit answers from the class but give feedback on improvements in use of language you noted earlier.

6c If you have only three groups in your class, you could put half of one group with each of the other two.

- Give students ten minutes to present their ideas and discuss which six *in total* (out of a maximum of 12) are the best.

5.5 STUDY AND WRITING SKILLS

Lesson topic and staging

This lesson focuses on describing graphs, charts and information in a table. Students match charts, a graph and a table to their descriptions and discuss which is best for different information. They then read about holiday destinations and draw a table and a pie chart to describe information and statistics before focusing on phrases for comparing figures. Next, students read a chart comparing airport freight and correct mistakes in a summary. Finally, students summarise statistics contained in a table.

Objectives

By the end of the lesson, students should have:

* extracted specific information and language items from reading texts and different graphs and charts
* practised interpreting and representing information and statistics in graphs and charts
* revised/extended their range of phrases for comparing and contrasting information and statistics
* written a short summary of statistics contained in a table.

Common European Framework

Students can write a brief report to a standard conventionalised format and link a series of discrete items into a connected linear sequence of points.

Timings

If short of time, you could set exercise 7 on page 57 for homework. Alternatively, you could drop exercise 3b and ask students to compare only their table in exercise 3c. A possible lesson break would be after exercise 3c on page 56.

WARM-UP

This activity introduces students to statistics for holiday destinations.

* Tell students they are going to find out about others' holiday destinations.
* Elicit the questions 1 'Did you stay in your country for your holiday last year?' and 2 'Have you ever been abroad?'
* Divide the class in two: ask one half to ask the first question and the other half to ask the second.
* Students move round the room asking their question to everyone in the class and noting the number of people who say 'yes'.

* Students then compare their results with another student who asked the same question and decide how to report this to the class (e.g. a percentage, a fraction, using the words *most, not many, nearly all*, etc.).
* Finally, elicit 'reports' from three or four students and ask others if their reports are the same.

STUDY SKILLS: describing graphs, charts and tables

1 Ask students which of the types of chart, graph and table they have used before.
* Then give them three minutes to read the options (1–4) and match them to the diagrams.
* Ask students to compare with a partner before you check answers with the class.

> 1 pie chart; 2 bar chart; 3 table; 4 line graph

2 Give students two minutes to think about their choices.
* Then put students in pairs to explain their choices and disagree with each other if necessary.
* Go through answers with the class. The answers below are ideal but you should accept reasonable alternatives.

> 1 bar chart; 2 pie chart; 3 line graph; 4 table

3a If you have a strong class, students can design the table *and* fill in the statistics. Students do not have to follow the design of the table on page 75 (in this book) and may, for example, choose not to rank the countries but just provide the percentages.
* If your students need help, draw a table on the board with just the headings and ask students to fill in the destinations and statistics.
* If you provide the table below 3c for students to use, tell them that *n/a* means *not applicable* and that you can't give a rank because these figures are not for one country but a collection of countries.
* Allow 15 minutes for this activity and monitor to check students are filling in the table correctly.
* Students can use their dictionaries to check vocabulary (e.g. *remain stable*) if necessary.
* Answers are checked after exercise 3c.

3b Remind students of the pie chart in exercise 1 and give them a maximum of five minutes to draw their own.
* Monitor to check students are drawing a reasonably clear chart.
* Answers are checked after exercise 3c.

3c Give students five minutes to compare the table (exercise 3a) and the pie chart (exercise 3b) and suggest improvements to each other if necessary.
* Draw the table and pie chart below on the board and ask students to compare them with their own.

- Students pie charts should look like the one below but their tables may vary depending, for example, on whether they decided to include ranking or not.

Suggested table:

Destination	Rank two years ago	% two years ago	Rank last year	% last year
Italy	1	22%	1	25%
North America	3	12%	2	22%
Spain	2	20%	3	20%
North Africa	4	10%	4	10%
France	6	5%	5	6%
Germany	6	5%	6	4%
Denmark and Sweden	8	2%	6	4%
The Netherlands	5	8%	8	2%
Other destinations	n/a	16%	n/a	7%

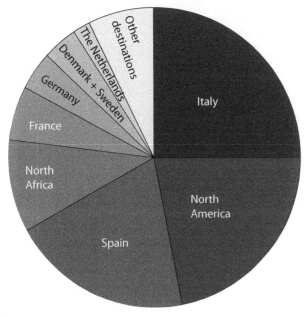

- If possible, reproduce the table and the pie chart above so that all students can see them (perhaps on an Interactive Whiteboard or an overhead projector). Show students the table/pie chart and ask them to compare these with their own.

WRITING SKILLS: describing information in a table

4a Give students two minutes to underline the phrases and then compare with a partner.
- Go through answers and the notes in brackets with the class.

the most (a superlative comparison); this compares with (comparison or contrast); Similarly (comparison, used at the beginning of a sentence and followed by a comma); compared with (comparison or contrast); in comparison with (comparison or contrast); while (comparison or contrast, preceded by a comma); On the other hand (contrast, followed by a comma and normally used at the beginning of a sentence); However (contrast, followed by a comma and normally used at the beginning of a sentence; whereas (contrast, preceded by a comma)

4b Comparison and contrast
- Students do this activity individually and then compare with a partner.
- Go through answers with the class and accept reasonable alternatives.

  1 while; **2** compare; **3** In comparison; **4** Similarly; **5** On the other hand

5 Students may be worried about reading tables and figures so allow plenty of time for this activity and, if necessary, tell students to work in pairs.
- Go through answers with the class and elicit/show where in the table the information comes from.

  1 Memphis International Airport; **2** Beijing Capital Beijing International Airport; **3** Frankfurt International Airport; **4** Hartsfield-Jackson International Airport; **5** Dubai International Airport; **6** Hartsfield-Jackson International Airport

6 Tell students to read the summary and stop after each sentence to check the table and compare information.
- Ask students to compare with a partner before you check answers with the class.
- Mistakes are crossed out and corrections are underlined in the answers below.

  Paragraph 2: increased its ranking by one place maintained its number one ranking between 2005 and 2006; Hong Kong airport, however, […] approximately four million three and a half million tonnes of cargo; an impressive 51% 5.1% in comparison with 2005; **Paragraph 3:** Frankfurt airport […]. It transported 21,127,979 2,127,797 tonnes of cargo; **Paragraph 4:** At both airports Beijing Capital Beijing International Airport; Paragraph 5: with freight up only down 2.8%

7 Give students five minutes to look at the table on page 172 and monitor to help clarify if necessary.
- Then, give students 30–40 minutes to write their summaries.
- Students use exercises 3 and 6 as models for organisation and some of the phrases in exercise 4.

- Monitor while students are writing to help with vocabulary and ideas if necessary.

- When they have finished, ask them to compare summaries with another student and make suggestions for improvement.

- If necessary, you can then give students another five minutes to make the necessary changes.

- Finally take the summaries in for marking, paying particular attention to the organisation and the use of language for comparison and contrast from exercise 4.

HOMEWORK OPTIONS

Students do the exercises on pages 37–38 of the Workbook.

Students conduct a survey on a topic of their choice but it must have a contrast of time (e.g. two different years, days, months etc.). They draw a table, pie charts, or a line graph to show the results and then write a summary of these. Alternatively, students give their table to another student who has to interpret it and write the summary.

Literature

6.1 THE NOBEL PRIZE

Lesson topic and staging

This lesson looks at the Nobel Prize for Literature. Students learn words related to literature and discuss their views on literary topics. Next, students read a text about the Nobel Prize for Literature and study vocabulary related to people in literature. Students then listen to people discussing a book and focus on the adjectives and phrases they use. Finally, students discuss a book they liked and one they didn't.

Objectives

By the end of the lesson, students should have:

- extracted specific information and language items from a reading and listening text
- extended their range of vocabulary related to literature
- participated in a group discussion to express their opinions about literature.

Timings

If short of time, you could drop exercises 4a and 4b on page 58 but make sure you lead in to the reading text before students do exercise 5 on page 59. Alternatively, you could cut the number of opinions for discussion in exercise 3 on page 58. A possible lesson break would be after exercise 5 on page 59.

WARM-UP

This activity introduces the topic of when and what people read.

- Write the following on the board: *a newspaper every day, a book on holiday, a book in the evening, a magazine in the doctor's surgery, a book or a magazine when travelling to school/college/work.*
- Tell students they are going to find people in the class who do the things on the board and elicit the question 'Do you read …?'
- Ask students to move round the room asking different students the questions. When someone answers 'yes', they should ask follow-up questions, e.g. 'Which paper do you prefer? What kind of book do you like?'
- When most students have found someone who does the things on the board, stop the activity.
- Get the names of students who do the different things from the class and ask for any extra information.

Woody Allen quote:

This quote refers to speed reading which is normally seen as a positive skill. Allen disputes this by showing that he had no real understanding of *War and Peace* having speed read it. The humour is in the fact that speed reading is not intended for works of literature.

i Woody Allen (born 1935) is an American film director and comedian known particularly for his depiction of a neurotic man.

VOCABULARY: literature

1a Give students a minute to think about their answers and then elicit ideas from the class.

1b Check students understand *fiction* (not real, about imaginary people and events) and *non-fiction*.

- Set the activity and students then work individually, using their dictionaries if necessary.
- Ask them to compare with a partner before you check answers with the class.
- Note: the answers below say what these types of writing normally are. However, it is possible, for example, for a play to be mostly non-fictional and a blog to be fictional. It depends on the content. A crime story can be either fiction or non-fiction.
- Check students' pronunciation of the stress on the following: *novels, poetry, romances, non-fiction, autobiographies, biographies, memoirs*.

> fiction: novels, plays, poetry, romances, science fiction, short stories, thrillers, crime stories; non-fiction: autobiographies, biographies, blogs, crime stories, diaries, essays, history, memoirs, travel writing

2 Put students in pairs or small groups to discuss these questions and give their reasons.

- Check students understand *great* in this context (generally believed to be culturally important) and elicit an example most students will have heard of (e.g. Shakespeare's plays, Cervantes' *Don Quixote*).
- When they have finished, ask the class about five of the types of writing and the reasons they think they're literature or not.
- Get a few ideas from the class about 'great' literature, but don't insist on a complete definition as students will think about this more in exercise 3.

☀ Don't mention the major religious books as examples of 'literature' (e.g. The Qur'an, The Bible).

3 Give students one minute to decide if they agree with each opinion, then put them into pairs and allow at least five minutes for the discussion.

- For feedback, choose five of the items and ask the class for their opinions and reasons.

- Tell students popular fiction is often not regarded as 'literature'. This helps students with exercise 4b.

- Finally, ask students if they would like to change the ideas they discussed in exercise 2 earlier.

READING

4a Elicit/tell students that the Nobel Prize for Literature is one of the most important awards for writing.

- Put students in pairs and ask them to tell each other about any of the writers in the list they know.

- Then ask them to discuss if each writer may have won the Nobel Prize.

- In feedback, elicit students' ideas but don't give the correct answers at this stage.

i Jane Austen (1775–1817) a British novelist (e.g. *Pride and Prejudice*); Leo Tolstoy (1828–1910) a Russian novelist, essayist and philosopher (e.g. *War and Peace*); Stephen King (born 1947) an American best-selling author of horror novels (e.g. *The Shining*); Agatha Christie (1890–1976) a British writer of crime fiction (e.g. the Hercule Poirot series); Vladimir Nabokov (1899–1977) a Russian-American novelist; J.K. Rowling (born 1965) the British writer of the best-selling Harry Potter children's stories; Ian Fleming (1908–1964) a British thriller writer (the James Bond series); William Shakespeare (circa 1554–1616) an English dramatist and poet; Winston Churchill (1874–1965) a British Prime Minister and writer of histories.

4b Read through the instructions and elicit/tell students that *can't have won* means it wasn't possible in your opinion, based on the evidence you have.

- Give students three minutes to read the text and then tick (has won), cross (hasn't won) or underline (can't have won, in my opinion) each author.

- Put students in pairs and give them five minutes to discuss whether each author has won the prize.

- Go through answers with the class and ask students if they're surprised that Winston Churchill won.

> Jane Austen: can't have won (she died before the prize began); Leo Tolstoy: hasn't won; Stephen King: can't have won (he writes popular fiction); Agatha Christie: can't have won (she wrote popular fiction); Vladimir Nabokov: hasn't won; J.K. Rowling: hasn't won (if students know this for sure) or can't have won (she writes popular children's fiction); Ian Fleming: can't have won (he wrote popular fiction); William Shakespeare: can't have won (he died before the prize began); Winston Churchill: has won

5 Ask students to read the instructions and the statements (1–6), and try to answer as many as possible before they read the text again.

- Ask students to compare with a partner before you check answers with the class.

> **1** True; **2** False (English is the most common language); **3** Not given; **4** False (it's annual, i.e. every year); **5** False (it's given for a body of work, i.e. a collection of writing); **6** True (Jean-Paul Sartre, a French philosopher and novelist, and Boris Pasternak, a Russian novelist, refused the award)

VOCABULARY: people in literature

6 Give students a minute to try to think of the words before they read the text again to check.

- Students then do this activity individually, using a dictionary if necessary.

- Ask students to compare with a partner before you check answers with the class.

- In feedback, check students' pronunciation of any difficult words (e.g. *biographer*).

> **1** author; **2** novelist; **3** biographer; **4** ghostwriter; **5** dramatist; **6** poet; **7** critic; **8** judge

7 Give students one minute to read the questions and think about their answers.

- Then put students into groups of three for the discussion before getting a few ideas from the class.

LISTENING AND SPEAKING

8a Write *The Da Vinci Code* on the board and ask students if they've read this or seen the movie.

- If nobody has heard of it, tell them it's an international, best-selling thriller by Dan Brown.

- Read through the instructions with the class and check students understand *book group* (people meet to discuss a book they have all read – this is a popular idea in the US and Europe).

- Warn students that they need to listen carefully to find out who is speaking. Sometimes the name is mentioned after a person has spoken.

- Play the track without pausing and then ask students to compare with a partner.

- Check answers with the class, but don't focus on difficult vocabulary because students will study this in exercises 8b and 9.

Michael liked it because it's a page-turner, a good and fast moving story, easy to read; Jenny liked it because the plot was exciting, really gripping; Jarvis didn't like it because he felt his intelligence was insulted, it was tedious, the ending was a real let-down; Erika didn't like it because it was really dull and didn't make her think, not a good story, hard-going at the beginning.

8b First, ask students to check any unknown vocabulary from the box in their dictionaries.

- Then set the activity and warn students that the words in the text are not in the same order as the list.

- Play the track without pausing.

- Ask students to compare with a partner before you check answers with the class.

- Tell students they can use all the words in the box in exercise 10 later.

- Check students can pronounce any difficult words (e.g. *tedious, disturbing*).

The following should be ticked: awful; brilliant; dreadful; dull; exciting; gripping; interesting; lightweight; overrated; tedious; thought-provoking. (Answers are bold in the audioscript below.)

9 Give students a few minutes to complete the sentences before you play the track again.

- Check answers with the class, ask if each one is positive or negative and elicit/read out the notes in brackets. (The phrases are underlined in the audioscript below.)

1 It's a real page-turner (positive – very exciting); **2** It's not my kind of thing (negative – not what I normally like); **3** I couldn't put it down (positive – very exciting, interesting); **4** The ending was a real let-down (negative – really disappointing); **5** I just couldn't get into it (negative – from the start I didn't find the story interesting); **6** It's light and easy to read (positive in the context of this track, but light can be a negative comment, i.e. not serious); **7** It was very hard-going at the beginning (negative – difficult to read because of the story or writing style); **8** It certainly lived up to all the hype (positive – the advertising said it was good, and it was).

Audioscript and answers to exercises 8–10:
Track 2.10
Jenny, Michael, Erika, Jarvis
J: Now if everyone's got a coffee, I think we should begin. Has everyone read this month's book?
M/E/JA: Yes, sure.
J: Well, Michael, I suppose as you chose this book for us to read you should start us off. Why did you choose it?
M: Yes, well …OK. I chose it because of all the publicity really. I thought we should all see what all the fuss was about. So, *The Da Vinci Code* by Dan Brown. What can I say? I really thought it was **brilliant**. <u>1 It's a real page-turner</u>. I read the whole thing in a day.
continued…

JA: Really??!! I thought it was **dreadful**; all that stuff about the Louvre being a museum, which is in Paris, which is in France. I felt insulted. And what was all that romantic stuff in the middle? No, I'm sorry, <u>2 it's not my kind of thing</u>. Jenny, what did you think?
J: OK Jarvis, I agree that was a bit odd, but you must agree the plot was **exciting**, all those twists and turns? <u>3 I couldn't put it down.</u>
JA: Really, Jenny, I'm surprised at you. It was really **tedious**. And <u>4 the ending was a real let-down</u>. After 500 pages nothing really happened. I found that Stephen King book we read last month much more **interesting**, and at least the characters were written with some imagination.
E: I agree with you, Jarvis – <u>5 I just couldn't get into it</u>. It was really **dull** and just not **thought-provoking**, which I was surprised about considering the subject matter.
M: Come on, Erika, it's a thriller. <u>6 It's light and easy to read</u>, just a good story.
E: Well, not for me. <u>7 It was very hard-going at the beginning</u> and then I just gave up. There were just too many people in it for me. And all those really short chapters about the different people – I suppose that was to make it easier to follow, except that for me it didn't work. I don't know if it was the way it was written.
J: Well, for me <u>8 it certainly lived up to all the hype</u> – I'd definitely read one of his others now. I agree with Michael. It was really **gripping**. I couldn't wait to see what would happen next.
JA: Not me. I mean, I like a good mystery but this was definitely **overrated**.
E: Yes, just **awful** … anyway, let's agree to differ on this one, but it's my turn to choose for next month and it's going to be something a bit less **lightweight**. How about a classic, perhaps something by Charles Dickens, you know with interesting characters?
J: Great.
M: Yes, I've never read any of his.
J: Sounds good.

10 Give students a few minutes to think about books they have read and choose two. If students haven't read much in their lives, ask them to think of books they read at school or movies they've seen.

- Put students into groups of three for the discussion and tell them to ask questions for further information.

- Allow ten to fifteen minutes for this activity.

- Monitor to notes mistakes with the vocabulary and phrases from this lesson.

- In feedback, ask students if they heard about any books they would like to read.

HOMEWORK OPTIONS

Students do the exercises on page 39 of the Workbook.

Students do exercises V1 5 and V2 6 on page 145 in the Language reference.

6.2 CHARACTERS IN DANGER

Lesson topic and staging

This lesson looks at fictional characters in books. Students listen to someone talking about a fictional character and then about a book that impressed them and focus on the vocabulary they use. Next, students read a brief extract from a novel and focus on sets of words in the text(s). Students then focus on narrative tenses from the texts and focus on the meaning and form of these. Finally, students write a short story using narrative tenses.

Objectives

By the end of the lesson, students should have:

- extracted specific information and language items from listening and reading texts
- extended their range of vocabulary related to describing a character, a book and light/darkness/fire
- revised/extended their understanding of the use of narrative tenses
- written a short story using narrative tenses.

Timings

If short of time, you could set exercise 11 for homework. A possible lesson break would be after exercise 6 on page 61.

WARM-UP

This activity introduces the topic of characters in books.

- Write the following on the board: *Sherlock Holmes, Harry Potter, James Bond (007)*.
- Ask students to discuss in pairs what they know about each character.
- Elicit answers from the class.

> Example answers: Sherlock Holmes: a detective, his friend is Dr Watson, lives at 21B Baker Street London; Harry Potter: a boy wizard, goes to Hogwarts School; James Bond: a British spy

SPEAKING AND LISTENING

1 Use the Warm-up activity as a lead in or focus students on the book cover showing Sherlock Holmes and tell the class that this character impresses a lot of people (they think he's a good character).

- Set the activity and put students into pairs to discuss the questions.
- Get a few ideas from the class.

2a Read through the instructions with the class and then play the track without pausing.

- Elicit answers from the class and ask students if they've read any of the stories.

> Sherlock Holmes wasn't a real person but a lot of people think he was.

ⓘ The Sherlock Holmes stories were written by the Scottish author, Sir Arthur Conan Doyle (1859–1930).

2b Set the activity and then play the track again, pausing at the points indicated in the audioscript below.

- Ask students to compare with a partner and then tell them to read the audioscript on page 181 to check.
- Go through answers with the class and tell them to underline the phrases in the audioscript.
- Then put students in pairs to decide if each is positive or negative, using their dictionaries if necessary.
- Go through answers with the class. (Answers are bold in the audioscript below.)
- Point out that we can use the adjectives in the phrases with other nouns (e.g. fascinating story, brilliant idea, incredible sense of humour).

> fascinating person (positive); someone we can all admire (positive); brilliant intellect (positive); incredible analytical powers (positive); amazing powers of observation (positive); supremely talented (positive); he has human failings (negative); he has character flaws (negative); he can be very arrogant (negative); Holmes is so brilliant (positive); he's a very courageous person (positive); He's knowledgeable (positive); he's talented musically (positive); he's very believable (as a character) (positive)

Audioscript and answers to exercise 2:
Track 2.11
Part 1
The Sherlock Holmes stories made a huge impression on me when I first read them, and the reason's simple. Sherlock Holmes himself is a **fascinating person** … **someone we can all admire.** He's got a **brilliant intellect** and **incredible analytical powers.** [PAUSE] He's also got **amazing powers of observation** – just by looking at people, he can deduce all kinds of things about them and their lives. He's **supremely talented** as a detective and can solve the most difficult cases. [PAUSE] But **he has human failings** as well. **He has character flaws**, like **he can be very arrogant** – especially in his relations with his sidekick, Dr Watson. [PAUSE] Watson accompanies him on most cases, and he isn't stupid, but **Holmes is so brilliant!** And **he's a very courageous person**, especially when dealing with some very dangerous men. [PAUSE] **He's knowledgeable** and **he's talented musically.** He often plays the violin when he's in an unhappy mood. [PAUSE]

continued…

He's very believable as the main character in the stories. A lot of people think he really exists. Tourists come to England and go to Baker Street to see where he lived, some don't realise he's a fictitious character. And I suppose I think of him as a real character too. I feel I know him well. When I was young, my uncle used to read extracts from the stories to me, and he could quote pages of the stories by heart. I love Sherlock Holmes and re-read the stories many times.

3a Focus students on the cover of *To Kill a Mockingbird* and tell them this is the book described in the listening.

- Ask students to read the questions and then play the track, pausing at the point indicated in the audioscript below.

- Ask students to compare with a partner before you check answers with the class.

- Check students understand *absurdity* (stupidity), *insight into* (understanding of), *perspective* (point of view) and *wise* (he knows a lot and understands people and the world).

> **1** It's heart-warming and it's a moral tale; it shows the absurdity of racism but we also get an insight into the world of the child.; **2** He's the father of the child, an incredibly fair, wise person – the moral centre of the book.; **3** We need to learn to see from other people's perspectives, try to understand them.

3b Ask students to read the word pairs and then play the track without pausing.

- Ask students to compare with a partner and then tell them to read the audioscript on page 181 to check.

- Students should use their dictionaries for unknown word pairs.

- Go through answers with the class (bold in the audioscript below). (Note: d) *read* is a noun and used here to mean *book*, *reading event*.)

> **1** c); **2** a); **3** e); **4** f); **5** d); **6** h); **7** b); **8** g)

> **Audioscript and answers to exercise 3:**
> **Track 2.12**
> **Part 2**
> One book that's made a huge impression on me is *To Kill a Mockingbird* by Harper Lee – so much so that it's a book I always buy for people as a present. The reason I like it so much is that it's **incredibly heart-warming** and it's a **moral tale**. Also, it's **extremely well-written** and in a subtle way it's a page turner. You want to know what happens to all the characters in the story.
> As well as that, the **language is very evocative**. It's a **charming read.** You really get the feel of a sleepy town in a hot summer during the great Depression in the United States. Something that's special about the book is that in a way it's written from a **child's perspective**.
>
> *continued…*

This gives a revealing view of the adult world; in particular, it shows the absurdity of racism but we also get an insight into the world of the child, especially the world of games and adventures during the summer. [PAUSE]
A **key character** in the book is Atticus, Atticus Finch – he's the father of the child and he provides the moral centre of the book. He's an incredibly fair, wise person. And from him we get the main lesson, as does young Scout, the child in the book. The main lesson from this book, I think, is that we need to learn to see from other people's perspectives – that we need to sympathise with their position and try to understand them. So, all round I think it's a marvellous book – the **characters are richly drawn** and it's a book that can teach us something in our own lives. It's certainly a lesson I learnt and an attitude of fairness that I try to carry with me through life.

READING

4 If possible, allow students to choose which extract they read. However, you must have an equal number reading A and B and may need to tell some students which to read.

- Ask students to read the questions and check they understand *is set* (the setting – the area/place the story happens) and *who tells the story* (i.e. which character, not the author).

- Give students five minutes to read their text and answer the questions.

- Monitor to help students with vocabulary essential to them answering the questions.

- Then put students into A/B pairs to ask/answer the questions.

- Go through answers with the class and tell them not to worry if they don't understand the story in the extract. (They could read the book to find out more.)

- If you have time and students want to, tell them to quickly read the other text.

> **Text A: 1** Dr Watson; **2** Dr Watson, Holmes; **3** in the house of the main suspect; **4** a young woman's life is in danger, Holmes and Watson are waiting in the house of the main suspect, someone lights a lantern in the next room, Holmes hits the bell rope, someone screams; **5** the probable killer may be in the house
> **Text B: 1** Scout Finch; **2** Scout, Jem (her brother), Atticus (her father); **3** at the prison in Maycombe County, a small town in Alabama, US; **4** Atticus is a lawyer defending a black man in racist Maycombe County, the townspeople want to attack the black man, Atticus waits for them and when they arrive, he tells them to leave; **5** the men may attack and injure or kill the prisoner, Tom, and Atticus

5 Put students into pairs or small groups to discuss the questions.

- Get a few answers from the class.

VOCABULARY: word sets

6 Tell students to underline the word sets they find.

- Elicit answers for the light/darkness and fire set before you ask students to look for others.

- Get answers from the class and tell students to use their dictionaries to check meaning.

- Keep students in their pairs to find other sets. See suggested answers but accept any reasonable answers.

> Light/fire/darkness: box of matches, candle, turned down the lamp, darkness, gleam of a light, smell of burning, heated metal, lit a dark lantern, struck a match, struck a light, glare flashing
> Sound and volume: gentle sound, silent, straining ears, audible, soothing sound, yelled, low, clear whistle, horrible cry, louder and louder, hoarse yell, dreadful shriek, cry, echoes, died away, silence

GRAMMAR: narrative tenses

7a Ask students if they can name any narrative tenses.

- Students then work in pairs before you check answers and go through notes in brackets with the class.

> **2** were taking = past continuous, came in = past simple; **3** got out, saw, closed, folded = past simple; **4** had lit = past perfect (lit = past participle of to light)

7b Keep students in their pairs and give them a maximum of three minutes for this activity.

- Go through answers with the class and briefly elicit the form of the past continuous (was/were + -ing) and the past perfect (had + past participle).

> **a)** past simple (sentence 3); **b)** past continuous (sentence 1); **c)** past continuous [first action], past simple [action that interrupts the first action] (sentence 2) (Note: in some sentences, the first action can continue simultaneously with the second e.g. We were sitting in the park when we saw the boy.); **d)** past perfect (sentence 4, i.e. the dark lantern was lit before they smelt the strong smell of burning)

8 Give students five minutes to do this activity individually and then compare with a partner.

- Tell students to look at exercise 7, and the Language reference on page 144 if they need help.

- Go through answers with the class and, if there is disagreement, ask why students chose a form.

- Finally, ask students if they've read any of the novels quoted in this exercise.

> **1** was playing, ran; **2** was trying, had seen; **3** were ticking, could not

9a Students do this activity individually and then compare with a partner before you check with the class.

- Use the example in this exercise to clarify meaning for the class or draw a timeline on the board.

> ongoing (i.e. continuous, in progress), before

9b Students use the example in exercise 9a to help them complete the gaps.

- Elicit the form from the class, write it on the board and highlight the possible contractions of had (I'd, you'd, s/he'd, they'd).

> had + been + -ing form of the verb

10 Give students five minutes to do this activity individually and then compare with a partner.

- Tell students to look at exercises 7 and 9, and the Language reference on page 144 if they need help.

- Go through answers with the class and, if there is disagreement, ask why students chose a form.

> **1** was sitting; **2** was shaking; **3** had been waiting; **4** heard; **5** came; **6** told; **7** had happened; **8** had borrowed; **9** had crashed; **10** had been driving; **11** rang; **12** was

For further practice, ask students to do exercise G1 1 and 2 on page 145 in the Language reference.

WRITING

11 Tell students they are going to write a story but will be given a lot of help.

- Ask them to read the introduction and then the notes on page 172.

- Give them five minutes to brainstorm ideas for each paragraph. If students have trouble thinking of ideas, you could ask the whole class to brainstorm ideas and write them on the board for students to use.

- Give students 30–40 minutes to write the story and monitor to help with vocabulary.

- Take the stories in for marking, paying particular attention to the use of narrative tenses.

HOMEWORK OPTIONS

Students do the exercises on pages 40–41 of the Workbook.

Students use the language in exercises 2 and 3 to write a short review of a book they have read (or a movie they have seen).

Students do exercises V3 7, and G1 1 and 2 on page 145 in the Language reference.

6.3 EVIL CHARACTERS

Lesson topic and staging

This lesson looks at evil characters in literature. Students describe evil characters they know of and then read two texts on famous bad characters. Students then focus on vocabulary and grammar (*used to /would*) in the texts. Students look at the meaning and form of the grammar and practise using it before focusing on pronunciation. Finally, students discuss things they used to do, think or believe as a child.

Objectives

By the end of the lesson, students should have:

- extracted specific information and language items from reading texts
- revised and/or extended their range of vocabulary using the reading texts as a source
- revised/learned about *used to* and *would* for past states and habits
- discussed things they used to do, think or believe when they were children.

Timings

If short of time, you could drop exercise 4b on page 63 and set it for homework. A possible lesson break would be after exercise 4b on page 63.

WARM-UP

This activity introduces the topic of evil characters in fiction.

- Focus students on the first photo on page 62 and ask them if they know of Dracula and elicit that he is an evil character (this should be obvious from the picture).
- Then write the following words on the board: *name, appearance, where he/she lives, what he/she does for a job, what he/she likes and dislikes*.
- Put students into pairs and tell them to make notes under the headings above to describe the perfect evil character (e.g. lives in an old castle in a dark and mysterious forest).
- When students have finished, ask them to read their notes to the class, who then vote on the best character.

READING

1 Use the Warm-up as a lead in to this activity.

- If you didn't use the Warm-up, first elicit the names of evil characters students know of.
- Then put students into pairs to talk about the character(s).
- Get a few ideas from some students and ask the rest of the class if they also know of the characters.

2 Focus students on the photos with the texts on page 62 and ask them if they know these stories.

- Then give students two minutes to read the texts and find the information.
- Ask students to compare with a partner before you check answers with the class.

> **Text A: 1** *Dracula*; **2** Bram Stoker; **3** a 15th-century Romanian ruler known as Vlad the Impaler; **4** he can become a wolf-like animal, he is a vampire (he sucks people's blood to survive), when he bites people they too turn into vampires
> **Text B: 1** *The Strange Case of Dr Jekyll and Mr Hyde*; **2** Robert Louis Stevenson; **3** Stevenson was thinking about the two sides to man (good and evil) and he had a dream that gave him the idea for the book; **4** he becomes an evil monster and murders people

3 Students do this activity in pairs or small groups.

- Get a few ideas from two or three pairs/groups and ask the rest of the class if they agree.
- If students are interested in question 4, encourage a whole class discussion and tell students to give reasons for and examples of their opinions.

4a Give students five minutes for this activity and tell them to use the context of the texts for help.

- Ask students to compare with a partner before you check answers with the class.
- Check students' pronunciation of any difficult words (e.g. *atrocities*).

> **1** sinister; **2** atrocities; **3** inflict; **4** tyrant; **5** brutal

4b If you used the Warm-up, students can use the notes they made to help them write the description.

- If not, elicit some ideas for appearance, what the character does, where they live, etc. from the class before you ask students to write their descriptions in 40–60 words.
- Allow about ten minutes for this activity and monitor to help with vocabulary if necessary.
- Take the descriptions in for marking, paying particular attention to the vocabulary students use. Alternatively, use the Task extension below.

When students have finished their descriptions, post them round the room, ask all students to read them and then vote on the best.

GRAMMAR: *used to, would*

5a Tell students to find and read all the examples in the text before they choose T or F for the statements.

- Check students understand *state* (e.g. I am happy, I live in a nice house, I want lunch).

- If students find this activity very difficult, ask them to read the Language reference on page 144.

- Ask them to compare with a partner before you check answers and elicit examples from the class.

- In feedback, emphasise that we can't use *used to* for single actions/events in the past, we have to use the past simple (e.g. 'I used to go to the cinema last week' is wrong).

> **1** True (used to inflict, used to sign); **2** True (used to be x 2); **3** False (it is always in the past and always something we did more than once, or regularly)

5b Tell students to look at the examples very carefully before answering the question.

- Ask them to compare with a partner before you check answers with the class.

- In feedback, write the examples on the board and underline the relevant parts to highlight form.

> Negative: we use auxiliary *did(n't)* + *used to* + infinitive (e.g. *read*). Questions: we use auxiliary *did* + *used to* + infinitive (e.g. *read*).

6 Tell students to find and read the examples before they answer the questions.

- If students find this activity very difficult, ask them to read the Language reference on page 144.

- Ask them to compare with a partner before you check answers and elicit examples from the class.

- Point out the contraction of *would* (*we'd*) in the second example, the position of the adverb in *would just burn* (Text A) and elicit the question form ('*Would you go* there a lot when you were young?').

> **1** Yes (e.g. would often talk, we'd watch, would capture, would burn); **2** No (we use *used to* to talk about past states); **3** No (we can't use *would* for states)

7 Students work in pairs and refer to exercises 5 and 6, and the Language reference if they need help.

- Monitor to point out mistakes if necessary.

- Go through answers with the class.

> **1** ~~would~~ used; **2** ~~use~~ used; **3** ~~was~~; **4** ~~is~~; **5** ~~use~~ used / ~~at the moment~~; **6** ~~used~~ use; **7** ~~used~~ use; **8** all used to suffer (Note: *all* can also come after *used to*.)

8 Orient students to the text, telling them to read it and decide if this is a travel guide they would buy for themselves or another (named) person and why.

- Students work individually, using exercises 5 and 6 and the Language reference for help if necessary.

- Tell students to think about the reasons for the answers they choose.

- Ask them to compare with a partner before you check answers and elicit reasons from the class.

> **1** used to/would (this is an example of where a time reference is not used with *would*); **2** used to/~~would~~; **3** used to/would; **4** use to/~~used to~~; **5** Did Lewis Carroll use to/Would Lewis Carroll go; **6** used to/~~would~~

pronunciation

9 Play the track and ask students to compare with a partner before you elicit answers from the class.

- Play the track again, pausing after each sentence to allow students to repeat. Correct pronunciation if necessary.

- Finally, point out that the pronunciation of *used to* and *use to* is exactly the same in English i.e. the /d/ sound disappears.

> **1** like the first 's'; **2** weak

💡 Students may not hear any difference between the two 's' sound. Model it as clearly as possible and, if necessary, place your hand on your throat to demonstrate the voiced sound /z/ of the second 's'.

SPEAKING

10 Set the activity and ask students to read through the ideas, checking they understand *scary* (frightening) and *giants* (huge and dangerous imaginary people).

- Tell students they can discuss some or all of the prompts in this activity or, if they prefer, think of ideas of their own.

- Put students in small groups and give them ten minutes to discuss their ideas.

- Monitor to note mistakes when using *used to* and *would*.

- When they have finished, get a few ideas from the class.

- Finally, correct some of the more common or important mistakes you noted earlier.

HOMEWORK OPTIONS

Students do the exercises on pages 42–43 of the Workbook.

Students write an email to a friend recommending a good horror film. In the email they have to describe an evil character from the film.

Student do exercises G2 3 on page 145 in the Language reference.

6.4 SCENARIO: A BOOK DEAL

Lesson topic and staging

This lesson focuses on the language of proposing, bargaining and talking about needs/expectations. Students read an article to introduce the scenario of a famous singer who is planning to write his memoirs. They then read a proposal he has written for these memoirs. Next, students listen to a conversation between the singer and his agent, and focus on the KEY LANGUAGE. Finally, the main TASK asks students to role-play the agent or a publisher and negotiate a contract.

Objectives

By the end of the lesson, students should have:

- learned useful phrases for proposing, bargaining and talking about needs/expectations
- used this language in a 'real-life' situation to negotiate a book deal between a literary agent and a publisher
- extracted specific information and language items from a reading and a listening text
- participated effectively in extended speaking practice.

Common European Framework

Students can use language effectively to express view and opinions, explain and give reasons for their plans and intentions.

Timings

If short of time, you could cut the number of options in exercise 5b on page 65. A possible lesson break would be after exercise 4 on page 65.

WARM-UP

This activity introduces the topic of famous people's memoirs.

- Ask students if they've read, seen a film/TV programme about a famous person's memoirs, who it was about, if it was good and why/not.
- Tell students to think of a famous person whose life would make a good book or film.
- Put them in pairs to discuss their choice.
- Finally, ask students if they would like to read the book or see the film about the person their partner chose.

SITUATION

1 Focus students on the photos on page 64 and ask them what they can see.

- Then explain they are going to read about a *lead singer* (the main singer in a band) who is going to write his memoirs.
- Ask students if they've read the memoirs of any famous pop stars.
- Ask students to read the questions and check they understand *resolve* (find a solution to something).
- Give students two minutes to read the article and answer questions 1 and 2.
- Ask them to compare with a partner before you check answers with the class.
- Then ask the pairs to discuss question 3 and elicit some ideas from the class.

> **1** because the band is going to split up (which means people will be interested in him again and he'll sell lots of books); **2** because he's had little formal education, he probably needs help with the writing process; **3** Answers depend on students' own ideas.

2 Read through the introduction and questions with the class.

- Give them three minutes to answer the questions before comparing answers in pairs.

> Answers depend on students' own ideas and opinions.

KEY LANGUAGE:
proposing, bargaining, talking about needs/expectations

3a Set the activity and play the track without pausing.

- Ask students to compare with a partner before you check answers with the class.

> Two topics: including more chapters on Lee Hart's personal background/family; how much money James Douglas he will be paid (the percentage).

3b Ask students to match the sentences to function and then compare with a partner.

- Play the track again and tell students to listen to check if their answers are correct. The context of the track will make it clear if they are bargaining or proposing. (Answers are bold in the audioscript.)
- Go through answers with the class and refer them to the context of the audioscript if there is disagreement.

> **1** a) (see also Other useful phrases); **2** b); **3** a); **4** c); **5** c); **6** a); **7** b); **8** c); **9** b) (and a) – the proposal is part of the bargaining); **10** b)

Audioscript and answers to exercise 3:
Track 2.14
Douglas, Hart

D: There are one or two points I'd like to discuss with you, Lee, before I contact a publisher.

H: OK. What do you want to talk about?

D: Well, you said you'd like to start with a short chapter about your family.

H: Yeah, it'll bring back some bad memories, so I don't want to make it too long.

D: I can understand it'll be difficult for you to talk about your childhood, but **1 a) if we included more chapters about your background, it'd add a lot of human interest to the book.** Readers would like to know about your childhood, your parents, and your two sisters. I believe your father left home when you were eight, didn't he? It must have been very difficult …

H: Yeah, it was. He was a terrible man, my father, violent, unstable, he made our lives a misery. I was really happy when he walked out on Mum. We all were. I don't want to upset her now by writing about that time.

D: I know how important your mother is to you, Lee. **2 b) Why don't you talk to her? 3 a) If you agreed to write two or three chapters about the family, you'd probably double or triple sales of the book.** It's a long time since your father left home, maybe you can persuade her that readers would be really interested in that part of your life.

H: OK, I'll try. If she and the rest of the family don't object, perhaps we can have more chapters about my family background.

D: Good, let's hope there's no problem there. Now, there's another important matter to discuss with you. Money! It's how I'll be paid for being your agent. As you know, agents are usually paid 10% of the money the writer receives from a book. That's 10% of the royalties you receive.

H: OK.

D: **4 c) But in this case, I think 15% is more appropriate.**

H: 15%? **5 c) Really, I wasn't expecting to pay as much as that.**

D: Well, it's a little bit above the market rate, but I'm very experienced in this kind of work. **6 a) You'll find I'm good value for money.** You see, I'll have more expenses than agents normally have. I'll have to go to a lot of international book fairs, set up interviews to promote the book, spend a lot of time negotiating with publishers, discussing TV and film rights and so on. The contract will be very complex and time-consuming.

H: I see.

D: There's going be a lot of interest in the book. Once it's launched, it'll be a full-time job for me to deal with everything…

H: OK, I get your point, but 15% still seems too high. **7 b) Look, I'd like to make a proposal. 8 c) I need time to think about this, and take some advice.** I'm seeing my financial adviser at the end of the week. **9 b/a) How about if I talked to him,** and after that we set up another meeting to discuss the financial details? If we agree, we can draw up a contract.

continued…

D: Fine, let's do that. **10 b) Could I suggest we meet towards the end of the month?** I'll be at the Cannes Film Festival for the next few days, and I'll be pretty busy for a while.

H: Yeah, I'm sure that'll be OK.

4 Give students five minutes do this activity individually and then compare with a partner.

- This activity is difficult so if students are undecided after eight minutes, stop them and go through answers with the class.

1 e); **2** h); **3** f); **4** c); **5** d); **6** a); **7** b); **8** g)

TASK: negotiating a contract

5a Lead in by asking students if they have ever had to negotiate in their jobs/at school and if they were successful.

- Read through the introduction with the class and then ask students to quickly read the points in exercise 5b to show them the purposes of the negotiation.

- Then divide the class into two groups, As and Bs, and ask them to read the relevant information on pages 159 or 164.

- Tell students to underline the main points they are going to make in the negotiation.

- Then go through the OTHER USEFUL PHRASES with the class.

- Next, ask students to compare what they have underlined in their information with another student in their group and discuss how they will negotiate these points (tell them to refer to the KEY LANGUAGE and OTHER USEFUL PHRASES).

- Monitor to help with vocabulary if necessary.

5b Put A/B pairs together and give them 15 minutes for the negotiation.

- If you have an odd number in your class, form groups with two publishers or two James Douglases.

- Monitor while students are speaking and note mistakes with KEY LANGUAGE and OTHER PHRASES.

- When they have finished, ask each pair who got the better deal in the negotiation.

- Finally, correct some of the more common or important mistakes you noted earlier.

HOMEWORK OPTIONS

Students do the exercises on page 44 of the Workbook.

Students write an imaginary email to a famous person of their choice proposing they write a memoir. The email should include the areas the book will cover.

Students do exercise KL 4 on page 145 in the Language reference.

6.5 STUDY AND WRITING SKILLS

Lesson topic and staging

This lesson focuses on improving listening skills and writing a travel blog. Students are introduced to the different types of informed guessing they do when listening in English: predicting what someone will say and guessing the meaning of words. They then do a series of listening activities to practise these. Next, students read a travel blog and focus on adverbs of degree. Finally, they write a travel blog about a given situation.

Objectives

By the end of the lesson, students should have:

- extracted specific information and language items from listening and reading texts
- practised/improved their listening skills
- revised/extended their range of adverbs of degree
- written a travel blog about a given situation.

Common European Framework

Students can write simple connected texts, narrate a story and write a description of an event.

Timings

If short of time, you could set exercise 9 for homework. Alternatively, you could drop exercise 8b on page 67 and rely on students' previous knowledge of adverbs of degree. A possible lesson break would be after exercise 5b on page 66.

WARM-UP

This activity introduces the topic of sources of information about travelling to foreign destinations.

- Tell students they are planning to travel abroad and write the following on the board: *blogs*, *friends*, *a travel guide*, *a piece of travel writing* (i.e. a non-fictional account of a journey), *a travel agency*.
- Tell them to rank the items from most to least useful for finding out information about a foreign destination.
- Then put students into pairs to compare and give reasons for their rankings.
- Finally, ask the class to vote on the most and least useful sources of information and elicit reasons.

STUDY SKILLS: improving listening skills

To lead in, ask students what kind of problems they have when listening to English.

- Elicit examples and include the problem of understanding the meaning of speakers' words.
- Then read through the introduction and the three types of guessing and ask students if they do these.
- Tell students they are going to practise all three.

1 Predicting from clues

- Check students understand *clues* (information that helps us guess something) and then set the activity.
- Put students in pairs and give them three minutes to discuss the questions.
- Students can use their dictionaries to check *bazaar* if necessary.
- Elicit answers from the class and refer to the Tip below.
- Finally, tell students that they have predicted the content of an extract from the book which they will hear in exercise 2.

☼ Tell students it doesn't matter if their predictions are not 100% correct, but they now have more idea what the text in exercise 2 may be about. Tell students they should predict content from clues every time they listen.

> 1 railway journey(s), perhaps a bazaar (market), perhaps journeys to places in Asia (*bazaar* has connotations of this part of the world); 2 southeast Asia because the women look as though they come from there

2a Guessing meaning of words

- Ask students to read the introduction and remind them that this is the same book as in exercise 1.
- Play the track without pausing and ask students if they heard any words they didn't understand.
- Tell students to look at questions 1 and 2, and use the words around the underlined item and the general context to help them guess.
- Ask students to compare with a partner before you check answers and go through the notes in brackets.
- Finally, tell students which is the correct answer.

> 1 either a) or c) (It can't be *sale* because we don't say *a shining sale*.); 2 either b) or c) (It probably isn't *asked her* because his voice wouldn't be heard at the station. It can't be *ordered her* because this isn't very polite.)
> **Correct answers: 1** c); **2** c)

2b Ask students to read the question and the options and check they understand *crab* (draw one).

- Put students into pairs to discuss their answer and give reasons.
- Elicit possible answers from the class and go through the notes in brackets.

> **Possible answers:** d), or perhaps a) (not chicken or crab because he would recognise them. Probably not grapes because he might recognise them even at a distance.)

2c Play Extract 2 so that students can check the correct answer.

> **Correct answer:** d)

3 Tell students they are going to hear the next part of the story and ask them to read items 1–5.

- Play the track and then put students into pairs to discuss their answers.
- Remind students of the procedure for guessing they followed in exercise 2 earlier.
- Elicit answers from the class and the reasons students chose them.

> **1** began to leave; **2** tied; **3** open a door; **4** stick; **5** small pieces with no special shape

4 Ask students to discuss this question in pairs and then play the track for them to check.

- Tell student the answer and ask them if they guessed correctly.

> Birds

5a Read through the instructions with the class and check they understand *obscured* (changed so that you can't hear them properly).

- Remind students to listen to the words around the obscured item to help them guess.
- Play the track and ask students to discuss their ideas in pairs and then fill in the gaps in sentences 1–3.
- Elicit ideas from the class. If some students don't know the word *whistle* others can draw or mime it.
- Then give them correct answers, emphasising it doesn't matter if they aren't 100% correct as long as they get the general idea.

> **1** luggage; **2** whistle; **3** platform

5b Ask students to try to answer the questions and then play the track again so they can check.

- Ask students to compare with a partner and then, if necessary, read the audioscript to check.
- Go through answers with the class.

> **1** people saying goodbye; **2** because there is an important person on it; **3** they bow and applaud; **4** it's an impressive and exaggerated way of saying 'goodbye'

WRITING SKILLS: a travel blog

6a Ask students to discuss the questions in pairs and then elicit answers from the class.

> A blog is an online and ongoing 'diary' about what you do and what you think about things.

6b Ask students to discuss the questions in pairs and then elicit a few answers from the class.

7 Give students one minute to brainstorm their predictions in pairs and then elicit a few ideas.

8a Give students one minute to read the blog and check their predictions from exercise 7.

- Ask students how many of their predictions were correct.
- Then give students five minutes to discuss the questions in pairs.
- Elicit answers from the class.

> **1** informal (*Wow!, by the way, take in, checked out* are examples of informal register. Blogs are often for friends and relatives to read and are therefore informal); **2 a)** completely full; **b)** very fast; **c)** visited, had a look at; **d)** took my wallet quickly; **3** Answers depend on students' own opinions (but probably the robbery)

8b Adverbs of degree

- Give students two minutes to find as many as possible, then go through answers and the notes in brackets with the class.

> extremely old (a strong adverb meaning very, very); incredibly noisy (strong, very, very); absolutely beautiful (strong, very, very); really impressive/really comfortable/really quickly (quite strong, very); pretty unlucky (not strong)

9 Ask students to choose the situation they want to write about. If students are studying in a foreign country, they can write about their current experiences.

- Give students 30 minutes to write their blog and monitor to check that the register is informal.
- Ask students to read each other's blogs and say what the most interesting event is.
- Take the blogs in for marking, paying particular attention to the register.

HOMEWORK OPTIONS

Students do the exercises on page 45 of the Workbook.

Students imagine they are Paul Theroux and write a blog or an informal email to you, describing the experiences from exercises 2, 3 and 4.

REVIEW

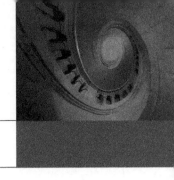

UNITS 4–6

GRAMMAR

1 Give students a few minutes to discuss the questions with their partner and tell them they will find some answers to numbers 2 and 3 in exercise 2.

2 Ask students to read the summaries and then give them five minutes to read the text and correct the summaries.

• Ask student to compare with a partner before you check answers with the class.

• Finally, ask students if they read any answers to questions 2 and 3 in exercise 1 and what they were.

> 1 People are surprised at how ~~light~~ heavy paperback books can be.; 2 The e-book can contain ~~one~~ many different books. 3 The e-book comes from ~~established~~ new (and superior) technology.; 4 E-books ~~will not be useful for many people~~ will be useful for many different people (e.g. people with poor eyesight and students).

3a Give students three minutes to underline the examples in the text. Make sure they underline the main verb used in each example as these will be useful in exercise 3b later.

• If students can't remember the form of these tenses, refer them to the appropriate page(s) in the Language reference.

• Ask student to compare with a partner before you elicit examples from the class.

• Finally, give students a few minutes to check the meaning of unknown vocabulary (e.g. *invent*).

> 1 are going to feel; 2 had been working; 3 had suffered; 4 were getting tired; 5 will be supplying; 6 will have to carry; 7 might want; 8 had to invent; 9 will be able to read; 10 won't have to spend

🔅 If possible, reproduce the text so that the whole class can see it (perhaps on an Interactive Whiteboard or an overhead projector). As you elicit examples, underline them in the text.

3b Tell students they may need to use phrases including the main verb (e.g. *had suffered*) and need to change the form of some phrases.

• Ask student to compare with a partner before you check answers with the class.

> 1 'm (am) going to / might want; 2 had suffered; 3 will have to carry; 4 had to invent; 5 won't have to spend; 6 will be supplying; 7 had been working; 8 will be able to read

VOCABULARY

4 Give students three minutes to complete the table.

• Ask student to compare with a partner before you check answers with the class.

> **Medical conditions:** arthritis; cancer; diabetes.
> **Forms of transport:** ferry; hydrofoil; scooter.
> **Types of writing:** biography; blog; memoir

5 Give students five minutes for this activity before comparing with a partner.

• Go through answers with the class.

> 1 painkiller; 2 radiologist; 3 contracted; 4 approve; 5 cable car; 6 seat; 7 short; 8 shrieked

KEY LANGUAGE

6 Tell students to read the statements first.

• Play the track without pausing.

• Ask them to compare with a partner before you check answers with the class.

> 1 False (she's fed up spending hours waiting at the bus stop); 2 False (this statement seems true at the beginning of the conversation but Sergei seems to start agreeing with Maria towards the end. He suggests Maria talks to her friend about how much car insurance costs and says they haven't seen a car they want to buy yet. He also says he wasn't expecting to pay so much which implies he's accepted they're going to buy a car.); 3 False (she says they would still have enough money to go on holiday and they could use the car instead of the train); 4 True ; 5 False (Maria's friend works for an insurance company) ; 6 False (Dennis works in a dry cleaner's and is selling his car privately); 7 True; 8 True

7a Give students five minutes to do this activity individually.

7b Play the track again for students to check their answers and, if necessary, ask students to read the audioscript on page 182.

• Answers are underlined in the audioscript below.

> 1 really; 2 be able to; 3 argue; 4 value; 5 don't; 6 way; 7 wasn't; 8 agree

Track 2.20

Maria, Sergei

M: I <u>really</u> think we need a car, Sergei.

S: Are you sure? What's wrong with the bus?

M: I'm fed up spending hours waiting at the bus stop. If we had a car, I'd <u>be able to</u> do everything much more quickly.

S: But I like the bus. It's cheap.

M: Well, we could get a cheap second hand car.

S: Yes, but if we spend the money on a car, we won't be able to afford other things, like holidays.

M: You can't <u>argue</u> that we won't have money for holidays. I mean, we could use the car for our holidays instead of going on the train. So it would be good <u>value</u> for money.

S: OK, Maria, but it's not just the cost of buying it. It'll probably cost quite a lot to insure.

M: Oh, I hadn't thought of that. How much is that going to be?

S: I don't know, but that friend of yours from the gym works for an insurance company, doesn't she? Why <u>don't</u> you talk to her? She'd probably know how much car insurance costs these days.

M::Oh yes, that's the best <u>way</u> to find out.

S: Anyway, we haven't even seen a car we want to buy yet.

M: Erm, you remember Dennis from the dry cleaner's?

S: I think so.

M: He's selling his old car. He only wants £1000 for it.

S: £1000! I <u>wasn't</u> expecting to pay as much as that.

M: But it's only five years old. Surely you must <u>agree</u> that's a very reasonable price …

LANGUAGE CHECK

8 Do the first sentence with the class.

- Then give students five minutes to do the rest of the activity.

- Check answers with the class after they have checked in the Coursebook.

> **1** ~~have~~ be; **2** ~~see~~ seeing; **3** ~~been~~ have; **4** ~~can~~ will be able to; **5** ~~could~~ might; **6** ~~must~~ had; **7** ~~getting~~ to get; **8** ~~had~~ was; **9** ~~did~~ had; **10** ~~use~~ used

LOOK BACK

9 The aim of this activity is to remind students of areas they looked at in Units 1–3. This will help reinforce any language or skills they had difficulties with or were particularly good at.

> find out who discovered X-rays: 4.1 exercise 5; study three ways to talk about future actions: 4.2 exercise 7; make predictions about your own life: 4.3 exercise 9; learn about using modal verbs for future possibility: 5.2 exercise 7; write a description of information in a table: 5.5 exercise 7; listen to people discussing The Da Vinci Code: 6.1 exercise 8; learn how to form the past perfect continuous: 6.2 exercise 9; write a travel blog: 6.5 exercise 9

If students have problems remembering these exercises, you could put them into small groups to remind each other (as appropriate) of the vocabulary learned, the content of the text, the topic they talked about.

To extend the activity, ask students to choose one of the exercises and write a test for other students. This could be a list of questions, a true/false, a gapfill, etc.

Architecture

7.1 FAVOURITE BUILDINGS

Lesson topic and staging

This lesson looks at architecture and people's favourite buildings. Students look at adjectives for describing buildings and practise the pronunciation before describing a building they know. Students then study verbs related to construction. Next, students read about three buildings and focus on vocabulary in the texts. Finally, students discuss buildings they like/dislike and write a paragraph to describe one.

Objectives

By the end of the lesson, students should have:

* extracted specific information and language items from reading texts

* extended their vocabulary related to architecture and construction, and practised using this

* participated in a discussion to express their opinions about a buildings

* written a paragraph describing a building that interests them.

Timings

If short of time, you could drop exercise 5 and set it for homework (students do not need this vocabulary to talk and write about buildings in subsequent exercises). Alternatively, you could set exercise 8b for homework. A possible lesson break would be after exercise 5b on page 70.

WARM-UP

This activity introduces the topic of famous buildings.

* Write the following buildings on the board, but not the dates in brackets: *The Colosseum* (about AD 80), *The Eiffel Tower* (1889), *Tower Bridge, London* (1894), *The Sydney Opera House* (1973), *The Empire State Building* (1931), *The Taj Mahal* (1648), *The Great Wall of China* (building began 500 BCE).

* Check that students know each building. It may help to elicit/tell students which cities they are in, take in photos/use the photos on pages 70–71 or find photos on the Internet.

* Put students in pairs and ask them to order the buildings from the earliest construction date to the latest.

* Elicit answers from the class (see dates in brackets).

* Finally, ask students if they've visited, like/dislike each building.

Le Corbusier quote:

This quote represents Le Corbusier's opinion of the function of buildings. It was innovative at the time because people generally considered buildings to also be artistic statements. The houses he designed were functional and ergonomic (designed so that humans could live in them and use them efficiently and easily).

i Le Corbusier (1887–1965) was a Swiss-born (later a French national) architect famous for his contributions to modern architecture. He was particularly engaged with providing better living conditions for people in crowded cities.

VOCABULARY: describing buildings

1 To give students some ideas for this activity, you could focus them on the photos on pages 70–71 or refer them to the Warm-up activity.

* Students discuss the questions in pairs before you elicit a few ideas from the class.

2a Tell students to do as many adjectives as possible before using a dictionary.

* Ask students to compare with a partner before you check answers with the class.

* In feedback, elicit/tell students that *classical* is a European style from the Roman (e.g. The Colosseum) or Greek periods (approx AD 1000–BCE 500), but that some modern buildings use this style.

* Tell students that the neutral adjectives can be either positive or negative depending on the opinion of the speaker/writer.

> **Positive:** elegant, graceful, impressive, magnificent, stylish, imposing, innovative;
> **negative:** derelict, dilapidated, run-down, ugly;
> **neutral:** ancient, classical, contemporary, ornate, traditional

2b Warn students that more than one adjective goes in some categories and a couple of adjectives can go in more than one category.

* Students work individually and then compare answers with a partner.

* Go through answers with the class and write the words on the board in preparation for exercise 3.

> **1** derelict, dilapidated, run-down; **2** ancient, classical, traditional; **3** ugly, (derelict, dilapidated); **4** innovative (stylish); **5** elegant, graceful, stylish, (magnificent); **6** ornate; **7** contemporary, (innovative); **8** imposing, impressive, magnificent

3 Word stress

• Focus students on the first adjective you wrote on the board in exercise 2b, elicit the main stress and mark it on the word (see answers below).

• Tell students to mark the stress on the other words in pairs, so they can say the word to each other if necessary.

• Check answers with the class.

• Then ask students to work individually to group the words according to their syllable stress.

• Warn students that one word has a stress on both first and second syllables.

• Ask students to compare and then play the track, pausing briefly after each word for students to check.

• Highlight that *contemporary* is pronounced as three syllables, *con-tem-pry*.

• Finally, play the track again, pausing after each word for students to repeat, and correct if necessary.

> **First syllable stress:** **an**cient; **class**ical; **der**elict; **el**egant; **grace**ful; **inn**ovative; **sty**lish; **ug**ly. **Second syllable stress:** con**tem**porary; di**lap**idated; im**pos**ing; im**press**ive; mag**nif**icent; or**nate**; run-**down**; tra**dit**ional.

4a Give students two minutes to look at the photos and decide their opinions.

• Put them into pairs to describe the buildings and discuss which they like.

🔧 When students have looked at both photos, ask them to describe one of the buildings from memory, without looking at the photos again. Their partner must guess which building is being described.

4b Give students a few minutes to think of a building they know (it doesn't need to be a famous building).

• Then put students in small groups to describe their buildings and ask each other questions for more information if necessary.

• They should begin their descriptions with the building's function (e.g. house, museum) and where it is.

• Finally, ask students if they would like to (as appropriate) visit/live in/stay in/etc. any of the buildings they heard described.

5a Tell students to match as many words as possible before they use their dictionaries to check meaning.

• Ask students to compare with a partner before you check answers with the class.

• In feedback, elicit the stressed syllable(s) on each word and ask students to mark this in their books. The main stress(es) are marked in the answers below.

> **1** g) **dam**age; **2** e) re**build**; **3** c) con**struct**; **4** h) de**mol**ish; **5** b) main**tain**; **6** a) re**store**; **7** d) com**mi**ssion; **8** f) de**sign**

5b To help students get started, elicit the first stage (*commission*) and then give them two minutes to order the other words.

• The order is not obvious, so put students into pairs to compare their lists and discuss the options.

• Elicit answers and write them on the board. Ask students if they agree with the order as you write each item. Accept any reasonable orders.

• Finally, give students the suggested order below.

> **Suggested answers: 1** commission; **2** design; **3** construct; **4** maintain; **5** damage; **6** restore; **7** demolish; **8** rebuild

💡 Take this opportunity to monitor for use of the passive structure while students are discussing the order of verbs (e.g. it's designed before it's built). This will help you assess their ability before the grammar focus in the next lesson.

READING

6a To lead in, (re)elicit the name of each building and where it is (The Colosseum, Rome, Italy; The Eiffel Tower, Paris, France; The Hajj Airport Terminal, Jeddah, Saudi Arabia).

• Explain students will read about each building later.

• Set the activity and give students one minute to guess the answers.

• Ask them to compare with a partner.

• Elicit a few guesses from the class.

6b Give students five minutes to read the texts and check their answers.

• Ask them to compare with a partner before you check answers with the class.

• In feedback, check students understand *gladiators* (Roman fighters for entertainment), but don't focus on other unknown vocabulary at this stage.

• Finally, ask students if they have visited/would like to visit any of the buildings and why/why not.

> **1** False (opened in AD80); **2** True (gladiator and animal fights); **3** True; **4** False (recently it has been renovated and partly restored); **5** False (it's a mixture of traditional architecture and high-tech *materials*. However, in the photo it appears there is a mix of architecture so accept True if students insist.); **6** False (it has no […] air-conditioning); **7** True (a low-energy building); **8** False (there was a lot of opposition from the public when it was built); **9** True (until about 1930); **10** True (built as a temporary structure)

🔧 To make activities 6a and 6b more communicative, divide the class in three and ask students to focus on only one text. In 6b, students read their text to check their guesses and then swap information with students who read the other texts. In exercise 7, you can either ask students to find the words in their text only and then swap information, or ask everyone to read all three texts.

7 Tell students there is more than one possible answer for number 8.

• Students do this activity individually and then compare answers with a partner.

• Go through answers and check the pronunciation of any difficult words (e.g. *amphitheatre*).

> 1 amphitheatre; 2 survived; 3 restore or renovate;
> 4 high-tech; 5 parasols; 6 landmark; 7 temporary;
> 8 eyesore

SPEAKING AND WRITING

8a Tell students that *interesting* here refers to the design (not, for example, the history).

• Give students a few minutes to think of a building for each adjective and then elicit a few ideas from the class.

💡 The research stage in this activity means that you will need to give students plenty of time during the lesson. Alternatively, ask them to research and make notes in their own time and then write the paragraph in class.

8b Students can use the Internet to research the building and make notes.

• Give students 15 minutes to write their paragraph, using the notes they made earlier.

• Monitor to help with vocabulary if necessary.

• Take the work in for marking, paying particular attention to the use of vocabulary from this lesson.

• Alternatively, post the paragraphs round the room and ask students to read them all. Then ask students which buildings they already knew and which they'd like to visit.

HOMEWORK OPTIONS

Students do the exercises on page 46 of the Workbook.

Students think about a building they visited on holiday in the past and write an email to a friend telling them why they liked/didn't like the building.

Students do exercises V1 5 and V2 6 on page 147 in the Language reference.

7.2 HOTELS IN SPACE

IN THIS LESSON

Lesson topic and staging

This lesson looks at the possibility of building hotels in space. Students discuss if they'd like a holiday in space. They then read an article on space hotels and focus on vocabulary in the text. Next, students study passive structures in the article and focus on meaning and form. Then, students listen to an architect talking about hotel design. Finally, students discuss if they believe space hotels are a waste of time and money.

Objectives

By the end of the lesson, students should have:

• extracted specific information and language items from a reading and a listening text

• extended their range of vocabulary related to competitive advantage and hotels

• revised/extended their understanding of the use of the present/simple future passive and the present continuous passive

• discussed the idea of space hotels and whether they are worth building.

Timings

If short of time, you could drop exercise 4 and set it for homework. A good lesson break would be after exercise 4 on page 73.

WARM-UP

This activity introduces the topic of hotels in different locations.

• Ask students if they like staying in hotels and what kind they prefer (e.g. large, small, family run).

• Write the following on the board: *a large, international/small family run hotel in the mountains/ in the desert/in a city/on a small island/under the sea/on a boat.*

• Ask students to decide what kind of hotel they would ideally like to stay in and where it should be. They can only choose from the options above.

• Then put students into pairs to explain their choice.

• Finally, elicit a few ideas and ask the class if they agree.

READING

1 Focus students on the picture on page 72 and ask them what they think it is.

• Tell students the picture shows a space hotel and then set the questions.

- Ask students to briefly discuss their ideas in pairs and then elicit a few ideas from the class.

2 Give students two minutes to read the article and compare the features with their ideas in exercise 1.

3 Give students five minutes to complete the gaps and warn them they will have to change the form of the sentences/words in the text.

- Students can use their dictionaries to check vocabulary if necessary.

- Ask students to compare with a partner before you check answers with the class.

> **1** substantial proportion; **2** bed and breakfast;
> **3** artificial gravity; **4** potential; **5** flexible walls;
> **6** inflated

4 Tell students to underline the expressions in the article before they answer the questions.

- Encourage students to use the context to guess meaning rather than their dictionaries.

- Ask students to compare with a partner before you check answers with the class.

- In feedback, check students' pronunciation of *cater*.

- Finally, ask students if they would like to stay in a space hotel now they have read about them.

> **1** b); **2** a); **3** a); **4** a); **5** a)

GRAMMAR: the passive (1)

5a Students may underline examples that are not passive. Allow them to do this at this stage and don't give them any guidance regarding form because they will look at this in exercise 5b.

- Give students three minutes to underline examples and then compare with a partner.

- Check that students have underlined all the correct examples (see answers below).

- Finally, give students a few minutes to find any unknown vocabulary from the examples.

> Correct examples: will the most innovative new hotel be built; is finally integrated; are already being made; hotel is expected; grown (this is a reduced relative clauses using the passive, i.e. which is grown); will be required; being strapped; is inflated; were designed; was cancelled; was given the right; could be used; will probably be called

5b Give students 30 seconds to circle the examples and then elicit these from the class (see below).

- Then give students a maximum of one minute to choose the correct words in the rule before comparing with a partner.

- Check answers with the class and tell students that *will be* is not given as an option in the rule because it is regarded as a form of *be*.

- Finally, elicit that *not* is used to make the passive negative, the contraction of *will not (won't)* and a few examples of past participles.

> Circled present simple passive and future passive: will be built; is integrated, is expected, (is) grown, will be required, is inflated, will be called
> We form the passive with *be* + the past participle.

6 First, ask students if they underlined any present continuous passive forms in exercise 5a and then focus them on the example in this activity.

- If students ask if *without being strapped* is present continuous passive, tell them they will read about this in the Grammar tip later.

- Give students 30 seconds to complete the gaps and then elicit answers from the class.

- Note: *already* is an adverb and not part of the basic structure, but highlight its position for students.

- Read through the Grammar tip with the class.

> We form the present continuous passive with the verb *be* + *being* + the past participle.

7 Students do this activity individually and then compare with a partner.

- Tell students to look at exercises 5 and 6, and the Language reference on page 146 if they need help.

- Monitor to point out mistakes but encourage students to self-correct if possible.

- Go through answers with the class and, if necessary, elicit the reasons for each one.

> **1** are being manufactured; **2** will be built; **3** being invested; **4** is being checked / will be checked (Note: the answer here depends on whether the construction is happening now or will be happening in the future.); **5** being constructed; **6** is being carried out / will be carried out; **7** will not/won't be finished; **8** being included

8 Tell students to read all four sentences (1–2 and a–b) before they match the items.

- Ask students to compare with a partner and refer to the Language reference if they need help.

- Check answers and go through the notes in brackets with the class.

> **1** a) (It's not important who builds it, the emphasis is on where, also we assume it'll be built by architects, designer, builders, etc; **2** b)

LISTENING

9a Set the context and play the track, pausing before each question.

- Tell students not to worry if they can't write the complete questions at this stage.
- Ask students to compare with a partner and then tell students to read the questions (but not the rest of the text) in the audioscript on page 183.
- Then play the track again, pausing as above to give students time to write notes.
- Tell students they do not need to write examples to support their answer (e.g. for question 3, students can write *facilities* instead of *cafeteria, brasserie, TV room*, etc.).
- Ask students to compare with a partner before you check answers with the class.

> 1 their role as architects, what they are trying to do; 2 the location, what kind of people it's designed for, the budget, access, the facilities, make it an enjoyable place to stay at; 3 aesthetic appearance of the interior, the function, a spacious and cosy lounge, the facilities available, good access; 4 she likes the idea, it'll be an example of human progress, a huge challenge, she's excited about it; 5 yes, definitely, in her opinion

9b Ask students to read the statements and answer as many as they can from memory.

- Play the track again or ask students to read the audioscript to check their answers before you go through them with the class.
- In feedback, ask students if they agree with the opinions expressed by numbers 1 and 5.
- Finally, ask students to read the audioscript on page 183 and use their dictionaries to find the meaning of unknown vocabulary (e.g. *brasserie, crucial, integrate*).

> The following statements reflect opinions expressed in the talk: 1, 5

SPEAKING

10 Ask students to read the statement and question and then give them five minutes to make some notes with examples to support their opinions.

- Then give students ten to fifteen minutes to discuss the statement in groups of three and decide, as a group, if they agree completely, not at all or partially.
- When they have finished, elicit how far each group agrees with the statement and their reasons.

HOMEWORK OPTIONS

Students do the exercises on pages 47–48 of the Workbook.

Students imagine they are going to interview Howard Wolff (see exercise 2) for a radio programme and need to write five questions to ask him.

7.3 BUILDING BRIDGES

IN THIS LESSON

Lesson topic and staging

This lesson looks at bridges around the world. Students read an article about important bridges and then discuss how these compare. Students then focus on idioms related to bridges and the use of prefixes on words in the text. Next, students look at passive structures in the text and focus on the meaning of these before practising them. Finally, students discuss two bridges using information provided and write a paragraph to describe one of them.

Objectives

By the end of the lesson, students should have:

- extracted specific information and language items from a reading text
- revised and/or extended their range of idioms and prefixes
- revised/learned about the past simple and present perfect passive
- discussed and written about two different bridges.

Timings

If short of time, you could drop exercise 4 on page 74 and set it for homework. A possible lesson break would be after exercise 5b on page 74.

WARM-UP

This activity introduces the topic of bridges and why people like/dislike them.

- Focus students on the photos on page 75 and ask students if they like the designs of these bridges.
- Then, ask students to think of a bridge they like or dislike and think about why.
- Put students into pairs to talk about their bridges giving information such as where it is, what river it crosses, how old it is, what it looks like, what it's used for, as well as why they like/dislike it. Students should ask each other questions for further information.
- Finally, ask a few students to tell the class about their bridges and why they like/dislike them.

READING

1 Focus students on the photos and ask them if they know anything about these bridges.

- Then ask students to briefly discuss the second question in pairs or small groups.
- Elicit a few ideas from the class.

2 Read through the instructions with the class and give students three minutes to read the introduction (above the photos) and tick the reasons.

- Ask students to compare with a partner before you check answers with the class.

> The following should be ticked: 2, 4, 5

3a Read through the questions with the class and check they understand *resist* (prevent the effects of something), *dimensions* (length, width, etc.).

- Give students five minutes to read the rest of the article and answer the questions.
- Monitor to help with vocabulary (i.e. words students must know to answer the questions, e.g. *harp*) or ask students to use their dictionaries.
- Ask students to compare with a partner before you check answers with the class.

> **1** Charles Bridge; **2** Akashi Kaikyo Bridge;
> **3** Golden Gate Bridge; **4** Alamillo Bridge

3b Give students two minutes to read the information on the bridges again.

- Then put them into pairs to discuss the similarities and differences.
- Ask two or three students to tell the class what similarities and differences they talked about with their partner.

☀ You could take this opportunity to monitor for students' use of comparative structures and phrases. In feedback, elicit corrections to some of the mistakes you noted and/or give students alternative ways of expressing themselves.

VOCABULARY: idioms, prefixes

4 When students read the first paragraph of the article, ask them to underline all the idioms they can find. Tell them the idioms all contain *bridge*.

- Check that students have found four idioms and elicit them from the class.
- Students then use the idioms to complete sentences 1–4. Remind them they need to change the form.
- Ask students to compare with a partner before you check answers with the class.
- Then, in pairs, ask students to try to express the idioms in other words. They can read the article for clues.
- Elicit ideas from the class (see below).

> **1** burn my bridges; **2** cross that bridge when we come to it; **3** all water under the bridge; **4** build (some) bridges
> **Idioms in other words: 1** lose something I've got when I may still need it; **2** deal with that when it happens; **3** it's already happened, let's forget about it; **4** make friends and form relationships

For further practice, ask students to do exercise V3 7 on page 147 in the Language reference.

5a Do the first part of this activity as a whole class by writing each word on the board and underlining the prefix.

- Give students one minute to match the prefixes and meanings.
- Go through answers with the class.

> **1** re; **2** in, un; **3** mis; **4** over

5b Students do this activity individually and then compare with a partner.

- Go through answers with the class and check students understand *insoluble* (e.g. sugar is soluble in water, sand is insoluble in water).
- In feedback, elicit/give the stress on the original words (e.g. im*portant*) and then on the prefix + word (e.g. **un**im*portant*).

> **1** unimportant; **2** misunderstand; **3** overcrowded;
> **4** insoluble; **5** redefine; **6** insensitive

For further practice, ask students to do exercise V4 8 on page 147 in the Language reference.

☀ Show students that prefixes are contained in the information about a word in a good dictionary.

GRAMMAR: the passive (2)

6a Give students three minutes to underline examples and then compare with a partner.

- Check that students have underlined all the correct examples (see answers and Tip on the next page).
- Give students a few minutes to find any unknown vocabulary from the examples.
- Then put them into pairs to discuss the form.
- In feedback, write one example of the past simple passive and the present perfect passive on the board and highlight the relevant parts to show the form. Alternatively, see the Tip on the next page.
- Finally, remind students of the contractions of *have* ('ve) and *has* ('s) and then elicit/tell them that adverbs generally come after the auxiliary (*was, were, have* or *has*), e.g. *has never been*. (Note: *tragically* is after *been* in the text because there are two adverbs in this sentence (*occasionally* is the other). It is a choice of style and makes the sentence easier to read.)

> Examples of past simple passive: was destroyed; was built; (was) named (Note: the auxiliary *was* is not used here, but the form is still passive.); was scheduled; was opened.
> Examples of present perfect passive: has since been rebuilt; has … been tragically misplaced; has never been shattered; has been built
> Past simple passive: *was/were* + past participle.
> Present perfect passive: *have/has* + *been* + past participle

⚙ If possible, reproduce the article so that all students can see it (perhaps on an Interactive Whiteboard or an overhead projector). When you check that students have underlined the correct examples, to highlight the form and for feedback in exercise 6b, highlight the relevant parts of the text.

6b Ask students if they found any other passive forms in the text and elicit examples (including those in this exercise if possible).

- Give students 30 seconds to match the sentences to the forms and then elicit answers from the class.

- Then, elicit the form of each from the class and write it on the board.

- Finally, give students the following active/passive transformation to show them when the passive infinitive might be used: We planned (scheduled) to complete it = it was scheduled to be completed.

> 1 b); 2 a) Form 1: *was/were* + *being* + past participle. Form 2: *to be* + past participle

For further information, ask students to read G2 in the Language Reference on page 146.

7 Tell students that the report is about complaints made by local residents during the building of a hotel.

- To orient students to the text, ask them to brainstorm what the complaints might be and then quickly read the text to check. (The complaints in the text are noise and pollution).

- Then give students five minutes to do the activity as per the Coursebook.

- Ask them to compare with a partner and use exercise 6, and the Language reference for help.

- Go through answers with the class and ask students to give reasons.

> 1 have *been* received; 2 was ~~completing~~
> *completed*; 3 was ~~constructing~~ *being constructed*;
> 4 were ~~delivering~~ *being delivered*; 5 were ~~digging~~
> *being dug*; 6 were ~~making~~ *being made*, or *made*;
> 7 was ~~doing~~ *done*; 8 ~~have been~~ *were* closed;
> 9 have *been* received; 10 has now *been* built; 11 is
> *to* be done; 12 to be ~~publish~~ *published*

For further practice, ask students to do exercise G1,2 1 and 2 on page 147 in the Language reference.

8a First, elicit/tell students that the subject in a passive sentence comes at the end of the sentence.

- Students do this activity in pairs before you check answers with the class.

- In feedback, ask students to underline the long subject expression (the new strange-shaped building in the City of London) in sentence 2 and the known information (it was designed) in sentence 1.

> 1 b); 2 a)

For further information, ask students to read G3 on page 146 of the Language Reference.

For further practice, ask students to do exercise G3 3 on page 147 in the Language reference.

ⓘ The 'Gherkin' (30 St Mary Axe OR the Swiss Re Tower) is a new building in London, completed in 2004. It has a strange shape (curved sides and pointed at the top) and is sometimes lit in green at night. People think it looks like a small cucumber (a gherkin).

8b Give students a few minutes to do this activity individually before comparing answers with a partner.

- Check answers with the class and elicit the long subject expression or the known information in each highlighted passive.

- Finally, give students a few minutes to find difficult vocabulary from the sentences in their dictionaries.

> The bridge is supported by a pylon and cables which form the graceful shape of a harp = a); this bridge has been built … = b); This work was scheduled … = b); The bridge was opened on 21 May […]. It was opened to traffic = b)

SPEAKING AND WRITING

9 First, tell students to look at the photo of their bridge.

- Tell them the information below the photo is about their bridge OR about another student's bridge.

- Give them a few minutes to tick the pieces of information they think are about their bridge, using their dictionaries if necessary.

- Then put students into pairs to tell each other the information they didn't tick in the previous stage.

- Students must not look at each other's photos but can ask questions.

- They should take notes while they are talking.

- When they have all the information about their bridge, give students 20 minutes to write their paragraphs, using the notes they made in the previous stage and the information they ticked earlier.

- Monitor to help with vocabulary and point out mistakes with the passive structure, if necessary.

- Finally, take the paragraphs in for marking, paying particular attention to the use of passive structures.

HOMEWORK OPTIONS

Students do the exercises on pages 49–50 of the Workbook.

Students write an account of a situation in their past using at least two of the idioms in exercise 4.

Students do exercises G1,2 1 and 2, G3 3, V3 7, and V4 8 on page 147 in the Language reference.

7.4 SCENARIO: ON THE HORIZON

IN THIS LESSON

Lesson topic and staging

This lesson focuses on the language of requirements. Students discuss facilities they expect to find at a good hotel. They are then introduced to the scenario by reading an invitation to tender for a contract to design a luxury hotel. Next, students listen to architects talking about designing part of the hotel and focus on the KEY LANGUAGE. Finally, the main TASK asks students to discuss and finalise the facilities for the ground floor of the hotel.

Objectives

By the end of the lesson, students should have:

- learned useful phrases for talking about requirements
- used this language in a 'real-life' situation to discuss and finalise facilities at a luxury hotel
- extracted specific information and language items from a reading and listening texts
- participated effectively in extended speaking practice.

Common European Framework

Students can use language effectively to express views and opinions, explain and give reasons for their and intentions.

Timings

If short of time, you could drop exercise 4b on page 77. A possible lesson break would be after exercise 4b on page 77.

WARM-UP

This activity introduces the topic of required facilities at luxury hotels.

- Ask students if they often stay in hotels/have ever stayed in hotels and if they like them.
- Put students in pairs and ask them to describe the best hotel they've stayed at or they know of (they should include facilities).
- Then elicit different facilities to the board and include the following: *cable/satellite TV in all rooms, swimming pool, restaurant, shops, hairdresser, gym.*
- In pairs, students then rank the facilities on the board from absolutely essential to not important.
- Elicit lists from a few pairs, with reasons, and ask the class if they agree and why/why not.

SITUATION

1 If you used the Warm-up activity, students can re-use some of the vocabulary here, but will need to add ideas for the conference centre.

- If you didn't use the Warm-up, ask students if they've stayed at/know of a top hotel and what facilities it had/has.
- Then put students into small groups to do the activity in the Coursebook.
- Get a few ideas from the class.

2a Focus students on the title of the text on page 76 and check they understand *Invitation to Tender* (a company invites others to try to win a contract by putting together a proposal, including costs, etc.).

- Tell students to read the questions and check they understand *reputation* (people's opinion of you) and tell them HHCC is the name of the company giving the invitation.
- Give them five minutes to read the text and answer the questions.
- Ask students to compare with a partner before you check answers with the class.
- In feedback, check students understand the difference between *conferences* (large meetings to discuss topics of interest, e.g. academic) and *congresses* (similar to conferences but to make important decisions on particular issues, e.g. a United Nations Congress).

> 1 It's famous for providing luxury accommodation and outstanding service; 2 L-shaped; 3 conferences and congresses; 4 the quality of the plan for the ground floor

2b Give students two minutes to discuss this question in pairs and then elicit ideas from the class.

- If only one or two students know where Dubai is or about its reputation, elicit ideas from them for the class to hear.
- If no students know about Dubai, tell them it is a wealthy and dynamic state (Emirate) in the Middle East (i.e. in a convenient location between China/India and Europe and easily accessible from both directions) and it has a reputation for rapid and extravagant building developments.

KEY LANGUAGE: talking about requirements

3a Focus students on the photos and the floor plan and ask them what the two people in the smaller photo on page 77 are doing (discussing plans).

- Read through the introduction and questions with the class, and check they understand *health-conscious* (you care about your health).

- Tell students that question 1 needs *specific* suggestions.
- Explain that the architects want to put in a tender to HHCC.
- Play the track without pausing and then ask students to compare answers with a partner.
- Go through answers with the class and check they understand *games room* (somewhere to play table tennis, etc.).

> **1** a games room, a sauna or a jacuzzi, an aerobics and dance studio (Note: *sports facility* and *somewhere to relax* are not specific suggestions.);
> **2** talk about plans the next day and get ideas from the rest of the team

3b Warn students that they need to use the information from the text and sometimes complete the sentences in their own words. Tell them it's not necessary to write all the information available.

- Play the track and, if students find this activity difficult, pause at the points indicated in the audioscript.
- Ask students to compare with a partner before you check answers with the class. (Answers are underlined in the audioscript below.)
- When you have checked answers, ask students to find all the italicised phrases in the sentences.

You could take this opportunity to highlight the form used with these expressions. Read through the information given below with the class and, if necessary, write it on the board (or see the Tip below) for students to copy.

> **Form: 1** *it's vital* + present simple form of the verb;
> **2** *it's absolutely essential* + infinitive; **3** *we've got to* + infinitive (without *to*); **4** *We certainly need* + noun (Note: the sentence here has a noun phrase.); **5** *we should offer* + noun; **6** *It might be a good idea* + infinitive; **7** *we'd have to* + infinitive (without *to*); **8** *we need to* + infinitive (without *to*)

If possible, reproduce the text so that the whole class can see it (perhaps on an Interactive whiteboard or an overhead projector). As you go through the answers (and the Task extension suggested above, if used), highlight the relevant parts of the text.

> **Audioscript and answers to exercise 3:**
> **Track 2.23**
> *Fatima, Yasmin, Richard*
> F: Let's talk about our plans for the ground floor, Yasmin. What ideas do you have?
> Y: Well, I need a little more time to think about it, but seeing that space won't be a problem, in my opinion, it's vital we have <u>1 some sort of sports facility on the ground floor, that's a priority, I think.</u> Also we'll need an area where people can relax. [PAUSE]
> F: How about you, Richard? What do you think?
> *continued…*

> R: I agree Yasmin's right. It's absolutely essential to offer a facility <u>2 for people who want to forget work for a while</u>, just chill out and the ground floor's the best place to provide it. But I'm not sure what sort of facility it should be. [PAUSE]
> F: So, Yasmin, any ideas?
> Y: Mmm, well, people are health conscious, they do want to relax, they're often very stressed. So… 3 <u>we've got to offer them something, that's for sure</u>. Off the top of my head, I suggest we have a games room on the ground floor, you know, table tennis, snooker. It'd be very popular with some of our guests. [PAUSE]
> F: Mmm, I don't know, Yasmin. We certainly need some kind of area 4 <u>where people can take it easy</u>, let their hair down a bit. But I'm not sure a games room is the answer. I mean, is it really the right choice for a business hotel?
> Y: OK, maybe not a games room, but we should offer <u>5 them something to help them relax</u>, maybe a sauna, a jacuzzi, that sort of thing. Don't you agree, Richard? [PAUSE]
> R: Yeah, a sauna, why not? And, erm, I've just thought of something. It might be a good idea to have <u>6 an aerobics and dance studio</u>. Of course, we'd have to find out first 7 <u>if our guests really wanted that kind of facility</u>. [PAUSE]
> F: Mmm, I like that idea, Richard. It would probably appeal to all age groups. I think most people would enjoy doing aerobics and dance. But we 8 <u>need to think this through. There are plenty of options</u> to meet the needs of groups who want to keep fit, and others who'll want to wind down. Let's talk about it tomorrow and get ideas from the rest of the team.
> F: Yes, they'll have plenty of ideas. Let's see what they come up with.

For further practice, ask students to do exercise KL 4 on page 147 in the Language reference.

4a Put students in pairs to discuss this question and then go through answers with the class.

- In feedback, elicit/tell students it's the adverb *certainly* that makes *need* strong.

> **Strong needs:** it's vital; it's absolutely essential; we've got to; we certainly need; we'd have to

4b Give students a couple of minutes to look again at the expressions (not the full sentences) in exercise 3b and ask you if they need help pronouncing any individual words.

- Then, put students in pairs to predict where the main stress will be in each phrase.
- Play the track, pausing after each expression, and ask students where the main stress is. Highlight the intonation of each expression, if necessary modelling it yourself.
- Play the track again and pause after each expression for students to repeat.
- Correct if necessary.

Track 2.24
1 ... it's vital we have ...
2 It's absolutely essential to offer ...
3 We've got to offer them ...
4 We certainly need ...
5 ... we should offer them something ...
6 It might be a good idea to have ...
7 ... we'd have to find out ...
8 But we need to think ...

TASK: deciding on facilities in a hotel

5a Read through the introduction with the class and then divide students into three groups of equal size.

- If you don't have the right number of students to form equal groups, make sure A and B are equal and put any extra students into group C. When they discuss the plans in exercise 5b, you can have two HHCC representatives in one or more of the mixed groups.

- Ask students to read their instructions and ask you if they need clarification.

- Then go through the OTHER USEFUL PHRASES box with the class and remind them of the KEY LANGUAGE.

- Give students 20 minutes to discuss facilities and plans.

- Monitor to note mistakes with the KEY LANGUAGE and OTHER PHRASES.

- When students have finished, correct a selection of the mistakes you noted earlier and tell students they have another chance to use this language in 5b.

5b Form new groups with an A, a B and at least one C student in each.

- Give them 15 minutes to try to agree on what facilities to include and where they should be.

- Tell A and B students they can't change the plans they decided on in exercise 5a.

- Tell C students, they can change their requirements if A or B students persuade them to do so.

- Monitor to note improvements in students' use of the KEY LANGUAGE and OTHER PHRASES.

5c Put C students back into their group from exercise 5a and give them ten minutes to decide which firm should get the contract.

- Put A and B students back into their groups and give them ten minutes to decide if they should change any of the plans they originally made.

- When they have finished, ask group C who should get the contract and why.

- Ask the losing team (A or B) if the changes they discussed might have helped them win the contract.

- Finally, tell students how their use of KEY LANGUAGE or OTHER PHRASES improved in this activity.

HOMEWORK OPTIONS

Students do the exercises on page 51 of the Workbook.

From exercise 5: Group C writes an email to the winning architects saying why they won; the winning group writes an email to HHCC accepting the contract and outlining their proposal again; the losing group writes an email to HHCC saying how they could change their proposal. Students should write their emails individually at home. Remind students about the language in this type of email, i.e. formal.

Students do exercise KL 4 on page 147 in the Language reference.

7.5 STUDY AND WRITING SKILLS

IN THIS LESSON

Lesson topic and staging

This lesson focuses on identifying fact and opinion in a text, and avoiding repetition when writing. Students read a review of an exhibition and identify facts and opinions. They then analyse the text to find ways of avoiding repetition of nouns, verbs and clauses before practising this themselves. Next, students read a description of a house and focus on organisation of the text. Finally, students write a description of a building.

Objectives

By the end of the lesson, students should have:

* extracted specific information and language items from reading texts
* extended their range of language items used to avoid repetition when writing and practised using these
* identified the organisation of a written description
* written a description of a building.

Common European Framework

Students can write simple connected texts, convey information/ideas on abstract and concrete topics, and write a description.

Timings

If short of time, you could set exercise 10 for homework. A possible lesson break would be after exercise 3b on page 78 or exercise 6 on page 79.

WARM-UP

This activity (re)introduces the topic of describing buildings.

* Focus students on the photo on page 79 and ask them to write three things they like and three things they dislike about it.
* Put students into pairs to compare their ideas and decide, on balance, if they like or dislike the building.

STUDY SKILLS: identifying fact and opinion

1   Focus students on the photo on page 79 and tell them this building was designed by the architect Frank Lloyd Wright. Tell students they will read about the building later.

* Ask students if they know anything about Frank Lloyd Wright and, if possible, elicit a few ideas.
* Set the activity and give students two minutes to read the review and answer the questions.
* Ask students to compare with a partner before you check answers with the class.
* Finally, ask students if this is an exhibition they'd be interested in visiting.

> **1** The writer likes the exhibition very much (it is exceptionally interesting and informative).;
> **2** The writer thinks Frank Lloyd Wright was truly a remarkable architect.

2a Give students a maximum of one minute to answer the questions.

* Get answers from the class but don't elicit reasons for these at this stage.

> **1** opinion; **2** fact; **3** fact; **4** opinion

2b Students do this activity in pairs.

* Elicit ideas from the class and elicit/tell students that the modifier *exceptionally*, the adjectives *interesting*, *informative*, and *the most important* are ideas that other people might disagree with (i.e. they are opinions).

> **1** exceptionally, interesting, informative; **4** In my opinion, the most important

2c Give students two minutes to underline opinions in the text.

* Ask them to compare with a partner before you check answers with the class.
* Go through answers and the notes in brackets with the class.
* Tell students they can use these ways of expressing opinion later in the lesson.
* Finally, give students a few minutes to check vocabulary from the examples in their dictionaries.

> it should not be missed (modal *should* expresses advice, i.e. the writer's opinion); the finest skyscrapers (adjective = opinion); innovative (this is the writer's and other people's opinion, but perhaps not everyone's); beautifully-crafted (descriptive adverb *beautifully* = opinion); must have learned (past deduction/certainty based on the writer's opinion of evidence); lovely (adjective = opinion); truly (modifier = opinion); remarkable (adjective = opinion)

If possible, reproduce the text so that the whole class can see it (perhaps on an Interactive Whiteboard or an overhead projector). When you check answers in this exercise and in exercises 3, 4 and 5, highlight the appropriate parts of the text.

WRITING SKILLS: a description of a building

3a Avoiding repetition – nouns

- Read through the introduction and instructions with the class.
- To remind students what a pronoun is, focus them on the examples in the list.
- Give students one minute to think of other pronouns and then compare their answers with a partner.
- Elicit answers and make sure each item is a pronoun. If students could not think of pronouns in a category, give some of the examples below.

> Personal pronouns: he, it, they, you, her, me, us, them; Possessive pronouns: theirs, his, ours; Demonstrative pronouns: those, these, this; Relative pronouns: that, when, where, whose; Other pronouns: anyone, nobody, myself

3b If necessary, do the first example as a whole class and underline the noun in the text it refers to.

- Then give students five minutes to do the other italicised pronouns.
- Tell students some pronouns refer to a noun clause and others refer to more than one noun/noun clause.
- Ask students to compare with a partner before you check answers and go through notes with the class.

> *It* (line 7) = the exhibition; *They* (line 13) = Adler and Sullivan; *which* (line 30) = EITHER the drawings and pictures OR Adler and Sullivan's buildings OR both; *They* (line 31) = the pictures and drawings; *which* (line 44) = Japanese prints; *ones* (line 48) = houses; *he* (line 53) = Wright.

4a Avoiding repetition – verbs

- Ask students to read the introduction and then give them a minute to answer the question.
- Elicit answers from the class and underline the appropriate part of the text.
- Check students understand *break away* (doing something in an innovative and untraditional way).

> do = design, break away

☼ You could ask students to do exercises 4a and 4b and then provide feedback for both.

4b Give students 30 seconds to read paragraph 4 again and then elicit the answer from the class.

> shows

5 Avoiding repetition - clauses

- Ask students to read the introduction and then give them two minutes to answer the questions.
- Check answers with the class and underline the relevant part of the text.

> So = go to a Frank Lloyd Wright exhibition; this = experiment with (verb)

6 Give students five minutes to re-write the text and then compare answers with a partner.

- Then elicit answers from the class and accept any that are correct. If necessary, go through the model answer below.

> The exhibition has a number of drawings and pictures. They are beautifully executed / which are beautifully executed, and the ones of large buildings are particularly impressive. Wright worked with engineers at the offices of Adler and Sullivan. He did so / this for many years and must have learned a lot from them, as their attention to detail clearly influenced his work. Many European thinkers, such as John Ruskin, also influenced his designs. However, Wright also developed his own ideas, and incorporated many of these / many of which were incorporated into the houses he built.

☼ If you use the model answer, you could reproduce it so that the whole class can see it (perhaps on an Interactive Whiteboard or an overhead projector).

7 To orient students to the text, focus them on the photo on page 79 and, in pairs, think of words to describe the house.

- Tell students to read the text quickly to see if the same or similar words are used.
- Set the activity in the Coursebook but make sure students read points a)–d) before they read the text.
- Ask students to compare with a partner before you check answers with the class.

> 1 d); 2 c); 3&4 a); 5 b)

☼ In feedback, tell students that writing of this sort in English normally moves from the general to the specific (see the text, for example). This is not true of a lot of other languages. Ask students if it's true of their language.

8 Give students three minutes to do this activity and then ask them to compare answers in pairs.

- Go through answers with the class.

> which = a natural rock; as do = verb phrase (emphasise the close connection between the inside and outside of the building)

⚠ After *the interior* there is an elided *of the living room*. Elision (missing out words and phrases that are understood from the context) is another way of avoiding repetition.

9 Give students two minutes to underline the verbs and then compare with a partner.

- Elicit answers from the class and tell students that verbs are often used in the passive in this kind of text.

- Give students a few minutes to find unknown vocabulary from the examples in their dictionaries.

> demonstrate, grow out of; fit in with; consist of; project over; are arranged in; seem; is built over; are incorporated into; emphasise; appear to be; is admired by; is considered by

10 You can choose which option students do, depending on their experiences and knowledge, or let students choose for themselves.

First option

- Give students ten minutes to write notes about their building and monitor to help with vocabulary.
- They can use the Internet to do further research about the building.

Second option

- Give students five minutes to read the notes and find difficult vocabulary in their dictionaries.
- If they use the Internet, you will need to give plenty of time or ask students to do it in their own time.

Both options

- When students have collected their information, give them 30 minutes to write their description.
- They can use the description in exercise 7 as a model of organisation, but tell them not to copy the style because the text is written by an architecture expert.
- Monitor to point out where students could use ways of avoiding repetition, if they aren't doing so.
- Take the descriptions in for marking, paying particular attention to ways of avoiding repetition and verbs introduced in exercise 9.

HOMEWORK OPTIONS

Students do the exercises on page 52 of the Workbook.

Students write a blog entry about a visit to an exhibition. They should avoid repeating nouns and verbs.

8 Globalisation

8.1 GLOBALISATION – GOOD OR BAD?

Lesson topic and staging

This lesson looks at different opinions on globalisation. Students define the term and discuss which causes or results of globalisation are important for them. Students then focus on word combinations related to globalisation and discuss some topical points. Next, students read postings on a message board and listen to podcasts of people's opinions before studying word combinations in these. Finally, students discuss the opinions and the impact on their own lives before writing their own posting.

Objectives

By the end of the lesson, students should have:

- extracted specific information and language items from a reading and listening text
- extended their range of vocabulary related to globalisation
- participated in a group discussion to express their opinions about globalisation
- written a message board posting expressing their opinions.

Timings

If short of time, you could drop exercise 6 on page 81 or set exercise 10 for homework. A possible lesson break would be after exercise 4b or 6 on page 81.

WARM-UP

This activity introduces the topic of the impact that economic growth can have on a population.

- Ask students to focus on the photo and elicit what it shows (extreme poverty next to extreme wealth).
- Put students into groups of four and ask them to think of problems that this situation might cause.
- Elicit answers from the class and tell students that will be looking at one possible cause in this lesson.

Bill Clinton quote:

This quote means that in the new global economy, workers, ideas, resources, technology, finance and everything else associated with an economy can be moved easily around the world. It also implies that there is movement (i.e. change) in people's understanding of what an economy is.

i Bill Clinton (born 1946) was the 42nd President of the United States, serving from 1993–2001.

SPEAKING

1 Write *globalisation* on the board and ask students how this word/concept makes them feel.
- Then put students into small groups and give them three minutes to decide on a definition of the term.
- Get a few ideas from the class and ask other students if their definition is similar.

2 Give students two minutes to do this activity and then compare their answers with a partner.
- Go through answers with the class and then ask students how similar this is to their definition in exercise 1.
- Finally, check students understand *multinational companies* (companies that operate all over the world, not just in one or two countries).

> 1 world; 2 improvements; 3 communications; 4 experience; 5 life

3 Give students one minute to read the list of causes/ results and tick the ones that are important for them.
- Give them a further minute to think of any they would like to add.
- Then put students into small groups to compare their lists, give reasons for their choices and ask each other questions to get as much information as possible.
- During the discussion, students can add other ideas to their lists.
- Elicit the most important points from two or three students and ask the class if they had the same choices.

4a Give students one minute to see if they can fill gaps before they look at the nouns in the box.
- Then give students four minutes to complete the gaps, using the nouns in the box.
- Ask students to compare with a partner before you check answers with the class.
- In feedback, check students' pronunciation of *environment* (with a silent second *n*).

> 1 workers, 2 gap; 3 poverty; 4 understanding; 5 cultures; 6 environment; 7 industry; 8 competition; 9 standards; 10 companies

4b First, ask students if the points in exercise 4a were positive or negative about globalisation (both).
- Ask students, without reading the list again, if they think they agreed with more positive than negative points, or vice versa.

- Then put students into groups of three to discuss each of the points.
- Students should say if they agree or not and give reasons.
- Encourage students to ask questions and to disagree with each other if necessary.
- Finally, choose four or five of the points and ask students if they agreed or not and why.

READING AND LISTENING

5a Lead in by asking students if they ever write on online message boards, giving their opinion on a topic. If so, ask which message boards they write on and on what topics.

- Then read through the introduction with the class and tell students the names of the writers are at the bottom of each message and they will hear the other messages in exercise 5b.
- Give students five minutes to write short notes in the chart about Mike, Cindy, Ingrid and Marco.
- Ask students to compare with a partner before you check answers with the class. Answers are below exercise 5b.

Take this opportunity to introduce some useful language from the text and the listening. Other words are taught in exercise 7.

Write the following words/phrases on the board: *cost effective* (goods are cheaper to produce because of efficiency and choosing a cheap place to make them), *consumer* (the people who buy products and services), *sweatshop* (a factory, normally in a poorer country, where people work very long hours for very little money), *migrate* (populations move from one country to another to live and work), *aspect of* (feature of), *evolution* (the natural development of humans and societies), *developing countries* (countries where industry is not fully developed yet), *a force for change* (something that makes changes happen) and *mobility* (easy movement).

Either ask students to check the words/phrases in their dictionaries or elicit/give the meanings in brackets above.

5b First, ask students what a podcast is (a short recording of someone speaking, which is posted online) and if they ever make or listen to podcasts.

- Then set the activity, play the track and pause after each podcast.
- Ask students to compare with a partner and then play the track again if necessary.
- Go through answers with the class and, if necessary, refer students to the audioscript on page 183.

Message	For or against	Reasons
1 Mike	For	Progress. Better, cost effective and cheaper products. Consumer choice. Communication and opportunity for travel, work, education. Faster development. Poorer countries benefit from investment.
2 Cindy	Against	Sweatshops in poor countries so rich ones have cheap goods. Inequality. Destruction of natural resources. Benefits rich countries. They control prices and affect poor countries and make people migrate.
3 Ingrid	For	A kind of evolution. Make products where it's efficient. Social/economic progress for developing countries. Free markets. Free movement of people.
4 Marco	Against	Good only for developed countries. Multinationals benefit – have more power than governments – some are richer than countries.
5 Michel	Against	World is smaller but unfair. Benefits for developed, not developing, world. Child labour and abuses of human rights. Some benefits but unfair. Bigger gap between rich/poor countries. Exploits poor. No respect for local cultures.
6 Doug	For	Access to information. Improved lives. Mobility to skilled workers. Fair trade reduces poverty. Countries share products and services. Developing countries have better employment. Increased competitiveness/efficiency.
7 Astrid	Both for and against	Better communications. TV and Internet improve people's lives. BUT gap between rich/poor countries is greater. Exploits workers to reduce costs. Corporate greed.
8 John	For	Benefits everyone. Communicate with the world. Benefits small businesses – they can compete better with big companies in foreign countries because of new technology and cheaper transport.
9 Maria	Against	Damages the environment. Global warming and climate change. Big business has no respect for environment, only money. No benefits for poor workers.

6 Give students five minutes to summarise the two messages they choose individually.

- If students find this difficult to do without writing it down, they could take notes but do not encourage them to write full sentences.
- Then put students into pairs to compare their summaries (if they have summarised the same messages) or read each other's summaries and compare these with the original messages.
- Students can comment on how accurate and how complete the summaries are.

VOCABULARY: word combinations

7a Students will probably know the meanings of most of these words, but may be less sure of the combinations.

- If students are worried about the exact meaning of some words, tell them they will be able to check in exercise 7b.
- Students work individually to complete the word combinations and then compare with a partner.
- Check answers with the class.

> **1** choice; **2** change; **3** greed; **4** trade; **5** rights
> **6** natural resources; **7** global warming;
> **8** multinational companies; **9** child labour;
> **10** free markets

7b Give students five minutes to check their answers and use their dictionaries if necessary.

- You may need to clarify the following: *fair trade* may not be in their dictionaries (richer countries pay a *fair* price for products, not just the cheapest price), *free market* (import/export without taxes).

SPEAKING

8 Give students five minutes to re-read the notes they made in the chart for exercise 5, decide which opinions they agree/disagree with and think about their reasons.

- Then put students into groups of three or four and give them ten minutes to discuss the opinions.
- Monitor to note mistakes with the vocabulary from the lesson.
- Ask each group for one opinion they all agreed or disagreed with, and their reasons.
- Finally, go through some of the more common or important mistakes you noted earlier.

9a Give students a few minutes to think about each category.

- Put them into pairs so that they are talking to a different student from those in exercise 8 and give them ten minutes for the discussion
- Monitor to note improvements in their use of vocabulary from this lesson.
- Ask two or three pairs to tell the class their ideas for one of the categories.
- Finally, tell students the improvements you noted earlier.

You could reverse exercises 9b and 10 so that students can post their written messages (exercise 10) around the room before they discuss their opinions with others. If you reverse the order, tell students to write a message in response to the instructions in 9b.

9b Give students five minutes to discuss their opinions and reasons in small groups.

10 Give students 15–20 minutes to write their message.

- Tell them to use the messages in exercise 5 as a model for informal register and to incorporate some of the vocabulary from exercise 7.

- Take the messages in for marking, paying particular attention to the register and use of vocabulary.
- Ask students to post their messages around the room so that the whole class can read them. Then put students into small groups to discuss their opinions (see exercise 9b).

HOMEWORK OPTIONS

Students do the exercises on page 53 of the Workbook.

Students write a message responding to one of the messages in exercise 5, either agreeing or disagreeing with the points made.

8.2 THE POWER OF THE INTERNET

IN THIS LESSON

Lesson topic and staging

This lesson looks at how the Internet is affecting our lives. Students read a text about the Internet changing our lives and then discuss various topics related to this. Students then look at abstract nouns and verb patterns (e.g. *remember* + *-ing*) taken from the text and practise using them. Finally, students discuss various situations using the verb patterns studied earlier.

Objectives

By the end of the lesson, students should have:

- extracted specific information and language items from a reading text
- extended their range of abstract nouns related to social relationships
- revised/extended their understanding of the use of different verb patterns
- discussed various personalised situations using these verbs patterns.

Timings

If short of time, you could drop exercise 3 on page 82. A possible lesson break would be after exercise 4b on page 83.

WARM-UP

This activity introduces the topic of how often and why people use the Internet.

- Tell students they are going to find out how often people in the class use the Internet.
- Write the following on the board: *Find someone who uses the Internet on average: for more than three hours a day, for more than one hour a day, every other day, once a week, once a month, never.*
- Elicit the question 'How often do you use the Internet?' and then ask students to move round the room talking to as many people as possible.
- Tell them to write the names of people in each category.
- After about five minutes, stop the activity and elicit the names of students in each category.
- Ask students if they were surprised at the amount of time people use the Internet.

READING

1a Focus students on the photos, elicit that these are Internet websites and ask how many students know them.

- Set the activity and put students in pairs to discuss.
- In feedback, ask students which sites they have heard of, but not to give answers to the question 'What kind of sites are they?' until they have checked in 1b.

1b Give students four minutes to read the text and check their answers to exercise 1a.

- Tell them not to worry about unknown vocabulary at this stage.
- Elicit answers from the class and check students understand *encyclopaedia* (a 'book' where you can read information about many different topics), *virtual* (not physically real) and *social networking* (talking to people socially – not business – to share information and help each other). (Note: *networking* is included in exercise 4a, but *social networking* is needed for exercise 3.)

> Google – finds and lists websites for you, a search engine; YouTube – you can upload and share videos made at home; eBay – you can buy from and sell things to other people, auctions; Amazon – shopping, retail; Wikipedia – encyclopaedia; MySpace – you can post information about yourself and meet new friends; Second Life – an electronic world where you can 'live', a large and complicated game

2 Tell students to read the questions first. Then give them eight minutes to read the text and answer the questions.

- Ask students to compare with a partner before you check answers with the class.
- In feedback, check students understand *unscrupulous* (dishonest).

> **1** because of cheap air travel, mobile phones, email and the Internet – all make communicating with others all over the world much easier than in the past; **2** friendships used to be formed during a lifetime, e.g. make a friend at school and keep them as adults, but now many young people find friends on the Internet; **3 a)** Internet shopping is very common now, millions of people buy and sell to strangers and set their own prices; **b)** Wikipedia has more content than any other encyclopaedia and it's free, people can add/change content; **c)** people meet new friends and find old friends on the Internet and it's much easier to share experiences; **4** there are unscrupulous sales people, Wikipedia content may be wrong

3 Give students one minute to read the questions and think about their opinions.

- Put students in their pairs and give them five to ten minutes to discuss the questions.
- Finally, get a few ideas from two or three pairs.

VOCABULARY: abstract nouns

4a Students do this activity individually and then compare answers with a partner.

- Go through answers with the class and check students' use of main stress in *networking, hierarchy, creativity* and *collaboration*. Also check students' pronunciation of *chy* in *hierarchy*.

  1 b); **2** a); **3** e); **4** c); **5** d)

4b Students do this activity individually and then compare answers with a partner.

- Go through answers with the class.

  1 creativity; **2** collaboration; **3** networking;
  4 hierarchy; **5** influence

GRAMMAR: verb patterns

5 First, ask students to read the verbs 1–4, find them in the text and underline the forms that follow them.

- Then give students three minutes to do this activity.

- Ask students to compare with a partner before you check answers with the class.

- In feedback, check students understand *potential* (the possible ability to do something), *double-check* (check again/twice), and the reference to *sabre boy* (light sabres are the weapons used in the famous *Star Wars* movies. They are large sticks of light – you could draw one on the board). You may also need to check *wielding* (holding a weapon, e.g. a gun, in a way to suggest you're going to use it), *antics* (the funny things he did).

  1 a); **2** c); **3** d); **4** b)

6 Put students in pairs and give them five minutes to discuss the sentences.

- Students may find this activity difficult, so refer them to the Language reference on page 148 for help.

- Go through the answers and the notes in brackets with the class.

- In feedback, elicit/point out the weak form of *to* in the relevant sentences.

  1 a) thinking about an earlier action (i.e. remember now about watching before), **b)** thinking about a future action (i.e. remember first and then lock the door); **2 a)** thinking about an earlier action (i.e. never forget in my whole life about meeting before), **b)** thinking about future action (i.e. not forget first, switch off the lights second); **3 a)** finish an action (i.e. driving), **b)** stop one action and start doing another (i.e. stop driving and start having a break); **4 a)** do something as an experiment (i.e. I didn't know if sending her flowers would be effective), **b)** make an effort to do something difficult (i.e. persuading her was a difficult thing to do).

⚠ For *remember* and *forget*: the answer says thinking about a future action. This is fairly clear in the examples in exercise 6 because the actions (to lock and to switch) are obviously in future time. However, in exercise 7 this is less obvious. Tell students that the action is in the future *from the point of view of the speaker*. For example, both *remember* and the second action may be in past time, but the second action is still in the future from the speaker's point of view (e.g. I remembered to lock the door, i.e. I remembered first and locked the door second).

7 Give students five minutes to do this activity individually.

- Monitor to points out mistakes but tell students to self-correct by referring to exercise 6 and the Language reference.

- Ask students to compare with a partner before you check answers with the class.

  1 to respond; **2** to get; **3** attending; **4** to post;
  5 hearing; **6** putting; **7** to bring

For further practice, ask students to do exercise G1 1 and 2 on page 149 in the Language reference.

SPEAKING

8 Give students three minutes to read the list of topics and think about possible answers, but tell them not to write sentences.

- Monitor to help with vocabulary or ask students to use their dictionaries.

- Then, put students into pairs and give them ten minutes to swap experiences.

- Encourage students to ask each other questions to get as much information as possible (e.g. 'Why did you stop doing that? Have you ever done it again?').

- Monitor to note mistakes with the forms and pronunciation of *remember* and *forget*.

- When students have finished, ask them for the most interesting/surprising/exciting thing they heard.

- Finally, correct some of the more common or important mistakes you noted earlier.

HOMEWORK OPTIONS

Students do the exercises on pages 54–55 of the Workbook.

Students write a message about one of their experiences from exercise 8 to include on a website like YouTube or MySpace. In the next lesson, they post these round the walls of the classroom. All students read the messages and decide on the most interesting/surprising/exciting.

Students do exercises V1,2 5 (note this contains vocabulary from lesson 8.1) and G1 1 and 2 on page 149 in the Language reference.

8.3 GLOBAL ROLE MODELS

Lesson topic and staging

This lesson looks at whether global role models are a good or bad phenomenon. Students read about the influence of global role models and discuss their opinions of this phenomenon. Students then focus on vocabulary associated with the media in the text. Next, students look at grammar in the text (*have something done*) and focus on its use before practising it. Finally, students talk about good or bad experiences, using the grammar from this lesson.

Objectives

By the end of the lesson, students should have:

- extracted specific information and language items from a reading text
- revised and/or extended their range of vocabulary using the reading text as a source
- revised/learned about the form *have something done* and practised using this form
- discussed personalised experiences using the form *have something done*.

Timings

If short of time, you could cut the number of questions students discuss in exercise 4 on page 84. A possible lesson break would be after exercise 4 on page 84.

This activity introduces the topic of famous people and the influence they have.

- Ask students to think of a very famous person and make notes about what they are famous for and how they influence ordinary people.
- Then put students into groups of three or four and ask them to discuss the people they chose.
- Each group must then decide the most famous and most influential person discussed in their group.
- Elicit the person chosen in each group and the reasons. Ask the rest of the class if they agree.
- Finally, ask the class to vote on the most famous and influential person from all the groups.

1 Ask students to read the questions and check they understand *global role models* (famous people who are known all over the world. Other people try to imitate their behaviour, their style and their opinions).

- Put students into groups with a maximum of four students in each.
- If students don't know all the people in the photos, they can restrict their discussion to the ones they do.
- When they have finished, elicit answers to the first and second questions from the class so that all students can find out who the people in the photos are.
- Then elicit answers to the third question from two or three groups and ask other students if they agree that these people are global role models.

> Clockwise from far left: Nelson Mandela (ex-President of South Africa and before that a leading person in the anti-apartheid movement that disagreed with separating black and white people); Arnold Schwarzenegger (Austrian-born American film actor and now a politician); Imran Khan (former captain of the Pakistani cricket team); Madonna (American pop singer); David Beckham (British footballer); Princess Diana (former wife of Prince Charles of Britain – he will be the next King. She was also famous for her charity work. She died in 1997.)

2 Read the instructions with the class and elicit/give the meaning of *scan* (finding particular words/information in a text).

- Ask students which words in the questions they will look for in the text (1 children/TV and a number; 2 governor of California; 3 World Cup).
- Then give students one minute to scan the text and answer the questions.
- Tell students not to worry about vocabulary at this stage because they will study it in exercise 5.
- Ask students to compare with a partner before you check answers with the class.
- Finally, ask students if they were surprised by any of the answers.

> 1 91%; 2 Arnold Schwarzenegger; 3 two billion (1 billion = 1,000 million) (Note: this is the football World Cup.); 4 Melrose Place, Beverly Hills, 90210

3 Ask students to read the questions first, then allow five minutes for them to read the text and answer the questions.

- Tell students they can use their dictionaries to find the following words as they read: *eating disorder, endorse, ban/banned, cultural imperialism* and *anorexia*.
- Ask students to compare with a partner before you check answers with the class.

> **1** False (he's more famous for playing the character Terminator in the movies of the same name); **2** False (the football World Cup is watched by two billion); **3** False (he endorsed products in Japan); **4** False (they were banned); **5** True (cultural imperialism, they say American TV programmes influenced people in Fiji); **6** True (anorexia)

4   Ask students to read the questions and check they understand *cross cultural boundaries* (be understood, popular and relevant in many varied cultures and countries) and *obsessed with* (completely and perhaps strangely interested in something).

- Put students in pairs or small groups and give them five minutes to discuss the questions.

- Get ideas for different questions from two or three groups.

VOCABULARY: the media

5a Allow students a maximum of three minutes for this activity.

- Tell students not to use dictionaries but to guess from the context if words are associated with the media.

- Ask students to compare with a partner before you get answers from the class.

- In feedback, write all correctly chosen words on the board so that all students can see them.

- Tell students to find and underline any words that they didn't find earlier.

- Don't give students the meaning for any words at this stage because they will study them in exercise 5b.

> Words associated with the media: film; television (TV); programmes; live ones (live sports programmes); audiences; watched; broadcast; televised; articles; newspaper; photo; paparazzi; news broadcasts; media coverage; local press; news conferences; foreign media

5b Students do this activity individually and then briefly compare with a partner.

- Go through answers and the notes in brackets with the class.

- Check students' pronunciation of difficult words (e.g. *paparazzi, coverage*).

- Finally, tell students to find any other difficult words from exercise 5a in their dictionaries.

> **1** broadcast; **2** paparazzi (Note: this noun is plural. The singular is paparazzo.); **2** media coverage; **4** the press (Note: the media is often used synonymously.)

For further practice, ask students to do exercise V3 6 on page 149 in the Language reference.

GRAMMAR: *have something done*

6a Ask students to read the two sentences and check they understand *clause* (a condition that makes something happen, e.g. a clause that lets you refuse to do something).

- Put students in pairs to answer the questions and, if necessary, refer them to G2 in the Language reference on page 148.

- Go through answers with the class and elicit the form *have* + object + past participle. Underline the appropriate parts of sentence 1 to demonstrate this.

- Then tell students that you can use this form in different tenses (e.g. I'm having my house cleaned, I'll have a new dress made, Have you had your hair cut?).

> **a)** someone else; **b)** someone else; **c)** 2; **d)** 1

> (!) There is no difference in the form to tell you that examples 1 and 2 have a slightly different meaning. The answers to questions c) and d) are implied by the context in examples 1 and 2. He probably didn't ask reporters to write the articles but he probably did ask someone (his lawyers?) to put the clause in the contract.

6b First, give students the information in the Warning! below.

- Then ask them to underline examples in the text and compare with a partner.

- Elicit examples from the class to make sure they are correct and write them on the board.

- Next, put students in pairs to decide if each example is type c) or d). (Note: the 'types' of clause are those referred to in questions c) and d) in exercise 6a.)

- Go through answers with the class and label each example on the board type c) or type d) (in brackets after each example in the answers below).

- Finally, read through the Grammar tip with the class.

> UNESCO had a survey conducted (type c); [Beckham] had his hair cut (type c); he had his photo taken (type d).

> (!) Students may confuse *have/had something done* with the present or past perfect. (Note: there is an object after the auxiliary in *have something done*, but not in the present or past perfect, e.g. I have/had finished it.)

For further information, ask students to read G2 in the Language reference on page 148.

7   Give students eight minutes for this activity and tell them to use their dictionaries if necessary.

- Monitor to point out mistakes, but ask them to refer to exercise 6 and the Language reference if they need help.

- Ask students to compare with a partner before you check answers with the class.

8.4 SCENARIO: SUPERMARKET SUPERPOWER

- Finally, elicit if each sentence is type c) or d) (see exercise 6).

> **1** The authorities had the protestors removed (type c); **2** We will have three new phone lines installed next month (type c); **3** The photographers had their bags searched at the airport (type d); **4** She is having her new book translated into Japanese (probably type c); **5** The demonstrators had their fingerprints taken by the police (type d); **6** He is going to have his eyes tested tomorrow (type c); **7** I haven't had the film developed yet (type c); **8** My brother had his passport stolen last year (type d).

SPEAKING

8 Give students one minute to think of a good or a bad experience.

- If students can't think of ideas, you could give them following prompts: while on holiday, when you were are school, the last time you went shopping/ decorated your house, when you wanted to give someone a really nice present or they gave you a nice one; when you wanted to surprise someone or they wanted to surprise you.

- Put students into groups and give them ten minutes to talk about their experiences.

- Tell them to give as much information as possible and to ask each other questions.

- While they are speaking, monitor to note mistakes with *have something done*.

- When they have finished, ask the class which was worst/best experience they heard about.

- Finally, correct some of the more common or important mistakes you noted earlier.

HOMEWORK OPTIONS

Students do the exercises on pages 56–57 of the Workbook.

Students write an email to you or another student in the class describing the experience/s discussed in exercise 8. (Students should not write the email to one of the students from their group in exercise 8.)

Students do exercises V3 6 and G2 3 on page 149 in the Language reference.

8.4 SCENARIO: SUPERMARKET SUPERPOWER

IN THIS LESSON

Lesson topic and staging

This lesson focuses on the language of clarifying what you have said, or asking someone for clarification. Students read two texts that introduce the scenario of a large supermarket chain moving into new markets and a TV debate to discuss the issues. Next, students listen to the chief executive of the chain and focus on the KEY LANGUAGE. Finally the main TASK asks students to take part in the TV debate.

Objectives

By the end of the lesson, students should have:

- learned useful phrases for giving and asking for clarification of something that's been said

- used this language in a 'real-life' situation to take part in a debate

- extracted specific information and language items from a reading and a listening text

- participated effectively in extended speaking practice.

Common European Framework

Students can use language effectively to express view and opinions, explain and give reasons, ask someone to clarify or clarify themselves what he/she/they have just said.

Timings

If short of time, you could cut role A, and possibly B, from the debate in exercise 5 on page 87. You will need to write the Chair's (role A) questions on the board. This will enable you set a shorter time limit for this exercise because fewer students will have to speak. A possible lesson break would be after exercise 3b on page 87.

WARM-UP

This activity introduces some of the advantages and disadvantages of large supermarkets.

- Focus students on the photos on page 86 and ask them if and how often they shop at supermarkets.

- Then divide the class into group A and group B.

- Tell group A to list the advantages of supermarkets and the disadvantages of small local shops, and group B to list the advantages of small local shops and the disadvantages of supermarkets.

- Make sure all students make notes.

- When they have decided their lists, put students into A/B pairs to discuss the advantages and disadvantages and tell them the objective is to persuade their partner that they are right.
- Encourage students to ask each other questions and to interrupt when they want to disagree.
- Finally, ask each pair whether supermarkets or small local shops won the argument.

SITUATION

1 If you didn't use the Warm-up activity, focus students on the photos on page 86 and ask them if and how often they shop at supermarkets.

- Put students in pairs and ask them to discuss questions 1 and 2 only.
- Elicit ideas from the class.
- Then, ask students to quickly read the extract (English language channel) and ask them when the programme is on (Thursday 10.00) and why people might be interested in it (students' own opinions).
- Next, ask students to discuss question 3 in pairs.
- Finally, elicit ideas for question 3 from the class.

2 Focus students on the title of the report and ask them what they think it means (Smithsons are developing/ expanding/growing/moving forward).

- Then ask students to read the questions before giving them three minutes to read the report.
- Students should note down their ideas for question 5 to use in exercise 3b later.
- Ask student to compare with a partner before you check answers with the class.
- Check students understand *acquisition* (buying a company), *rebranding* (changing the public image of a company), *direct market entry* (opening new stores in places where there are none), *vast* (enormous) and *everything from* (this is used to imply that it sells a lot more than the items listed).
- Ask students if there are supermarket chains similar to Smithsons in their countries. In what ways are they similar?

> **1** over 85 years ago; **2** a vast range of goods, books, DVDs, electrical goods, financial services, fuel, insurance, household items, can organise weddings and funerals; **3** all over the world; **4** acquisition and rebranding of established store chains, direct market entry into new markets; **5** answers depend on students' own opinions

3a Read through the introduction with the class, and tell students that this recording is not of the TV debate mentioned in exercise 1 but is from another programme.

- Ask students to read the list of options and check they understand *unions* (an association of workers to protect their rights) and *treatment* (the way you behave/act towards people).
- Tell them the items in the list are in a different order on the track.
- Play the track without pausing.
- Ask student to compare with a partner before you check answers with the class.

> The following should be ticked: Consumer choice; Staff unions; Competition; Treatment of staff.

3b Put students in pairs to see if they can remember what was said about the ticked items in exercise 3a.

- Then play the track again, if necessary pausing at the points indicated in the audioscript below exercise 4a to give students time to make notes.
- Tell students not to worry if they can't note everything.
- Ask students to compare with a partner before you check answers with the class. (Answers are bold in the audioscript.)
- Then ask students to look at the notes they made in exercise 2, question 5 and decide if the criticisms are the same as those in the radio programme.

> Consumer choice: range of products, lower prices is part of the choice, Smithsons believes customers have the right to choose where they shop; Staff unions: accused of being anti-union, he doesn't think unions are a good idea for staff or the company; Competition: accused of forcing competitors out of business with low prices, you can't make people pay more just to keep other businesses going; Treatment of staff: they pay low wages, accused of having suppliers who use child labour and sweatshops, he says they pay their workers over the minimum wage

KEY LANGUAGE: clarifying

4a Give students a few minutes to see how many gaps they can fill before you play the track again.

- Play the track again without pausing and then ask students to compare with a partner.
- If necessary, ask students to look at the audioscript on page 184.
- Go through answers (underlined in the audioscript below) with the class and write the answers to 7, 8 and 10 on the board so that students can see the spelling.
- Finally, check students understand *specific* (exact, giving more details), *rephrase* (say something again in a different way) and *precise* (exact and correct).

1 mean; **2** saying; **3** know; **4** want; **5** put; **6** explain; **7** specific; **8** rephrase; **9** give; **10** precise

Audioscript and answers to exercises 3&4:
Track 2.26
Presenter, CEO

P: Good evening everyone and welcome to this week's edition of 'In the Hot Seat', with me Louise Falcon. Tonight my guest is Bob Craven, chief executive of the supermarket giant Smithsons.

CEO: Good evening, everyone.

P: Welcome to the programme Bob, It's good to finally have you on the show to answer a few questions.

CEO: It's my pleasure, Louise.

P: Could I start off by asking you about the success of Smithsons – why do you think it is so successful?

CEO: Well, Louise, I think it's because of our **range of products** and because we have always meant good value for money.

P: Yes, but 1 what do you mean by good value? Surely in some markets, and for some people, you are very expensive?

CEO: Well, I don't think so actually. 2 Basically, what I'm saying is the customer is at the heart of our business. We always charge lower prices than our competitors.

P: Ah, yes, but some people accuse you of **using low prices to force the competition out of business.**

CEO: 3 Sorry, I don't know what you mean, Louise.

P: Well, there've been examples where you have destroyed small businesses by keeping prices low, which of course you can do because of your size.
[PAUSE]

CEO: That's ridiculous, Louise. What we're doing is **offering the consumer a choice ... and part of that choice is lower prices.** And we're proud of that. Now, **you could force people to use higher-priced competitors to keep them in business, but that doesn't seem right to me.** 4 What I really want to say was that **we believe in the customers' right to choose where they shop.**

P: I see, but ...

CEO: 5 Or to put it another way, businesses come and go. The world changes. Nothing lasts forever. [PAUSE]

P: OK, but that's a very arrogant thing to say when you consider the impact on people's lives. If you don't mind, I'd like to move on now to your staff. There have been criticisms of the fact that as a company **you pay low wages and also, there are accusations that some of your clothing suppliers may use child labour and sweatshops.**

CEO: Right, well I can't comment on our suppliers, but what I can tell you is that in many markets **our workers are paid over the minimum wage** and as a company we do a lot for charity. [PAUSE]

P: 6 Could you explain that in more detail, please? What do you actually do for charity?

CEO: Certainly. I can tell you that Smithsons gives about 2.5 % of its profits to local community projects.
continued...

P: 7 Could you be more specific? Because many people have claimed they haven't seen the results of these community projects.

CEO: Yes, well, er, for example, if we build a new store, we, er, also, er, set aside money for a community centre or park. People like Smithsons, Louise. We do a lot for people.

P: Yes, but what about the negative impact of Smithsons?

CEO: Sorry I don't follow you.

P: OK. 8 Let me rephrase that. What I'm talking about is economic and social damage which big multinational companies like yours can do around the world.

CEO: 9 Could you give me an example?

P: Yes, the fact that as a company **you are anti union. You don't let employees join workers organisations.**

CEO: Yes, that's true. We **don't think that unions are a good idea for staff or the company** as a whole.

P: But why not? What I mean is ... what are you worried about?

CEO: I don't think we're worried at all. I'm sorry, I don't see what you mean by all this damage you talk about. I see only benefits. Perhaps in some ways we are victims of our own success. We are almost too successful, but that is down to our customers. Statistics show that in the markets we have entered recently it is actually the poorest sections of society who benefit most. 10 To be more precise ... we really appeal to everyone and alienate no one.

P: ... Right. Another question for you now ...

4b Students work individually and then compare answers with a partner.

• Go through answers with the class and check students can pronounce *basically* (three syllables ba-si-cly) and *specific*.

> **a)** 2, 4, 5, 8, 10; **b)** 1, 3, 6, 7, 9

For further practice, ask students to do exercise KL 4 on page 149 in the Language reference.

TASK: a TV debate

5a Focus students on the photo on page 87 and ask them what kind of programme this is (a live TV debate) and if they can remember what it is called from exercise 1 (*Vista*).

• Ask students to read the introduction.

• Divide the class into five groups (A, B, C, D and E) and tell them to read the relevant role card.

• Give students five minutes in their groups to discuss ideas for what they could say in the debate.

• Monitor to help with vocabulary if necessary.

5b Form new groups of five with an A, B, C, D and E student in each.

- Remind students of the KEY LANGUAGE and go through the OTHER USEFUL PHRASES box with the class, checking they understand *chairing* (leading, controlling a debate).
- Then ask each person in the group to tell the others what their role is and give students 15–20 minutes to hold their debate.
- Monitor to note mistakes using the KEY LANGUAGE and OTHER PHRASES.
- When they have finished, ask each group who (i.e. which role) was most successful during the debate.
- Finally, correct some of the mistakes you noted earlier.

🔧 If you don't have enough students to form equal groups of five, remove one or more of roles A, B and E. If you remove role A, you will need to write the Chair's questions on the board at the beginning of the debate or chair the debate yourself. If you have too many students to form equal groups of five, give one role (but not role A) to more than one student. For example, the debate will then have two students with role C.

HOMEWORK OPTIONS

Students do the exercises on page 58 of the Workbook.

Students write an email to the producers of *In the Hot Seat* (exercise 3) either agreeing or disagreeing with some of the opinions expressed in the programme. Students must also include their own opinions.

Students do exercise KL 4 on page 149 in the Language reference.

8.5 STUDY AND WRITING SKILLS

IN THIS LESSON

Lesson topic and staging

This lesson focuses on summarising skills and writing a summary. Students discuss a list of statements about writing summaries. They then look at different techniques for summarising: identifying topic sentences and paraphrasing. Next, students practise these techniques and the skill of editing to shorten texts before writing a summary of their own.

Objectives

By the end of the lesson, students should have:

- extracted specific information from a reading text
- extended their range of techniques for summarising written texts and practised using these
- written a summary.

Common European Framework

Students can write simple connected texts and notes conveying simple information.

Timings

If short of time, you could set exercise 8 for homework. Alternatively, you could ask students to paraphrase only one paragraph in exercise 3b on page 88. A possible lesson break would be after exercise 6b on page 89.

WARM-UP

This activity reminds students of the content of the article in lesson 8.2, exercise 1.

- Focus students on the photo on page 88 and ask them how old the people are (teenagers) and where they come from (lots of different countries).
- Remind students they read an article earlier in this Unit about how teenagers are communicating with each other nowadays.
- Put students in pairs to try to remember as much as possible about the article.
- If you have students who didn't read the article, make sure they are in a pair with someone who did.
- Elicit ideas from the class and tell them they will be summarising this article later in the lesson.

STUDY SKILLS: summarising

1a Focus students on the title of this section (summarising) and ask them if they have ever written a summary in English and if they found it easy or difficult.

- Then ask students to give you two or three things you should do when summarising.

- Ask students to quickly read the list of statements to see if they can find the ideas they gave you above.

- Then, give students three minutes to do the activity in the Coursebook and compare their answers with a partner.

1b Students can check their answers individually before you go through answers with the whole class.

> **1** True (most summaries should be about a third of the original length); **2** True (if you do not understand the text, your summary will not be accurate); **3** True (if you do not use your own words, you could be accused of plagiarising); **4** False (you may have to use certain technical words in your summary. It may be more convenient to do so); **5** False (it should only include important information, i.e. the key points); **6** False (a complete summary will include all the important points); **7** False (a summary does not include additional information); **8** False (you may include a limited number of quotations); **9** True (it is the original writer's opinion which is important); **10** False (you may change the order or ideas if this makes the summary clearer or more readable)

For exercises 2–7 it will be useful to reproduce summaries from the Coursebook and model answers from the Teacher's Book so that the whole class can see them. You could use an Interactive Whiteboard or an overhead projector. When you check answers in these exercises or analyse model answers, highlight the points you have made in the texts.

2 Topic sentences

- Ask students what a topic sentence is and get a few ideas from the class.

- Then ask students to read the Summarising tip on page 88 and compare their ideas.

- If you did not do the Warm-up activity, tell students they are going to use a text from lesson 8.2, exercise 1 in the next few exercises and then follow the procedure in the Warm-up.

- If your class have not read the article in lesson 8.2, exercise 1, ask them to do this exercise now. Students will not need to do any of the other exercises in 8.2.

- Then, read through the instructions and example in exercise 2 in this lesson.

- Give students five minutes to this activity individually and then compare answers with a partner.

- Elicit answers from the class and then give students the suggested answers below.

> Paragraph 2: Topic sentence: *For example, up until recently ... but that has now changed*. Supporting idea: Through the Internet, young people can meet other people with similar interests from all over the world.
> Paragraph 3: Topic sentence: *The Internet has also greatly influenced how people buy and sell goods*. Supporting idea: People can buy and sell things they couldn't before and sometimes from/to complete strangers.

3a Paraphrasing

- Tell students to read the paragraph in the article (lesson 8.2, exercise 1) before they read the paraphrases.

- Ask students to discuss their ideas in pairs, then elicit answers and reasons from the class.

- Then go through the answers below with the class.

> Paraphrase A is better than B because it is shorter and expresses clearly the key ideas in the paragraph. Paraphrase B gives too much detail and repeats phrases from the original text. It also does not highlight the main idea of the paragraph.

3b Ask students to paraphrase paragraph 2 only and then compare with a partner. This will give some guidance for paraphrasing paragraph 3.

- While students are writing, monitor to suggest improvements.

- When they have written both paraphrases, ask two or three students to read theirs out loud.

- Then ask students to compare their paraphrases with the models below.

> Paragraph 2: People used to make friends at school and keep them all their lives. Now many people, especially the young, find friends on the Internet through shared interests.
> Paragraph 3: The Internet has also influenced how people shop. They can now buy many more things and even buy from or sell to strangers. However, Internet shopping can be risky.

4 Read through the instructions with the class and emphasise students are looking for reasons why this is *not* a good summary.

- Allow about five minutes for the discussion and then elicit ideas from the class.

- Go through the answers below.

> The reasons are: the summary repeats too many phrases from the original; it is too long (44 words); there is no mention in the original that Google is a major success; it doesn't tell you what Wikipedia is/does; it's not accurate; the original doesn't say that Google is more reliable, but that Wikipedia does contain errors

WRITING SKILLS: a summary

5 Ask students to read options a)–c) before they read paragraph 5 of the article.

- Put students into pairs to discuss the best option and their reasons for thinking this.

- Go through answers with the class.

> The best option is c) because it sums up the main idea without being too specific or too general. a) and b) are too specific.

6a This is not a difficult activity, so elicit the answer immediately from the class.

> Topic sentence: *Probably the biggest impact that the Internet has had is the way in which it has influenced social networking.*

6b Give students a few minutes to read paragraph 5 again and underline the key supporting ideas.

- Ask students to compare with a partner before you check answers with the class.

> Supporting ideas: People can meet new friends, renew old acquaintances and play games with each other.

7a Editing to shorten

- Ask students to read paragraphs 5 and 6 of the article in lesson 8.2, exercise 1.

- Read through the introduction to this activity with the class. Then ask students to read the examples a)–c), paying particular attention to the kinds of changes made in each text.

7b Ask students to edit only the first paragraph (number 1) and then compare their answers with a partner.

- Show or read out loud the model answer below and ask them to notice how their editing is similar/ different.

- Then give students five minutes to edit the remaining two paragraphs (numbers 2 and 3) and compare with a partner.

- Ask two or three students to read their edited paragraphs to the class and then show or read them the models below.

> Model answer 1: International shopping is now common with people buying goods from online sites such as Amazon, the online retail site, and the international auction site, eBay.
> Model answer 2: The Internet helps solve crimes, it helps raise money for charities and it even helps find missing children through websites designed for that purpose.
> Model answer 3: Google, a major sources of information, finds the web pages you need and ranks them according to the number of links made to them. = Google finds and ranks web pages according to the number of links made.

8 Explain that students are going to write and edit a summary of an Internet page about eBay.

- First, orient students to the text by asking them to brainstorm in pairs things they know about eBay.

- Then ask students to read the text and to find out how many of their ideas are mentioned.

- Ask students to look again at the work they did in exercises 2–6 and tell them to follow the same procedure when summarising the web page about eBay.

- Give students 30 minutes to write their summaries.

- Then ask them to read through the work they did in exercise 7 again and give them ten minutes to edit their summaries.

- When they have finished, ask students to compare their summaries in pairs and make any final suggestions for improvement.

- Give students three minutes to make any final changes.

- Finally, ask students to compare their summary with the model below.

- Alternatively, take the summaries in for marking, paying particular attention to the skills, techniques used and the criteria for writing a good summary from exercise 1.

🔧 Instead of asking students to edit their own summaries, ask them to swap with a partner and edit each others'.

> Model summary: eBay is a website where people can buy and sell goods. It is a cheap, easy method, and a huge quantity of goods is sold on it daily. People can sell anything from valuable objects to items they would normally throw away. People send goods themselves to buyers. Some well known companies sell new products on eBay. eBay has been criticised: certain sales have been considered unethical, and the system of feedback is not liked by everyone. There is also a risk that users might be offered copies of products. (90 words)

HOMEWORK OPTIONS

Students do the exercises on pages 58–59 of the Workbook.

Students find an article, a web page or a story that interests them and summarise it in 100 words. In the following lesson, these are posted round the room for all students to read. Students decide which article, etc. they would like to read in its full form.

Art

9.1 WHAT IS ART?

Lesson topic and staging

This lesson looks at the different kinds of art people like. Students discuss art that they like, what they think is 'real art' and the purposes of art. They then read a leaflet about exhibitions and focus on vocabulary related to art. Next, students listen to people talking about exhibitions they have seen and focus on language to describe these. Finally, students discuss exhibitions/art they have seen and write an email describing these.

Objectives

By the end of the lesson, students should have:

- extracted specific information and language items from a reading and listening text
- extended their range of vocabulary related to art
- participated in group discussions to describe and express their opinions about art and exhibitions
- written an email describing and expressing their opinions about art and exhibitions.

Timings

If short of time, you could drop exercises 2a and 2b on page 90 as the discussion in exercise 8 can still take place without these ideas. Alternatively, you could set exercise 9 for homework. A possible lesson break would be after exercise 5 on page 90.

WARM-UP

This activity introduces different kinds of art, where they can be found and useful vocabulary for exercise 1.

- Focus students on the painting on page 90 and ask them to give you a few words to describe it.
- Make sure you elicit *painting* and then ask students where they could see it. Elicit *gallery*.
- Then write the following on the board:

  1 paintings, 2 graffiti, 3 monuments, 4 political cartoons, 5 graphic designs, 6 performance art, 7 tattoos, 8 mosaics, 9 religious icons, 10 murals

  a) walls in streets, b) galleries, c) someone's body, d) walls in streets and important buildings, e) churches, f) floors, g) streets, h) theatre, i) newspapers, j) advertisements

- Put students in pairs and tell them to match each type of art to the place it can be found.
- Some places apply to more than one kind of art, so tell students they can only choose one place for each.

- Students can use their dictionaries if necessary.
- Go through answers with the class, but avoid discussion about whether a *tattoo*, a *cartoon* or *graffiti* are art because this is the focus of exercise 1b.

  1 b); **2** a); **3** g); **4** i); **5** j); **6** h); **7** c); **8** f); **9** e); **10** d)

i Salvador Dali (1904–1989), a Catalan (Spanish) artist particularly famous for his surrealist paintings. The painting on page 90, *The Persistence of Memory*, is an example of his art.

Anonymous quote:

This quote has two levels of meaning: 1 the surface meaning is as the words suggest; 2 the implied meaning is a criticism of art you're looking at or know about. It means 'I may not understand it but I don't think this is art. I know what kind of art I like (normally, 'traditional' portraits and landscapes) and this piece isn't it.'

SPEAKING

1a Focus students on the painting on page 90 and elicit/ tell them it's a famous painting by the Spanish artist Salvador Dali.

- Ask students if they like this painting and why/why not.
- Then ask students to read the questions and put them into small groups for the discussion.
- Elicit a few ideas from two or three of the groups.

1b If you used the Warm-up activity, students will already have used their dictionaries for some terms here.

- If you didn't use the Warm-up, ask students to read the list and use dictionaries for unknown words.
- Keep students in the same groups as exercise 1a and give them five minutes to discuss the options.
- Elicit a few answers and reasons for each item.

2a Ask students to read and rank the list individually before discussing their answers in pairs.

- Tell pairs they should produce one list that they can both agree on.
- Elicit a ranking from one pair and ask the rest of the class if they agree.

2b Give students a few minutes to think of examples but tell them not to worry if they can't (see Tip).

⊛ Students may not know enough about art to give examples for all or any of the purposes. You could prepare some photos of different kinds of art (each demonstrating different purpose) and show these to the class. Students then say which purpose each exemplifies. Some photos may exemplify more than one purpose.

READING

3 Before students look at the leaflet, elicit/tell them what *skim* means (looking at/reading quickly to get the general/overall idea).

• Set the questions, ask students to look at the leaflet and almost immediately, elicit answers.

• Then ask the class if they go to galleries to see art exhibitions (or any kind of exhibition).

• Ask one or two students to briefly tell the class about the last exhibition they went to.

> It's advertising forthcoming exhibitions at a gallery; It's aimed at people who like different kinds of art.

4 Warn students that this time they will need to read the text carefully and give them eight minutes for this activity.

• Tell students not to use their dictionaries except for questions 3 and 6 (to check *ceramics*, *bronze*, *oils* and *watercolours*).

• Ask students to compare with a partner before you check answers with the class.

• If students are unsure of a particular answer, go through the notes in brackets.

> 1 Shaping the World (an opening day talk by the artist, Start of the New (including a series of lectures); 2 Tomorrow Now!, Shaping the World (Cynthia Marlow is still alive so there will probably be some up-to-date art), Easy on the Eye (may contain recent photos of current film and TV stars) (Note: The Start of the New is not included here because Modern Art does not refer to up-to-date art.); 3 Forever Autumn; 4 Shaping the World (Cynthia Marlow); 5 Easy on the Eye; 6 Shaping the World (ceramics, stone, bronze)

5 Give students a few minutes to decide on their exhibition and then put them in pairs to compare ideas.

• If students aren't interested in any of the exhibitions, ask them to discuss their reasons.

VOCABULARY: art and artists

6a Give students five minutes to read and find the words.

• Tell students they can use dictionaries but to try to guess meaning from context.

• Ask students to compare with a partner before you check answers with the class.

• In feedback, elicit/give the main stress on each word (highlighted in the answers below).

> 1 groundbreaking; 2 preview show; 3 retrospective; 4 masterpiece; 5 controversial; 6 thought-provoking (Note: -sial is pronounced ʃəl.)

6b Tell students to underline all the words in the text before they choose the answers.

• Ask students to compare with a partner before you check answers with the class.

• In feedback, elicit/give the main stress on each word (highlighted in the answers below).

> 1 Realism; 2 Modern art; 3 Contemporary art (pronounced as three syllables – con-tem-pry); 4 Abstract art

6c Ask students to read the text quickly and circle all the people connected to art.

• Elicit ideas from the class and write correct suggestions on the board.

• Ask the class to copy the list from the board and check unknown vocabulary in their dictionaries.

• Finally, check that students understand *critics* (people whose job it is to give their opinions on art) and *art lovers* (people who love art, not lovers shown in art).

> critics, collectors, art lovers, sculptor, artist, painters

For further practice, ask students to do exercise V1 5 on page 151 in the Language reference.

⊠ As a final activity, you could ask students to look at the purposes of art in exercise 2a and match types of art (and people connected with art) from exercise 6 to the purposes (e.g. controversial art = to make people think and stimulate ideas, a collector = to make money). Students discuss their answers in pairs.

LISTENING

7a First, focus students on the last section of the leaflet and ask them what a *Friend of the Gallery* is (someone who pays an amount of money each year and then receives discounts, invitations to previews, etc.).

• Then ask students to read through the options and discuss in pairs which they know/like/dislike.

• Tell students to read the questions and then play the track without pausing.

- Check answers with the class. (Answers are bold in the audioscript below exercise 7b.)
- Finally, if students are interested in knowing more about any of the artists or kinds of art in the list, you could ask them to look on the Internet.

> **1** The following should be ticked: Matisse; Rembrandt; Pop Art; the photo exhibition; **2** Yes

You could prepare some photos of the different kinds of art and pieces by the artists in the list and show these to the class.

7b Give students a couple of minutes to try to complete some of the gaps.

- Play the track, if necessary pausing at the points indicated in the audioscript below.
- Ask students to compare with a partner before you check answers with the class (underlined in the audioscript).
- In feedback, check students understand *(not) into something* (I like/dislike [doing] it) and *reviews* (reports written by critics).

> **1** impressed; **2** into; **3** expectations; **4** reviews; **5** effort/fee; **6** exhibitions; **7** recommend

> **Audioscript and answers to exercise 7:**
> **Track 3.2**
> *Monica, Jane*
> M: So Jane, do you think you'll renew your membership? I was just looking at the programme for next year.
> J: I'm not sure really. I didn't get to see as many exhibitions as I'd hoped to last year. I only went to a couple. **I saw the Matisse** exhibition. It was fantastic – so inspiring. <u>1 I was really impressed by it.</u>
> M: I didn't get to see that. <u>2 I'm not really into that sort of thing</u> but I heard it was something special, though. I also heard the **Monet one was excellent, but I didn't see it.** [PAUSE]
> J: No, neither did I. The only **other one I got to was the Pop Art** one which <u>3 didn't really live up to my expectations.</u> How about you? Did you see it?
> M: No, I didn't actually, but <u>4 the reviews weren't very good.</u> [PAUSE]
> J: Well, you didn't miss much at all. <u>5 It wasn't worth the effort, or the entrance fee</u> for that matter. Yeah, it was very expensive, now I think about it.
> M: Oh, I'll tell you what **I really liked – the Rembrandt exhibition** at the start of the year. It was excellent, although it was really packed. I even had to queue up for half an hour. <u>6 It was one of the best exhibitions I've ever seen.</u> But I think the other thing I really enjoyed last year was the **portrait photos exhibition** in the café exhibition, which is free anyway. [PAUSE]
> J: Mmm. The thing is, the membership is expensive if you don't go to most of the exhibitions. So, how about it then? Are you going to rejoin, or what?
> M: I don't know. What are you going to do? What's on that looks interesting?
>
> *continued...*

> J: The 'Tomorrow Now' exhibition in January looks fab! If it's anything like the exhibition I saw in Paris last summer – I think some of the works on show will be the same – it should be wonderful. <u>7 I'd really recommend it.</u>
> M: What about the Cynthia Marlow exhibition?
> J: Oh, let's give that a miss – she's boring.
> M: Well, I think **we should rejoin**, but make sure we go to almost everything next year.
> J:: **OK, then, that's what we'll do.**

SPEAKING AND WRITING

8 Read through the instructions and give students a few minutes to choose an exhibition, gallery or work of art.

- Give pairs ten minutes to discuss their choice and ask each other questions if necessary.
- Monitor to note mistakes in using the vocabulary and phrases from this lesson.
- Then ask students to tell the class if they'd like to see the exhibition/work they heard about and why.
- Finally, correct some of the more common or important mistakes you noted earlier.

9 Give students 15–20 minutes to write their emails.

- Monitor to point out mistakes and help with vocabulary if necessary.
- When they have finished, post the emails round the room, ask students to read them all and decide which exhibitions/works they would like to see.
- Finally, take the emails in for marking, paying particular attention to the use of vocabulary and phrases from this lesson.

HOMEWORK OPTIONS

Students do the exercises on page 60 of the Workbook.

Students think of an exhibition they would really like to see (it can be imaginary). They then write a short leaflet describing the exhibition to attract people. In the next lesson, post the leaflets round the room. Students read them and decide which exhibition(s) they'd like to go to.

Students use the Internet to research one of the artists or types of art from this lesson. They then write a description of the artist and/or art.

Students do exercise V1 5 on page 151 in the Language reference.

9.2 PHOTOGRAPHY

Lesson topic and staging

This lesson looks at photography and whether people think it is art. Students read an article about photography and discuss whether they think it's art. Students then look at adverb/adjective combinations in the text and practise using these. Next, students learn about gradable/ungradable adjectives and adverbs used with them before practising their use. Finally, students discuss photos they have taken and photos they have seen.

Objectives

By the end of the lesson, students should have:

- extracted specific information and language items from a reading text
- extended their range of common adverb/adjective combinations
- revised/extended their understanding of gradable/ungradable adjectives and the adverbs that collocate with these
- described photographs they have taken and seen.

Timings

If short of time, you could drop exercise 6b on page 92. A possible lesson break would be after exercise 6b on page 92.

WARM-UP

This activity introduces the topic of appreciating photos.

- Bring a small set of photos to the lesson (they could be taken from the Internet and projected on the Interactive Whiteboard or from photos you have at home).
- Ask students to look at the photos and decide why they like/dislike them.
- Divide the class into small groups and ask students to take it in turns to tell the others why they like/dislike a particular photo, but students must not point at or hold the photo they are talking about.
- The other students in the group guess which photo is being talked about and then agree/disagree with the first student's opinion.

READING

1 Use the Warm-up activity to lead in to this exercise.

- If you didn't use the Warm-up, focus students on the photos on pages 92–93 and ask if they like them.

- Then put students into small groups to discuss the questions.
- Get a few ideas from two or three groups.

i The photo with the bicycle and steps was taken in the Var department, Hyères in France, in 1932. The other photo was taken at a Picasso Exhibition in New York City.

2 Give students two minutes to read the text.

- Ask them to briefly compare with a partner before you check answers with the class.

> c)

3 Give students two minutes to find and underline the parts of the text that support this idea.

- Elicit answers from the class and then give students three minutes to check vocabulary in the parts of the text they have underlined. Students need to understand *moving* (affects you emotionally) for exercise 5.

> The photographer is creative; the camera can't decide between an ordinary, functional, regular photo and a really excellent, cleverly composed photo (but the photographer can); it is the photographer who picks out the essential qualities of the subject at a particular moment; photos taken for other purposes, e.g. news photography, can be iconic works of art; [the photo described at the end of the article] is deeply moving (and this is an aspect of art).

If possible, reproduce the text so that the whole class can see it (perhaps on an Interactive Whiteboard or an overhead projector). As you check answers to this and subsequent exercises, highlight the relevant information and language items in the text.

4 Tell students to do questions 1 and 2 first, underlining the relevant parts of the text.

- Warn students that answers to these questions may overlap.
- Ask them to compare with a partner before you check answers to these two questions with the class. (Note: because answers to questions 1 and 2 overlap, they are given together in the answers below.)
- Then put students into pairs or small groups to discuss question 3 and give reasons for their opinions.
- Elicit some ideas from the class.

> 1 & 2 more can be captured in a photograph than intended by the photographer (unlike a painting); the photograph had not passed through the brain of the photographer (unlike painting and painters); the painter decides what and how to paint, and how to make it interesting; photo-taking can be an automatic process; 3 Answers depend on students' own opinions.

VOCABULARY: common adverb/adjective collocations

5   Elicit/tell the class what a *collocation* is (words that commonly go together e.g. *deeply* [not *heavily*] sad).

•   Show students that *deeply* is the adverb in the example above.

•   Give students one minute to find the words and adverbs and underline them in the text.

•   Elicit answers from the class and explain that these are common collocations, but they may see other adverbs used with these adjectives.

•   Finally, explain that there are no definite rules for which adverb commonly collocates with an adjective.

> entirely unexpected; completely different; completely wrong; deeply moving

6a First, elicit/tell students that all the adverbs have the same meaning (completely).

•   Then give students three minutes for the activity and tell them to guess the answers if necessary.

•   Students can use their dictionaries to check the meaning of the adjectives.

•   Elicit answers to the board so that students can copy the correct collocations.

•   Explain that these are common collocations but they may see other adverbs used with these adjectives.

> highly praised; heavily criticised; utterly impossible; highly qualified; painfully shy; totally unbelievable; totally unjustified; utterly useless

6b To make the activity more challenging, ask students to do it without looking at exercise 6a.

•   Elicit answers from the class.

> 1 was highly praised; 2 was highly qualified; 3 was totally unbelievable; 4 a painfully shy; 5 often heavily criticised; 6 was totally unjustified

GRAMMAR: ungradable adjectives

7a Read the instructions and adjectives with the class and tell students that *unusual* here means *not the usual/normal kind*, not *strange* in a negative way.

•   Give students 30 seconds to match the adjectives and compare answers with a partner.

•   Check answers with the class and explain that the adjectives in pairs have similar meanings.

> unusual/unique; good/excellent; important/essential

7b Give students two minutes to do this activity individually.

•   Ask them to compare with a partner before you check answers with the class.

•   In feedback, check students' pronunciation of *furious, exhausted, fascinating* and *tiny*.

•   Then read through the information below this exercise and check students understand *the end of the scale* (the most cold it is possible to be).

> angry/furious; bad/terrible; big/enormous; cold/freezing; upset/devastated; tired/exhausted; hungry/starving; interesting/fascinating; small/tiny

7c Ask students to read the examples and then elicit answers from the class.

> *unusual* is gradable (and the adverb *very* can collocate with it); *unique* is ungradable (and the adverb *absolutely* can collocate with it)

8   Students do this activity individually and then compare with a partner.

•   Write the table on the board, then elicit answers and write them in the table.

Gradable	Ungradable
unusual	unique
good	excellent
tired	exhausted
hungry	starving
cold	freezing
upset	devastated
bad	terrible
big	enormous
important	essential
angry	furious
small	tiny
interesting	fascinating

9a Give students two minutes to find the examples and underline the correct option.

•   Elicit answers and then tell students that *utterly, totally* (exercise 6a) and *completely* (in the text on pages 92–93) are examples of adverbs that collocate with ungradable adjectives.

•   Read through the GRAMMAR TIP with the class.

> 1 gradable; 2 ungradable

(!) Tell students *absolutely* (and other adverbs that go with ungradable adjectives) emphasise the adjective, but cannot change the degree because the adjective is already the most it can be.

For further information, ask students to read G1 in the Language reference on page 150.

9b Students do this exercise individually and then compare answers with a partner.

•   Go through answers with the class.

1 a ~~very~~ really excellent photograph (Note: you can also use *absolutely* here but need to change *a* to *an*.); **2** correct; **3** I was ~~very~~ absolutely/really devastated when they […]; **4** were ~~extremely~~ absolutely/really terrible; **5** correct

10 Tell students to underline the adverb/adjective combinations and then check these are correct.

- Then put students in pairs to answer the questions and give reasons for their answers.

- Elicit answers and reasons from the class.

very excellent (*very* collocates with gradable adjectives, *excellent* is ungradable); very cheap (correct); very enormous (*very* collocates with gradable adjectives, *enormous* is ungradable); absolutely hungry (*absolutely* collocates with ungradable adjectives, *hungry* is gradable); extremely fascinating (*extremely* collocates with gradable adjectives, *fascinating* is ungradable); absolutely interesting (*absolutely* collocates with ungradable adjectives, *interesting* is gradable); really wonderful (correct – *wonderful* is an ungradable adjective)

For further practice, ask students to do exercise G1 1 on page 151 in the Language reference.

SPEAKING

11 Give students one minute to think of the two photos.

- Put students into groups to describe the photos and to ask each other questions.

- Students can ask about the photo itself (e.g. 'Why do you think the photographer chose that angle?') or about the situation ('Where were you when you took it? Was it a nice day?').

- Finally, students to tell you the most interesting/funniest/strangest photo they heard about.

- Many people can access photos on the Internet. You could ask students to sit at a computer and show other students the photos or print them out at home and show them in the next lesson.

HOMEWORK OPTIONS

Students do the exercises on pages 61–62 of the Workbook.

Students look at the description of the Robert Capa photo in the text on page 93. They then write a description of one of the photos they chose in exercise 11. In the next lesson, post these round the room and ask students to read them all and decide which photo they think they like best.

Students do exercises G1 1 and V2 6 on page 151 in the Language reference.

9.3 CONTEMPORARY SCULPTORS

IN THIS LESSON

Lesson topic and staging

This lesson looks at different contemporary sculptors. Students discuss their opinions of contemporary art and then read texts on three sculptors. Students then look at adjectives in the text and focus on adjective order. Next, students focus on the position of adverbs in a sentence, using the texts as a source before practising positioning adverbs themselves. Finally, students discuss a work of art they really like.

Objectives

By the end of the lesson, students should have:

- extracted specific information and language items from reading texts

- revised and/or extended their range of vocabulary using the reading text as a source

- revised/learned about the order of adjectives and the positioning of adverbs in sentences

- discussed their opinions of contemporary art and a piece of art they like.

Timings

If short of time, you could cut the number of items students do in exercises 5 and 7, as this is not a complicated language area for students to grasp. A possible lesson break would be after exercise 5 on page 94.

WARM-UP

This activity reintroduces some vocabulary related to people in the broader area of art.

- Write the following on the board: *renaipt, grphrhopotae, clportsu, epto, nstiooract, ftiiafgr rittsa.*

- Tell students these are all artists in a broad sense (i.e. not only painters).

- Put students in pairs to rearrange the letters to make words.

- The first pair to finish wins.

painter; photographer; sculptor; poet; cartoonist; graffiti artist

READING

1   Ask students to read the statement and clarify it for them if necessary.

• Students then discuss the statement in groups of three or four.

• Get a few opinions from two or three groups.

☀ To make exercises 2 and 3a more communicative, you could put students into groups of three and ask each student to read a different text. After each exercise, they swap the information they found. You should, however, ask students to look at all three texts from exercise 3b onwards.

2   First, focus students on the names at the top of each profile and ask if they've heard of these people.

• Then give them three minutes to read the texts and answer the question.

• Elicit answers from the class.

> Anish Kapoor: sculpture (and architecture); Antony Gormley: sculpture; Yoko Ono: sculpture (and film making, poetry, music)

3a Ask students to read the sentences and tell them that *criticism* in number 5 means negative comments.

• Give students eight minutes for this activity.

• Ask them to compare with a partner before you check answers with the class.

> 1 Antony Gormley; 2 Yoko Ono; 3 Yoko Ono;
> 4 Anish Kapoor; 5 Yoko Ono; 6 Antony Gormley;
> 7 Anish Kapoor (Note: Yoko Ono often mixes art with poetry and music, but the text doesn't specifically say she is currently doing this.)

3b Give students a minute to look at each photo and then put students into pairs to discuss the questions.

VOCABULARY: order of adjectives

4a First ask students to identify the adjectives in each highlighted phrase.

• Tell students that some of the words can also be nouns in other contexts (e.g. *metal, steel*) but they are used as adjectives here.

• Then ask students to read the headings and tell them that *function/class* means the purpose or type of the adjective.

• Tell students there may be no adjectives for some of the headings.

• Give students three minutes to put the adjectives in groups using their dictionaries if necessary.

• Ask them to compare with a partner before you check answers with the class.

> age: no examples; material: steel, metal, clay; colour/pattern: brown; opinion: outstanding; nationality: no examples; function/class: art; size: huge, enormous, small; shape: fully-extended; other: famous, stainless, rich, aristocratic

4b First, ask students to add the adjectives to the headings in exercise 4a and check answers with the class.

> age: antique; material: silk; colour/pattern: dark, colourful; opinion: beautiful; nationality: Japanese; function/class: Cubist; size: huge; shape: no example; other: well-known

• Set the activity and give students five minutes to decide on the order.

• Ask students to compare with a partner before they check their answers on page 173.

• To reinforce the answers, write one of the example sentences on the board and demonstrate the order.

> The order is: opinion; size; most other qualities; age; colour/pattern; nationality; material; function/class

5   Put students in pairs so they can discuss answers as they do them rather than compare at the end.

• Students can use their dictionaries if necessary.

• Monitor to point out mistakes with word order and refer students to the table on page 173.

• Finally, elicit answers to the board so that all students can clearly see the order.

> 1 fabulous, large, bronze; 2 large, rectangular, coloured; 3 fine, ancient, Javanese; 4 British Impressionist; 5 hard, coloured, heat-resistant; 6 dreary, modern, urban; 7 square, Japanese, origami

GRAMMAR: position of adverbs

6a Ask students to find all the examples before they add them to the lists.

• They can use their dictionaries if necessary.

• Ask students to compare with a partner before you check answers with the class.

> 1 Time: then, in May, in 1972, nowadays; 2 Place: there, at home, in Hampstead, England, to New York; 3 Manner: quickly, carefully, creatively, dramatically; 4 Frequency: sometimes; never; often; frequently; 5 Certainty: definitely; perhaps; probably; certainly; 6 Degree: a lot; mostly; mainly; strongly

6b Students look at the examples in the text and answer questions 1–4.

- If they find this very difficult, tell them to work with a partner.
- When they have finished, ask them to check by reading G2 in the Language reference on page 150.
- Elicit answers and examples from the class.
- Finally, read through the Grammar tip with the class and elicit/tell them that if the adverbial is at the beginning of a sentence, it is normally followed immediately by a comma.

> **1** at the end of the clause; **2** in the middle of the clause; **3** before the verb (and after the subject) but after the verb *be* and auxiliaries (e.g. I have often seen that artist); **4** if the sentence uses *been* as part of a perfect structure, the adverb comes after the auxiliary *have/has/had* but before *been*

For further information, ask students to read G2 in the Language reference on page 150.

7 First, ask students to read sentences 1–6 and discuss with a partner how many of these artists and art types they know.

- Students can use their dictionaries if necessary.
- Elicit answers from the class and then refer to the Tip below.
- Next, set the activity in the Coursebook and give students five minutes to order the adverbs.
- Ask them to compare with a partner and refer to exercise 6, the Grammar tip and page 150 in the Language reference if they need help.
- Go through answers and notes in brackets with the class.

> **1** Van Gogh often painted outdoors; **2** Picasso has strongly influenced many artists; **3** Leonardo da Vinci sketched technical designs very skilfully; **4** The French post-Impressionist Paul Gauguin died alone in Tahiti (Note: we can't put *in Tahiti* at the beginning of this sentence because we don't want to emphasise the place more than the action *died*.); **5** [....] expression of art deco is probably in the huge skyscrapers in the USA; **6** Nowadays, the batik effect is produced by [...] being hand-made [nowadays] (Note: *nowadays* can go at the end of the sentence but it is usually more natural to use it at the beginning.)

You could suggest students use the Internet to find out more about the artists and types of art in exercise 7.

SPEAKING

8 Give students a couple of minutes to think of a work of art and note down adjectives and adverbs to describe it.

- Then put students into groups of three and give them ten minutes to describe and discuss each piece.

- Tell students to ask questions to get as much information as possible (e.g. 'When did you first see it? How does it make you feel?').
- Monitor to note mistakes with adjective and adverb order.
- When they have finished, ask students for the most interesting/best/worst piece they heard about.
- Finally, correct some of the more common or important mistakes you noted earlier.

You could also ask students to sit at a computer and show other students pictures of the work of art. If students can't think of a work of art or have little interest in art, you could bring some photos into class or find them on the Internet and project onto the Interactive Whiteboard.

HOMEWORK OPTIONS

Students do the exercises on pages 63–64 of the Workbook.

Students write a description of the work of art they chose in exercise 8. If possible, students could print out a copy of the work of art and include it with their description. In the next lesson, post these round the room and ask students to read them all and decide which piece they like best/least.

Students do exercises G2 2 and 3 on page 151 in the Language reference.

9.4 SCENARIO: THE NEW EXHIBITION

Lesson topic and staging

This lesson focuses on the language of sequencing information and moving to a new point. Students read a text to introduce the scenario: a gallery planning exhibitions. They then listen to the gallery's director and experts discussing artists to exhibit. Next, students listen to an employee suggesting an artist and focus on the KEY LANGUAGE. Finally, the TASK asks students to present artists and discuss who to exhibit.

Objectives

By the end of the lesson, students should have:

- learned useful phrases for sequencing information and moving to a new point when speaking
- used this language in a 'real-life' situation to make presentations and discuss options
- extracted specific information and language items from a reading and listening texts
- participated effectively in extended speaking practice.

Common European Framework

Students can use language effectively to express views and opinions, explain and give reasons, agree/disagree politely, and link discrete items into a connected linear sequence of points.

Timings

If short of time, you could cut the number of artists in listening exercise 2 and then the same artists from exercise 7. This will create small groups of students, fewer presentations and a shorter discussion. A possible lesson break would be after exercise 5b on page 97.

This activity revises adjective order from lesson 9.3.

- Focus students on the photo on page 96 and ask them what they can see.
- Write the following on the board: *shape*, *age*, *size*, *colour*, *style*.
- Put students into pairs and tell them to describe the picture in the photo, using one adjective in each of the categories above. They have one minute.
- Stop the activity after a minute and elicit sentences from the pairs.
- The pair with the most creative/inventive/interesting sentence wins.

1 Focus students on the photos on page 96 and ask them what is happening (men are moving a picture, probably to hang in a gallery, as in the inset photo, for an exhibition).

- Focus students on the card and ask who it is written by and for (by the Marco Giordano Gallery, for Friends of the Gallery). Elicit/remind them what 'friend of a gallery' is and what they receive.
- Tell students to read the questions and then the text in one minute.
- Put them into pairs to discuss the questions and then elicit answers from the class.
- Finally, ask students if they have ever been to exhibitions like this and/or bought contemporary art.

> **1** because they like art by young, contemporary artists, the opportunity to buy affordable, new art (private individuals and people from institutions, people who don't have much money to spend); **2** someone who buys for a large gallery, a government, a company, etc.; **3** an artist who is becoming increasingly famous; **4** answers depend on their own opinions

2a Set the context and give students 30 seconds to look at the chart.

- Suggest that students draw a bigger version of the chart to give them space to write notes.
- Play the track, pausing briefly after each expert to give students time to write.

2b Give students two minutes to compare answers and then play the track again if necessary.

- Go through answers with the class and check they understand *murals* (paintings on walls).
- The audioscript for this activity is on page 184 in the Coursebook.

	Artist	Type of art	Best-known work of art
1	Savanna Charles	huge glass and metal sculptures	Spiderwoman
2	Alberto Cassini	abstract paintings	Chaos
3	Ingrid Tauber	photographs, mostly of people's faces	Homeless Woman
4	John Leach	graffiti murals (i.e. on walls)	Battleground

3 Keep students in the same pairs as exercise 2 and give them three minutes to discuss the question.

- Students can use additional information they heard but didn't note in exercise 2 if they want to.
- Elicit answers and reasons from two or three pairs and ask the rest of the class if they agree.

KEY LANGUAGE: sequencing
information, moving to a new point

4a Read through the introduction with the class and tell
students the photo on page 97 is of Marta Villanueva.

- Ask students to read the questions and tell them that
question 1 is covered first in the text so they don't
need to worry about question 2 at the beginning.

- Tell students that *reputation* refers to what people
think about her personality.

- Tell students there is a lot of information for question
2, but they shouldn't worry if they can't note it all
because they will compare with other students later.

- Play the track without pausing and ask students to
compare in small groups and if necessary, play the
track again.

- Check answers with the class. (Answers are bold in
the audioscript below exercise 4b.)

> **1** 1 basic facts; 2 style of painting; 3 reviews
> by critics; 4 the artist's reputation/personality;
> **2** an up-and-coming artist, Portuguese, 28 years
> old, lives/works in Paris, married to a French
> businessman, paints in her spare time, works
> full-time for a United Nations organisation, speaks
> fluent Portuguese, English, Spanish and French

4b Set the activity and check students understand
sequence (put in order) her information.

- Play the track again without pausing and ask students
to compare in the same groups as in exercise 4a.

- Elicit answers from the class (underlined in the
audioscript below) and write them on the board.

> First; then; after that; finally

Audioscript and answers to exercise 4:
Track 3.4
Part 1
Hello everyone, I hope you enjoyed your lunch. I'm
going to talk to you now about Marta Villanueva, as I
think she could be the artist we're looking for for one
of our exhibitions. First, I'll give you a few basic facts
about her. Then, I'll talk about her style of painting.
After that, I'll mention some reviews she's received.
Finally, I'll describe what she's like as a person. I've got
some photos of her work, you can look at them after I've
finished. One other thing, please feel free to interrupt me
at any time, if you have questions.
OK, I take it not many of you have heard of Marta
Villaneuva. Right? Well it doesn't surprise me really, but
she is an **up-and-coming** artist, and that's why she's so
exciting. Let me give you a few facts about her: she's
Portuguese, 28 years old, living and working in Paris.
She's married to a French businessman. At the moment,
she paints in her spare time, she's got a full-time job
working in a United Nations organisation. By the way,
she speaks fluent Portuguese, English, Spanish and
French – quite a linguist. OK? *[fade]*

5a Ask students to read the questions and tell them to
note answers to 1 and 2 while they are listening. They
will discuss question 3 with other students after the
listening.

- Play the track without pausing and then ask students
to compare answers to 1 and 2 in pairs.

- Go through answers with the class.

- Then ask students to discuss the answers to question
3 before you check these with the class. (Answers are
bold in the audioscript below.)

- Finally, check students understand *worth watching*
(pay attention to her because she has potential).

> 1 landscapes and cityscapes; 2 worth watching,
> amazing colours that explode from the canvas; 3
> charming, modest, sociable

5b Set the activity and play the track again pausing at the
points indicated in the audioscript below.

- Ask students to compare in the same groups as
exercise 4.

- Elicit answers from the class (underlined in the
audioscript below) and write them on the board.

- Words in brackets show where students can substitute
their own words when they use these phrases.

> Right, I've told you a bit about ...; So, moving on
> now to ...; OK, that's all I have to say about ...
> What do (the critics) say about ...?; OK, that's it for
> the critics. Let's go on to ...

Audioscript and answers to exercise 5:
Track 3.5
Part 2
Right, I've told you a bit about her, I've given you a few
basic facts. So, moving on now to her style of painting;
1 she paints mainly landscapes and cityscapes, using
bright colours and light and shade to create the mood of
her paintings. Her paintings are really beautiful. Many of
her landscapes and scenes of everyday life remind me of
Monet and some of the other French impressionist painters.
[PAUSE]
OK, that's all I have to say about her style. What do the
critics say about her? Well, *Art World*, a magazine you all
know, described her as **2 'an artist worth watching'.** And
the *Modern Art Review* said recently, **2 'Her colours are**
amazing. They explode from the canvas. Collectors are
beginning to take a great interest in Marta Villanueva.' Need
I say more? [PAUSE]
OK, that's it for the critics. Let's go on to her personality and
reputation. Well, I've met her several times. I think I know
her quite well now. She's **3 charming, modest and sociable,**
and she can talk intelligently about a wide range of subjects.
She's extremely knowledgeable, not just about art. Right,
now you know a bit about the kind of person she is.
To conclude now. Let me remind you of my main points.
Marta Villanueva's paintings are eye-catching and colourful.
There's a lot of interest in her work. She's a linguist, and she's
got a friendly personality and good communication skills.
Just what we need for our first exhibition.

6a Give students three minutes to do this activity individually before comparing with a partner.

- Go through answers with the class.

> **1** a); **2** a); **3** b); **4** c); **5** b); **6** b); **7** c); **8** b)

For further practice, ask students to do exercise KL 4 on page 151 in the Language reference.

6b First, give students two minutes to decide where the main stress should be. Emphasise they are only looking for one word in each phrase.

- Play the track, pausing after each phrase to give students time to check and mark the stress.

- Ask students to compare with a partner and then check answers with the class. (Stressed words are bold in the audioscript below.)

- Elicit the important intonation on each phrase (each phrase begins with a high pitch).

- Play each phrase again and pause after each for students to repeat. Correct them if necessary.

> **Audioscript and answers to exercise 6b:**
> **Track 3.6**
> 1 **First**, I'll give you a few basic facts ...
> 2 **Finally**, I'll describe what she's like as a person.
> 3 **Right**, I've told you a bit about her, ...
> 4 **So**, moving on now to her style of painting ...
> 5 **OK**, that's all I have to say about her style.
> 6 **OK**, that's it for the critics.
> 7 **Let's** go on to her personality and reputation.
> 8 **Right**, now you know a bit about the kind of person she is.

TASK: giving an informal presentation

7a Read through the introduction and instructions and then divide the class in four groups (A, B, C and D).

- Tell students to read their information, using a dictionary if necessary, and emphasise they should not use the final piece of information they've been given for this activity (it is for exercise 8 later).

- Ask students to make notes for their presentation.

- Monitor to provide additional vocabulary if necessary.

- Ask students to compare their notes with other students from their group (e.g. with other A students) and then make improvement to their own notes.

7b Put students into new groups with an A, B, C and D student in each.

- Read through the OTHER USEFUL PHRASES box with the class and remind them of the KEY LANGUAGE.

- Then allow 15–20 minutes for the presentations but tell students they should not discuss the different artists at this stage.

- Monitor to note mistakes with the KEY LANGUAGE and OTHER PHRASES.

- Finally, correct a selection of the mistakes you noted earlier.

8 Keep students in the same groups as exercise 7b and give them 15 minutes to discuss the artists.

- Tell students they can introduce the additional points they were given in the Coursebook.

- Monitor to note mistakes with phrases for agreeing/ disagreeing, and persuading.

9 Ask each group to decide on two artists.

- Elicit decisions and the reasons for these from the class.

HOMEWORK OPTIONS

Students do the exercises on page 65 of the Workbook.
Students write an email to the director of the Marco Giordano Gallery, saying which artists their group decided on in exercise 9 and explaining why.
Students do exercise KL 4 on page 151 in the Language reference.

9.5 STUDY AND WRITING SKILLS

IN THIS LESSON

Lesson topic and staging

This lesson focuses on expanding your vocabulary and writing an online review. Students look at a list of sentences using *nice*, replace it with other adjectives and then read about expressing yourself well. Students then match adjectives to uses of *nice* before finding alternatives for another set of basic adjectives and focusing on common collocations. Next, students discuss what a good review contains, then read and analyse the organisation and language of a film review. Finally, students write a film review themselves.

Objectives

By the end of the lesson, students should have:

- extracted specific information and language items from a reading text
- learned about extending their range of vocabulary and practised this with different basic adjectives
- written a film/DVD review.

Common European Framework

Students can write simple connected texts, link a series of discrete items into a connected linear sequence of points and described a film.

Timings

If short of time, you could set exercise 9 for homework. A possible lesson break would be after exercise 4b on page 98.

WARM-UP

This activity introduces the topic of films and asks students to use adjectives to describe films they like/dislike.

- Ask students how often they go to the cinema or watch DVDs.
- Write the following on the board: *horror, thriller, love story, historical drama, comedy, documentary*.
- Tell students to rank the types of film from favourite to least favourite. They can use their dictionaries.
- Then ask students to think of one adjective for each type of film that describes why they like it or not (e.g. *thriller – exciting*).
- Put students into pairs to compare their lists and give reasons.

1 Ask students if they overuse any particular adjective and elicit *good/nice* and other examples.

- Read the instructions with the class and give students five minutes to decide the meaning of *nice* in the different phrases.
- Ask students to compare with a partner before you elicit answers from the class.
- Finally, tell students that phrases 1, 2 and 5 are fixed expressions and not normally used with adjectives other than *nice*.

> Possible answers: 1 enjoyable, productive; 2 pleasant, enjoyable; 3 friendly, charming, I like her; 4 fashionable, it suits you; 5 refreshing, to make us feel better; 6 friendly neighbours, pleasant environment

2 Give students one minute to read the text and then elicit if it is true of their language.

- Focus on the fact that precision is more important in writing than in speaking.

3 Set the activity and tell students they can use their dictionaries if necessary.

- Ask students to compare with a partner before you check answers with the class.
- In feedback, check students' pronunciation of difficult words (e.g. *picturesque, stylish*).

> 1 beautiful, picturesque; 2 delicious, tasty;
> 3 relaxing, restful; 4 stylish, trendy; 5 charming, friendly; 6 productive, useful

4a Give students eight minutes for this activity and tell them to use their dictionaries if necessary.

- Warn them that some adjectives are more difficult to put in the lists than students will initially think.
- Ask students to compare with a partner before you check answers with the class.
- Check students' pronunciation of difficult words (e.g. *monotonous, appalling*).
- Then ask students to read the paragraph and check they understand the difference between a dictionary and a thesaurus (bring copies of each to the lesson).

> 1 brilliant, outstanding, terrific; 2 appalling, awful, dreadful; 3 absorbing, compelling, gripping;
> 4 heartbreaking, moving, touching; 5 monotonous, repetitive, tedious, 6 amusing, hilarious, witty;
> 7 exhilarating, nailbiting, thrilling; 8 absurd, laughable, ridiculous

4b Collocations

- Put students in pairs or small groups so they can brainstorm the collocations.
- Tell students not to worry if they are unsure about answers, but, to read the Longman Language Activator entry on page 174 to check.

- Go through answers and the notes in brackets with the class.
- Finally, emphasise that the adjectives here all have the same basic idea and it is the collocations that show the use of each.

> 1 absorbing, gripping, compelling (Note: a book can be fascinating if it is factually based.); 2 fascinating; 3 gripping, compelling (Note: a film can also be absorbing, although this is not mentioned in the dictionary entry.)

WRITING SKILLS: an online review

5a If you used the Warm-up, students will have used vocabulary for different films already. Make sure you put students into different pairs from the Warm-up.

- Give students five minutes to discuss the questions and encourage them to give as much information as possible for number 3.
- Elicit a few ideas from the class.

5b Give students one minute to tick the items they think should be included.

- Ask students to compare with a partner.
- As you elicit ideas from the class, ask students if they agree and why/why not?

> All the items are possible in an online review except what happens at the end.

6a Focus students on the photo and ask them if they have seen this film and if it was good. Give/elicit the name (*Casino Royale* – a Bond/007 movie).

- Then give students one minute to read the review and answer the question. Students do not need to use dictionaries in this activity.
- Elicit an answer from the class.

> A positive review overall (with some negative criticisms)

6b Ask students to read the list (1–8) and then give them five minutes to read the text.

- Ask students to compare with a partner before you check answers with the class.
- Finally, if students have seen the film, ask them if this is a fair review.

> 1 Paragraphs A and C; 2 Paragraph A; 3 Paragraph A; 4 Paragraph D; 5 Paragraph B; 6 Paragraphs A and D; 7 Paragraph B; 8 Paragraph D

7 Explain that online reviews normally use interesting adjectives because they are expressing an opinion and want the reader to understand exactly what the writer thought.

- Ask students to find all the italicised adjectives (seventeen).

- Read the instructions and tell students that if they use a replacement adjective once if may be too repetitive to keep using it.
- Give students ten minutes to change the adjectives.
- While they are working, write all the adjectives on the board for use in feedback.
- Ask students to compare with a partner before you elicit answers from the class.
- Write the suggestions students make next to the appropriate adjective on the board.

> Answers depend on students' own choices but you should check that each one is appropriate for the noun, and has the correct basic idea (see exercise 4).

8a Adverbs

- Give students a few minutes to find the adverbs and then match them.
- Ask students to compare with a partner before you check answers with the class.

> totally – completely; particularly – especially; generally – usually; really – truly; definitely – certainly

8b Students do this activity individually and then compare with a partner.

- Go through answers with the class and check students' pronunciation of *particularly* and *especially*.

> 1 totally, completely; 2 definitely, certainly, 3 generally, usually; 4 particularly, especially, 5 really, truly

9 Give students one minute to choose the film they are going to write about.

- Ask them to read the review in exercise 6 again to remind them of the organisation and style.
- If student can't remember the actors, director, etc., tell them to leave this information out or give them time to do research on the Internet.
- Then give students 30–40 minutes to write their reviews.
- Monitor to help with vocabulary and point out serious mistakes if necessary.
- When they have finished, ask them to read their work again to see if they have used a variety of adjectives and adverbs.
- Take the reviews in for marking, paying particular attention to the organisation, register and use of a variety of adjectives and adverbs.

HOMEWORK OPTIONS

Students do the exercises on pages 65–66 of the Workbook.

Students find a film review on the Internet and practise replacing the adjectives it uses with alternatives.

REVIEW

UNITS 7–9

GRAMMAR

1a Ask students to read the two paragraphs and check they understand *the wealth of the oceans* (the ocean's resources).

- Put students into pairs and give them five minutes to discuss the ideas in the paragraphs.
- Elicit ideas from two or three pairs and ask the rest of the class if they agree and why/why not.

1b Keep students in the same pairs as exercise 1a and give them three minutes to discuss this question and give reasons for their opinions.

- Elicit ideas from two or three pairs and ask the rest of the class if they agree and why/why not.

2a Focus students on the title of the text and the picture and ask them what they think it is about.

- Then ask students to read the first paragraph and see if their prediction was correct.
- Tell students not to worry about vocabulary and the gaps in the text at this stage.
- Next, ask students to read the five headings and show them A, B, C, D and E in the text.
- Give students two minutes to read the text and write the appropriate number in the space provided.

  1 D; **2** C; **3** B; **4** E; **5** A

2b Give students ten minutes for this activity.

- Ask students to compare with a partner before you check answers with the class.

  1 b) (Note: c) is also possible, but not normally accepted as 'correct' English.); **2** a); **3** c); **4** c); **5** a); **6** a); **7** c); **8** c); **9** b); **10** b); **11** a); **12** a)

VOCABULARY

3 Focus students on the title of the text and elicit what they know about Brad Pitt.

- Then give them ten minutes to read the text and choose the correct answers.
- Ask students to compare with a partner before you check answers with the class.

  1 celebrities; **2** paparazzi; **3** restored; **4** run-down; **5** innovative; **6** commission; **7** collaboration; **8** contemporary; **9** thought-provoking; **10** controversial; **11** traditional; **12** overcome

4 Ask students to match all the words and then compare their answers with a partner.

- Go through answers with the class.

  1 c); **2** e); **3** a); **4** b); **5** h); **6** d); **7** g); **8** f)

KEY LANGUAGE

5 Set the context and then read through the instructions with the class.

- Ask students to read the statements and then play the track without pausing.
- Ask students to compare with a partner before you check answers with the class.

  1 True (I'm not exactly clear); **2** False (we can make the necessary changes); **3** Not given; **4** True (low running costs) (Note: whether the lights are expensive to *buy* is not given.); **5** True (a legal requirement to provide disabled access in public buildings); **6** Not given (but there will be a lift for wheelchair users *near* the entrance).

6a Give students ten minutes to complete the sentences.

- Ask them to compare answers with a partner.

6b Play the track for students to check their answers.

- Ask students to compare with a partner and, if necessary, ask them to look at the audioscript on page 185.
- Go through answers with the class.

  1 moving on; **2** be a good idea; **3** Let's go; **4** we certainly need; **5** that's it for; **6** be more specific; **7** you mean by; **8** explain that in

Track 3.7

Architect, Directors

A: Good morning everyone. I'm here to talk about the plans for extending the gallery. First I'd like to talk about some queries we have with your brief. Then I'd like to go through one or two of the planning issues. Finally, I'll be asking for your contributions to the discussion. So, moving on to the brief. I'm not exactly clear on the number of visitors you expect each day. This has quite a big impact on the provision of toilet facilities and cloakroom space. So perhaps you could give us a more precise indication, so we can make the necessary changes. We also need to know if you want any exterior lighting on the building – I think it might be a good idea to have that. OK, that's all I have to say about the brief. Let's go on to the planning issues. I've noticed that you haven't mentioned disabled access in your brief. Perhaps you aren't aware that it is now a legal requirement to provide disabled access in public buildings? So, we certainly need to make provision for that – I don't think it's going to be a problem but I just wanted to make you aware of it. OK, that's it for the planning issues; now I'd like to invite any questions or comments.

D1: Yes. You mentioned exterior lighting. Could you be more specific?

A: Of course. It's absolutely essential to make the public aware of the extension and having a building lit up at night does attract a lot of attention. There are several new types of spotlight that are very effective but have low running costs.

D 1: I see.

D 2: And what do you mean by disabled access? Could you explain that in more detail please?

A: Sure. Basically, what I'm saying is that we need to provide a lift for wheelchair users near the entrance area and the bookshop …

LANGUAGE CHECK

7 Do the first example with the class.

- Then give students eight minutes to add words to the other sentences. (Note: students may want to put two words in number 2 (*all water*) as this is the phrase on page 74 in the Coursebook. Emphasise they should only put one word and monitor to check they have chosen *water*.)

- Ask students to compare with a partner before you check answers with the class.

1 Reservations are being <u>made</u> for the hotel.; 2 Don't worry – it's <u>water</u> under the bridge (Note: *all water* is perhaps more common than just *water* but both are possible.); 3 The new office was scheduled <u>to</u> be finished within six months.; 4 It might <u>be</u> a good idea to discuss it first.; 5 The website allows people <u>to</u> contact their old school friends.; 6 Clare <u>had</u> her handbag stolen on the bus.; 7 That film didn't really live <u>up</u> to my expectations.; 8 To get this job you have to be highly <u>qualified.</u>; 9 It's absolutely <u>unique</u>. There's nothing like it.; 10 OK, that's <u>it</u> for the designs.

LOOK BACK

8 The aim of this activity is to remind students of areas they looked at in Units 7–9. This will help reinforce any language or skills they had difficulties with or were particularly good at.

learn about the present continuous passive: 7.2, exercise 6; study how prefixes change meaning: 7.3, exercise 5; write about a building that interests you: 7.1, exercise 8b; study which verbs are followed by an object and infinitive: 8.2, exercise 5; learn about a structure we use to talk about a bad experiences that has happened to us: 8.3, exercise 7; listen to people's views on globalisation: 8.1, exercise 5b; read about Henri Cartier-Bresson: 9.2, exercise 2; study adverb-adjective collocations: 9.2, exercise 5; practise putting adverbs in the correct place: 9.3, exercise 8

If students have problems remembering these exercises, you could put them into small groups to remind each other (as appropriate) of the vocabulary learned, the content of the text, the topic they talked about.

To extend the activity, ask students to choose one of the exercises and write a test for other students. This could be a list of questions, a true/false, a gapfill, etc.

10 Psychology

10.1 GROUP PSYCHOLOGY

IN THIS LESSON

Lesson topic and staging

This lesson looks at how well groups work together. Students discuss teams they've been in and then focus on adjectives to describe people before practising the pronunciation of these. Students then read a web page about how teams function and listen to a lecture about group dynamics. Next, students focus on vocabulary taken from the listening and finally discuss who in the class would take different roles in a team.

Objectives

By the end of the lesson, students should have:

- extracted specific information and language items from a reading and a listening text
- extended their range of vocabulary related to describing people's personalities and working together
- participated in a group discussion to decide who would be good in which role in a team.

Timings

If short of time, you could drop exercise 8b on page 103. A possible lesson break would be after exercise 5 on page 102 or exercise 7 on page 103.

WARM-UP

This activity introduces the idea of describing people's personalities (and appearance).

- Elicit the names of four famous people and write them on the board. The people must be known to all students in the class.
- Then tell them to think of three adjectives to describe this person. They must use at least two personality adjectives and can use their dictionaries if necessary.
- Put students into small groups and tell them to take it in turns to say their three adjectives.
- The others in the group must guess who is being described.

Sigmund Freud quote:

This quote means that, like an iceberg, most of what constitutes someone's psychology is hidden from other people. We only see a small part of a person's 'mind', the background experiences and feelings that influence it.

i Sigmund Freud (1856–1939) was one of the most influential psychologists of the 19th and 20th centuries and his ideas are still very much used and discussed today. He founded the psychoanalytical school of psychology and placed great emphasis on the influence of people's previous experiences on the way they behave.

SPEAKING

1 Focus students on the title of this lesson (Group Psychology) and elicit that this is about how people in groups relate to one another.

- Then give students a few minutes to think of their answers to questions 1–4 before putting them into groups of three or four for the discussion.
- Tell students number 3 means Did the people work/play well together or were there problems?
- Get a few ideas from the class and take this opportunity to elicit/give *group dynamics*.

2 Ask students to read the adjectives and tick any they used.

- Then set the second question and tell students they can use their dictionaries if necessary.
- Ask students to compare ideas with a partner before you elicit a few ideas from the class.

pronunciation

3a Stress patterns

- Do the first example with the class (*ambition – ambitious*) to demonstrate what the rubric means by 'nouns related to these adjectives'.
- Then give students ten minutes to find the nouns and write adjective–noun pairs.
- If you are short of time, put students into pairs and ask students to do half the words each.
- When they have finished, ask them to compare their answers with a partner (or another pair).
- Elicit answers from the class and write them on the board for use in exercise 3b.
- For adjective–noun pairs, see the audioscript below exercise 3b.

3b Give students a few minutes to mark the stress and then compare with a partner.

- Note: students may not know if the stress pattern changes unless they have marked the stress correctly. This will not be done until students have listened and checked their answers. It may be better to tell students to answer the question after they have listened to check.

- Set the question about changing stress patterns and, if possible, elicit a few answers from the class.
- Play the track, pausing after each pair of words to allow students to check their answers.
- Go through answers with the class, marking the correct stress on the board and eliciting/showing students where the stress pattern changes.
- Play the track again, pausing after each pair of words for students to repeat. Correct if necessary.

> **Audioscript and answers to exercise 3:**
> **Track 3.8**
> ambitious – ambition authoritative – authority
> conscientious – conscientiousness creative – creativity
> diplomatic – diplomacy energetic – energy
> knowledgeable – knowledge objective – objectivity
> practical – practicality resourceful – resourcefulness

READING

4 Focus student on the title of the introductory paragraph in the text (Belbin Model) and ask students if they've heard of this.

- Give students one minute to read the introduction only and find out how may people Belbin says you should have in a team.
- Students then work individually to read the table and answers the questions in exercise 4.
- Note: only put students in pairs to say if they agree with their partner's choices if your students know each other fairly well. Students may not be happy if their partner doesn't agree.

5 Give students five minutes to match the adjectives.

- Ask them to compare with a partner before you check answers with the class.

> Plant = creative; Resource investigator = resourceful; Coordinator = authoritative; Shaper = energetic; Monitor-evaluator = objective; Teamworker = diplomatic; Implementer = practical; Completer-finisher = conscientious; Specialist = knowledgeable. The extra adjective is *ambitious*.

LISTENING

6a Set the context and give students a few minutes to order the stages.

- Ask them to compare with a partner.
- Answers are checked in exercise 6b.

6b Give students two minutes to match the names and stages but tell them not to worry if they are unsure.

- Play the track without pausing and then ask students to compare answers in pairs.
- Go through the answers below with the class. (The audioscript is below exercise 7.)

- To follow up, ask students if they experienced these stages in the teams they discussed in exercise 1.

> **1** forming – b); **2** storming – c); **3** norming – a);
> **4** performing – e); **5** adjourning – d)

7 Ask students to read the questions and try to answer them from memory.

- Then play the track again and ask students to compare answers in pairs.
- Go through answers and the note in brackets with the class. (Answers are bold in the audioscript below.)

> **1** a) 1940s, 1950s; b) 1960s; **2** the period when everyone likes everyone else at the beginning of something (a *honeymoon* is literally the holiday a married couple take immediately after their wedding, i.e. when they are completely happy and in love); **3** pop groups, football teams, reality TV shows

> **Audioscript and answers to exercises 6 and 7:**
> **Track 3.9**
> Good morning everyone. Our topic today is group dynamics. I want to talk about how groups develop over a period of time. So I'll describe the stages that groups often go through.
> Erm, first of all, I'd like to mention an academic who did some interesting early work on groups. His name's Kurt Lewin, you spell Kurt, K.U.R.T, by the way. Lewin was one of the first researchers to study groups scientifically, so he's important. **1 He [*Lewin*] published his results during the 1940s and 1950s.** And he created the term 'group dynamics' to describe how groups and individuals act and react in changing situations.
> OK, the next really important contribution came from a researcher, Bruce Tuckman. **1 Tuckman developed a theory about groups in 1965.** He argued that groups went through four stages.
> Now I'd like to look briefly at each of the stages in turn: First, 'Forming'. **2 This is the stage when the group pretends to get on well with each other and everyone seems to be happy. It's a kind of honeymoon period.** Next is the 'Storming' stage. As the name suggests, at this stage, members of the group are less polite to each other and they try to resolve their issues, even if they lose their tempers at times. Individual group members may fall out with each other as the true personalities of group members become clearer at this time.
> 'Norming' is the stage after that. Members get used to each other at this stage. They begin to trust each other, share information and are much more productive as they get down to the job of working together.
> The final stage is 'Performing'. The members of the group have common goals. The atmosphere in the group is good. They work efficiently together and cooperate effectively with each other.
> Those are the four stages in the development of the group. Maybe I should say too, Tuckman added a fifth stage. He called it 'Adjourning'. That's the stage when the group breaks up. Of course, some groups never even reach the 'Norming' stage. If they don't trust each other, and members find they cannot put up with each other the group may break up early, before the 'Norming' stage.
> *continued...*

Tuckman's theory is useful and of practical value. Think for a moment about **3 pop groups** you know, the Beatles, for example. They went through all five stages. During the 'Performing' stage, they were very effective, and wrote and performed some of their best songs, but eventually John Lennon moved away from the group and after Paul McCartney left, the band began to break up. You can also think of successful **3 football teams** which go through those stages. After early struggles, they have a period of success, they win championships, and then the team breaks up – for whatever reason. Finally, a very contemporary example would be in **3 reality TV shows** such as Big Brother, where the way the group works is actually the most interesting part of the programme. So Tuckman's model is a good one, and it's useful for analysing group dynamics.

Now are there any questions so far...(*fade*)

VOCABULARY: working together

8a Students do this activity individually and use their dictionaries if necessary.

- Ask students to compare with a partner before you check answers with the class.

  1 f); **2** e); **3** c); **4** a); **5** d); **6** b)

8b Check students know the form *get used to + -ing/* noun for number 2.

- Students do this activity individually and then compare answers with a partner.

- Encourage students to ask follow-up questions to get as much information as possible for each sentence.

- Elicit answers from a few students and ask them for further information if possible.

SPEAKING

9 Ask students to read the instructions and decide in their groups whether to organise a party or a wedding.

- Then give them 15–20 minutes to do activities 1–3.

- Monitor while students are speaking and note mistakes with vocabulary.

- When they have finished, elicit a few ideas for number 3 only from two or three groups.

- Finally, correct some of the mistakes you noted earlier.

HOMEWORK OPTIONS

Students do the exercises on page 67 of the Workbook.

Students do exercise V1 6 on page 153 in the Language reference.

10.2 PEER PRESSURE

IN THIS LESSON

Lesson topic and staging

This lesson looks at peer pressure and how it affects people. Students discuss the meaning of *peer pressure* and then read a leaflet about teenage bullying. They then look at idioms with the word *mind* and practise using these. Next, students look at relative clauses taken from the text, focus on their use and practise using them. Finally, students use relative clauses to talk about a personalised situation.

Objectives

By the end of the lesson, students should have:

- extracted specific information and language items from a reading text

- extended their range of idioms using the word *mind*

- revised/extended their understanding of relative clauses and practised using these

- discussed various personalised situations using relative clauses.

Timings

If short of time, you could drop exercise 4a and 4b and set them for homework. A possible lesson break would be after exercise 4b on page 104.

WARM-UP

This activity introduces the topic of doing things because we want to or because other people want us to.

- Ask students if they always do what they want to or if they sometimes do what others want.

- Then give students three minutes to think of two things they regularly do because they want to and two things because other people want them to.

- Put students into pair or small groups to compare their answers.

- Finally, ask the class if they chose similar activities and elicit a few reasons we do things because others want us to.

READING

1 Focus students on the title of this lesson and elicit that *peers* are people around your age in the same social group and *peer pressure* is the influence others have on your actions and opinions.

- Give students two minutes to tick the items they believe are examples of peer pressure. They can use dictionaries if necessary.
- Then put students in pairs or small groups to discuss their answers and give reasons.
- Finally, elicit an answer and reasons for each item in the list and check students understand *bullying*.

> Any of the items might be examples of peer pressure. Answers depend on students' own opinions.

2 Focus students on the title of the leaflet and the photo on page 104 and ask them who it's written for (parents and children).

- Ask students to underline the four questions in the leaflet
- Then give them one minute to read the text but not to underline or take notes.
- Put students into pairs to discuss answers to the four questions, but tell them not to read the text in detail.
- Elicit possible answers from the class, but don't insist on complete accuracy at this stage.

> 1 doing/thinking something that other want you to do/think because you want to be accepted; 2 how they dress, talk, music they listen to, attitudes they adopt (their opinions), and how they behave; 3 yes, definitely; 4 they need to know who their children are socialising with and encourage them not to enter situations where they will be pressurised

3a Give students five minutes to read the text and take short notes if necessary.

- Ask students to compare with a partner before you check answers with the class.
- In feedback, check students understand *self-esteem* (the level of confidence you feel about your own abilities), *conform/conformity* (behaving the same as the majority of people) and *going against the grain* (not conforming).

> 1 children and young adults; 2 a student who gave the wrong answer to a question because all the others in class gave the wrong answer, even though he knew it was wrong; 3 no, sometimes people like them; 4 feel lonely, have low self-esteem, become depressed; 5 parents: know the people children are socialising with, make children stay out of situations where they will be pressurised; children: learn to say 'no', choose friends wisely, talk to someone they trust, think about the results of their actions, be true to themselves

3b Students discuss this question in small groups and give examples from their (or people they know) experience.

VOCABULARY: idioms with *mind*

4a If necessary, elicit what an *idiom* is (an expression where the meaning is not completely clear from the individual words).

- Give students three minutes to do this activity and compare answers with a partner.
- Check answers with the class and tell them that *out of your mind* can also mean *extremely worried*.

> 1 b); 2 d); 3 c); 4 e); 5 a)

4b Tell students they will need to change the form of some idioms when they put them in the gaps.

- Give students three minutes to do this activity and compare answers with a partner.
- Check answers and read through the notes in brackets with the class.

> 1 make up my mind (+ *about* + something); 2 peace of mind; 3 keep an open mind; 4 out of your mind (+ *with* worry/fear); 5 in two minds (+ *about* something)

For further practice, ask students to do exercise V2 7 on page 153 in the Language reference.

GRAMMAR: relative clauses

This grammar focus might be mainly revision at this level. In exercises 5 and 6, make sure you elicit rather than give students information, and encourage them to work as independently as possible.

5 Remind students that a relative clause adds more information to a sentence and elicit an example from the class (e.g. 'He's the man that I spoke to yesterday.').

- Don't elicit/give any further information about relative clauses at this stage.
- Give students three minutes to underline the clauses in the text and ask them compare with a partner.
- Elicit answers from the class and that the relative pronoun is not being used in Part 2.

> Part 1: when we are influenced to do something; who are about the same age; with whom they socialise; which is the most common form of social influence; Part 2: which means peer pressure can be powerful and hard to resist; who are low on confidence and unsure of themselves; (that) they would not normally do; who knew the correct answer to a question; Part 3: which means others are less likely to call the behaviour bullying; when their children are being bullied; Part 4: with whom their children are associating; in which they know they would be pressurised

☀ If possible, reproduce the leaflet so that the whole class can see it (perhaps on an Interactive Whiteboard or an overhead projector). As you check answers to exercises 5, 6 and 7, highlight the relevant parts of the text.

6a It may be easier to reorder the stages in this exercise as below:

- First, ask students to underline the correct word in definitions 1 and 2 (this should be revision at this level).
- Second, check answers with the class.
- Third, ask them to identify which clauses from exercise 5 are defining/non-defining.
- Finally, check answers with the class, but don't elicit further information about these clauses at this stage.

> Choose the correct words: **1** non-defining; **2** defining. All the clauses from exercise 5 are defining relative clauses, except *which means peer pressure can be powerful …* and *which means others are less likely … .*

6b Emphasise that students do not need to use all the words in the box.

- Give students five minutes to complete the rules, referring to the examples in the text for help.
- Ask students to compare with a partner and if necessary look at G1 on page 152 in the Language reference.
- Go through answers with the class and refer to the leaflet for examples.
- Read through the Grammar tip with the class.

> **1** non-defining; **2** whom; **3** which; **4** before; **5** that

7a Give students a maximum of one minute to think about the question and then elicit an answer from the class.

> b)

7b Give students a maximum of one minute to find the example and then briefly compare with a partner.

- Elicit the answer from the class and remind students that this kind of relative clause is non-defining.

> … which means others are less like to call the behaviour bullying.

☀ Ask all students to read G1 in the Language reference on page 152 because this may contain other information they need reminding of. Monitor to provide clarification of points.

8 Set the task and focus students on the example (1–f) at the bottom on the options.

- Tell students that some relative clauses may come in the middle of sentences 1–9.
- Give students ten minutes for this activity.

- Monitor to point out mistakes but encourage students to look at exercises 5, 6 7, and the Language reference to help them self-correct.
- Ask students to compare with a partner before you check answers with the class.

> **1** f) We are seeking a counsellor to whom we can refer special cases.; **2** e) Even the bullies were crying, which was surprising.; **3** i) Kurt Lewis, who many see as the father of social psychology, fled to the USA from Germany.; **4** h) Teenagers like to turn for advice to other young people who they sympathise with.; **5** d) People who are easily influenced will follow someone else's lead first.; **6** c) The type of peer pressure that leaves you feeling confused or hurt is never good.; **7** g) Peers are the individuals with whom a child or an adolescent identifies most.; **8** b) We took all the teenagers to the seaside, which made a good break for them.; **9** a) The bullying problem (,) about which we had a lot of discussion (,) has now been resolved. (Note: this could be defining OR non-defining.)

☀ If possible, produce the complete sentences so that all students can clearly see where the relative clause is inserted and the punctuation.

SPEAKING

9 Ask students to read the instructions and the relative clauses, and check they understand *relief* (the feeling when you expect something to go wrong which doesn't).

- Then ask students to read the example before putting them into groups for the activity.
- Allow ten to fifteen minutes for this activity and encourage students to make their sentences without writing them down.
- Finally, get a few ideas from the class.

HOMEWORK OPTIONS

Students do the exercises on pages 68–69 of the Workbook.

Students write a blog message describing one of the situations from exercise 9 and using relative clauses to comment. In the next lesson, they post the messages round the room for everyone to read. Others then decide on the most interesting/amusing/disappointing situation described.

Students do exercises G1 1, 2, 3 on page 153 in the Language reference.

10.3 PSYCHOLOGY AT WORK

Lesson topic and staging

This lesson looks at the psychological profiling of criminals. Students read a about a person you wouldn't normally expect to commit a crime. They then read about criminal profiling before focusing on vocabulary related to this topic. Next, students look at the use of reduced relative clauses in the text and then practise using them. Students then discuss a book/film they have read/seen about profiling or serial killers. Finally, students write a summary of the text on psychological profiling they read earlier.

Objectives

By the end of the lesson, students should have:

- extracted specific information and language items from reading texts
- revised and/or extended their range of vocabulary related to criminal profiling
- revised/learned about reduced relative clauses and practised using these
- discussed a book or film about profiling or serial killers
- written a summary of a text about criminal profiling.

Timings

If short of time, you could set exercise 10 for homework. A possible lesson break would be after exercise 6 on page 107.

This activity introduces the topic of people we think shouldn't commit crimes.

- First, elicit a few reasons why people commit crimes (they are angry about something, depressed, need money, insane, etc.).
- Then write the following on the board: *politician, business person, police office, lawyer, prison guard.*
- Tell students to rank the people from most to least likely to commit a crime.
- Put them into pairs to discuss their answers and give reasons.
- Finally, elicit ranking from one student in the class and ask the others if they agree and why/why not.

1a Use the Warm-up as a lead-in to this exercise and/or explain that the short text is about a person we wouldn't normally expect to commit a crime.

- Ask students to read the text very quickly and elicit why we wouldn't expect him to commit a crime.
- Check that students understand *devoted to his mother* (loved very much, always did things for her) and *stable marriage* (no problems with the relationship).
- Then give students three minutes to discuss the possible crime before checking on page 173.
- Ask students if they are surprised he committed this crime and why/why not.
- Finally, tell students that this is a true case that happened in the UK.

1b Set the question and elicit ideas from the class.

2 Focus students on the title of the article and check they understand it (looking at the background, habits, interests of a person and deciding what they are like and what they might do).

- Ask students to read the questions and check they understand *criminal profiler* (the person who looks at the psychological profile of criminals or possible criminals).
- Put students into pairs to discuss the questions.
- Then give them two minutes to read the text and compare their ideas. Tell them not to worry about unknown vocabulary at this stage.
- Go through answers with the class and check they understand *motives* (reasons for doing something) and *offender* (a criminal).
- Finally, ask students if their ideas were similar to those in the text.

> by investigating behaviour, motives and background of criminals; it can identify actual or potential offenders

3 Give students eight minutes for this activity.

- Tell them to underline the relevant information in the paragraphs they identify.
- Ask students to compare with a partner before you check answers with the class.
- Check students' pronunciation of *minute* (adjective).
- Finally, ask students if they have read books or seen movies/TV shows about criminal profiling, if they liked them and why.

> **1** Paragraph D: by investigating behaviour, motives and background of criminals; **2** Paragraph D: place of residence; **3** Paragraph B: serial killers, mass murderers; **4** Paragraph C: James Brussels; **5** Paragraph D: minute details of the crime scene; **6** Paragraph B, C, E: serial killers, aeroplane hijacking, suicide bombers, mass murderers, bomber; **7** Paragraph A: criminal profiling

VOCABULARY

4 Give students a maximum of five minutes for this activity.

- Go through answers with the class and check their pronunciation of *psychiatrist*.

> **1** motive; **2** deduce; **3** psychiatrist; **4** profile; **5** case file; **6** assessment

GRAMMAR: reduced relative clauses

5a Give students one minute to find the sentences in the text.

- Write them on the board (or see the Tip below).

> a number of letters mailed by the suspect; the crime scene, enabling them to describe the ...

5b Give students a couple of minutes to discuss this question in pairs.

- Elicit answers from the class and highlight the relevant parts of the sentences on the board.

- Explain that reduced relative clauses are often used to improve the style of a piece of writing. Also, we can use reduced relatives for clauses which use other relative pronouns (e.g. *who*, *that*).

> Sentence 1: (Note: this is a passive structure.) The relative pronoun *which* and the auxiliary *were* are dropped. Only the past participle *mailed* is used here.; Sentence 2: the relative pronoun *which* is dropped and the verb (*enables*) is changed to the *-ing* form.

If possible, reproduce the text so that the whole class can see it (perhaps on an Interactive Whiteboard or an overhead projector). As you check answers to exercises 5 and 6, highlight the relevant parts of the text.

6 Tell students there are seven reduced relative clauses in the text (in addition to the two examples in 5a), but they only need to find four. They should, however, try to find some which use the past participle and some which use the *-ing* form.

- Elicit the examples from the class and write them on the board (or see the Tip above).

- Then put students in pairs to answer questions 1 and 2 (see Tip below).

- Go through answers with the class and in each case elicit the full relative clause.

- This is a fairly complicated area of language, so give students a few minutes to read the information in G2 on page 152 in the Language reference.

> Examples from the text: [most commonly] referred to as ...(*which is most commonly referred to as ...*); lead detective profiling the offender (*lead detective who profiles the offender*); traced back to work done (*to work which was done*); methods used to detect criminals (*methods which are used to ...*); profiles performed in the last century (*profiles where were performed in ...*); Buttoned (*which will be buttoned*); the arresting officers (*the officers who arrested* [the bomber]).

Active clauses use the *-ing* form, passive clauses use the past participle.

Students may find number 2 difficult. If necessary, use the first sentence in exercise 5a and *lead detective profiling the offender* as examples. Show students how the full relative clause is formed (i.e. 1.*which were mailed by the suspect*, and 2 *lead detective who profiles the offender*. Then ask which is passive (number 1) and which active (2). Then ask students to look again at how these are written in the text and answer question 2 in exercise 6.

7 Give students five minutes for this activity, referring to exercises 5 and 6, and the Language reference if necessary.

- Ask students to compare with a partner before you check answers with the class.

> **1a** taken; **1b** taking; **2a** making; **2b** made; **3a** developing; **3b** developed; **4a** built; **4b** building

8 Focus students on the photo in this exercise and ask if they've seen this image before. Elicit that it is from the movie *The Silence of the Lambs* and ask students if they've seen it and, briefly, what it's about.

- It they haven't seen it, ask them to predict from the previous content of this lesson and the photo what they think it's about.

- Ask students to read the text quickly to check their ideas.

- Read through the instructions for exercise 8 and remind students that the present participle is the *-ing* form.

- Then give students five minutes to do the activity. Most examples simply involve crossing out the pronoun and auxiliary.

- Ask students to compare with a partner before you check answers with the class.

- Finally, ask students who haven't seen the movie if they would like to, and/or ask the class if they have seen movies or read books similar to this.

> [...] movies ~~which focus~~ focusing on profilers ~~who are~~ investigating criminal cases.; [...] is a film ~~which is~~ directed by [...]; Clarice Starling ~~who is~~ played by Jodie Foster [...]; [...] serial killer, ~~who is~~ named Hannibal Lecter. Lecter, ~~who is~~ currently serving nine [...]; performance of Lecter, ~~who was~~ played by Anthony Hopkins, [...]; Kay Scarpetta series, ~~which was~~ written by Patricia Cornwell.; [...] an FBI criminal profiler ~~who works~~ working for the FBI.

If possible, reproduce the text so that the whole class can see it (perhaps on an Interactive Whiteboard or an overhead projector). As you check answers, highlight the relevant parts of the text.

For further practice, ask students to do exercise G2 4 on page 153 in the Language reference.

SPEAKING

9 Give students a few minutes to think about a book/film they have read/seen and what they would like to say about it.

- Then put students into groups of three or four and ask them to take it in turns to describe the book/film.

- After each description, other students should ask questions to get as much information as possible.

- If others in the group have read/seen the book/film, they should discuss their opinions of it.

- Monitor to note mistakes using the vocabulary from the lesson and relative clauses.

- When they have finished, ask students which of the books/films the would like to read/see.

- Finally, correct some of the more common or important mistakes you noted earlier.

WRITING

10 Set the activity and give students five minutes to underline the key points in the text on psychological profiling.

- Ask them to compare with a partner.

- Then ask students to read the relevant parts of lesson 8.5 again to remind themselves of techniques for summarising.

- Give students 30 minutes to write their summaries.

- Ask them to read the summary and edit if necessary.

- Take the summaries in for marking, paying particular attention to points covered in lesson 8.5.

HOMEWORK OPTIONS

Students do the exercises on pages 70–71 of the Workbook.

Students write a short review of a crime TV programme or movie they have seen. They can look at lesson 9.5 for ideas. In the next, lesson post the reviews round the room and ask all students to read them and decide which programme/movie they would like to see.

Students do exercises G2 4 and V3 8 on page 153 in the Language reference.

10.4 SCENARIO: ASK VANESSA

IN THIS LESSON

Lesson topic and staging

This lesson focuses on the language of giving advice. Students are introduced to the scenario of an agony aunt who gives advice to people on a radio programme and discuss different aspects of this kind of show. Next, students listen to the agony aunt talking to a caller and then focus on the KEY LANGUAGE. Finally, the main TASK asks students to give each other advice on problems provided in the Coursebook and then discuss the problems in groups.

Objectives

By the end of the lesson, students should have:

- learned useful phrases for giving and responding to advice

- used this language in a 'real-life' situation to offer each other advice

- extracted specific information and language items from a listening text

- participated effectively in extended speaking practice.

Common European Framework

Students can use language effectively to express and respond to feelings, express views and opinions, and explain and give reasons.

Timings

If short of time, you could drop exercise 1 but make sure you ask students to read the situation and then lead in to exercise 2. Alternatively, drop exercise 6 as students will have practised the KEY LANGUAGE in exercise 5. A possible lesson break would be after exercise 4c on page 109.

WARM-UP

This activity introduces the topic of problems, advice and who to talk to when you have problems.

- Ask the class what kind of personal problems people have in developed societies and elicit/give all of the following and write them on the board: *financial, relationship with partner, relationship with children, problems with your boss, stress because you're too busy, health problems*.

- Then write the following on the board: *a counsellor, your partner, your friend, your boss, your children, your doctor, a financial advisor*.

- Check students understand *a counsellor* (an independent and neutral person whose job it is to help people with their problems).

- Ask students to decide who they would talk to and why they would choose this person if they had any of the problems listed on the board.

- Put students into small groups to explain their answers.

SITUATION

💡 Throughout this lesson, avoid asking students to refer to their own personal problems but, if necessary, you can ask them to refer to hypothetical situations, e.g. if you knew someone with this problem.

1 Use the Warm-up as a lead in to this activity by telling students they are going to read about someone whose job it is to help people with their problems.

- If you didn't use the Warm-up, elicit different people to talk to if someone had a problem and then focus students on the photo. Elicit that she deals with problems on a radio show.

- Give them one minute to read the situation and then five minutes to discuss the questions in pairs.

- Go through answers with the class.

> 1 a person whose job is giving people advice on the radio, the TV, in a newspaper or magazine. They are not normally psychologists or psychiatrists.; 2–5 Answers depend on students' own ideas.

2 Read through the introduction and questions with the class and ask students to read the summaries.

- Play the track without pausing.

- Ask students to compare with a partner and discuss the reasons for their answer.

- Elicit answers from the class. (The audioscript is on page 186 of the Coursebook.)

> Summary B = correct. (False information in Summary A: early in their marriage he went bankrupt so they didn't have a lot of money; she isn't planning to divorce him. False information in Summary C: It's not only since he retired that he's been spending too much money; she doesn't say he's worried about his debts.)

3a Give students five minutes for this activity.

- While they are speaking, monitor to note what language they use when giving advice. This will help you decide how much of the KEY LANGUAGE they already know and what their weaknesses are.

- Elicit a few ideas from two or three pairs.

3b Set the activity and play the track without pausing.

- Keep students in the same pairs as exercise 3a to discuss the similarities between their advice and Vanessa's.

- Ask two or three pairs if their advice was similar or different. (The audioscript is below exercise 4b.)

KEY LANGUAGE: giving advice

4a Set the context and give students a few minutes to see if they can fill gaps before they listen again.

- Then play the track again, if necessary pausing at the points indicated in the audioscript below.

- Ask students to compare with a partner. Answers are checked in exercise 4b. (Answers are bold in the audioscript below.)

4b Give students a maximum of five minutes to check their answers, using the audioscript on page 186.

- Go through answers with the class.

> 1 f); 2 g); 3 e); 4 h); 5 a); 6 d); 7 b); 8 c); 9 i)

Audioscript and answers to exercises 3 and 4:
Track 3.11
Vanessa, Michelle
V: Well, it's obviously very difficult for you, Michelle, no wonder you're confused and upset.
M: Mmm, I don't know which way to turn, to be honest, that's why I've phoned you. I need some good advice.
V: OK, **1 First of all, I think you need to talk to someone about the debts you have.** A real professional.
M: Yes, but I don't know any professional person who could help us.
V: But I do, Michelle. At the end of the programme, I can give you the name of someone who can advise you how to deal with your debts.
M: Great, thanks very much.
V: **2 And you could also contact your local Citizens Advice Centre** – their services are free. If possible, you should both go there. OK?
M: Mmm, OK.
V: Another thing. Could I ask you, do you have a joint account with your husband?
M: Yes, actually I do. Our account's in both our names.
V: **3 Well, you know, it might be a good idea to have a separate bank account.** Just for the time being. Until your husband gets his finances in order. And tell me, do you have access to the Internet?
M: Yes, I use it at work. And also at home, when my husband isn't using the computer.
V: **4 Great! Well, if I were you, I'd check the Internet to see if there are some websites offering help** – for free, of course. **5 And there's another thing you can do. I'd advise you to contact a finance company.** They might be able to help you. Why don't you look into it? Your bank might be able to advise you and recommend a reputable company.
M: All right, I'll think about that. But what about my husband's spending problem? What can I do about it?
continued...

V: **6 Mmm, it's a serious problem, it's vital that you do something about it. 7 Or should I say, it's vital he does something about it. Why don't you have a serious talk with him?** Tell him his spending is threatening your marriage, because it is. Advise him to seek professional help. There's an association he can join, they have experts who'll help him to control his addiction. I'll give you details later.

M: Thanks, Vanessa. You've given me some good ideas. I must say, I feel a lot better talking to you.

V: Good. I'm pleased to hear it. **8 One final bit of advice. You might consider getting some counselling yourself.** You've had a tough time recently, life's been difficult. You know, you need to think about your relationship with your husband. If he goes on destroying your life, you may have to consider divorce. **9 I know you don't want to do that**, and I hope it doesn't come to that, **but it's essential that your husband changes his behaviour** or it'll make you very unhappy, and possibly destroy your marriage. Think about it.

M: Mmm. Well, thanks very much, Vanessa. Please give me the addresses you mentioned.

V: Of course I will. My staff will contact you at the end of the programme, and you'll get everything you need. Goodbye Michelle, and good luck!

4c Students can do this activity in pairs or groups of three.

- Go through answers with the class and emphasise it is the phrases in exercise 4a that make the advice strong, neutral or tentative, not the content of the advice given.

> **1** f) neutral; **2** g) neutral; **3** e) tentative; **4** h) neutral; **5** a) neutral; **6** d) strong; **7** b) neutral; **8** c) tentative; **9** i) strong

For further practice, ask students to do exercise KL 5 on page 153 in the Language reference.

TASK: an advice phone-in

5a Set the context and divide the class into two groups (A and B).

- Give students two minutes to read their two emails and choose one to discuss later.
- Then give students five minutes to read the email they chose and make a few notes (e.g. on the most serious part of the problem, how the problem started, etc.).
- Put students into A/B pairs and give them five to ten minutes to discuss the problems, decide what content to include in any advice they might give and how strong the advice should be.
- Students do not need to use the phrases from exercise 4 at this stage.
- Monitor to make suggestions and help with vocabulary if necessary.

5b Keep students in the same pairs as exercise 5a.

- Remind them of the KEY LANGUAGE in exercise 4 and go through the OTHER USEFUL PHRASES with the class.
- Give students five minutes to role-play the first situation.
- Monitor to note mistakes with the KEY LANGUAGE and OTHER PHRASES.
- Then give another five minutes for students to swap roles, monitoring again for mistakes.
- When they have finished, ask students for the best piece of advice they received.
- Finally, correct some of the more common or important mistakes you noted earlier.

6 Put the pairs together and give them five to ten minutes for this activity.

- Elicit a few ideas from one or two groups and then ask the class to vote on the most interesting problem and if this problem is common.

HOMEWORK OPTIONS

Students do the exercises on page 72 of the Workbook.

In their roles as agony aunts, students write replies to one of the emails they discussed in exercises 5 and 6

Students do exercise KL 5 on page 153 in the Language reference.

10.5 STUDY AND WRITING SKILLS

IN THIS LESSON

Lesson topic and staging

This lesson focuses on writing a bibliography and referencing, and writing a discursive essay. Students discuss statements about including references in texts. Students then read about a referencing system and identify when this has been used incorrectly. Next, students read parts of an essay and focus on content in the introduction/conclusion and on linking words. Finally, students write an essay giving their opinion on the topic.

Objectives

By the end of the lesson, students should have:

- extracted specific information and language items from reading texts
- learnt about referencing sources in texts and how to write a discursive essay
- written a discursive essay.

Common European Framework

Students can write simple connected texts, link a series of discrete items into a connected linear sequence of points and convey information and ideas on abstract and concrete topics.

Timings

If short of time, you could set exercise 7b for homework. A possible lesson break would be after exercise 2 on page 110.

WARM-UP

This activity introduces the topic of using books as sources of information.

- Put students into pairs and tell them to list all the different things you can use information from books for (e.g. finding someone's telephone number).
- They can list any ideas as long as they are reasonable.
- Tell students they have one minute to do this activity and they need to think of as many ideas as possible.
- Stop them after a minute, ask how many each pair found and then elicit ideas from the class.

STUDY SKILLS: writing a bibliography, referencing

1 Focus students on the photo on page 110 and ask them why they think this man is carrying so many books and what he uses them for.

- If possible, elicit writing an academic essay as one of the ideas.
- Then ask students to read the sentence above exercise 1 and use this as a lead in to the exercise
- Give students ten minutes to discuss the statements and decide if they are correct.
- Elicit students' ideas and go through the answers below. Emphasise that these are the accepted answers in most academic cultures that follow a European/American style.

> 1 correct; 2 correct; 3 correct; 4 incorrect – a quotation can be longer; 5 correct – loose paraphrases are acceptable without referencing; 6 correct (probably); 7 incorrect – you must reference the author; 8 incorrect – as teachers usually want to read their students' opinions too, not just those drawn from others

2 Read the instructions with the class and elicit/tell students that Harvard is one of the most respected universities in the USA and worldwide.

- Ask students to read the extract from the Harvard System of Referencing and then ask them if they are familiar with this system.
- Then give students five minutes to identify which of the entries in the bibliography are incorrect.
- Ask students to compare with a partner before you check answers with the class.

> Incorrect entries are: 2 (because there is no date in brackets, volume and issue number are not given, pages from journal not given); 3 (because there is no date in brackets, no place of publication, or name of publisher); 5 (because it doesn't say when the site was last accessed)

WRITING SKILLS: a discursive essay

3a Focus students on the title of this section of the lesson and ask what a *discursive essay* is (an essay that discusses a point of view or an opinion).

- Ask students if they have to write discursive essays now or if they have ever written one in English.
- Then ask what problems they have/might have if/when they write a discursive essay.
- Read the instructions with the class and check that students understand *only child* (a couple has only one child).

- Put students into groups to do the activity.

3b Give students five minutes to discuss their ideas with other groups.

- Elicit advantages and disadvantages from the class and write them on the board. Students will be able to use these later in the lesson.

💡 If you have any only children in the class and they are willing to do so, they may be able to give the rest of the class some ideas they wouldn't normally think of.

4 Ask students to read the questions and then give them two minutes to read the text and discuss their answers with a partner.

- Elicit answers from the class and emphasise that a discursive essay gives both sides of an argument.

> **1** because it is becoming more common in many parts of the world and people have very different views on this topic; **2** to present the arguments for and against, and decide if it's truly an advantage.

5 Linking words

- To orient students to the next two paragraphs of the essay, ask them to read it and find two advantages and two disadvantages to being an only child.

- Ask them to compare answers with a partner and then elicit ideas from the class.

- Then ask students if they agree with the advantages and disadvantages mentioned in the text.

- Set the activity in the Coursebook and give students two minutes to underline the linking words.

- Ask them to compare with a partner and then discuss which linking words go with uses a)–c).

- Check answers with the class and point out the commas after *In addition*, *As a result*, *Furthermore*, *On the other hand*, *Moreover*, *However*, and before and after *therefore*. Tell students all of these words are normally used at the beginning of a sentence, although it is possible to use them after the subject (see *therefore*).

> **a)** In addition, Another advantage of, Furthermore, Moreover, especially (Note: students may also give *and* as an answer here. This is correct.); **b)** On the other hand; However; **c)** so that, As a result, as, therefore

6 Conclusions

- First ask students what they would expect to find in a conclusion to a discursive essay.

- Then ask them read options 1–4 and see if their ideas are similar.

- Give students one minute to read the conclusion and tick the relevant options.

- Go through answers with the class and emphasise that it is standard practice to include these ideas in a conclusion.

> The following are contained in the text: 1, 2, 4

7a Ask students to read the quote and use their dictionaries if necessary.

- Give them a minute to think about their own opinion.

- Then put students into pairs to discuss the quote.

- Tell students to note the reasons they and their partner agree and disagree.

- Elicit ideas from the class and write them in two columns on the board (agree/disagree).

- Tell students that in a discursive essay you have to give both sides of the argument before reaching a conclusion in your opinion.

7b Ask students to read the instructions and tell them the essay should be about 500 words long.

- Give them plenty of time to research the essay. It might be better for students to do this after the lesson as research may take a long time.

- Tell students to use the extracts in exercises 4, 5 and 6 as a model and to make sure their referencing follows the conventions in exercise 2.

- If students write the essay in class, allow about 40 minutes.

- Monitor to point out mistakes and help with vocabulary if necessary.

- Take the essays in for marking, paying particular attention to referencing, linking words and the content of the introduction and conclusion.

💡 If you think your students will not want to spend a long time researching, tell them they only need to include two or three referenced sources in their essay. All the other ideas can be their own or their partner's from exercise 7a.

HOMEWORK OPTIONS

Students do the exercises on pages 72–73 of the Workbook.

Students write an email to the author of the essay in exercises 3–6 saying they enjoyed reading it, but that they disagree with his/her conclusion. They should write a paragraph saying why they disagree.

11 Cultures

11.1 DEFINING CULTURE

IN THIS LESSON

Lesson topic and staging

This lesson looks at what we mean by *a culture*. Students discuss the term *culture* and features of their own. They then read about defining culture and focus on vocabulary in the text related to this topic. Next, students listen to six people saying what they miss about their cultures and discuss which views they share with these people. Finally, students discuss what items to put in a time capsule to represent their culture(s).

Objectives

By the end of the lesson, students should have:

- extracted specific language items and/or information from a reading and a listening text
- extended their range of vocabulary related to defining culture
- participated in a group discussions to choose objects representative of their culture(s).

Timings

If short of time, you could cut the number of items students need to put in the time capsule in exercise 8 on page 113. A possible lesson break would be after exercise 4 on page 113.

WARM-UP

This activity introduces the topic of culture with a specific reference to customs.

- Focus students on the photos and give them a couple of minutes to decide what is happening in each, what the people look like, etc.
- Put them in pairs to describe the photos to each other but not say which picture they are describing.
- Their partner has to guess which photo is being described.
- Then elicit that all the photos show people drinking tea and ask them to discuss which country/region each photo is of and if they think this is typical.

Ludwig Wittgenstein quote:

This quote means that people's experiences and attitudes are expressed by their language – and their language defines and limits their experiences and attitudes. If there is no word for an idea/action/thing, then it does not exist in a person's experience.

READING AND VOCABULARY: culture

1a If you didn't use the Warm-up activity, focus students on the photos and elicit that all the photos show people drinking tea.

- Put students into pairs to briefly discuss which country/region each photo is of and if they think this is typical of that country/region.
- Set the activity and give students two minutes to note words that immediately come into their minds.
- Put students into pairs to compare and then elicit a few ideas from the class.

☀ In all the speaking exercises below, *don't* encourage others to say what they find strange about each other's cultures as this may offend. Instead, ask them what they find interesting.

1b Give students two minutes to think about this question.

- If necessary, write the following prompts on the board: people, music, religion, food.
- Put students into pairs to compare their ideas and encourage them to ask each other for more information (e.g. 'What does that [food] taste like? Why do people do that?').
- Don't spend long on this discussion as students will talk about their culture in exercise 3c.
- Finally, elicit a few ideas from the class.

2 First, ask students to read quickly and elicit if this is similar to students' ideas in exercise 1.

- Ask students to read the headings in the box.
- Tell students not to worry about unknown vocabulary at this stage.
- Then give them three minutes to read the text again and match the headings.
- Ask students to compare with a partner before you check answers with the class.
- In feedback, check students' pronunciation of *cuisine* and *rituals*.

> 1 Geography; 2 Climate; 3 Language; 4 Cuisine; 5 Values; 6 The arts; 7 Religion; 8 Rules of behaviour; 9 Customs/traditions; 10 Historical events; 11 Life rituals; 12 Institutions; 13 Architecture

3a Tell students to use the headings to predict where to find the words/expressions but not to read the text.

- Students can choose more than one heading, if appropriate.

- Get a few ideas from the class but don't give students the answers as they will find out in exercise 3b.

  > Answers depend on students' predictions.

3b Give students five minutes to read the text and find the words or expressions, using their dictionaries if necessary.

- They may need to read more than one section if any of their predictions in exercise 3a were wrong.

- Ask students to compare with a partner before you check answers with the class.

- In feedback, check students' pronunciation of *terrain*, *dialects*, *etiquette* and *heritage*.

- Finally, ask students if their predictions in exercise 3a were correct.

  > a) staple diet; b) dialects; c) rules of etiquette; d) superstitions; e) terrain; f) commemorations; g) sects; h) heritage

3c Give students one minute to choose three or four words from exercise 3b.

- Put them into pairs or groups of three, if possible not with the student they talked to in exercise 1.

- Allow ten to fifteen minutes and encourage students to ask each other for further information if possible.

- Monitor to note mistakes with vocabulary from exercise 3b and help with additional vocabulary.

- For feedback, ask a few students for the most interesting thing they heard.

- Finally, correct a selection of the mistakes you noted earlier.

For further practice, ask students to do exercise V1 6 on page 155 in the Language reference.

4 Give students a few minutes to read the questions and think about their answers.

- Tell students they only need to think of two or three examples for questions 3 and 4.

- If possible put students into different groups from exercise 3c and allow ten minutes for the discussion.

- Monitor to provide additional vocabulary and note mistakes with the vocabulary from exercise 3b.

- For feedback, elicit two or three answers for each question and ask the rest of the class if they agree.

- Finally, correct a selection of the mistakes you noted earlier.

LISTENING

5 Set the question using *do* or *would*, as appropriate for your students' current situation.

- Give students a minute to think of the first things that come into their heads.

- Put them into pairs to compare and give reasons for their answers.

- Then elicit a few ideas from the class and ask other students if their ideas were similar.

6a Ask students to read items a)–f) and to look at exercise 6b for the spelling of people's names (or see the Tip below).

- Play the track without pausing.

- Ask students to compare with a partner before you check answers with the class.

☀ You could ask students to write a)–f) next to the names in exercise 6b as this will prevent them being distracted by having to copy the spelling.

  > a) Danielle; b) Alessandra; c) Ayla; d) Anna;
  > e) Nancy; f) Carola

6b Ask students to read the questions and then play the track, pausing after each person if necessary.

- Ask students to compare with a partner, then check answers with the class. (Answers are bold in the audioscript below.)

- In feedback, check students understand and can pronounce *anonymous* (you are alone and nobody knows you personally), *intimate* (very private), *dive* (move suddenly into a situation – literally, it means jump head-first into water) and *comfort zone* (a situation where you feel relaxed, secure and happy).

  > **1** it's wonderful, people try hard to make guests feel comfortable; **2** there are many small, local ones you can walk to, you can get everything, they're not anonymous; **3** you can discuss personal and intimate problems with your friends, friends are expected to forget their own problems to help you; **4** everything is fresh, you can get everything from the natural environment, she misses the spices; **5** she dives into a very private comfort zone (i.e. she quickly develops a feeling of love, trust, comfort and being home); **6** you don't need to make arrangements a long time in advance, you call someone and then meet them immediately

> **Audioscript and answers to exercise 6:**
> **Track 3.12**
> *1*
> *Ayla, from Turkey*
> When I'm outside Turkey, travelling for my job, I miss the smell of strong Turkish coffee, and the smell of the food. I really miss our typical Turkish breakfast of white cheese, bread, eggs, honey and olives. I think also of the rain in my home town, and holidays where my family and relatives come together. I miss the prayers we hear five times a day from the mosques. I also think **Turkish hospitality is wonderful**. I miss visiting friends, relatives and neighbours and the way that **Turkish people really try hard to make their guests feel comfortable.** Another thing I miss about Turkish culture is the respect for older people.
> *continued...*

2

Carola, from Germany

When I lived abroad, I missed cycling to places. I didn't see many people on bikes, everyone used cars all the time, even for short distances. Children were taken to school by their parents, and my host father drove to a nearby petrol station to get his newspaper. I thought about getting a bike, but there were no cycle paths in my area, and I felt I'd be a kind of 'outsider' if I cycled to work in the morning.

I also missed small local supermarkets where **you can walk to do your shopping**. In Germany, we have **many small supermarkets in all parts of cities or towns, and you can get everything you need there.** They are **not huge and anonymous,** like the big supermarkets in some other countries.

Talking of food, I missed German bread and German rolls. Bread tastes a lot better in my country, I can tell you.

3

Anna, from Russia

When I worked abroad what I missed most was certain emotional aspects of our culture, not material ones. I certainly missed the Russian style of friendship. In my country, people will **discuss all kinds of very personal problems, even intimate problems** with you. And **they expect friends to forget their own problems and do everything to help you out.** But outside Russia, I noticed people are more individualistic, and even with good friends, the conversations are more superficial, they take less time, and people tend to be more focused on their own problems.

Also, I missed Russian jokes and loud laughter. Russians often organise parties at someone's home, old friends come together and spend hours eating and drinking around a big table, discussing things, singing, dancing. One final thing. I missed our traditional Russian winter, going down snow covered hills on a toboggan with my young son, skiing and skating, playing snowballs and making snowmaidens with our fluffy snow.

4

Danielle, from Cameroon

What did I miss when I was abroad? Definitely the food. In Cameroon, **everything we eat is fresh**, no processing, artificial stuff or colouring. I remember we had to literally chase the chicken, kill it, and then cook it. It took almost the whole afternoon. And then I missed the **spices. We took the tomatoes, basil and peanuts straight out of the field,** it was wonderful! When we wanted a treat, all we had to do was go to the mango or guava or avocado tree and pick it. And if we wanted a snack, we would go to the corn field to get some corn. I tell you, I had no problem keeping slim.

continued...

The weather, I missed that too. Cameroon is a tropical country, so we had some very good weather. Believe it or not, what I missed most was the sun of course, but also the tropical rain. I tell you, when it beats down on top of a tin roof, it produces a sound that's like a lullaby, it makes you feel sleepy.

5

Alessandra, from Italy

I feel comfortable living in foreign countries, especially in Europe. I like the variety of cultures you meet just travelling a few hundred kilometres. But I miss something that just isn't there. It's the sound of my typically Italian language where I grew up. It took me a long time to realise its effect on me. **When I hear people speaking my Italian dialect, then I let myself dive into a very private comfort zone.** It's a blend of feelings consisting of love, trust, comfort, and being 'home'. For me, I've lived and worked in various places around the world, but I've never experienced that anywhere else, except in my home country.

I'm studying in England now and I definitely miss not being able to express my ideas as soon as they come into my mind. I just can't communicate easily and precisely what I think in English, and that frustrates me.

Of course, I miss knowing where to go to find what I need. Being Italian, it means I miss good food, the sun and friendly people. I miss so much, but I'm really enjoying being in England.

6

Nancy, from Argentina

I've travelled all over the world. What do I miss? Well, the first thing that comes to mind is the more relaxed atmosphere we have in the streets, you know, socialising and meeting friends for coffee or dinner. It's a very spontaneous culture. **You don't need to make arrangements a long time in advance. You just phone a friend, and then meet them at home or outside only a few minutes after your phone call.** I should mention our drink, I miss it a lot when I'm overseas. It's called *mate*, it's a traditional drink in a special container. You pour a kind of green tea herb (called *Yerba Mate*) into the container, you add boiling hot water and then sip the tea. It's a kind of ritual. You pass the container around with a group when you get together at someone's home – it's a bit like the Indian tribes used to pass round the 'pipes of peace'. You chat, have fun and talk philosophically about life, the state of the world, and so on. Friendship and bonding are very important in Argentina. I missed all that socialising when I was in England and the United States.

7   Ask students to read the questions and give them one minute to think of some answers.

• Elicit answers from the class.

SPEAKING

8a First, elicit ways that cultures record/present items that represent them (e.g. museums, exhibitions).

• Then ask students to read the rubric and the text in the box and ask students if they have heard of time capsules.

• Put students into groups of three or four, making sure that you have a even number of groups for exercise 8b. Emphasise they must agree on the choices and give reasons.

• Allow ten to fifteen minutes for the discussion and monitor to help with vocabulary if necessary.

• Finally, ask each group for its list and the reasons for choosing one or two of the items.

☼ For multi-national classes, you could make sure there is a mix of nationalities in each group so that the capsule becomes representative of different cultures (e.g. students choose three items each and give reasons). For mono-national classes, if possible make sure there is a mix of ages and sexes in each group. If you are short of time, cut the number of items students can put in the capsule.

8b Each group should now join with another group to share their ideas for the time capsule, and their reasons.

• Monitor to help with vocabulary if neccessary.

• In feedback, ask students if any of the choices were unusual or surprised them.

HOMEWORK OPTIONS

Students do the exercises on page 74 of the Workbook.

Students imagine they are living abroad and write an email or a blog message for friends saying what they miss about their culture. If students really are living abroad they can use real experiences.

Students do exercise V1 6 on page 155 in the Language reference.

11.2 CULTURE SHOCK

IN THIS LESSON

Lesson topic and staging

This lesson looks at culture shock. Students discuss a quote about culture and then read a leaflet about culture shock. They then discuss their experiences of foreign cultures before focusing on adjectives in the text. Next, students listen to someone talking about culture shock and then use this as a source for studying reported speech. Then students read and discuss blogs about studying in a foreign country and finally write a letter giving advice on this topic.

Objectives

By the end of the lesson, students should have:

• extracted specific information and language items from a reading text and a listening text

• extended their range of vocabulary related to personal feelings

• revised/extended their understanding of the uses of reported speech

• discussed the effects of culture shock and studying in a foreign country

• written a letter giving advice on studying in a foreign country.

Timings

If short of time, you could drop exercise 1 and begin the lesson with exercise 2. Alternatively, you could set exercise 11 for homework. A possible lesson break would be after exercise 5b on page 115.

WARM-UP

This activity introduces feelings people experience when they are different from everyone else.

• Focus students on the photo on page 114 and elicit that the black sheep is different from the others.

• Put students in pairs and imagine what the black would say if it could talk (e.g. 'I feel lonely').

• Give them three minutes to think of as many things it might say as possible.

• Elicit ideas from the class and ask students to vote on the best idea.

READING

1   Use the Warm-up as a lead in to this activity and ask students if they think the black sheep might say 'I miss my own culture'.

- Ask students to read the quote and use a dictionary for *sustain* if necessary.

- If students don't understand the quote, paraphrase it: 'Our culture is necessary for us to live and understand the world'.

- Put students into pairs to discuss the quote and then elicit a few ideas from the class.

2 Ask students why it might be difficult living in a foreign culture and elicit *culture shock*.

- Set the activity and remind students that *skim* means to read very quickly and get the general idea.

- Give students one minute for this activity and tell them not to worry about unknown vocabulary.

- Ask students to briefly compare with a partner before you elicit answers from the class.

- The answers below are suggestions only. Accept any reasonable answers from students.

> Suggested answers: A What is culture shock?; B The phases/stages of culture shock.

3 Give students five minutes to re-read Extract B and do the activity.

- Tell them not to worry about unknown vocabulary because they will study this in exercise 5.

- Ask them to compare with a partner before you check answers with the class.

> a) 4; b) 5; c) 3; d) 1; e) 2

4 Give students five minutes to discuss the questions in pairs and then elicit a few ideas from the class.

- For question 3, elicit/give a definition of *reverse culture shock* (feeling culture shock in your own country, e.g. when you return from a long period in a foreign country).

- Tell students they will hear someone talking about this later.

VOCABULARY: adjectives

5a First, tell students to find the adjectives in the leaflet.

- Give them three minutes to do the activity, using the context of the leaflet to help.

- Tell students not to use their dictionaries at this stage.

- Ask them to compare with a partner before you check answers with the class.

- In feedback, elicit/give the stress on each adjective (highlighted in the answers below).

> Positive adjectives: stimulated; intriguing.
>
> Negative adjectives: isolated; inadequate; frustrated; hostile

5b Give students a maximum of five minutes for this activity.

- Ask them to compare with a partner before you check answers with the class.

- When you elicit answers, check students' pronunciation of each adjective and correct if necessary.

> 1 intriguing; 2 stimulated; 3 hostile; 4 isolated; 5 inadequate; 6 frustrated

For further practice, ask students to do exercise V2 7 on page 155 in the Language reference.

LISTENING

6a Set the context and emphasise students should only note the *main* problems.

- Play the track without pausing and elicit answers from the class.

- In feedback, elicit and check students understand *doesn't fit in* (he feels he is different from others).

> He didn't like the weather conditions and the air-conditioning in Chicago; everything's changed in England and he doesn't fit in.

6b Give students a minute to see if they can answer any questions before you play the track.

- Play the track without pausing and give students a minute to finish answering the questions after the track has finished.

- Ask them to compare with a partner before you check answers with the class. (Answers are bold in the audioscript below exercise 7a.)

- Finally, ask students if his experiences are similar to the ones they discussed in exercise 4.

> 1 True (the whole time); 2 False (the countryside was stunning and the people wonderful, he probably liked the ice-hockey); 3 False (he disliked them both); 4 False (they were too cold because of the air-conditioning); 5 True (he doesn't fit in); 6 True (I haven't heard of most of the [football] players)

GRAMMAR: reported speech

7a Elicit that we can use reported speech when we are telling someone what someone else said.

- Then elicit a few other pieces of information about reported speech (e.g. the tense change, use of reporting verbs), but don't go into detail because students will revise/learn this in exercise 7b.

- Give students a couple of minutes to read sentences 1–5 and underline the text.

- Check that students have underlined the correct sentences (underlined in the audioscript below).

- If possible, reproduce the text so that the whole class can see it (perhaps on an Interactive Whiteboard or an overhead projector). As you check answers to exercises 7 and 8a, highlight the relevant parts of the text.

> **Audioscript and answers to exercise 6:**
> **Track 3.13**
> 1 I emigrated to Chicago just over ten years ago. I think **I suffered from culture shock the whole time I was there.** 3 The countryside outside the city was stunning and the people were wonderful but I just couldn't get used to the weather conditions. **The winters were bitterly cold and they seemed to last for a lifetime.** Before I went to work, I usually looked out of the window to see what the weather was like. Sometimes the sky was blue and cloudless, and there was plenty of sunshine. 'Ah,' I would think, 'a nice, mild winter day.' But 4 when I went outside, the cold would hit my face within minutes. My face went numb, and really hurt, and if the wind was strong, I was soon shivering with the cold. I used to hate that walk to the subway, it was so painful.
> **But the summer wasn't much better.** It was quite hot, and often humid, it made me feel really uncomfortable. And then when you went into a café to cool down, **the air conditioning was always on and most places were freezing cold.** I just couldn't put up with the heat outside and the icy conditions in the buildings – it drove me crazy. One day I woke up and said to myself 2 'I don't enjoy living here.'
> I've been back in England for a few months now. **That's been a bit of a culture shock as well.** I'm still trying to adjust to my home country. People talk about TV programmes they loved, and I can't join in the conversation because I've haven't seen them. And a lot of the TV presenters and personalities look strange to me. So much older, I remember them as young men and women, now they're middle aged. And take sport, for example, **I followed ice hockey in Chicago** but everyone here talks about **football. I haven't heard of most of the players,** so I can't pretend to be interested.
> 5 I'm just not fitting in at the moment, I feel like a fish out of water, to be honest. I've no idea how long it'll last. But if I don't adjust soon to conditions here, I'll start to wish I was back in Chicago!

7b Students discuss this question in pairs, using the underlined parts of the text to help.

- This should be revision for most students. Encourage them to work without asking you for help.

- Go through answers and the notes in brackets with the class.

- To remind students further, ask them to read G1 to the end of the table on page 154 in the Language reference.

> Change the subject (e.g. *I* to *he*), use reporting verbs (e.g. *said*) and sometimes *that*, change the tenses one step back into the past (e.g. *emigrated* – *had emigrated*, *don't enjoy* – *didn't enjoy*), change adverbs (e.g. *here* – *there*, *ago* – *before*)

8a Give students one minute to read the sentences and answer the questions individually.

- Get answers from the class.

> The tenses do <u>not</u> change to one step back in the past (e.g. *was stunning* – *was stunning*), adverb doesn't change (*at the moment*). However, note the change in form *am* – *is* because the subject changes *I* – *he*.

8b Give students two minutes to match the reason to the example (3–5) and then compare answers in pairs.

- Check answers with the class and refer to the relevant parts of the audioscript above.

> **3** b); **4** c); **5** a)

(!) Sentence 4, exercise 7a: The sentence doesn't change because of the time conjunction *when*, but also because we do not usually change *would* when we transform direct into reported speech.

For further information, ask students to read G1 on page 154 in the Language reference.

9 Read the introduction and emphasise that Susan is in England now and she said these things in England.

- Put students in pairs for this activity to encourage them to discuss the changes necessary.

- Allow at least ten minutes and monitor to point out mistakes, but encourage students to self-correct.

- Students can use G1 in the Language reference if they need help.

- Go through answers with the class and write the sentences on the board so students can see the form.

- Finally, tell students that it is common to not change the tenses at all when reporting what someone has said in an informal situation (e.g. to another friend). For example, 2 She said she lived in a [...].

> **1** She said she had studied the language before she went (time conjunction); **2** She said had lived in a tiny studio flat while she was there (time conjunction); **3** No changes because this is still true and the subject/verb agreement stays the same; **4** She said she had given chocolates to her boss once – and he had been really surprised; **5** She said she really misses Japan and would love to go back (situation unlikely to change / *would*); **6** She said she often goes to Japanese restaurants to eat Japanese food (the action still happens – *often*, not just once); **7** She said that she had bought a ticket for [...] the day before (Note: if this is reported soon after the time Susan said it and reported in an informal situation, e.g. to a another friend, the tenses are unlikely to change.); **8** She said she can't wait to get back (still true because he hasn't returned to Japan yet).

10 Give students five minutes to make notes about their information, paying attention to whether these actions/situations are still true, happening now, use a modal, etc. Check they don't write these in reported speech.

- Put students into pairs to discuss what their blog said. Tell them to use reported speech when possible.

- Monitor to note mistakes with tenses, use of adverbs, etc.

- When students have finished, correct some of the mistakes you noted above.

- Finally, ask students for the best idea their blogs had for helping with culture shock. Ask them to tell you this using reported speech.

11 Ask students to read the instructions and check they understand *pen friend* (someone you write to but may never have met).

- Give students a few minutes to think about what a foreigner might find difficult in their country.

- Then give them a few minutes to think about what might help with these difficulties.

- Allow students 30 minutes to write their letters.

- Tell them they can report ideas from the blogs in exercise 10.

- Monitor to help with vocabulary and register/style (it should be informal).

- Take the letters in for marking, paying attention to the vocabulary and grammar from this lesson.

Students do the exercises on pages 75–76 of the Workbook.

Students research advice on travelling to a foreign country and write an advice sheet. In the next lesson, students post these round room. All students read them and report the best pieces of advice to a partner.

Students do exercise V2 7 on page 155 in the Language reference.

11.3 UNDERSTANDING CULTURES

IN THIS LESSON

Lesson topic and staging
This lesson looks at cultural differences and how they lead to misunderstandings. Students listen to people talking about mistakes they made abroad and then focus on the verbs they use to report what was said. Students then look at the form of these and practise using them. Next, students read two texts about cultural awareness and study their (in)formality. Finally, students have a debate about cultural awareness.

Objectives
By the end of the lesson, students should have:

- extracted specific information and language items from a listening and reading texts

- revised/learned about common verbs for reporting what someone said

- analysed texts for features of (in)formality

- participated in a debate about cultural awareness.

Timings
If short of time and your students are confident using the reporting verbs, you could drop exercise 5. A possible lesson break would be after exercise 5b on page 116.

WARM-UP

- This activity introduces different customs around the world.

- Write the following on the board:

      1 don't point the soles of your feet at people
      2 accept business cards with two hands
      3 don't blow your nose in public
      4 shake hands when meeting someone
      5 don't give someone an uneven number of flowers

      a) USA; b) China; c) Thailand; d) Austria; e) Japan

- Tell students these are all customs in different countries.

- Put students in pairs and ask them to match the custom to the country.

- Go through answers with the class and ask students which they'd heard of before.

    1 c); **2** b); **3** e); **4** a); **5** d)

LISTENING

1   Use the Warm-up as a lead in. Alternatively, focus students on the title of the lesson and tell them a quick story (imaginary if necessary) about someone you know making a cultural mistake in a foreign country.

*   Then ask students to read the questions and put their hands up if they've had an experience like this.

*   If a lot of students have, put them into pairs to discuss these. If not, elicit a few examples in open class.

2a Set the context and the question. Play the track, pausing after the first speaker to give students time to write notes.

*   Elicit answers from the class and ask students if they have similar customs in their countries.

> 1 Turkey; he took money from an old woman on a bus but didn't know he should give it to the driver; 2 Spain; she didn't know that in Spain people eat very late, so ate before she went out.

2b Set the activity and then play the track, pausing at the points indicated in the audioscript below.

*   Ask students to compare with a partner and, if necessary, play the track again.

*   Go through answers with the class and write them on the board so that students can see the spelling. (Sentences containing the answers are underlined in the audioscript below.)

*   Finally, give students a few minutes to check unknown verbs in their dictionaries.

> 1 persuaded me to travel; 2 admitted taking/ apologised for not giving; 3 warned me /regretted travelling; 4 refused to do; 5 insisted on picking/ agreed to meet; 6 encouraged me to order; 7 told me to

Audioscript and answers to exercise 2:
Track 3.14
1
When my wife and I were on holiday in Istanbul, Turkey, we decided to visit a market. <u>1 My wife persuaded me to travel there by *dolmus*</u> – one of the small minibuses which hold about 20 passengers. [PAUSE] We sat in the middle of the bus, and after about ten minutes, an old woman came from the back seats, tapped me on the shoulder and put two coins in my hand, muttering something in Turkish. I didn't understand, but thanked her and put the coins in my pocket. A few minutes later, the bus driver stopped and spoke to the old woman. She pointed at me, and didn't look very pleased. The bus driver started waving his arms about and shouting at me in broken English, 'You bad person. You get off my bus, you don't give me money.' I suddenly realised that the woman had given me the coins to pass on to the driver to pay for the journey. I was so embarrassed. <u>2 I admitted taking the money and apologised for not giving it to him.</u> He just wouldn't listen [PAUSE] <u>3 He warned me not to get on his bus again.</u> I regretted travelling by *dolmus* and we never did it again. During the rest of our holiday, we travelled by taxi and ferry boat! [PAUSE]

continued...

2
I made a terrible social gaffe in Spain the first time I went there for work purposes. <u>4 I'd refused to do the orientation programme because I'd been to Malaga</u> for a week a few years before [PAUSE] – it was great: sunny beaches and loads of other expatriates – really enjoyed myself. But when I went there for a week to work it was totally different. I'd arrived in the afternoon and there was a car to take me to the hotel from the airport. I'd missed lunch so I had a snack at about 3 o'clock. Then, knowing that <u>5 my hosts had insisted on picking me up at 9 o'clock and that I'd agreed to meet them</u> in the hotel lobby, I thought I would have my supper before going out for the evening. Big mistake! I hadn't realised that the Spanish eat very late. [PAUSE] So there I was in a very nice restaurant having to choose a meal at 11 o'clock when I felt stuffed full from my supper earlier. <u>6 They encouraged me to order lots of different dishes.</u> I tried to eat but couldn't manage more than two or three mouthfuls. [PAUSE] My hosts thought I must be unhappy or ill. I could see that they were very concerned so I decided to tell them the truth. <u>7 They nearly fell off their chairs laughing and told me to forget about eating any more food.</u> In a funny way, my social gaffe worked out OK in the end because everybody was laughing so much that we were able to talk business in a friendly atmosphere. But I never went anywhere new ever again without a full briefing.

GRAMMAR: reporting verbs

3   Give students five minutes to complete the chart and compare answers with a partner.

*   Go through the answers with the class.

Verb + *to* + infinitive	Verb + object + *to* + infinitive	Verb + *-ing* form	Verb + preposition + *-ing* form
offer; refuse; agree	invite; persuade; warn; tell; encourage	consider; admit; regret	insist on; apologise for

4   Read through the introduction and, if necessary, do number 1 as an example with the class.

*   Give students eight minutes to re-write the sentences.

*   Monitor to point out mistakes, but encourage students to self-correct by using the chart in exercise 3.

*   Ask them to compare with a partner before you check answers and go through notes with the class.

> 2 I admitted sounding a bit rude; 3 She/he insisted on us treating everyone equally (note the position of the object); 4 She/he persuaded me to think about it; 5 She/he warned me not to come into his/her shop again; 6 She/he regretted leaving university early; 7 She/he refused to resign; 8 He/she apologised for being late.

5a Divide the class into three groups (A, B and C) and ask students to look at the prompts provided. Tell students to work together in their groups to make sentences.

- Monitor to help with vocabulary if necessary.

5b Put students into groups of three with an A, a B and a C student in each.

- Use a strong group to demonstrate the activity.
- Then give students five to ten minutes to do the activity. Monitor to note mistakes with the form of reporting verbs.
- Finally, correct some of the more common or important mistakes you noted earlier.

READING

6a This question is about multicultural societies. If your students are in a country where there is only one dominant culture, ask them to think of the different cultures within a country they know of (e.g. the USA).

- Elicit answers from the class but don't ask if these cultures live well together as this may elicit controversial opinions.
- Take this opportunity to elicit/give the term *multicultural* (many different cultures in a country).

6b Explain that both texts are about cultural differences and cultural awareness.

- Give students three minutes to read the texts without using dictionaries or taking notes.
- Put them into pairs to briefly discuss their answer to the question.
- Elicit an answer from the class and then ask which text they agree with more.

> Text A believes cultural awareness is the key to living and working effectively in a globalised world. Text B believes cultural awareness is not important if people and their families are secure.

7 Give students five to eight minutes for this activity and tell them to use dictionaries if necessary.

- Ask students to compare with a partner before you check answers with the class.

> **1** c); **2** b); **3** c); **4** a)

8a First, ask students if they think one text is more formal than the other (students should have noticed this).

- Then give students two minutes to do the activity, using their dictionaries if necessary.
- Ask students to compare with a partner before you check answers with the class.

> Text A: textbook; essay; formal; distant. Text B: blog; email; informal; chatty

8b Give students about five minutes to read the texts again and find examples of the items in the list.

- Ask students to compare with a partner before you check answers with the class.
- Tell students that the features in the answers below are typical of formal/informal texts.

> pronouns: Text A – one's, one, Text B – we, you; vocabulary and grammar: Text A – more formal (e.g. *possess* not *have*, *superficial* not *basic*), more complex sentences (e.g. *More important than superficial behaviour is the value system ...*); Text B – more informal/colloquial (e.g. *mucking in together*, *kids*), simpler sentences (e.g. *We don't like to feel threatened*); questions in the text: Text A – no questions; Text B – direct questions (e.g. *You know what it does?*)

9 Give students five minutes to decide how formal the five texts are.

- Ask students to compare with a partner and give reasons for their answers.
- Check answers with the class.

> **A** Text A; **B** Text B; **C** Text A; **D** Text B; **E** Text A

SPEAKING

10 Divide the class into groups of four. If you have an odd number of students, you can add more 'for' or 'against' students to form larger groups.

- Elicit that presentations in debates are quite formal, but that the discussion afterwards is informal.
- In each group, tell students A/B and C/D to work together and give them ten minutes to prepare their presentations, but to make notes rather than write it.
- Monitor to help with vocabulary and style if necessary.
- Then give students three minutes to present their arguments and monitor to check formal style.
- When the presentations are finished, ask all the students in each group to discuss the issue for about five minutes. (Note: they can use informal language.)
- Monitor to check informal style.
- When they have finished, ask which students had the stronger arguments and then comment on the change from formal to informal style.

HOMEWORK OPTIONS

Students do the exercises on pages 77–78 of the Workbook.

Students do exercise G2 3 on page 155 in the Language reference.

11.4 SCENARIO: KALEIDOSCOPE WORLD

IN THIS LESSON

Lesson topic and staging

This lesson focuses on language for creating impact in a formal presentation. Students read an article introducing the scenario: a company that organises foreign exchanges and wants to find destinations for their clients to visit. They then listen to a tourist board representative giving a presentation on his city and focus on the KEY LANGUAGE. Finally, the TASK asks students to give a presentation on their city or region.

Objectives

By the end of the lesson, students should have:

- learned useful phrases for creating an impact when giving a formal presentation
- used this language in a 'real-life' situation to give a presentation on their city or region
- extracted specific information and/or language items from a reading and listening text
- participated effectively in extended speaking practice.

Common European Framework

Students can use language effectively to give a straightforward description of a familiar subject.

Timings

If short of time, you could drop questions 2, 3 and 4 from exercise 3 as these are not required to introduce the scenario. A possible lesson break would be after exercise 5b on page 119.

WARM-UP

This activity introduces the idea of travelling to learn about aspects of countries.

- Write the following on the board: *food*, *music*, *art*, *nature*, *history*.
- Ask students to decide which country they would visit to find out about these different things, e.g. 'I'd go to China because I know nothing about Chinese music', 'I'd go to the UK because it has a varied history'.
- Put students into small groups to discuss their choices, giving reasons and asking each other questions.
- Finally, ask the class for one or two examples in each category.

SITUATION

1 Focus students on the photos and elicit that these show people visiting foreign countries.

- Ask the class why people visit other countries and elicit ideas (including interest in culture, etc.).
- Put students into pairs to do the activity in the Coursebook and then elicit a few ideas from the class.

2 Ask students to read the question and the examples, and then brainstorm more ideas in pairs.

- Get a few ideas from the class and write them on the board for students to use in exercise 6.

3 Ask students to read the questions and tell them that for question 3 they should add more benefits, and for question 4 there are no actual criticisms in the text – they should decide what these might be.

- Give students five minutes to read the article and the advert, using their dictionaries if necessary.
- Ask students to discuss their answers with a partner.
- Go through answers with the class and ask students if they have been on an exchange trip.

> 1 operating cultural exchange programmes (i.e. young people visit a country, maybe stay with a family, and then people from that country visit theirs); 2 government grants and donations; 3 benefits in text = experience new cultures, possible benefits = learn tolerance, understand people better, gain some independence, see how your country affects others, start learning a new language; 4 possible criticisms = short time means people get a very simple idea of the country, may try to force cultures on people; 5 the company is expanding rapidly

4a Remind students that *Kaleidoscope World* wants to find other destinations and have asked for presentations from tourist boards.

- Read through the introduction and ask students where Toronto is (Canada) and if they have/would like to visit Canada.
- Ask students to read the questions and then play Part 1 of the track.
- Ask students to compare with a partner before you check answers with the class. (The audioscript is below exercise 5b.)

> 1 three; 2 he'll leave them until the end of the presentation; 3 population, location, type of city (an industrial, commercial and cultural centre)

4b Play Part 2 of the track and give students a few minutes at the end to finish taking notes.

- Ask students to compare with a partner before you check answers with the class.

CN Tower (it's the tallest structure in the world with a fantastic view of the city), City Hall (it's beautifully designed and there's entertainment in the square in front of it), Casa Loma (many interesting architectural features)

4c Play Part 3 of the track and give students a few minutes at the end to finish taking notes.

- Ask students to compare with a partner before you check answers with the class.

- In feedback, write key vocabulary on the board (e.g. *waffles, ice hockey*) and ask students to check this in their dictionaries.

have waffles for breakfast, see an ice hockey match, go to the Caribana festival (one of America's largest street festivals)

KEY LANGUAGE: creating impact in a presentation

5a Focus students on the title of this section of the lesson and elicit/tell them it's important to make people listen to what you say.

- Focus students on the three techniques and tell them these can make your presentation sound interesting.

- Warn students that the answers to 1–5 do not occur in the same order as the questions.

- Play Parts 1 and 2 again, if necessary pausing after each phrase to give students time to write.

- Ask students to compare with a partner before you check answers with the class. (Answers are numbered and underlined in the audioscript below.)

1 commercial/cultural; 2 lively/cosmopolitan;
3 better/better, more/more; 4 what/sights;
5 why/worth

5b Give students five minutes to underline other examples and then compare with a partner.

- Elicit answers from the class and make sure all the examples in the audioscript below are included.

- If possible, reproduce the text so that the whole class can see it (perhaps on an Interactive Whiteboard or an overhead projector). As you elicit/give examples, underline them in the text.

Audioscript and answers to exercises 4 & 5:
Track 3.15
Part 1
Hello, everyone. My name's James and I'm from Canada. This morning I'm going to talk to you about my fascinating home town of Toronto. I've divided my presentation into three parts. First of all, I'll start with some background information, then I'll move on to the main sights. Finally, I'll outline some other experiences a visitor should try when they come to Toronto. If you don't mind, we'll leave questions to the end.

continued...

OK, I'll start with some basic information. Toronto is the capital city of the province of Ontario, and it's situated on Lake Ontario. Until 1934, it was called York. It's got a population of approximately 2.4 million, so it's a fairly large city. It's an important industrial, 1 commercial and cultural centre.
Toronto's getting 3 better and better these days, as 3 more and more people come from all over the world to settle here. They enrich our city greatly with their skills and talents and they help to create the 2 lively, friendly, cosmopolitan atmosphere the city is famous for.

Track 3.16
Part 2
So 4 what are the main sights of the city? Well, there are many things to see, but let me focus on three: the CN Tower, City Hall and Casa Loma.
OK, 5 why is the CN Tower worth seeing? Well, [REPETITION] it's a tall building, a very tall building. Actually, it's the tallest structure in the world; it's 1,815 feet high. Built in 1976 by Canadian National Railways, it overlooks the city and you can see it wherever you are in the city. It's [TRIPLING] truly gigantic, incredible, and awe-inspiring. Go up the tower and you get a fantastic view of the city. And if you're very brave, [QUESTION] why don't you stand on the glass floor, 342 metres off the ground, then look down? And if you can do that, [QUESTION] why not take the elevator and go on up to the Sky Pod? That's another 34 storeys higher!
Another great sight is the City Hall. There was a world wide competition in the 60s to design it, and a Finnish architect, Vilja Revell, won the competition. Unfortunately, he died before it was opened in 1965. It's beautifully designed, and far ahead of its time. Now it's a very popular tourist [REPETITION] attraction, in fact it's probably the most popular attraction. In front of it is Nathan Phillips Square. The Square is an entertainment venue, it offers [TRIPLING] free concerts, ice skating and on New Year's Eve, a huge celebration takes place there.
Finally, Casa Loma. [QUESTION] What can I say about this extraordinary castle? It was called a 'rich man's folly'. People thought Sir Henry Pellatt, the owner, was crazy to spend so much money on building the castle in 1914. It cost 3.5 million dollars, a huge sum in those days. And he went bankrupt trying to maintain and develop it. Ten years later, its value was just 27,000 dollars. It has so many interesting architectural features: 60 large rooms, an immense Great Hall, where 2,000 people can be entertained, [TRIPLING] a beautiful library, secret underground passages and magnificent gardens. It's a *must* place to visit.

Track 3.17
Part 3
Finally, I'll talk about some things a visitor should definitely do when they come to Toronto.
Well, [QUESTION] how about trying some waffles for breakfast? They're sort of pancakes – with maple syrup – delicious, and typically Canadian food.
Secondly, if you like sports, you should go to see an ice hockey match featuring the local Maple Leaf team. They've won many championships and are one of the top ice hockey teams in North America. Ice hockey is [TRIPLING] physical, fast and exciting. It's a rough game, a contact sport, but thrilling and skilful.

continued...

I'd also like to suggest that visitors should try and experience the Caribana festival, which takes place every year from mid-July to early August. It is one of America's largest street festivals and is based on the Trinidad carnival. The first one took place in 1967, when the city's Caribbean community celebrated the 100th anniversary of Canada. It just got [REPETITION] <u>bigger and bigger</u> so that today it attracts more than a million visitors.
To sum up, I'd just like to say that Toronto is a [TRIPLING] <u>modern, exciting, and welcoming</u> city just waiting to be explored. I do hope you will be able to add it to your list of destinations and we look forward to showing you the very best which Toronto has to offer. That's all from me. Any questions?

TASK: giving a formal presentation

6a Read the instructions with the class and remind them of the KEY LANGUAGE.

- Go through the OTHER USEFUL PHRASES with the class.

- Then give students 20–30 minutes to prepare their presentations.

- Monitor to help with vocabulary and point out mistakes if necessary.

6b Divide the class into groups of three or four.

- Students take turns to give their five-minute presentations and answer questions at the end of each.

- Take notes on students' use of the techniques in exercise 5.

- When they have finished, ask each group to decide which was the best presentation and why.

- Finally, comment on students' use of techniques from exercise 5, using the notes you made earlier.

HOMEWORK OPTIONS

Students do the exercises on page 79 of the Workbook.

Students write a fact sheet on the city/town/region they presented in exercise 6. In the next lesson, post these round the room, ask students to read them all and then say which places they would like to visit.

Students do exercise KL 5 on page 155 in the Language reference.

11.5 STUDY AND WRITING SKILLS

IN THIS LESSON

Lesson topic and staging

This lesson focuses on improving reading skills and writing a formal letter. Students discuss techniques for reading and then listen to an expert giving tips for effective reading. Students then look at some techniques in more detail and practise using these. Next, students look at the layout of a formal letter and focus on formulaic expressions. Finally, students read an advertisement and write a formal letter in response.

Objectives

By the end of the lesson, students should have:

- extracted specific information and language items from a listening and reading texts

- learned about different techniques for effective reading and practised using these

- learned about some conventions of formal letters and written a formal letter.

Common European Framework

Students can understand the main points and information in articles and everyday reading materials, guess the meaning of words from their context, and understand a writer's specific attitudes and points of view. Students can write simple connected texts and reply in written form to adverts.

Timings

If short of time, you could set exercise 8 for homework. Alternatively, you could limit the type of prefixes/suffixes/linkers students find in 4b. A possible lesson break would be after exercise 4b on page 120.

WARM-UP

This activity focuses students on some of the difficulties they have when reading in English.

- Ask students how often and if they enjoy reading in English.

- Write the following on the board: *getting the general meaning, understanding specific points, understanding the writer's opinion, unknown vocabulary, reading quickly.*

- Tell students these are difficulties people may have when reading and elicit other suggestions if possible.

- Then tell students to order the items from more to least difficult.

- Ask them to compare with a partner and give their reasons.
- Finally, elicit lists from a few students and tell the class this lesson will help them with reading skills.

> ## STUDY SKILLS: improving reading skills

1a Use the Warm-up as a lead in or elicit some of the difficulties students have when reading in English.

- Give students five minutes to discuss the list and then elicit which students use.

1b Allow two minutes to choose the most important techniques and then compare with a partner.

- Ask a few students for the techniques they chose and why.
- Finally, ask students which of the techniques could help them with the difficulties they identified in 1a.

2a Set the context and ask students to read the questions.

- Tell them to listen for general advice in question 3 rather than specific tips.
- Play the track and then ask students to compare with a partner.
- Go through answers with the class and check students understand *acquiring* (obtaining) and *reasoning* (thinking critically, analysing).
- Finally, ask students if they think the advice is useful.

> **1** Professor Mary Robinson, a book on improving reading skills; **2** it may help you express yourself better, it may be the best way of acquiring knowledge, it keeps your reasoning abilities working well; **3** the more reading you do, the better

2b Set the activity and play the track again.

- Ask students to compare with a partner before you check answers with the class. (Parts of the text containing the answers are bold in the audioscript below.)
- Make sure students understand that the ticked items are all good tips and the un-ticked ones are not.
- Finally, tell students that the ticked items will help their reading.

> The following should be ticked: 1, 4, 5, 6 and **7** (this is implied in the listening - *I think students are often not selective enough about what they choose to read* – i.e. they need to decide first what they want to know).

Audioscript and answers to exercise 2:
Track 3.19
Presenter, Guest

P: *[applause]* ... and welcome to today's edition of 'Daybreak', where my guest is Professor Mary Robinson, the author of a new book on improving reading skills.

G: Hello, Pam, and good morning everyone.

P: Yes, hello, Mary, and thanks for joining us. Perhaps we could start with you telling us a bit about why you wrote the book?

G: Yes, sure. Well, I've noticed that among the sort of students I meet at the university, there seems to be a decline in the amount of reading they do, both for their studies and for pleasure. This is a real shame because there is a clear link between the amount you read and your ability to express yourself. Also, it seems that reading is the best way of acquiring knowledge. For example, research into how people acquire knowledge has shown that people who watched more TV were more likely to get general knowledge questions wrong, and this is independent of intellectual ability.

P: Really, how interesting.

G: Yes, it seems the more reading you do, the better, whatever it is. Reading increases vocabulary, improves your general knowledge and keeps your memory and reasoning abilities working well.

P: That's got to be a good thing! So what tips can you give for improving reading?

G: Obviously, it depends on the sort of reading you're doing. However, **I think students are often not selective enough about what they choose to read** and then they focus too much on details. **It's very important to get an overall idea about what you're reading and to make full use of any headings and subheadings to help guide your reading, and stop you wasting time reading unnecessary information.** Also, I think it's crucial to **engage with what you read.** People often think of reading as a one-way process, but in fact it should be a two-way process ...

P: Can you explain what you mean there?

G: Of course. To be an effective reader, **you should always be thinking about what the writer may say next, and also questioning what you read. Think about if you agree or disagree with what you are reading, with the opinion of the writer, with their logic, conclusions and arguments** ... that sort of thing.

P: Right. Anything else?

G: Well, one particular problem that I've noticed is foreign students who focus too much on unknown vocabulary. This can make reading very time consuming as they constantly stop to look up words in their dictionaries.

P: Yes, I see. In fact, I think people often do that in their own language too.

continued...

G: When they're studying, indeed. However, often, **you can work out the meaning of the word by reading on and looking at the context it's used in, or at least make an educated guess.** For people who want to **improve their reading speed**, a good tip is to use your finger, but not to follow the words on the line. No, the secret here is **to move your finger down the page as you read**, as this will train your eyes to move more quickly down the text and keep you moving forward.

P: That's a good tip. Well, thank you very much, Professor, and good luck with the book.

G: Thank you, Pam.

3 Ways to improve your reading

- Lead in by telling the class they are going to look in more detail at techniques for reading.

a Reading and chunking

- Ask students if they want to be able to read faster in English (they will probably say 'yes') and tell them that 'chunking' groups of words is a way of doing this.
- Ask students to read the examples and set the first question.
- Elicit/tell students the chunks are usually divided before (or just before) the main sentence stress, e.g. *All cultures / develop from / a range of / diverse influences.* This will also affect intonation, i.e. intonation rises on the stress in each chunk. Chunks are often clauses (but not always, if a particular clause is very long).
- Then put students in pairs and allow them eight minutes to divide sentences 1–3 into chunks.
- It may help if students decide where the stress is and/or read the sentence aloud to each other.
- Elicit answers from the class and write them on the board to clearly show the chunks.
- Then ask students to read the sentences using chunking.

1 He wrote / a brief history / of Western culture; **2** Many people / argue that /American culture / will soon / take over the world; **3** Cultural studies / is becoming / an increasingly popular / university course.

b Reading and vocabulary: guessing unknown words

- Read the introduction with the class and elicit/tell them that prefixes/suffixes are useful because they give you the 'sense' (e.g. positive, negative, strong, weak, many, opposite) of the word.
- Give students three minutes to do only the first activity and then ask them to compare with a partner.
- Go through answers and the notes in brackets with the class.

1 b) **2** c); **3** a); **4** d); **5** h) (Note: the prefix here also means *a smaller thing within a large thing*, e.g. subheading.); **6** e); **7** g); **8** f)

- Then ask students to do the second activity and add more examples.
- Go through answers and the notes in brackets with the class.
- Write extra examples on the board for students to copy if necessary.

1 *-logy*, noun, e.g. *biology, psychology* (academic subjects); **2** *-ism*, noun, e.g. *racism, socialism*, (concepts/ideas); **3** *-less*, adjective, e.g. *hopeless, useless* (without something); **4** *-able*, adjective, e.g. *reliable, sociable* (qualities); **5** *-ible*, adjective, e.g. *possible, flexible* (qualities); **6** *-ment*, noun, e.g. *apartment, argument* (concrete or abstract); **7** *-ion*, noun, e.g. *election, direction* (concrete or abstract)

- Give students three minutes to underline prefixes and suffixes in the texts on page 117.
- Ask them to compare with a partner before you get examples from the class.

Examples from text B (prefixes and suffixes are in bold): cultur**ally**; **non**sense; concen**trate**; sit(t)**ing**; off**ence**; invad**ing**; physic**al**; call**ed**; trivi(a)**al**; **un**important; polite**ness**; pati**ence**

c Reading and understanding: linkers

- First, get a few examples of linking words/expressions from the class.
- Give students five minutes for the matching activity and then compare with a partner.
- Go through answers with the class.
- Students then work in pairs to write sentences using the words/expressions.
- Elicit examples and write those that best exemplify the linkers on the board.

1 e); **2** h); **3** f); **4** a); **5** g); **6** d); **7** c); **8** b)

4a First, ask students to briefly look again at the techniques in exercise 3.

- Give students five minutes to read their texts (using the techniques above) and note the main points.
- Set the question and put students into pairs to summarise the main points for each other, using linkers if possible.
- Tell students to use their notes but not to read the text again.
- Elicit similarities from the class.
- Finally, ask students if they know anyone who has been part of a subculture and which one.

Both texts talk about subcultures (youth culture is the focus of B and an example in A), their fashions, how business uses them for commercial interests, commercialism doesn't kill subcultures, the tastes and preferences of youth culture/subculture change very quickly

4b It is better to reverse the order of activities in this exercise because focusing students on specific prefixes/suffixes will not encourage them to chunk the text.

- First, ask students to discuss how they chunked the text when they read it in exercise 4a.
- Then ask students to look at the text again and find prefixes, suffixes and linking phrases.
- Ask them to discuss with a partner how these helped them guess meaning.
- Finally, elicit a few ideas from the class.

WRITING SKILLS: a formal letter

5 Letter layout
- Lead in by asking if/when students need to write a formal letter in English (exams, applying for a job).
- Focus students on the formal letter diagram and ask them if the layout looks the same as in their cultures.
- Then give students five minutes to do the activity and compare with a partner.
- If students find this activity very difficult, stop them after two minutes and go through answers with the class.

1 E; 2 G; 3 A; 4 F; 5 B; 6 L; 7 J; 8 K; 9 D; 10 C; 11 I; 12 H

6a Formulaic language
- Read through the introduction with the class and give students three minutes for the activity.
- Ask them to compare with a partner before you go through answers and notes with the class.
- Elicit/tell students the language used is formal, e.g. with *reference to* instead of *about*.
- For a reminder of this, students can look at lesson 5 in Unit 1.

1 forward/future; 2 writing/reference; 3 assistance/hesitate; 4 enclosed (Note: in an email *attached* is used.)/information; 5 question; 6 contacted

6b Give students two minutes for this activity and then get answers from the class.

a) 2; b) 6; c) 4; d) 1; e) 3; f) 5

7 Elicit/remind students the texts they read in exercise 4 were about youth (sub)cultures.
- Ask students to read only the first paragraph of the advert and then elicit what it is advertising and what kind of people might be interviewed in this series (e.g. business people, young people, parents, etc.).
- Set the activity in the Coursebook and put students in pairs to discuss the questions.
- Get a few opinions on three or four of the questions from the class.

8 Set the activity and elicit the register of formal letters from the class, e.g. vocabulary (see above), no contractions, no colloquial language, e.g. 'I can't stand youth culture.'
- You could ask students to look at lesson 5 in Unit 1 for more ideas.
- Give students ten minutes to make notes on what to include in the body of the letter.
- Then focus them again on exercises 3c, 5, 6 and give them 30 minutes to write their letters.
- Take the letters in for marking, paying attention to organisation, expressions, linkers and content.

HOMEWORK OPTIONS

Students do the exercises on pages 79–80 of the Workbook.
Students write a letter to Professor Robinson (from exercise 2), saying they heard her advice on the radio and have (or have not) found it useful. If they don't think it's useful, they should say why (politely).

Technology

12.1 DEVICES AND GADGETS

Lesson topic and staging

This lesson looks at technology used in everyday life. Students discuss technology they use and focus on vocabulary related to machines. They then listen to people saying what they like/dislike about gadgets and discuss technology they like/dislike. Next, students read a text on unknown inventors and swap information with others. Finally, students discuss statements about technology before writing an essay on one of these topics.

Objectives

By the end of the lesson, students should have:

- extracted specific information from a listening and reading texts
- extended their range of vocabulary related to technology and machines
- participated in a group discussion about various aspects of technology
- written a 'for and against' essay on an aspect of technology.

Timings

If short of time, you could cut set exercise 8 for homework. A possible lesson break would be after exercise 4b on page 123.

This activity introduces the topic of useful technology.

- Write the following on the board: *a parent, a teenager, yourself, a person aged 80+, your teacher*.
- Tell students they are going to buy a piece of technology for each of these people.
- This does not need to be something for entertainment (e.g. a DVD player): it can be any machine.
- Give them three minutes to decide what they would buy for each person.
- Then put them into small groups to compare ideas and give reasons.
- Finally, ask students if they thought of similar gifts.

Ken Olson quote:

This quote is humorous because it has been proved to be very wrong. The meaning of the quote should be easily understood by students. The picture on page 122 is an obvious example of why Ken Olsen was so wrong, as it shows graphics from a computer game.

VOCABULARY: technology

1   Use the Warm-up as a lead in to this activity and for question 1, tell students to discuss technology they use in and outside the home (e.g. a car, a bus, a washing machine, an MP3 player).

- Alternatively, focus students on photos A–D page 123 and ask if they own any of these items.
- Ask students to read the questions and check they understand *technologically minded* (understand how technology works, can fix it if it breaks) and *technophobe* (the opposite of technologically minded, can't use technology very well).
- Then give students five minutes to discuss the questions in groups of three or four.
- Elicit answers from three or four students and for question 3, ask the rest of the class if they agree.

2a Read through the instructions and elicit/tell students how a dictionary shows if a noun in (un)countable and the common collocations.

- Give students five minutes for the activity and then elicit answers from the class.
- If necessary, use the following to clarify gadget: normally small, clever, and often exciting to own.

> apparatus (normally used as uncountable but can be countable); appliance (countable); device (countable); engine (countable); equipment (uncountable); gadget (countable); machine (countable)

💡 To demonstrate how a dictionary gives the information above, reproduce an entry so the whole class can see it (perhaps on an Interactive Whiteboard or an overhead projector). As you elicit/tell students the information, highlight the relevant parts.

2b These questions contain common collocations of the nouns above. If students didn't find them in their dictionaries earlier, highlight them in feedback.

- Give students five minutes to fill the gaps and then compare answers with a partner.
- Check answers with the class and if necessary clarify *cash machine* with *ATM*.

> 1 appliances; 2 equipment; 3 machine; 4 device; 5 gadgets; 6 apparatus

2c Give students eight minutes to discuss the questions and then elicit answers from a few pairs.

> 1–5 Answers depend on students' own opinions and experience; 6 oxygen tank, mask

3a Students can use their dictionaries for this activity.

- Ask students to compare with a partner before you check answers with the class.
- In feedback, clarify *obsolete* (the technology is no longer used), and *durable/hard-wearing* (also mean difficult to damage/destroy).
- Check students' pronunciation of *environmentally, obsolete* and *durable*.

> **1** environmentally friendly, green; **2** cutting edge, state-of-the-art; **3** obsolete, out of date; **4** easy to use, user-friendly; **5** durable, hard-wearing; **6** handy, practical

3b Ask students which of the devices in the photos they own or used to own and elicit the name of each one (A sat nav; B a Walkman for playing cassettes; C a Blackberry (phone and mini-computer); D an old style mobile or cell [US English] phone).

- Put students in pairs for this activity so they have to say the adjectives aloud and practise pronunciation.
- Elicit a few ideas from three or four pairs and ask the rest of the class if they agree.

3c Give students one minute to choose a few pieces of technology. Tell them they can include examples of any of the nouns in exercise 2a.

- Then put students into small groups to compare ideas.
- Monitor while students are speaking and note mistakes with the adjectives.
- Get a few ideas from the class and then correct some of the mistakes you noted earlier.

LISTENING

4a Set the activity and tell students they should be able to guess unknown words from the context.

- Play the track, pausing briefly after each speaker.
- Ask students to compare with a partner before you check answers with the class. (Answers are bold in the audioscript opposite.)

> **1** Person 1: mobile phones; Person 2: portable DVD player; Person 3: a shredder; **2** Person 1: Like (reluctantly) = good in emergencies, Dislike = people use them on the train, in restaurants, speak too loudly and talk all about their lives; Person 2: Like = easy to use, durable, handy, portable, Person 3: cheap, user-friendly, Dislike = reminds him what kind of world we live in (where people look in your rubbish to get letters and then steal your identity), not environmentally friendly

Audioscript and answers to exercise 4:
Track 3.20

1

I absolutely detest **mobile phones … cell phones**, whatever you want to call the horrible things. OK, yes, they're **practical in emergencies**, like when your car has broken down. But most of the time they're a pest, an absolute nuisance, and a pain in the neck. I loathe them. I was sitting on the train this morning and at least five people were shouting into their phones – **why does everyone have to speak so loudly?** And why do some of them give you their life story? It's so incredibly rude. I just want to sit in peace on the train and read my newspaper. I had to put my headphones on to listen to my state-of-the-art MP3 player just to drown out their noise. And restaurants, don't get me started on that. **People shouting on phones in restaurants** – so incredibly inconsiderate –why don't they just go outside to take their stupid calls?

2

What's my favourite piece of technology? That's easy, my **portable DVD player**. I've used it so much since I bought it, the chrome surface is really worn and the machine looks old. I don't care, I won't change it. It's really **easy to use and it's certainly durable.** It never breaks down, not even if I drop it, and that often happens. I love films, it's my main interest. As soon as I buy a new DVD, I want to watch it right away. The DVD player is so **handy** for that. It takes me just a few seconds and I'm watching the film. **I even take it on the train with me.** I have an hour's journey to work, so I'm never bored with my **portable** player. My fellow travellers seem to like it too. I've often caught them sneaking a look at the film I'm watching. So… three cheers for portable DVD players. What a great invention!

3

I suppose the last piece of technology I bought was a **shredder**, you know, for shredding documents and things like that. Everyone kept telling me to buy one because they, … because of identity fraud – other people finding out information about you and using it to, I don't know, to steal from your bank account or get a passport in your name, that kind of thing. So I've just bought a shredder, and it's all right. It was **cheap** enough and it's pretty **user-friendly**, but **I don't like it** … the idea, I mean. I don't like the idea of having to destroy important documents so other people can't use them. It's just that **it shows what kind of world we live in now**, I suppose, **and I don't want to believe it.** The other thing about the shredder that I don't like is the fact that it **isn't very environmentally friendly** – it uses quite a lot of electricity which isn't very green to start with, and apparently, you **can't put shredded paper in the recycling bin.** I think it's different from council to council, but where I live, they won't take shredded paper because the pieces are too small and can't be sorted mechanically for recycling.

4b Give students one minute to choose the technology and think about what they like/dislike.

- If students have talked about items they like in other exercises, ask them to think of one they dislike.

- Put students in groups of three and allow five minutes for the discussion. Encourage students to ask each other questions for more information.

- In feedback, ask students which was the best/worst/oldest/newest item they talked about.

READING

5 Students work in pairs to decide all the inventors they know and what they invented.

- Then, if necessary, put the pairs together to swap information on any they didn't know.

- Finally, go through answers with the class.

> Alexander Graham Bell – telephone; W.H. Hoover – vacuum cleaner (often called a Hoover in the UK); King Camp Gillette – safety razor (for shaving facial hair); John Boyd Dunlop – pneumatic (inflatable) tyre; Orville and Wilbur Wright (the Wright Brothers) – engine powered flying machine (a plane); Lazlo Biro – ballpoint pen, also called a Biro; Elisha Otis – lifts (UK)/elevators (US)

6a Focus students on the title of the article and ask students what they think it is about.

- Then ask them to read only the introduction to check (people who don't get recognition for inventions).

- Check students understand *take out a patent* (register an invention with the government so nobody can 'steal' it).

- Put students into groups of three and give them eight minutes to read their text and answer the questions.

- Tell students reading the text on page 166 not to worry about the word *caveat*, they only need to understand *patent*.

- Students can use their dictionaries if necessary.

6b Keep students in the same groups as exercise 6a and give them eight minutes to exchange information.

- Tell them to ask each other questions if necessary.

- Go through answers with the class.

- Finally, ask students which story they are most surprised by and if they feel sorry for these men.

	Text A (page 123)	Text B (page 166)	Text C (page 168)
1	Percy Pilcher	Antonio Meucci	John J. Loud
2	Built and flew a glider, then built a plane with an engine.	Invented the *teletrophono* and made 30 prototype telephones.	Invented a pen with a rotating ball
3	Glider 1890s, plane 1899	Prototypes 1856–1870, patent 1871	Patented 1888

	Text A	Text B	Text C
4	The engine broke, Pilcher flew his glider instead, crashed and died from his injuries	Had an accident, became ill, no money to renew patent, Bell registered patent, Meucci sued but died before case finished.	He didn't exploit his patent commercially; Biro patented the ballpoint pen 1938–1943
5	In 2003 someone built the plane using Pilcher's design – it worked and flew for longer than the Wright brothers.	In 2002 US House of Representatives recognised his achievements should be acknowledged.	Biro licensed pen to BiC, which now sells 14 million Cristal pens a day, annual sales of 1.38 billion euros

SPEAKING AND WRITING

7 To prevent students spending too much time on each statement, tell them they need only think of two 'for' and two 'against' arguments for each.

- Allow ten to fifteen minutes for the discussion.

- Monitor to note mistakes with the vocabulary from this lesson.

- Elicit ideas from each group and write them on the board for use in exercise 8.

- Finally, correct some of the mistakes you noted earlier.

8 Remind students there are 'for' and 'against' arguments for each statement on the board.

- Give them one minute to choose which statement to write about.

- Then give them 30–40 minutes to write their essay.

- If necessary, students can look at lessons 5 in Units 3 and 10 for ideas on language and organisation.

- Monitor to help with vocabulary and point out mistakes.

- Finally, take the essays in for marking, paying attention to the use of vocabulary in this lesson

HOMEWORK OPTIONS

Students do the exercises on page 81 of the Workbook.

Students research one of the inventors in exercise 5 (excluding those mentioned in the texts in exercise 6) or choose an inventor they know about. They then write a fact sheet about their inventor. In the following lesson, post the fact sheets around the room and ask students to read them all. Ask students if they learned anything new from reading the fact sheets.

Students do exercise V1 6 and V2 7 on page 157 in the Language reference.

12.2 LIVING WITHOUT TECHNOLOGY

Lesson topic and staging

This lesson looks at people living without technology. Students read about the Amish community and discuss their attitude to technology. They then focus on words with prefixes in the text and practise using these. Next, students look at conditional tenses and focus on the meaning and alternative conjunctions to *if* before practising them. Finally, students discuss how they would manage without technology.

Objectives

By the end of the lesson, students should have:

- extracted specific information and language items from a reading text
- extended their range of vocabulary using prefixes to convey opposite meaning
- revised/extended their understanding of first and second conditional
- discussed how they would manage without technology in their lives.

Timings

If short of time, you could drop exercise 10 if students are confident using the grammatical forms. A possible lesson break would be after exercise 6 on page 124.

WARM-UP

This activity introduces the topic of technology in our everyday lives.

- Focus students on the photos on pages 124 and 125 and elicit that they show people using old technologies (e.g. horse-drawn carriages).
- Put students into small groups and ask them to discuss what life would be like without the following modern technologies: *cars, planes, computers, mobile phones and TV*.
- Elicit ideas from the class.

READING

1 Students discuss these questions in pairs or groups of three. (Note: you could tell students that all three photos were taken in present day North America. Students may not find them unusual if they think they are of a developing country.)

- Take this opportunity to introduce the Amish community, who use horse-drawn ploughs and drive carriages like these.

> The farmer is using horses to plough the field. The children are dressed in a 19th-century European style. There is a horse-drawn carriage on the same road as a truck. All of these are unusual in North America and in developed societies in general.

2a Read through the instructions and tell students each paragraph is an answer.

- Give them two minutes to do the activity in the Coursebook and compare with a partner.
- Go through answers with the class and tell students that Pennsylvania is a State of the USA.

> 1 A; 2 D; 3 C; 4 B

2b Give students five minutes to read the text again and make *brief* notes.

- Tell students they do not need to include all the information available in the text when answering the questions.
- Ask students to compare with a partner before you check answers with the class.

> 1 plain clothes, limited use of technology, simple way of life, separate themselves from mainstream society; 2 search the Internet, watch the movie *Witness*; 3 yes, they do if strictly necessary, e.g. phones (never in the house), planes, cars to go to hospital, modern farm equipment (but only if pulled by horses); 4 they value simplicity and self-sufficiency, believe technology will take Amish away from the community, mistrust modern things (especially technology)

3 Check students understand *close-knit* community (close, supporting each other).

- Give students five minutes for this activity.
- Then give them another five minutes to discuss and justify their answers in small groups.
- In feedback, elicit if each idea is valued or not, but ask for justification for only a few.
- Students do not need to quote large parts of the text to justify their answers but you should accept any that are reasonable. Justifications are not included in the answers below because they will vary.

> Valued: simplicity; self-sufficiency; independence from the outside world; close-knit community; equality; privacy
> Rejected: material comforts; modern technology

4 Students discuss this question in groups of three or four.

- Elicit a few ideas from the class.

VOCABULARY: opposites

5a Ask students to predict what the opposites of these words might be before they check the text.

> inappropriate; inconvenient; inefficient; inequality; dislike; unlikely; mistrust

5b Put students in pairs and give them three minutes to brainstorm possible answers.

- Elicit answers and write any words that may be unknown to the rest of the class on the board.

6 Explain that the text is about problems with the health service in the USA.

- Elicit a few problems with the health service in students' own countries (e.g. waiting for treatment).

- Ask students to read the text quickly without filling the gaps, then do the activity as per the Coursebook.

- Ask students to compare with a partner before you check answers with the class.

- In feedback, check students understand *insensitive* (not caring about people's feelings).

- Finally, ask students if they have now found more problems similar to the ones they thought of earlier.

> **1** ineffective; **2** unnecessary; **3** inefficient; **4** mismanagement; **5** inaccurate; **6** inequality; **7** unable; **8** insensitive (Note: answers 1 and 2 could be reversed.)

For further practice, ask students to do exercise V3 8 on page 157 in the Language reference.

GRAMMAR: conditionals (1)

This area should be revision for most students at this level. Get answers from the class rather than give them. They should only use the Language reference to check answers.

7a Students complete the sentences individually and then briefly compare with a partner.

- Monitor to find out how many students use the first and second conditionals.

- Ask students to underline the sentences in the text and correct their answers if necessary.

- Check answers with the class.

> **1** If you visit an Amish area, you'<u>ll see</u> women in long dresses.; **2** If you <u>were</u> invited into an Amish home, you '<u>d find</u> no televisions …

7b & 7c Put students in pairs to discuss the questions in these exercises and find examples.

- Check answers with the class and ask students for examples from the text to show the meaning of each conditional and its form.

- Then give students a maximum of five minutes to write down what the form of each is (e.g. *if* +....).

- Monitor to point out mistakes but encourage students to self or peer-correct.

- Finally, ask students to check their answers by reading G1 on page 156 in the Language reference.

- Take this opportunity to elicit negatives, question forms, and possible contractions and the comma after the *if* clause if it comes first in a sentence. If students are unsure, answer any questions at this stage.

> **7b and 7c 1** = first conditional (future possibility); **2** = second conditional (imaginary or unlikely situation). Further example of first conditional: If you pass an Amish area, you'll notice farm equipment being pulled.; Further examples of second conditional: … supposing that an Amish had to make an important telephone call, they would go to …; … if they had to go to hospital, they would be able to ride…

It may be better for students to answer the questions in 7a *and* 7b before they find more examples in the text. In this way, they will have discussed meaning, which will help them (along with form) to find examples.

In part C, the sentence beginning 'The Amish do compromise with the modern world, as long as ...' is an example of the so-called 'zero' conditional. This uses a present tense in both clauses. It is used for actions/events/facts that are always/generally true, unlike the first conditional which refers to future time.

8 Students do this activity individually and then compare with a partner.

- Elicit answers from the class and write them on the board so students can see the form.

> **1** 's, is / 'll, [or will, might, may, could, should] fire; **2** wait / 'll [or will, can] call; **3** had / 'd buy; **4** buy / 'll, [or will] give (Note: second conditional is also possible here, depending on how possible it is that they will buy the MP3 player.); **5** have / 'll [or will] call; **6** knew / 'd [or would, could] tell

9a When students have found the conjunctions in the text, elicit the answer from the class.

- Then elicit that *when* can replace *if* in the first conditional, making the meaning more certain.

> They can all replace *if*. Also, see the Warning after exercise 7b & 7c above.

9b Students refer to the examples in the text and briefly discuss this question in pairs.

- Elicit answers from the class and check students' pronunciation of the weak form of *as*.

> **strict conditions:** as long as, provided that; **imaginary situations:** imagine, supposing that

10 Ask students to read the instructions and clarify that *correct in two ways* means they may be able to correct some sentences in two ways (i.e. using both the first and second conditional).

- Give students five minutes to do this exercise individually.
- Ask them to compare with a partner before you check answers with the class.
- In feedback, tell students you can drop *that* after the relevant conjunctions and check students understand *computer crashed* (the technology broke, stopped working).

> **1** ~~I'd~~ I'll buy you an MP3 player as long as you agree to …OR I'd buy you an MP3 player, as long as you agreed to…; **2** Would you be interested in investing in more technology if you ~~have~~ had the chance?; **3** If I ~~start~~ started this technology course again, I think I'd do it differently; **4** Imagine you had a million pounds, what ~~will~~ would you do with it?; **5** Supposing that the computer crashed, who ~~will~~ would you phone? OR Supposing that the computer crashes, who will you phone? **7** You can borrow my MP3 player, provided that you ~~would~~ bring it back tomorrow (Note: this sentence uses the present tense in both clauses but is a first conditional because it refers to future time).

11 Ask students to read the instructions and emphasise they can choose first or second conditional, but they must justify their choice.

- Give students ten minutes to write their sentences.
- Monitor to point out mistakes but encourage students to self-correct.
- Then ask students to compare with a partner and justify their answers.
- Elicit one example for each sentence and ask for justification. Ask the rest of the class if they agree.
- Accept any grammatically correct, meaningful and reasonably justified answers.

SPEAKING

12 Give students a couple of minutes to think about their ideas. Then put them into groups of three or four and allow ten minutes for the discussion.

- Monitor to note mistakes with the first and second conditional.
- In feedback, ask students if they'd all miss the same thing(s) and how they might replace it.
- Finally, correct some of the mistakes you noted earlier.

HOMEWORK OPTIONS

Students do the exercises on pages 82–83 of the Workbook.

Students imagine they have visited an Amish area. They write a travel blog describing the experience, using the first and second conditionals when possible. They must not refer to the text in exercise 2.

Students do exercises V3 8 and G1 1, 2 and G2 3 on page 157 in the Language reference.

12.3 PRO OR ANTI?

IN THIS LESSON

Lesson topic and staging

This lesson looks at the effects of technology on how food is produced. Students read an article on genetically modified food and focus on how the writer shows his opinion. Students then look at third and mixed conditionals in the text and focus on the meaning and form before practising these themselves. Finally, students participate in a debate on whether technology has improved our lives.

Objectives

By the end of the lesson, students should have:

- extracted specific information and language items from a reading text
- extended their range of techniques and language for expressing their opinions
- revise/learned about third and mixed conditionals
- participated in a debate on whether technology has improved our lives.

Timings

If short of time and your students are confident using mixed conditionals, you could drop exercise 8 and move to the freer practice in exercise 9. A possible lesson break would be after exercise 5 on page 126.

WARM-UP

This activity introduces different methods for producing food.

- First, ask students where they buy their food and if they grow any themselves.
- Write the following on the board:
  - ○ 1 *processed*; 2 *free range*; 3 *battery farming*; 4 *genetically modified*; 5 *organic*; 6 *home made*
  - ○ a) animals are kept in buildings all their lives; b) food has other things added in factories; c) animals move around where they want; d) cook food from basic ingredients; e) no chemicals are used; f) the natural plant/animal is changed using biological technology.
- Put students in pairs to match the phrases to their meanings, using dictionaries if necessary.
- Check answers with the class.
- Then put students into groups and ask them to discuss what kind of food they prefer to eat and why.
- Elicit a few ideas from the class.

> **1** b); **2** c); **3** a); **4** f); **5** e); **6** d)

READING

1 You could drop this exercise if you used the Warm-up activity.

- Ask students to read the questions and check they understand *genetically modified* (the natural plant/animal is changed using biological technology).
- Then put students into groups of three or four and give them five minutes to discuss the questions.
- Elicit a few ideas with reasons from the class.

2a Focus students on the photo and ask what they think the article is about.

- Give them one minute to read the paragraph and answer the questions.
- Ask them to compare with a partner but don't check answers at this stage.
- Answers are given in exercise 2b.

2b Give students five minutes to read the whole article but tell them not to worry about unknown vocabulary.

- Tell them to change their answers in exercise 2a if necessary.
- Elicit answers from the class and ask a few students which is closest to their opinion.

> Closest to author's opinion: c); What many other people think: a)

i Bob Dylan is an American singer and song-writer. His song *The Times They Are A-changing* is one of his most famous. He is particularly known for his opposition to the Vietnam War.

3 Ask students to read the questions and check they understand *regulate* (control).

- Tell students that number 6 isn't asking for a time/date, but a condition.
- Give students eight minutes to read the text, using their dictionaries, and answer the questions.
- Ask students to compare with a partner before you check answers with the class and elicit/tell students that *a toxin* (e.g. gossypol) is a poison – a substance that will make you ill or kill you if you eat it.
- Finally, ask students if their opinion on this topic has changed since reading the text.

> **1** the telephone; **2** search engines; **3** the size of a blood cell; **4** gossypol is a toxin – removing it would make cotton seeds safe to eat; **5** a variety produced through genetic engineering; **6** if they were driven underground (secretive and unofficial)

4 Ask students to read the items 1–6 first and then give them eight minutes to find the examples.

- Ask students to compare with a partner before you check answers with the class.
- Write the examples on the board so the whole class can see them (or see Tip below).

- In feedback, check students understand *obstacle* (something that stops you doing something) and *hold someone back* (stop someone making progress).
- Finally, tell students that these are techniques and phrases they can use in exercise 10 later.

> **1** imagine that now …; **2** Will that make us less human? I don't believe so; **3** Such attitudes are unfortunate because they are a major obstacle to relieving suffering; **4** This is a bad idea; **5** we; **6** We should not let anti-technologist groups hold us back.

If possible, reproduce the text so the whole class can see it (perhaps on an Interactive Whiteboard or an overhead projector). When you check answers for exercises 4–7, highlight the relevant parts of the text.

5 Give students five minutes to underline sentences in the text.

- Ask students to compare with a partner before you check answers with the class.
- In feedback, accept any correct examples and write them on the board (or see the Tip above).

GRAMMAR: conditionals (2)

This area may be revision for some students at this level. If necessary, ask stronger students to help weaker ones. Get answers from the class rather than give them and challenge students to do exercises to test what they can remember about the structures.

6 Students work in pairs for this activity.

- Elicit answers from the class.

> If these groups <u>had</u> not opposed …, it would <u>have been</u> produced …
> **1** Yes; **2** No; **3** third conditional; **4** for unreal situations in the past, situations that are the opposite of the facts

7a Students work individually and then compare their answers with a partner.

- Check answers with the class.

> **a)** 2; **b)** 1

7b Students work individually and then compare their answers with a partner.

- Check answers with the class or ask them to look at G2 on page 156 in the Language reference.
- Elicit that sentence 1 is a mix of third + second, and sentence 2 is second + third.
- Take this opportunity to elicit negatives, question forms, possible written (e.g. *'d* for *would* or *had*) and spoken (e.g. *I'd've, would've, might've*) contractions and the comma after the *if* clause if it comes first.

- If students are unsure, answer any questions or ask them to read the Language reference at this stage.

> In sentence **1** we use *if* + past perfect (*had* + past participle), + *would/should/might/could* + infinitive.
> In sentence **2** we use *if* + past simple + *would/ should/might/could* + *have* + past participle.

8 Allow students about five minutes for this activity.

- Ask them to compare with a partner before you check answers with the class.

> **1** c); **2** g); **3** b); **4** e); **5** a); **6** d); **7** f)

i Sir Tim Berners-Lee invented the Internet in the late 1980s/early 1990s.

For further practice, ask students to do exercise G2 4 on page 157 in the Language reference.

9 Give students ten minutes to do this activity individually, using their dictionaries if necessary.

- Monitor to point out mistakes with form but encourage students to self-correct by looking at exercises 6 and 7 or at G2 on page 156 in the Language reference.

- Ask students to compare with a partner, correct mistakes if necessary and discuss the sentences.

- Elicit an example of each sentence from the class, correct it if necessary and ask other students if they agree with the idea expressed.

SPEAKING

10 Read the introduction with the class and elicit/ tell them that a *debate* is a formal argument and discussion.

- Check they understand *rapid rate* (fast moving/ changing).

- Go through the following format of a debate, writing it on the board if necessary: 1 People give their arguments for the motion; 2 The opposition gives their arguments against the motion; 3 Both sets of people ask each other questions, discuss the points, disagree, etc.

- Divide the class into two groups (A and B) and tell them to look at their information but not to read the other group's information.

- Tell them to follow the instructions in the Coursebook and that all students must speak in the debate later.

- Remind students of the language in exercise 4 and tell them to use conditionals when appropriate.

- Monitor to help students with vocabulary and ideas if necessary.

- When students have finished preparing, put the groups together so that everyone can see everyone else.

- Remind students of the debate format you introduced earlier and give the following timings: 1 five minutes; 2 five minutes; 3 ten minutes. You must give groups equal time in stages 1 and 2. If the 'for' and 'against' groups are large, allow more time in stages 1 and 2.

- While students are speaking monitor to note mistakes with language from exercise 4 and conditionals.

- When the debate and discussion are finished, ask students to vote for or against the motion. Emphasise they don't have to vote for their group if they think the other group's arguments were stronger.

- Finally, correct some of the more common and important mistakes you noted earlier.

If you have a very large class, you could form two A groups and two B groups. Then hold two simultaneous debates in separate parts of the room so that the noise doesn't distract groups.

HOMEWORK OPTIONS

Students do the exercises on pages 84–85 of the Workbook.

Students research a piece of technology that has changed people's lives. They write an email to the author of the article in exercise 2, supporting his view and describing the consequences of their chosen technology *not* being developed.

Students do exercises G2 4 on page 157 in the Language reference.

12.4 SCENARIO: COMPUTER CRASH

Lesson topic and staging

This lesson focuses on language for reassuring and encouraging people. Students read an article that introduces the scenario of a car breakdown company in trouble because its state-of-the-art computer systems are not working properly. Next, they listen to some members of staff commenting on working conditions at the company and then rank some of the company's problems. They then listen to the director talking to a staff member and focus on the KEY LANGUAGE. Finally, the TASK asks them to role-play a staff meeting to discuss the problems and decide on solutions.

Objectives

By the end of the lesson, students should have:

- learned useful phrases for reassuring and encouraging people
- used this language in a 'real-life' situation to take part in a staff meeting
- extracted specific information and/or language items from a reading and listening texts
- participated effectively in extended speaking practice.

Common European Framework

Students can use language effectively to agree and disagree politely, ask someone to clarify what they've said and make their opinions clear as regards finding solutions to problem.

Timings

If short of time, you could drop exercise 3b on page 129. A possible lesson break would be after exercise 3b.

WARM-UP

This activity introduces the idea of technology breaking down and what to do about it.

- Write the following on the board: *home telephone, cooker, car, TV, cell/mobile phone, fridge, home computer.*
- Ask students to imagine that they own all these items and they suddenly stop working.
- Tell them to rank the consequences of these items stopping working, from most to least serious.
- Put students in pairs to compare answers and give reasons.
- Elicit a couple of lists from students and ask the rest of the class if they agree.
- Take this opportunity to introduce *computer crash.*

- Finally, elicit what they would do and/or who they would call if each item stopped working.
- Elicit answers and include *breakdown service.*

SITUATION

1 If you used the Warm-up, tell students the article is about problems caused because the computer systems are not working properly.

- Focus students on the photo and elicit what kind of company it is (a car breakdown company).
- Then ask students to read the questions before giving them five minutes to read the text and answer.
- Ask students to compare and discuss with a partner before you check answers with the class.

> **1** Very serious because the company has fallen from first to fourth place for customer satisfaction, services are rated 'poor' and not 'value for money', customers complaints have risen sharply, many have moved to other companies, it's clearly facing a crisis; **2** a building controlled by a sophisticated computer system that makes decisions about the building's facilities, environment, databases, etc.; **3** Answers depend on students' own opinions.

2a Ask students to read items a)–d) before you play the track.

- Check answers with the class.

> **a)** 3; **b)** 4; **c)** 1; **d)** 2

2b Tell students to make short notes and not to try to write sentences.

- Play the track, pausing after each speaker to give students time to write.
- Ask students to compare with a partner before you check answers with the class.
- In feedback, elicit the meaning of *sprinkler system* which students will be able to guess from context.
- Finally, ask students which problem they think is most serious. (Answers are bold in the audioscript below.)

> Complaint 1: not enough room for everyone's car in the company car park, but they still let you drive in when it's already full, you spend ages looking for a space when there isn't one, a waste of time. Complaint 2: boiling hot during the winter and icy cold some days during the summer, the system just doesn't work properly. Complaint 3: can't use the kitchen because when you heat food, the fire alarm goes off and you get wet from the sprinkler system. Complaint 4: the lighting system is too sophisticated, it often turns off the lights when he's in the office working.

Audioscript and answers to exercise 2:
Track 3.21

1
I come to work by car. Parking's a terrible problem. There's **not enough room in the company car park for all the cars, but they still let you drive in,** and then you **spend ages looking for a space**, and there just isn't one. It's so annoying, such a **waste of time.** If the computer's so good, why can't it stop people going in if there's no space?

2
I like the general office, it's open plan and very friendly. But goodness, the air conditioning's awful. The office gets **boiling hot during the winter and it's icy cold some days during the summer.** Would you believe it, I had to put on a thick jumper while I was working in the middle of August. **The system just doesn't work properly.** You can keep your new computer, it's no good at all for controlling the temperature. I'm fed up with it. I preferred my old office – it was fine, and I always felt comfortable in it.

3
We'd all like to use the little kitchen for a quick coffee or to heat up a pizza. It was a good idea to have the **kitchen** next to our office. But we **can't use it, because when you heat something up, the fire alarm goes off and you get a cold shower from the sprinkler system.** Last week, I was soaked to the skin before I could get out! I tell you, the new computer system is no good, and never will be.

4
It's the **lighting system** that bothers me, it's **too sophisticated.** When I leave the office, it turns off the light, that's great. But the trouble is, it **often turns off the lights when I'm in the office, working**, that's really annoying. I never had a problem with the lights until the new computer was introduced. It's so sensitive. If you don't move around, it often switches off the light – it really drives me crazy at times.

3a Tell students that the ranking will depend on their own opinions.

- Allow students eight minutes to rank the problems, using dictionaries if necessary.

3b Groups should have a maximum of four students.

- Give students five minutes to compare lists and give reasons if necessary.

- Ask students if their lists were similar or different (and why).

KEY LANGUAGE:
reassuring and encouraging

4a First, ask students how they think the staff feel and include *upset* and *worried* in the items you elicit.

- Focus students on the title of this section and elicit that this is language to make worried people feel less so.

- Set the context and ask students to read the questions before you play the track.

- Ask students to compare with a partner before you check answers with the class (sections containing the answers are bold in the audioscript below exercise 4c).

- In feedback, check students understand *get the blame* (be told it's you that did something wrong) *had a go at me* (criticised me, verbally attacked me).

> **1** losing her job, she's got a family and her husband's unemployed; **2** she can't work with the computer system, and when it goes wrong, she gets the blame; **3** it crashed; **4** the team leader had a go at Rosa, told Rosa she was no good at her job; **5** there's an informal staff meeting for people to talk about how they feel and to make suggestions

4b First, ask students to try to fill gaps before you play the track.

- Then play the track, if necessary pausing at the points indicated in the audioscript below.

4c Ask students to compare with a partner before reading the audioscript on page 189.

- Check answers with the class (underlined in the audioscript below) and elicit that the director is using this language to make Rosa feel better.

- Then elicit/tell students that *I assure*, *I guarantee* and *you have my word* all mean *I promise*.

- Finally, check students' pronunciation of *assure* and *guarantee*.

Audioscript and answers to exercise 4:
Track 3.22
Director, Rosa
D: Hello, Rosa, can I join you?
R: Oh, …yes, certainly.
D: I'd like to have a chat with you, is that OK?
R: Yes, of course, how can I help?
D: Well, it's about work really. You see, I know a lot of staff aren't happy at the moment. Could I ask you, how do you feel about everything?
R: Well … er …
D: You can be frank with me, Rosa, <u>1 I promise you, it won't go any further.</u> [PAUSE]
R: OK, well actually, I'm really worried. I read that article, someone showed it to me, and, I don't know, **I'm worried about my job. I've got three children, and my husband's unemployed, I can't afford to be out of work.**
D: <u>2 Look, I understand how you feel.</u> [PAUSE] <u>3 But I can assure you</u>, we're going to put things right. [PAUSE] Please don't lose faith in us, even if you are a bit down at the moment.
R: It's not just me, I think we're all unhappy at the moment. We feel, I don't know, let down. **Everything's changed so much.**
D: How do you mean, changed? Is it because you're not happy with the move to this building?

continued…

R: No, it's not that, it's **the new computer system.** I just can't work with it. I think I'm doing the right thing, you know, operating it correctly, then **something goes wrong, and I get all the blame, when really it's the fault of the computer.**

D: Mmm, it's true, there's certainly been a lot of teething problems with the new systems – no doubt about that.

R: Yeah, but please don't blame it on us when things go wrong.

D: So, … what's gone wrong recently then?

R: Lots of things. Like, last week the **computer crashed** – it took almost a day and a half before we could use it. Subscriptions started piling up, **I had to do overtime to cope** with all the extra work, and did I get any thanks? No, **I entered the wrong details a couple of times, and my team leader had a go at me. Said I was no good at the job.**

D: Mmm, 4 that doesn't sound very fair to me, I must say. [PAUSE] Anyway, 5 don't worry, Rosa, we know you're one of the best workers in the company. Everyone knows that. [PAUSE] And 6 I guarantee we'll sort out the problems. [PAUSE] You won't be out of a job, 7 you have my word for that.

R: I hope you're right. [*sighs*].You know, with the old computer system, I was always on top of my work. People used to say what a great worker I was. [PAUSE]

D: 8 I can see how you feel and we're going to do something about it, I promise. [PAUSE] Tell me, are you free next Wednesday? There's going to be **a meeting after work. An informal one, a chance for people to say how they feel, and make suggestions.** I've asked the Head of Human Resources to lead the discussion. Would you be willing to represent the admin staff? You're very popular with your colleagues, I know you'd be a good choice.

R: Well, I suppose so – if they all agree.

D: Great. I'll talk to them, but I know they'll be happy for you to represent them. And stop worrying about your job. 9 Things'll get better, I guarantee that. We've contacted the supplier of the computer systems. They're confident they can sort out the problems and get things working again soon. Please tell your colleagues that.

R: OK, I'll do that.

D: Right. I hope you have a good meeting on Wednesday. I'll get my assistant to send you details.

TASK: problem-solving meeting

5 Remind students of the staff meeting mentioned in exercise 4a.

- Read through the instructions with the class and divide them into groups of four.
- Ask each student to choose a role or decide for them.
- Remind students of the KEY LANGUAGE and decide if they need to reassure others in the meeting.

- Give students about ten minutes to prepare and monitor to help if necessary.

- If you have at least eight students, first you could put them into groups with others with the same role. They can then help each other prepare for the meeting. Then form new groups with one of each role represented.

6 Read through the instructions with the class and check they understand *staff morale* (level of happiness).

- Go through the OTHER USEFUL PHRASES and tell students they will also need to (choose as appropriate to your class) agree, disagree, argue, persuade, as well as sometimes reassure people.
- Allow ten to fifteen minutes for the meeting and remind students to note down decisions.
- Monitor to note mistakes with any of the language you previously mentioned as useful.

7 If you have a very large class, form two groups to do this activity simultaneously.

- Tell students to read out their decisions from exercise 6 and discuss these as a class (or in their groups if you have a very large class).
- Monitor to note mistakes with any of the language you mentioned as useful in exercise 6.
- When they have finished, elicit what students have decided to do and why.
- Finally, correct some of the mistakes you noted in this exercise and exercise 6.

HOMEWORK OPTIONS

Students do the exercises on page 86 of the Workbook.

Students write a short letter to the staff of EBS saying what decisions were made and why.

Students do exercise KL 5 on page 157 in the Language reference.

12.5 STUDY AND WRITING SKILLS

Lesson topic and staging

This lesson focuses on how to avoid plagiarism and writing an article. Students discuss a list of examples of plagiarism and then listen to a lecture on this topic. Students then read a paragraph and four short texts based on it and decide which are plagiarised. Next, students brainstorm ideas on writing an article on technology. They then read an article and focus on language used to show the writer's opinion. Finally, students write an article of their own.

Objectives

By the end of the lesson, students should have:

- extracted specific information and/or language items from a listening and reading texts
- learned about plagiarism and how to avoid it
- learned language for positioning (making your point of view clear)
- written an article for a scientific journal.

Common European Framework

Students can understand the main points and information in articles, and understand a writer's specific attitudes and points of view. Students can write simple connected texts to convey ideas on abstract and concrete ideas and link a series of discrete items into a connected linear sequence of points.

Timings

If short of time, you could set exercise 8 for homework. Alternatively, you could drop exercise 2c on page 130 as this does not add to students' understanding of plagiarism. A possible lesson break would be after exercise 3 on page 130.

This activity introduces the idea of quoting what other people say.

- Write the following questions on the board: 'How long have you lived in this town/city? Do you like it?'
- Tell students to speak to five others in the class but not to write their answers. Instead, they must remember who said what.
- When they have spoken to five students, put them into pairs to tell each other who said what.
- Then ask the class if anyone remembers what everyone said and elicit the answers they heard.

- Finally, elicit that it is difficult to remember who said what, but then ask in what situation it is essential to quote sources (when writing academic essays, articles, etc.).

STUDY SKILLS: plagiarism – what it is and how to avoid it

At no point in these activities try to personalise by asking *Have you been caught plagiarising?* etc.

1 Focus students on the title of this section of the lesson and ask if students know what *plagiarism* is.

- Check students' pronunciation of *plagiarism*.
- Ask students in what situations plagiarism is considered a very serious offence.
- Set the activity, putting students into groups of three or four for the discussion.
- Answers will be checked in exercise 2a.

2a Set the activity and tell students to make extra notes next to statements in exercise 1 if they need to.

- Ask students to compare with a partner.
- Ask the students if they guessed correctly in exercise 1 and then go through answers with the class. (Sections containing the answers are bold in the audioscript below.)

> The following should be ticked: 1; 4; 5; 6. Example 2: Probably not plagiarism if it's completely *in your own words*, but if it's a close paraphrase, it is plagiarism. Example 3: It depends. If it's an idea generally known by everyone, it's not plagiarism. But if it's an idea only described by one person, you need to acknowledge.

Audioscript and answers to exercise 2a:
Track 3.23
Part 1
So, what is plagiarism? Well, basically, it's using the work of other people without saying where you got your information from, in other words, without acknowledging the author. If you use the same words that someone else has used in an article or lecture, for example, you are guilty of plagiarism. Of course, you're free to use the same words provided that you give a reference to the author and the source of the quote, I mean the article or book or whatever. **If you just rewrite sentences from another text in your own words, completely different from the original, you're probably not plagiarising.** You're doing a loose paraphrase, and that's OK, it's acceptable. **You're plagiarising too if you use other people's ideas without saying whose ideas they are; obviously some ideas are just general and known by everyone, but ideas described by one person must be acknowledged.**

continued…

Now, something that often surprises my students – you're also not allowed to copy work from another student, even if they give you permission, and submit it as your own. So, for example, if you discuss an essay with a friend of yours and then compare what you've written, you really must not take sections from your friend's essay and then use them in yours. **It's not collaboration – it's plagiarism.** I think it goes without saying that **you can't take a chunk of text from the Internet and put it in an assignment, without acknowledgment.** It's totally unacceptable. So, to sum up, you mustn't quote, copy or **paraphrase closely** what you've read or heard, without giving the source.

You know, I've heard of cases where students not only don't write the material they submit, but they don't even read it before giving it in! Incredible! The main problem is, some students often plagiarise without realising they're doing it. That of course is why I'm doing this lecture.

2b Ask students to read points 1–4 and then play the track.

- Elicit answers from the class and ask if this is the same in their country/countries.

  The following should be ticked: 1, 4

2c Ask students to read the questions and emphasise they only need to note a few words.

- Play the track and then ask students to compare with a partner.
- Check answers with the class.

  1 little confidence in their own ability, a competitive academic environment, they're lazy; **2** because of computer software that can detect plagiarism

Audioscript and answers to exercises 2 b and c: Track 3.24
Part 2
I'm often asked if you should use quotations from your source material. The answer is 'yes' **but not too many, if possible.** A lecturer wants your own thoughts and ideas about a subject, not just the ideas of other writers. They also want you to evaluate critically the material you've used. They're interested in your response to the topic. If you quote, however, you must write the words accurately, and **use quotation marks around the words you're quoting**, and of course, you should put a reference to the source with each one, in brackets.
continued…

Why do people plagiarise? I think, often, it's **because they don't have confidence in their own ability or ideas.** They feel safer using the ideas of other writers or speakers. Or it could be that **the student's studying in a very competitive environment. So, they feel they have to copy the work of well-known writers to get a good mark or high grade.** Another reason is, **some students are just too lazy to think about the material they're reading; it's too much effort for them to write notes in their own words.** OK, those are some of the reasons why people plagiarise. What's wrong with plagiarising? Well, it's a kind of stealing, isn't it? It's intellectual theft, and that's not acceptable.

These days, students use the Internet a lot for research. That's understandable, but it makes plagiarism very easy. It's also very risky now for students to plagiarise material from Internet sources and from any other sources, such as books or other students. **There's software available now, such as Turnitin, to spot plagiarism.** Staff can check quickly and effectively if they feel a student has copied material. So, the answer is, don't plagiarise, as you'll probably get caught!

3 Read through the introduction and instructions and then ask students to find out the topic of these texts by quickly reading the original paragraph.

- Give students eight minutes to read the four texts and discuss which are examples of plagiarism.
- Go through answers with the class.

  Versions A and D are not acceptable. A is worded too closely to the original. D starts with different wording but includes an unacknowledged quote.

WRITING SKILLS: an article

4 Read through the instructions with the class and ask students to read the example provided.

- Put students into pairs and give them three minutes to brainstorm pieces of advice.
- Elicit answers from the class and include the suggestions below.

  Suggested advice: read the journal to find out what style they like; make sure you use an appropriate style (probably formal); choose a topic that really interests you; decide what your point of view (your position) is before you write; brainstorm the content in note form; organise it into paragraphs; write a first draft; check and write a final draft; use clear topic sentences and linking; make sure your introduction states the purpose of the article, make sure your conclusion states your position; be very careful not to plagiarise.

5a Ask students to read the introduction and then give groups eight minutes to discuss and note arguments. Don't elicit ideas from the class at this stage.

5b Give students eight minutes to think of examples and monitor to prompt with ideas if necessary.

- Put groups together to compare and tell them to note down each others' arguments and examples.

- Tell students they will be able to use some of these arguments/examples later.

- If students have very few arguments/examples, elicit ideas from the whole class and write them on the board for students to use later.

6 Give students five minutes to read the article and answer the questions.

- Tell them not to worry about difficult vocabulary at this stage.

- Ask students to compare with a partner before you check answers with the class.

> **1** This article will present some of the disadvantages of technological advances (para 1); **2** Technology is developing too fast and it's essential to control it before it controls us (para 6).

7 Identifying the writer's position

- Elicit/tell students that the writer says there are advantages, but it is clear from his style that he thinks there are more disadvantages and his position is anti-technology.

- Then ask students to read the introduction, instructions and examples.

- Give them five minutes to find other examples and then compare with a partner.

- Elicit ideas from the class and write them on the board (or see the Tip below).

- Students may have ideas in addition to those below. Accept any reasonable suggestions.

- Note: 'chatting' is in inverted commas to show the writer does not believe this activity is like chatting.

- Numbers in brackets refer to the paragraph.

- ☼ If possible, reproduce the article so the whole class can see it (perhaps on an Interactive Whiteboard or an overhead projector). As you elicit ideas, underline them in the text.

- ⓘ Big Brother is the all-powerful, all-seeing, oppressive leader in George Orwell's novel *1984*. His face is seen everywhere with the slogan *Big Brother Is Watching You*. He probably does not exist but is an image used by the government to control people. The government watches the population through 'TV' screens.

Possible answers
Emphatic statements: People lose opportunities (2); Technology … creates isolated people (3); Young people sit … (3); we have no privacy any more (4); Someone is always spying on us (4); rich countries are using technology to dominate poor countries (5); It is essential to control technology (6)
Strong adverbs: undoubtedly (1); often (2); any more (4); everywhere (4); always (4); throughout (5); much too (6)
Strong adjectives: isolated (3); no [no privacy] (4) (Note: 'no' can also be labelled a determiner or a quantifier here.); ubiquitous (4); extreme (5); essential (6)
Strong language/images: sit for hours … like zombies (3); Big Brother (4) – see background information; spying (4); dominate (5); servant/master (6); before it is too late (6)
Rhetorical questions: But what is the result of 'chatting' with friends over the Internet for hours? (2); … does the technology benefit people in those countries? (5)

8 Ask students to read the instructions and then look again at the article in this lesson and lesson 12.3.

- Remind students of the advice in exercise 4 and the arguments/examples from exercise 5 and ask them to decide on their position

- Give them 15 minutes to brainstorm ideas and organise these into paragraphs.

- Remind them of the language in exercise 7 and then give them 30–40 minutes to write the article.

- Monitor to point out mistakes and help with vocabulary if necessary.

- Encourage them to write a first draft and to check it for mistakes before writing a final one.

- Take the articles in for marking, paying attention to positioning, and plagiarism.

HOMEWORK OPTIONS

Students do the exercises on pages 86–87 of the Workbook.

REVIEW

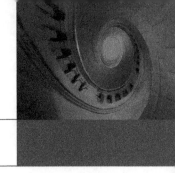

UNITS 10–12

GRAMMAR

1 Focus students on the photo on page 132 and elicit that this is an audience in the cinema, and they are wearing 3D glasses.

• Set the questions and give students three minutes to discuss them in groups of three.

2 Tell students to read items 1–5 and then give them two minutes to find the information in the text.

• Ask students to compare with a partner before you check answers with the class.

> 1 a film director (famous for *Titanic*); 2 a movie (a new version of Jules Verne's *Journey to the Centre of the Earth* – a novel published in 1864); 3 U2's (a world-famous Irish rock band) 3D film of their latest tour; 4 the number of US cinemas that have invested in 3D technology; 5 a Disney (famous, mostly children's film, production company) film

3 Give students eight minutes to do this activity individually and then compare with a partner.

• Go through answers with the class and elicit that the two answers in 3–5 have exactly the same meaning.

> 1 b); 2 a); 3 a) or b); 4 a) or c); 5 b) or c); 6 b) ; 7 b); 8 c); 9 a); 10 c)

VOCABULARY

4 Ask students to work in pairs for this activity.

• If they are unsure of any answers, they can skim the vocabulary sections in units 10–12 for help.

• Go through answers with the class.

> 1 technophobe; 2 environmentally; 3 used; 4 hard wearing; 5 stimulated; 6 psychiatrist; 7 inadequate; 8 frustrated; 9 cuisine; 10 intriguing; 11 fall; 12 equipment

5 Students work individually and then compare answers with a partner.

• Go through answers with the class.

> 1 make his mind up (about what to do); 2 out of her mind; 3 keep an open mind; 4 in two minds; 5 peace of mind

KEY LANGUAGE

6 Set the context and ask students to read statements 1–6.

• Play the track and then ask students to compare with a partner.

• Go through answers with the class.

> 1 False; 2 False (almost every evening); 3 True (that's the time when I [...] work on my assignments); 4 False (once); 5 True; 6 True

7 Give students ten minutes to do this activity individually.

• Ask them to compare with a partner before you play the track again.

• Check answers with the class.

> 1 You can be frank ~~of~~ with me ...; 2 Why don't you ~~say~~ tell me all about it?; 3 Look, I understand how you feel ~~it~~; 4 That ~~isn't~~ doesn't sound very fair to me ...; 5 ... good idea to ~~explain~~ tell them how you feel; 6 If I ~~be~~ were you, I'd ...; 7 ... talking to your landlord ~~for~~ about this; 8 Stop ~~worry~~ worrying about it.

Track 3.25
Tara, Henry
T: Can I have a word with you, Henry?
H: Sure.
T: I'm very behind with my coursework.
H: Are you finding the course too difficult?
T: Not really. That's not the problem.
H: Well, is there something wrong at home?
T: Erm ...
H: You can be frank with me, Tara. I promise you, it won't go any further.
T: Things have been quite difficult recently with ... with my flatmates.
H: Why don't you tell me all about it?
T: It's hard to explain. It seems so stupid ...
H: Look, I understand how you feel. Just tell me in your own words.
T: OK. It's the evenings really. You see they love listening to music and they have really powerful stereo systems. In fact they play music almost every night. But that's the time when I need to work on my assignments.
H: But why is that a problem for you?
T: Well, the music is so loud I can't really concentrate on my work.
H: Mmm, that doesn't sound very fair to me, I must say. It might be a good idea to tell them how you feel.

continued...

T: I'm not sure. I mean … I don't want to stop them enjoying themselves.

H: If I were you I'd just ask them to turn down the volume.

T: Well, I did ask them once and they turned it down. But they just started playing the music loudly again the next night.

H: You might consider talking to your landlord about this. He probably doesn't know about this noise problem.

T: Maybe. I suppose I could try talking to him.

H: And stop worrying about it. Things'll get better, I'm sure about that.

If students have problems remembering these exercises, you could put them into small groups to remind each other (as appropriate) of the vocabulary learned, the content of the text, the topic they talked about.

To extend the activity, ask students to choose one of the exercises and write a test for other students. This could be a list of questions, a true/false, a gapfill, etc.

LANGUAGE CHECK

8 Give students ten minutes to complete the gaps and then check their answers.

• Ask students to compare with a partner before you go through answers with the class.

> **1** a playwright about whom historians know; **2** something in which we all believe; **3** a strange man taking pictures of us …; **4** He said he had ('d) never been to …; **5** … insisted on inviting us …; **6** … apologised for not finishing …; **7** warned us not to go into …; **8** I'm sure you will ('ll) enjoy it …; **9** you would ('d) be offered food …; **10** many children would not be suffering …(Note: we do not normally contract *would* in writing after a proper noun e.g. *children*.)

LOOK BACK

9 The aim of this activity is to remind students of areas they looked at in Units 10–12. This will help reinforce any language or skills they had difficulties with or were particularly good at.

> read about nine key roles in management terms: 10.1, exercise 4; complete the rule about when we can omit *that* in relative clauses: 10.2, exercise 6b study the phrases which we can use to give advice: 10.4, exercise 4; decide on items to put into a time capsule: 11.1, exercise 8; listen to someone taking about life in Chicago: 11.2, exercise 6; learn about reporting verbs followed by the infinitive with *to*: 11.3, exercise 3; study examples of the first and second conditional: 12.2, exercise 7; practise talking about past conditions with present results: 12.3, exercise 9; listen to a lecture about plagiarism: 12.5, exercise 2

Unit 1
G1 1
1 a; 2 a; 3 a; 4 b; 5 b; 6 a
G2 2
1 Do you prefer ...; 2 Are you reading ...; 3 Does this mobile phone belong ...; 4 Is your course getting ...; 5 Does anyone know...; 6 Do you agree with ...; 7 Are the students learning ...; 8 Do your parents know ...
G3 3
1 c; 2 a; 3 c; 4 b; 5 a; 6 c; 7 a; 8 b; 9 c; 10 b
KL 4
1 rather; 2 vicious; 3 sort; 4 trouble; 5 solution; 6 situation; 7 deal; 8 solve
V1 5
1 pace; 2 appearance; 3 cultures; 4 charisma; 5 vocabulary; 6 nerves
V2,3 6 1 c; 2 f; 3 d; 4 a; 5 g; 6 b; 7 e

Unit 2
G1 1 1 b; 2 a; 3 a; 4 a; 5 b
G1 2
1 've looked at; 2 've been reading/'ve read; 3 've been worrying; 4 've been living/'ve lived; 5 's been raining; 6 've bought
G2 3
1 he works; 2 if they are; 3 it is; 4 we can get; 5 it is; 6 she does
G2 4
1 Could you tell me how much it costs?; 2 I'd like to know when the film starts; 3 Do you know whether she's coming to the party?; 4 Can you tell me if this model is available?; 5 I wonder where they put the keys?; 6 I'd like to know what causes earthquakes.
KL 5
1 e; 2 a; 3 f; 4 c; 5 g; not needed: b & d
V1 6
1 vandalism; 2 crime; 3 detached; 4 blocks; 5 open; 6 connections; 7 abandoned; 8 stunning
V2 7
1 satellite images; 2 scientific journals; 3 significant effects; 4 global warming; 5 false impression; 6 climate change
V3 8
1 relatively; 2 deliberately; 3 comparatively; 4 mainly; 5 pensively; 6 normally

Unit 3
G1 1
1 a few; 2 students; 3 hardly any; 4 none of; 5 Several of; 6 a little; 7 little; 8 Few; 9 much
G2 2
Quidditch is a fictional sport invented by the author J.K. Rowling for the best-selling Harry Potter books. It is a ball game in which the players try to score goals. There are four balls and two teams of seven players. Usually the players are wizards and witches and play the game by flying on their broomsticks. The goals are ring-shaped and are above the ground. The object of the game is to score more goals than the opposing team.
G2 3
1 the; 2 the; 3 The; 4 the; 5 –, – ; 6 the
KL 4 1 d; 2 f; 3 b; 4 e; 5 a; 6 g; 7 c
V1 5
1 Steve; 2 Caroline; 3 Lucy; 4 David; 5 Miranda; 6 Walter
V2 6
1 d; 2 b; 3 e; 4 a; 5 c
V3,4 7
1 agility; 2 illegal; 3 coordination; 4 expert; 5 dramatic

Unit 4
G1 1
1 1b 2a; 2 1b 2a; 3 1a 2b; 4 1b 2a; 5 1b 2a
G2 2
1 won't have seen; 2 will have had; 3 won't have finished; 4 will have arrived; 5 won't have left; 6 will have returned; 7 will have listened; 8 will have spent
G2 3
1 c; 2 f; 3 b; 4 h; 5 g; 6 e; not used: a, d

KL 4
1 If we **spend** the money on the buildings ...; 2 I'm not sure about that. It'd **probably** cost quite a lot ...; 3 We'll have to think about that. It **could** have an effect ...; 4 I'll **be talking** to the manager ...; 5 I'm not sure about that. What **angle** do you think ...; 6 We need to be careful. That might have a big **impact** on our sales.
V1,2 5
words in puzzle: anaesthetist; antibiotic; arthritis; cancer; diabetes; ether; fever; infection; injection; midwife; morphine; mould; painkiller; parasite; pharmacist; physiotherapy; psychiatrist; radiologist; surgeon; symptom; transplant; vaccine

Unit 5
G1 1 1 d; 2 c; 3 e; 4 b; 5 a
G2 2
1 managed; 2 didn't have to; 3 weren't able to; 4 in getting; 5 couldn't; 6 to find; 7 was able to; 8 could
G2 3
1 I couldn't/wasn't able to ....; 2 I could/was able to sing ....; 3 Juan didn't have to wear ...; 4 We were able to get ...; 5 I had to pay ...; 6 I succeeded in borrowing/managed to borrow ....
KL 4
1 really; 2 agree; 3 mind; 4 sure; 5 that; 6 way; 7 answer; 8 need
V1 5 1 d; 2 f; 3 b; 4 e; 5 c; 6 a
V2 6
1 fogbound runway; 2 turbulence; 3 rough weather; 4 puncture; 5 tailback; 6 platform alteration
V3 7
something inside or part of a car: airbag, anti-lock brakes, seat belt; something on the road: one-way street, speed cameras, traffic lights; a law: speed limit
V4 8
1 tycoon; 2 elevated; 3 freight; 4 shuttle; 5 fleet; 6 emit

Unit 6
G1 1 1 b; 2 a; 3 a; 4 a
G1 2
1 was sitting; 2 looked; 3 had been sitting; 4 had/had brought; 5 was; 6 had been working 7 hadn't had; 8 went; 9 brought; 10 sat; 11 was looking; 12 had/had brought
G2 3
A When I was a child I ~~use~~ *used* to read ...Then I would to read by ....; B Years ago I ~~would~~ *used* to live .... It ~~would~~ *used to* be such good fun.; C ... Didn't you ~~used~~ use to live i ... I ~~would~~ *used to* live ...
KL 4
1 Oh, I wasn't expecting ~~for~~ to pay so much.; 2 How about if I talked to her?; 3 ✓; 4 You'll find I'm good **value** for money.; 5 Look, I'd like **to** make a proposal.; 6 Could I suggest we to meet in November?; 7 ✓; 8 I need more time **to** think about this ...
V1 5
1 blogs; 2 poetry; 3 biographies; 4 history; 5 memoirs; 6 autobiographies; 7 romances; 8 novels
V2 6
1 judge; 2 poet; 3 biographer; 4 dramatist; 5 critic; 6 novelist
V3 7
1 candle, lamp, lantern, flash; 2 cry, whistle, yell, shriek; 3 gleam, glare, flash; 4 darkness, silence; 5 silent, audible

Unit 7
G1,2 1
1 has been stolen; 2 was being watched; 3 am being kept awake at night; 4 was given a watch; 5 is required; 6 can't be explained
G1,2 2
1 was being established; 2 was given; 3 was built; 4 being allowed; 5 have been influenced; 6 have been constructed; 7 was/is inspired; 8 is being damaged; 9 to be restored
G3 3 1 a; 2 b; 3 b; 4 a
KL 4
1 got; 2 through; 3 vital; 4 absolutely; 5 idea; 6 find; 7 offer; 8 need
V1 5
1 ornate; 2 innovative; 3 ancient; 4 ugly
V2 6
1 rebuilt; 2 damaged; 3 commission; 4 demolish; 5 designed; 6 maintain; 7 restore; 8 construct

V3 7 1 d; 2 a; 3 c; 4 b

V4 8

1 insoluble; 2 overcrowded; 3 revitalised; 4 misunderstood;
5 unimportant

Unit 8

G1 1

1 Our teacher allowed us to use calculators.; 2 We stopped the car
to look at the beautiful view.; 3 Would you consider ~~give~~ giving us
a larger room? ; 4 I'm afraid I forgot ~~locking~~ to lock the door ...;
5 The door seems to be locked. ... 6 ... I'll try ~~send~~ sending him a
text message.; 7 Did you remember ~~turning~~ to turn off the lights?;
8 I always try to stay in touch ...

G1 2 1 1b, 2a; 2 1a, 2b; 3 1b, 2a; 4 1a, 2b

G2 3

1 has had his/her house searched; 2 am having my car washed;
3 had his watch repaired; 4 have my hair cut; 5 has had her
contract cancelled; 6 had our bags searched

KL 4

1 d; 2 f; 3 a; 4 h; 5 b; 6 g; 7 e; 8 c

V1,2 5

Clues across: 6 multinational; 8 rights; 10 corporate. Clues down:
1 influence; 2 creativity; 3 collaboration; 4 networking; 5 hierarchy;
7 resources; 9 fair

V3, 6

1 celebrity; 2 press; 3 paparazzi; 4 broadcast; 5 newspaper;
6 coverage

Unit 9

G1 1

1 absolutely; 2 really; 3 absolutely; 4 really/very; 5 slightly/
extremely; 6 very; 7 good; 8 enormous/big; 9 interesting; 10 hotter;
11 starving; 12 upset

G2 2

Bridget Riley is probably the most famous living painter of op art
(optical art). These are works which usually feature patterns ... In
these large paintings she skilfully used black and white lines to
create amazing illusions. Her first big exhibition was in London
in 1962. The paintings on display were so powerful that viewers
frequently complained ... she used colour imaginatively. In the late
1980s, she began to experiment ...

G2 3

1 is mainly; 2 opened the envelope carefully; 3 In 2004 I; 4 usually
get home; 5 certainly know; 6 have often seen; 7 did you get there;
8 finished his essay quickly

KL 4

1 f; 2 c; 3 b; 4 g; 5 d; 6 a; not needed = e

V1 5

1 artist, art lover, collector, critic, painter, sculptor; 2 abstract,
realist, contemporary, modern; 3 thought-provoking, controversial,
groundbreaking; 4 preview, retrospective; 5 masterpiece

V2 6

1 moving; 2 painfully;3 useless; 4 criticised; 5 highly; 6 entirely;
7 totally; 8 highly; 9 totally; 10 different; 11 wrong; 12 utterly

Unit 10

G1 1

1 That's the man I met yesterday.; 2 This is the DVD player which/
that doesn't work very well.; 3 Janine is the woman whose house
was destroyed in the earthquake.; 4 My sister, who is a doctor,
lives in an old house./My sister, who lives in an old house, is a
doctor. ; 5 This is the computer game I told you about. /This is the
computer game about which I told you.; 6 The course, which began
in September, is very difficult./The course, which is very difficult,
began in September

G1 2

1 I don't fully understand the problem on which he's working.;
2 Protecting the environment is a cause in which she really
believes.; 3 This is the bill about which we disagreed.; 4 This is the
course for which they applied.; 5 That hotel is the one in which we
often stayed.; 6 Constance is the architect for whom I work.; 7 That's
the team for which my brother plays football.; 8 Do you remember
the project on which we used to work together?

G1 3

1 Do you know the person about ~~who~~ whom I am talking?; 2 This
phone, ~~that~~ which was very expensive, has never worked properly.;
3 I'm visiting the place where I grew up ~~in~~.; 4 Michael, who is very
intelligent, isn't very good at solving puzzles.; 5 The students, who
are from many different countries, are learning English.; 6 She's a
woman that ~~she~~ never admits she's wrong.

G2 4

1 designed; 2 left; 3 standing; 4 recommended; 5 giving; 6 bought

KL 5

1 c; 2 g; 3 d; 4 h; 5 f; 6 a; 7 e; 8 b

V1 6

1 get on with; 2 get used to; 3 broke up; 4 fall out with; 5 put up
with; 6 get down to

V2 7 1 c; 2 b; 3e; 4 d; 5 a

V3 8

1 psychiatrists; 2 case files; 3 assessment; 4 profiles; 5 motive; 6 deduce

Unit 11

G1 1

1 was working; 2 had lived; 3 should see; 4 would see ... the next/
following day; 5 had been...his... their; 6 his ... had received... the
day before/the previous day.

G1 2

1 she doesn't have a job at the moment.; 2 the weather there is
always cold in the winter.; 3 they're going to France when they've
finished the course.; 4 had been to a terrible school when she was a
child.; 5 they had watched the final episode of ER the night before.;
6 pollution from cars causes global warming.

G2 3

1 warned; 2 refused; 3 apologised for; 4 offered; 5 persuaded; 6 agree

G2 4

1 He offered to carry my case.; 2 She regretted getting married
so young.; 3 Mike warned me not to buy anything from that
shop.; 4 She apologised for shouting at me.; 5 My parents always
encouraged me to learn the guitar.

KL 5

(suggested answers): 1 Why is Cambridge worth seeing?; 2 It is an
important educational, cultural and business centre.; 3 Facilities for
tourists are getting better and better each year.; 4 Its buildings, parks
and countryside make it a beautiful place to live.; 5 The university is
becoming more and more popular with international students.;
6 So, what are the main historical sights of the city?

V1 6

1 language; 2 institutions; 3 cuisine; 4 religion; 5 the arts;
6 architecture 7 rituals/traditions; 8 climate

V2 7

1 d; 2 a; 3 e; 4 b; 5 f; 6 c

V3,4 8

1 valuable; 2 responsible; 3 international; 4 multicultural;
5 misunderstanding; 6 antisocial; 7 predates; 8 timeless

Unit 12

G1 1 1 d; 2 b; 3 c; 4 c; 5 c; 6 b; 7 c; 8 b

G1 2

1 If I~~'ll~~ go tomorrow ...; 2 Supposing we ~~are~~ were rich, ...; 3 I'd be
much happier if I ~~can~~ could ...; 4 As long as you ~~would~~ look after it,
...; 5 ... if she ~~would bring~~ brings her camera.; 6 ... ~~won't~~ wouldn't
it be amazing?

G2 3

1 h; 2 c; 3 f; 4 b; 5g; 6a; 7e; 8 d

G2 4

1 would have talked; 2 had done; 3 had had; 4 would be; 5 had
gone; 6 wouldn't have been

KL 5

1 d; 2 c; 3 f; 4 h; 5 b; 6 e; 7 g; 8 a

V1 6

1 appliances; 2 device; 3 apparatus; 4 equipment; 5 gadget

V2 7

1 user-friendly; 2 state-of-the-art; 3 durable; 4 obsolete; 5 handy;
6 environmentally friendly

V3 8

1 unable; 2 inequality; 3 dislikes; 4 inaccurate; 5 mistrust;
6 unnecessary; 7 inefficient; 8 inappropriate

List of photocopiable worksheets

1 A	Who's a good communicator?	Pair/group work	Vocabulary related to communication skills
1 B	What are you doing? What have you done?	Pair work	Continuous and perfect aspect in past and present; present and past simple
2 A	Let's move to …	Pair/group work	Vocabulary to describe city living environments
2 B	Ask me indirectly!	Individual, then whole class	Indirect questions in different tenses
3 A	Winning's a certainty!	Pair work	Abstract nouns made from adjectives
3 B	Did you get all of them or hardly any?	Individual, then pairs	Selected quantifiers in the context of sport
4 A	Medical word search	Individual/pair work	Knowledge and recognition of medical terms
4 B	The first day of the rest of your life	Whole class	Present continuous, *going to*, future continuous, *will* and future perfect
5 A	Not sure we'll get there but it's worth the try	Group work	Vocabulary for transport and transport problems
5 B	It's all in the planning	Individual, then pairs	Modal verbs for past and future ability, possibility and obligation
6 A	I'd love a good book!	Individual, then groups	Vocabulary related to types of literature and writing
6 B	I like a good mystery!	Pair/group work	Narrative tenses and creating their own ending to a story
7 A	Architectural comparisons	Pair/group work	Positive, negative and neutral vocabulary for describing buildings
7 B	Important buildings	Individual, then pairs	Passive structures in the context of buildings and architecture
8 A	Verb patterns scrabble	Group work	Verbs which take the infinitive or *-ing*
8 B	What have you had done?	Individual, then whole class	*have something done* in a personalised and guided context
9 A	How do you feel?	Whole class	Ungradable adjectives and their gradable equivalents
9 B	Describe it to me again?	Pair/group work	Adjective order to describe works of art
10 A	It's all in the mind	Individual, then pairs	Idioms using *mind*
10 B	A relative nightmare	Individual/pair work	Non-defining, defining and reduced relative clauses
11 A	How do you feel? What's it like?	Individual, then groups	Vocabulary to describe feelings and situations
11 B	Networking	Whole class	Reported speech in the context of travel and culture
12 A	Prefix snap	Pair/group work	Opposite adjectives formed with prefixes
12 B	What if …?	Individual, then whole class	First, second and third conditional, present and past condition with past results

Teaching notes for photocopiable activities

1a Who's a good communicator? (use after Lesson 1.1)

Aim: to provide further practice of vocabulary related to communication skills

Grouping: pairs or groups of four

Procedure:

- Divide the class into pairs or groups of four (with two pairs in each group).
- Explain that they work for an international PR (Public Relations) company and are part of a committee deciding on a new recruit for their customer relations department. They need to recruit someone who is a good communicator with people from all kinds of communities and cultures
- The candidates have already been interviewed and a summary email has been sent to the committee about each person. The committee has decided to invite one candidate back for a final interview and needs to decide which one.
- Give students the summary emails (a different one for each student in a pair, or for each pair in a group of four).
- Tell students to read their email and write the appropriate word or phrase on the comments (+/–). E.g. if their email says 'Couldn't look at me and was always looking out of the window', students should write 'can't maintain eye contact' or 'poor eye contact' in the – column.
- If students aren't sure about how to interpret some of the information, they should note it as something to look for in the final interview e.g. 'How charismatic?'.
- When students have completed they +/– sheets, put them into pairs (or groups of four) and tell them to discuss which of the two candidates should be invited for the final interview and why.
- Finally, ask each group who they decided should be invited back and why.

1b What are you doing? What have you done? (use after Lessons 1.2 and 1.3)

Aims: to provide further practice of continuous aspect and perfect aspect in the past and present, the present simple and the past simple within the context of communications

Grouping: pairs

Procedure:

- Give each student one role card and a copy of the interview form.
- Explain that you are going to put them into pairs and they are going to ask each other questions about the roles.
- Ask them to read their information and think about the answers they will give. Help students with problem vocabulary or ask them to use their dictionaries.
- Then give students five minutes to decide what questions they need to ask to get information from their partner. Either go through questions with the whole class or monitor to check that individual students' questions are accurate, e.g. Job? = 'What do you do?' Currently working? = 'Where are you currently working?' OR 'Who are you currently working for?'

- Put students into pairs and tell them to ask each other questions and note the answers in the second column on the interview form. Stress that students should only write notes and not full sentences. Encourage students to ask follow-up questions to get as much information as possible.
- If students don't have an answer to a question, tell them to invent something interesting.
- When they have finished, ask students which of the two jobs they would prefer to have and which of the two people they would prefer to be.

2a Let's move to … (use after Lesson 2.1)

Aim: to provide further practice of vocabulary to describe city living environments

Grouping: pairs or groups of four

Procedure:

- Explain that the students are going to move to another part of their city and share a flat/house together, but first they must decide where to go.
- Tell students they are going to read blog postings on the city's *Residents' Website* which gives information on what it's like to live in different areas.
- Give each student (or pair) one blog card and tell them to make notes to summarise the information. Students cannot use the same words as the blog but must use vocabulary from exercises 2a and 2b on page 16 of the Coursebook, e.g. 'Stanton's got a good mix of people from all over the world.' = 'Stanton – cosmopolitan/ cosmopolitan atmosphere'.
- Monitor to help students with the informal vocabulary if necessary (e.g. *I guess – I suppose, hang out – meet and do things together*).
- When they have finished making their notes, put students into pairs (or groups of four) and ask them to tell their partner/others in their group the pros and cons of moving to the area they read about.
- Students then discuss and decide which area they should move to and why.
- Finally, ask the class to vote on which area is better.

2b Ask me indirectly! (use after Lesson 2.3)

Aim: to provide further practice of indirect questions in different tenses within a personalised context.

Grouping: individual and then whole class

Procedure:

- Give each student a copy of the question sheet and tell them to note their answers to the direct questions.
- Explain that students are journalists doing research for an article on the types of people who study English/ travel abroad.
- Because they don't personally know the people they're speaking to, some of the questions will sound more polite if they are asked indirectly (e.g. 'How old are you?' = 'Can I ask how old you are?') and some require facts or opinions in the answers (e.g. 'Do many people in your country go abroad for a holiday?' = 'I'd like to know if many people […]').
- Then give students a maximum of ten minutes to rewrite the direct questions in the space provided so that they become indirect. Monitor the class to make sure

Teaching notes for photocopiable activities

students are writing the questions accurately and that the indirect phrases they are using are appropriate for the question (e.g. 'Do you know how old you are?' = inappropriate). Alternatively, if your class is fairly strong, move to the next part of the procedure without asking students to write the questions first.

- Ask students to move round the room asking others the questions and noting their answers. Encourage them to ask follow-up questions to get as much information as possible. If students don't want to answer a particular question, tell them to reply 'I'd rather not say, if that's okay'.

- Finally, ask a few students for the most interesting or surprising piece of information they could include in their article.

3a Winning's a certainty! (use after Lesson 3.2)

(Note: The vocabulary in this activity is taken from the text on page 28, and exercises 4–6 on page 29.)

Aim: to provide further practice of the form of abstract nouns made from adjectives

Grouping: pairs

Procedure:

- Give one set of cards to each pair who should divide them equally between them. Tell students they can look at their own cards but make sure that their partner can't see them.

- The first student lays either an adjective or a suffix card face up on the table. The second student then places a card with the appropriate noun ending after the adjective on the first card (e.g. *violent* – *-ence*), OR a card with the appropriate adjective before the suffix on the first card (e.g. *polite* – *-ness*). Students have to say what changes they need to make to the adjective to form the noun (e.g. *courteous* – drop the *-ous* and add *-sy*). Students can challenge each other if they think a card has been placed wrongly.

- Students then take turns and repeat the procedure above. If a student does not have an appropriate card to place, the turn passes back to the first student.

- Students continue placing their cards on the table until one student has no more cards left. The student who uses all their cards first, wins the game.

> Answers: violent – viol**ence**; polite – polite**ness**; aggressive – aggres**sion**; flexible – flexibi**lity**; agile – agi**lity**; courteous – cour**tesy**; supple – supple**ness**; calm – **no suffix needed**; coordinated – coordinat**ion**; confident – confid**ence**; developed - develop**ment**; considerate – considerat**ion**; excited – excite**ment**; certain – certain**ty**

3b Did you get all of them or hardly any? (use after Lesson 3.2)

Aim: to provide further practice of selected quantifiers in the context of sport and exercise

Grouping: individual then pairs

Procedure:

- Tell students they are going to read a summary of a newspaper report about how much exercise school children are doing and they will then replace some words and phrases with quantifiers.

- Give each student a copy of the summary and a copy of the sentence card.

- Ask them to underline the words and phrases they think will be useful when deciding which quantifiers to use (this should include words such as *worryingly*, and *alarming*).

- Tell students to think about which quantifiers might go in each gap on the sentence card, but not to write anything yet.

- Put students into pairs, cut up the quantifier cards and put them separately and face up on the table in front of each pair. Students then take cards to fill the gaps on their sentence cards. Warn students there aren't enough cards for all the gaps on both students' cards so they must be quick.

- When all the cards have been used, students check each other's sentences. If a card does not make sense or is grammatically incorrect in a particular gap, they must give it to the other student.

- When they have finished, go through answers with the class and tell students to remove any cards that do not make sense or are grammatically incorrect in a particular gap.

- The student with most quantifier cards at the end wins the game.

4a Medical word search (use after Lesson 4.1)

Aim: to test and reinforce students' knowledge and recognition of medical terms

Grouping: individual or pairs

Procedure:

- This activity is best given to students as revision some time after having studied the vocabulary in the Coursebook – either later in the same lesson or at the beginning of the following lesson.

- Give each student or pair a copy of the word search grid and tell them there are 14 items of vocabulary in the box. The words can run horizontally or vertically and students need to find them and circle each one.

4b The first day of the rest of your life (use after Lessons 4.2 and 4.3)

Aim: to provide further practice of the present continuous, *going to*, future continuous, *will* and future perfect

Grouping: whole class (but students only need to find out about three other students' roles)

Procedure:

- Give each student one role card and explain that the table contains information about their job and their future life. Other students are going to ask them about their future lives.

- Ask students to read the information on their role card and ask you or use their dictionaries for unknown vocabulary.

- Tell students to look again at the grammar on pages 41 and 42–43 in the Coursebook to remind themselves of the uses of the present continuous, future continuous, *will* + infinitive (without *to*), *going to* and the future perfect.

- Give students a maximum of ten minutes to decide what grammar they will use when answering others' questions. Monitor to check that students' ideas are accurate.

- 💡 If students find it difficult to decide what grammar to use, explain that *intend* means they need to use *going to*, *probably* = *will*, *arranged* = present continuous, *By 2020* = future perfect, and usually, if the time is a period in the future, the grammar is future continuous. However, some periods of time referred to in the grids use *intend* or *arranged* so students will need to use the appropriate grammar.

- Write the following suggested questions on the board: 'What do you do?', 'What are you doing this evening?', 'What about next year?', 'And next August?', 'How about in 5 years time?', 'Tell me about the time between then and 2020.', 'And after that – what about the rest of your life?'

- Then ask students to move around the room talking to as many people as possible. Tell students there are three future lives to find out about (other than their own). Students do not need to take notes.

- When they have found out about all three lives, ask the class which one they think is most interesting and if they would like a life like this.

5a Not sure we'll get there but it's worth the try (use after Lesson 5.1)

Aim: to provide further practice of vocabulary for transport and transport problems

Grouping: groups of three (or maximum four)

Procedure:

- Cut up the cards, keeping the three piles separate. Each group in your class will need one set of Places, one of Transport and one of Problems.

- Give each student in a group two cards from each pile and place the remainder on the table face up in front of the students. Make sure the three piles of cards remain separate. Students can look at their cards but should not show other students.

- Explain that students are going to try to travel to different places using different transport but that other students are going to try and stop them.

- 💡 It may be a good idea to demonstrate the game with one group while the rest of the class watches.

- One student looks at his/her cards and tries to make a meaningful sentence from the cards in their hand, e.g. *abroad* + picture of a plane = 'I want to travel abroad by plane'. If they can't make a sentence, they can take a card from the top of either the Places or Transport piles on the table and replace it with one of their own at the bottom of the pile. They can then try to make a sentence again but if this is still impossible, it's the next student's turn to try.

- If a student can make a sentence, they place their cards face up on the table and tell the others what their sentence is. The others decide if it's meaningful (e.g. 'Hovercraft' + 'to school and back' is NOT meaningful and the turn passes to the next student.

- If the sentence is meaningful, any other student in the group can then block the journey by using one of their Problem cards e.g. the picture of a 'fogbound runway' will block a 'plane' journey, the picture of a

'puncture' will block a 'quad bike' journey and so on. If the journey is blocked, the cards are discarded (NOT put back into the piles) and the student who played the Problem card takes a replacement from the top of the Problem pile on the table.

- If the sentence is not blocked, the student who made it keeps the cards to one side but cannot use them again. He/she then takes a card from the Places and Transport piles to replace the ones he/she has used.

- When all the cards are finished or it becomes impossible to make any further sentences, the game is over. The students with the greatest number of meaningful sentences wins.

5b It's all in the planning (use after Lessons 5.2 and 5.3)

Aim: to provide further practice of modal verbs for past and future ability, possibility and obligation

Grouping: individual, then pairs

Procedure:

- Explain that students are going to read about a journey they wanted to do/did last year and later plan another journey for next year.

- Divide the class in half (with an equal number of As and Bs) and give each student a copy of either Journey A or Journey B.

- Tell students to read about their journey and use their dictionaries or ask you for any difficult vocabulary.

- Then put students into pairs (one student A and one student B) to summarise their information for each other using *was able to*, *could*, *had to*, *needed to*, *managed to*, or *succeeded in*. If necessary, give students about five minutes to think about what they will say before you put them into pairs.

- When both students have talked about their journeys, explain that they will be trying to do another trip next year and give a copy of Plan A to student A and Plan B to student B. Ask students to tell each other what their plans are. (Note: students will need to use *might* when there is a possibility mentioned.)

- Then ask students to give each other advice about these plans or to check information they heard during the summarising stage earlier. Students need to use *will be able to*, *might*, *could*, *will need to*, or *will have to*.

- Finally, ask the class which journey they think sounds more exciting and if they'd like to go on a trip like these.

6a I'd love a good book! (use after Lesson 6.1)

Aim: to provide further practice of vocabulary related to types of literature and writing

Grouping: individual, then groups (maximum five students)

Procedure:

- Explain that students are going to decide what kind of book to buy for a friend's birthday.

- Write the following on the board: a poetry book, a romance, some travel writing, a play, some diaries, a collection of essays, a collection of short stories, a thriller, some memoirs, a novel, a biography, a history book, a science fiction novel, a crime story, an autobiography.

Teaching notes for photocopiable activities

- Give each student a 'birthday present' card and ask them to read the information and decide which type of book would be their first and second choice to buy as a birthday present.
- They can combine genres if necessary (e.g. a collection of short science fiction stories).
- When they have decided, put students into groups so that there is at least one student who read about Sam, one who read about Jane, and so on.
- Ask students to tell each other their first and second choices and why they chose these types of book.
- When they have finished, tell students there is only one copy of each type of book available to buy and students cannot buy the same book as another student.
- As a group they must decide which person (Sam, Jane, etc.) gets which type of book.

6b I like a good mystery! (use after Lesson 6.2)
Aim: to provide further practice of narrative tenses and allow students to create their own ending to a story
Grouping: pairs or groups of three
Procedure:
- Give one set of picture cards to each pair or group and explain that students are going to tell a story using the picture cards to help them.
- Write your own suggested beginning of the story on the board or provide a copy of it for the class.
- Ask students to decide/discuss what is happening in each picture before they begin telling the story. Help with vocabulary if necessary.
- Then give students 20–30 minutes to discuss the pictures and decide on the story. They need to include an ending of their own and use all the narrative tenses covered in the Coursebook at least twice. They can take notes to help them remember the story if necessary.
- Put students into larger groups and ask them to swap stories.
- Finally, ask the class to tell you which ending they thought was best.

7a Architectural comparisons (use after Lesson 7.1)
Aim: to provide further practice of positive, negative and neutral vocabulary for describing buildings in preparation for exercises 4a and 4b on page 70 of the Coursebook (Note: students need to know the meaning of each word *and* whether they are positive, negative or neutral to do this activity.)
Grouping: pairs or groups of four
Procedure:
- Cut up the vocabulary cards and put them face down in a pile on the table in front of the students.
- Each student takes five cards. If you have formed pairs, students can play the game twice.
- Students have to describe an imaginary building using the vocabulary they have on the cards. They can use *and* or *but* to join the words in sentences (e.g. It's a contemporary building *but* with a classical design, or It's innovative *and* stylish).
- Students can swap two of their cards but they can't choose which two cards another student gives them.

- They then make their sentences using as many of their cards as possible. If they can't use some cards because a sentence would not have meaning, they must put them to one side.
- Student/s then read out their sentences to the other students who must decide if they are meaningful. If they decide a sentence is not meaningful, the cards are discarded.
- When both/all the students have read out their sentences, they count the number of cards each of them has used (they cannot include the discarded cards).
- The student who has used most cards wins the game.
- Students can then return all the cards to the pile and start the game again.

7b Important buildings (use after Lessons 7.2, 7.2 and 7.3)
Aims: to provide further practice of passive structures in the context of buildings and architecture; to provide further practice of vocabulary for describing buildings
Grouping: individual and pairs
Procedure:
- Explain that students are going to be the judges of a competition to decide the winner of a prize for the best tourist attraction in their city. The category they are judging is Art and architecture. The two buildings they will consider are the finalists in this competition. They are both historically and culturally important, and attract a large number of tourists each year.
- Give one information card to each student (or to each pair if you want students to work together at this stage) and tell them to plan a presentation about their building. Because this is a formal presentation, they need to use passive structures whenever possible (e.g. 'Art shop' = 'Part of the building is used as an art shop', 'Renovations to chapel' = 'The chapel is currently being renovated'). If necessary, help students while they are planning.
- Students can use their dictionaries to check difficult vocabulary (e.g. *neo-classical*). (For Modernist/Modernism you could tell students this is a style of architecture that first appeared in the early 20th century, although most Modernist buildings were built in the second half of the 20th century. Modernist buildings are generally designed as living or working 'machines' for people. The buildings are functional rather than ornate.)
- Then put students into pairs (or groups of four if you used pairs in the previous stage) and ask them to give their presentations to each other. Students can ask questions for further information if necessary.
- When the presentations are finished, ask students to discuss the buildings using the criteria below and decide which building should win the prize:
  - Historical and cultural importance
  - Architectural importance
  - Attractions for tourists
  - Income and future potential for income
- Finally, ask the class which building they chose and why.

Photocopiables 181

Teaching notes for photocopiable activities

8a Verb patterns scrabble (use after Lesson 8.2)

Aim: to provide further practice of verbs which take the infinitive or -ing

Grouping: groups (minimum three, maximum five students)

Procedure:

- Cut up the tiles and give one set of subjects, main verbs and secondary phrases to each group. Tell students to separate the tiles into three piles (subjects, main verbs and secondary phrases) and then put them face down and separately on the table.

- Each student takes a total of six tiles and places them face up in front of them. They can choose how many tiles to take from the subjects, main verbs and secondary phrases piles. It doesn't matter if other students can see their tiles.

- Explain that the number on each tile is how much that word scores.

- The first student tries to make a sentence using a minimum of two of the tiles they have and places it in order on the table in front of all the students in their group. If they can make a sentence, they must explain the context in which this might be said. If the other students are happy with the context and think the structure of the sentence is correct, the first student adds up the scores on the each card to get a final score for their sentence. The first student then takes tiles from any of the piles on the table in front of them to replace the ones he/she has used.

- The turn passes to the next student who repeats the procedure above.

- If a student cannot make a sentence, they can put up to three of their tiles face down on the table at the bottom of the appropriate pile and take an equal number to replace them.

- A student can double the points they score by making use of one of the tiles already in a sentence on the table. In this case, the new sentence must intersect with the original one using one of the tiles already on the table as part of the new sentence.

- The game finishes when all the tiles have been used or when it is impossible to make any more sentences. The student with the highest score wins.

8b What have you had done? (use after Lesson 8.3)

Aim: to provide further practice of 'have something done' in a personalised and guided context

Grouping: individual then whole class

Procedure:

- Give a copy of the question sheet to each student in the class and explain they are going to find out the information by talking to other students.

- Ask them to think about the questions they need to ask. If necessary, do one or two examples with the class first.

- When they have thought about the questions, elicit these from the class and check they are accurate.

- Then ask students to move round the room asking and answering the questions to as many people as possible. They need at least one name next to each question. They should ask follow-up questions to get extra information and make notes if possible.

- While they are talking, monitor to check they are using 'have something + past participle' in their answers and note any common or important errors.

- When they have written information for each question on the sheet, stop the activity and elicit/provide corrections of some mistakes you noted earlier.

- Finally, ask the class what was the most surprising/interesting thing they found out.

9a How do you feel? (use after Lesson 9.2)

Aim: to provide further practice of ungradable adjectives and their gradable equivalents

Grouping: whole class

Procedure:

- Cut up the cards and give one to each student in the class. If there are more students than cards, provide enough cards so that some students have the same one. If there are more cards than students, give some/all students more than one.

- Remind students of lesson 9.2 Grammar: ungradable adjectives, then elicit and write the following ungradable adjectives on the board: *fascinating, devastated, starving, exhausted, freezing, furious, terrible, enormous, tiny* and *unique*.

- Ask students to copy the list of adjectives on to a piece of paper.

- Explain that the cards give a scenario. Tell students to read their card and decide how they felt or what the situation/object mentioned was like (e.g. angry, interesting, big, small).

- Students then move round the room reading their scenario to others who comment using an ungradable adjective (e.g. 'You must have felt absolutely devastated.'). The first student replies using the gradable equivalent (e.g. 'Not really, but I was very upset.'). Note: students will need to listen carefully to the scenario to decide how to comment (e.g. 'It [not 'you'] must have been absolutely fascinating.'). They do not have to use the adverbs *absolutely* and *really*.

- As students use each adjective, they cross if off their list.

- When students have used all ten adjectives, the activity finishes.

9b Describe it to me again? (use after Lesson 9.3)

Aim: to provide further practice and reinforcement of adjective order to describe works of art

Grouping: pairs or groups of four (two pairs in a group)

Procedure:

- Give each student or pair of students in a group a large sheet of paper (or ask them to turn to a blank page in their note books) and tell them to write 'A' 12 times down the left hand margin.

- Mix up the word cards and put them face up on the table in front of the students.

- Individual students have to take one card at a time to make a phrase, using a noun, plus a minimum of one and a maximum of three adjectives, e.g. *A beautiful Chinese clay figurine*. However, all students can take cards at the same time and do not need to take turns.

- The cards must be placed on the piece of paper next to each 'A' with all the words in the correct order.

Teaching notes for photocopiable activities

They can only have one card in their hand at a time and if they decide not to use it, they must return it to the table for other students to use.

○ They must finish one phrase before beginning the next (so they can't take all the 'colour' words at once).

○ They can move cards from one phrase to another when they have more than one phrase but must replace any they move with another appropriate card (they cannot have half-finished phrases, e.g. *a figurine*).

○ All the phrases must have a realistic meaning (e.g. *an enormous French silk figurine* is unlikely because figurines are small and not made of silk).

• If students don't know a particular word, they can ask you or look it up in their dictionary.

• The game finishes when all the cards have been used, so students have to be fast. When the game finishes, students can no longer move cards from one phrase to another.

• Ask students to check each other's phrases for correct word order and for meaning.

• The winner is the student/pair of students with the most correct phrases.

10a It's all in the mind (use after Lesson 10.2)

Aim: to provide personalised practice of idioms using *mind* and introduce a further idiom and adjective using *mind*

Grouping: individual and then pairs

Procedure:

• Ask students to look again at the idioms with *mind* they studied on page 104 of the Coursebook. Tell students that *go out of your mind* or *be out of your mind* can also mean be extremely angry or worried and give an example (e.g. 'He went out of his mind with worry when his son was very late home from school.').

• Introduce the idiom *put your mind to it* (really try hard to solve a problem or difficult situation) and the adjective *mindless* (no reason for something or boring/repetitive).

• Give each student a copy of the worksheet and tell them to read the six prompts, asking you for help for vocabulary or using their dictionaries if necessary.

• Then tell them to note two to four words in the circles to remind them of their answers to the prompts. Answers should be written randomly in the circles and not in the same order as the prompts.

• Put students into pairs and tell them to look at each other's notes. They should try to guess which notes refer to which prompt (e.g. 'Is this something you're in two minds about?') and ask questions to get as much additional information as possible.

• When they have found out what all the notes refer to, ask the class for the most interesting/surprising thing they found out.

10b A relative nightmare (use after Lessons 10.2 and 10.3)

Aim: to provide further practice of non-defining, defining and reduced relative clauses, including those used to add comment to the main clause

Grouping: individual or pairs

Procedure:

• Tell students they are going to read a true story that happened to the author last year on holiday. Give one worksheet to each student and ask them to read the story quickly and tell you why the family needed a holiday, where they went and what went wrong.

• Elicit or tell students that the story would be more interesting if more information was added. Ask them to read the box on the additional information card, helping with vocabulary if necessary.

• Students then work individually or in pairs to insert the information into the story following these rules:

○ They must use a non-defining or a defining relative clause.

○ They must use a reduced relative clause whenever they can.

○ They must change the grammar and use appropriate punctuation when necessary.

○ The story must make logical sense when the clauses have been inserted.

• When they have finished re-writing the story, put students into larger groups to compare and correct if necessary.

• Finally, give students a copy of the answers to compare. Note: students' stories may not be exactly the same but all stories that make sense are acceptable.

Answer:

(Note: 'which was stressful for all of us' could also go after 'had been studying really hard for weeks'.)

This is a true story **that happened to me and my family last year**. My wife and I had been working very hard for months and spending time away from the children, **which was stressful for all of us**. The kids, **who were taking important exams**, had been studying really hard for weeks. We were all tired, getting on each others' nerves and generally having a pretty bad time of it. One Sunday I was reading the paper, **which was something I rarely had time for**, and saw an ad for a holiday villa in Italy, **where my wife and I went on our honeymoon**. The villa was fabulous – big and spacious with its own pool and stunning views over a wooded valley. It was also cheap, **which added to the attraction of it a lot**. So, I called the number and two weeks later we were driving from the airport to the villa in a car [**that**] **I'd decided to hire instead of taking a taxi or the bus**.

When we arrived at the villa, it all looked just as it did in the ad [**that**] **I'd seen in the paper** except for one thing: there was nothing on top **where the roof should have been**. We just sat in the car and stared in disbelief.

By this time it was getting dark and we couldn't all sleep in the car, so we got our bags and went inside. In the living room was a man [**who was**] **sitting on a chair by the window**, [**who was**] **smoking a cigarette**. 'Er … hello', I said. 'Do you know what's happened to the roof?', **which was a strange question to ask when you first meet someone**.

'Si', said the man, 'I sold it to pay for the swimming pool.'

11a How do you feel? What's it like? (use after Lesson 11.2)

Aim: to provide further practice of vocabulary to describe feelings and situations

Grouping: Individual then groups of four

Procedure:

- Put students into groups of four and explain that they have all been studying the language and culture of a country which is very different from their own. Four people from their class have gone to live in the country for a while and have all written an email about their experiences.

- Give one email to each student in the group and tell them to make short notes on how the writer and any other people mentioned feel, what kind of experiences they've had, what they think the locals are like and so on. Students must use adjectives from 11.2, exercise 5 in their notes but can also use any other vocabulary they think appropriate.

- If necessary, give students an example of the kind of notes they could make, e.g. 'I can't make friends. I feel all alone' = *isolated*.

- Monitor to help with vocabulary in the emails (e.g. *whinge* = colloquial expression for complain) or ask students to use their dictionaries.

- Students then tell each other about the email they received and as a group discuss the following: 'Who is suffering most from culture shock? What should they do to help?'

- Finally, get answers to these questions from each group.

11b Networking (use after Lesson 11.2)

Aim: to provide further practice of reported speech in the context of travel and culture

Grouping: whole class

Procedure:

- Explain that students are tour guides working for big travel companies and are living and working all over the world. At the moment, they are at a conference in New York and are at a party organised so they can network.

- Give one role card to each student. If you have more students than cards, give the same card to more than one student.

- Tell students to read the information on the card (names can be male or female) and either use their dictionaries or ask you if they need help with vocabulary.

- Then ask students to decide how they will give the information e.g. 'food fantastic' = 'I thought the food was fantastic', 'No definite plans' = 'I don't have any definite plans' or 'I've no definite plans'. If necessary, help students structure their information.

- Then explain that at the networking party they might meet or hear about people who are living, have lived, or want to live in the same countries as them. They need to find out what the others thought of the place and what there is to do. Some of the information will be reported because the person they are speaking to will have heard it from someone else. For this information they need to use reported speech e.g. 'Pat said he/she had lived in Mumbai and thought the food was … ,etc.'.

- Ask students to move around the room asking and answering questions. They can form questions by using the heading of each column on the role card. There are five people to speak to or hear about (Pat, Les, Sam, Val and Terry). They should take notes on what is said so they can report it to others at the party.

- When students have got all the information they need, ask them to decide if they still want to live in the countries under 'future plans' on their cards and why/not?

- Finally, ask the class if anyone has really been to any of these countries.

12a Prefix snap (use after Lesson 12.2)

Aim: to provide further practice of opposite adjectives formed with prefixes

Grouping: pairs or groups (maximum four)

Procedure:

- Cut up the cards and place them face down on the table in front of students (one pile of adjective cards and one pile of prefix cards).

- The first student turns over an adjective card and a prefix card simultaneously. If the cards match (e.g. *in + efficient*), any of the students in the group can shout 'Snap!'. The first student to shout 'Snap!' wins the cards.

- If the cards do not match, the next student turns over two cards and puts them on top of the cards already face up on the table.

- Once all the cards have been turned over, the piles are turned back over and the procedure continues as above.

- When all the cards have been won, the game finishes. The winner is the student with most cards.

12b What if …? (use after Lessons 12.2 and 12.3)

Aim: to provide further practice of first conditional, second conditional, third conditional, present condition with past results, and past condition with past results

Grouping: individual, then whole class

Procedure:

- Give a copy of the worksheet to each student and ask them to think about their answers to the questions and make notes. Tell them that they can answer the questions in any way they want but it must make sense in terms of time reference and be grammatically correct.

- If necessary, refer students to pages 125 and 126 in the Coursebook to remind themselves of the different structures (first, second and third conditionals) and possible combinations of conditional and result clauses (mixed conditionals). Monitor while students are deciding on their answers to help with grammar.

- When students are prepared, ask them to move round the room asking and answering the questions. They should speak to as many different people as possible. The aim is to find someone who has a similar answer to themselves.

- Students write the name of a student with a similar answer to theirs, but don't need to make notes on the answer.

- When they have finished, ask students if anyone in the class had a similar answer to any of the questions. If possible, ask students if they can remember the answer they were given or, alternatively, ask the student who gave the answer to give a bit more information.

SUBJECT: INTERVIEW NOTES – JOHN BAILEY

Pleasant man. Made us laugh a lot. Never dominated the interview. Everyone liked him and we all felt we wanted to listen when he spoke. Expect he'll be popular with colleagues. He understood all the questions and thought about them carefully. Clothes very smart. Obviously had his hair cut for the interview! When asked about experience of other communities/cultures he started crossing and uncrossing his legs, looked uncomfortable, maybe sweating a bit? His reply was long and he didn't really answer the question – talked about other things instead. When relaxed, he looked straight at us. When uncomfortable, looked out of the window a lot.

Comments: +/–

+	–

Things to look for in final interview

SUBJECT: INTERVIEW NOTES – JANE ANDERSON

Pleasant woman. Completely relaxed. Very confident during the interview – but not very warm. Some colleagues will like her a lot, but not sure about everyone. Sat calmly with legs crossed. Always looked at the person she was speaking to. Chose her words very carefully. Spoke clearly. Never said more than absolutely necessary. Answered questions well. Obvious she could interpret what was being asked. But she didn't smile very much. Never laughed (even when I made a joke). Dressed a bit too casually for an interview. When asked about experience of other communities/cultures, she stayed very relaxed but said that she didn't have much – could learn? We really liked her honesty.

Comments: +/–

+	–

Things to look for in final interview

ROLE CARDS

Franco/Franca

You are a journalist currently working for an important newspaper (*The Chronicle*) in your country. You've worked at *The Chronicle* for three years, but worked for a number of smaller papers before this job. You studied journalism at the top media school in your country; while you were studying you wrote articles for local papers and set up a student newspaper. By the time you finished your studies, you'd won a number of awards for your journalism and last year you won an important international prize. You usually travel overseas four or five times a year to find news stories.

Gene/Jean

You're currently working for a large, international media company as a Communications Advisor and have been with the company for one year. Before this job, you worked as an assistant producer for a TV company, which you liked but decided you needed more variety. You studied English at one of the best universities in your country, but while you were there you became interested in communications – by the end of your second year you'd changed your course to Communications and Media. You enjoy working for your company but are hoping to go freelance in the near future.

INTERVIEW FORM

Questions for your partner	Notes
Job?	
Currently working?	
How long worked for current company?	
Previous job?	
Where studied?	
What studied?	
Do anything else while studying?	
Anything important happened by the time he/she had finished university?	

PEARSON
Longman

Jo's blog – Where I live: Stanton

Hi. I've lived in Stanton for years and wouldn't live anywhere else. If you're thinking of moving here, you've made the right decision! Stanton's got a good mix of people from all over the world. It's really alive in the evenings and at weekends when people get together in the parks (there are loads!) to hang out with friends, chat, do sports and that kind of stuff. There's always something going on.

Okay, I guess it can get a bit too busy when people are going to work in the morning, or coming home again and, yes, there are a lot of cars blocking the roads at these times, but that's like lots of other places, isn't it? Better trains and buses would help, but you can't have everything.

Something I'd change? Well, there aren't many houses – it's mostly old flats and that means you can't mind too much if you hear what's going on next door! And you often get the sound of cars and stuff happening on the streets. But I can live with that because in these old blocks you get to see right across the city from the top floor flats – yes, I've got one of those and it's fantastic, especially at night when the lights come on.

And one more thing I'd change – just recently people have been leaving their old cars in streets around the main park. I guess they don't want to pay to get them taken away, which I can understand. But it's irritating. And the council isn't doing much about it, which is even more irritating. But don't get me wrong, it's a safe area with very little crime. I've got two kids, so safety is a big issue for me.

I've just read what I wrote and it sounds like I'm criticising Stanton! I'm really not. I don't think it's got more problems that anywhere else and I really, really love it.

Jan's blog Where I live: Brockton

Hello, I really want to say something about where I live – Brockton. I love it! And so does everyone else I know! First, it's one of the few places in this city you can still get individual houses with gardens. Okay, they're not cheap, but it suits most people here because they like to hang out with friends at home. And if they don't, no problem, they can go to the park – it's quiet but nice. And they can get into the city centre really easily on all the buses and trains that come through Brockton. We've got three stations with a really good service – I think that's more than any other area. And because there are all those trains and buses, people don't use cars – most people I know don't even have one! So, the air's clean and that's a big advantage in this city.

Something I'd change? Well, it's not that safe after dark because there aren't many people around on the streets – not many cafés or places for people to go to because they like their own homes or going into the city. So, quiet and dark streets mean crime. And I guess it can get pretty bad around the stations – I wouldn't like to walk around those bits at night alone. But that's the same anywhere, isn't it?

I guess there's another thing I'd change. Groups of young kids, teenagers really, get together around the stations at night and the buildings sometimes get damaged. It doesn't look good with the broken windows. I don't know why they do it – bored, I guess.

But, like I say, I really do love it here. If you decide to move to Brockton, believe me, you've made the right choice!

ASK ME INDIRECTLY!

Direct questions	Indirect questions
1 How old are you?	**1**
2 When's your birthday?	**2**
3 Are you married or single?	**3**
4 Do you have any children?	**4**
5 Do you think you're good at English?	**5**
6 Why are you studying English?	**6**
7 What do you do for a living?	**7**
8 How much paid holiday do you get a year?	**8**
9 Have you ever been on holiday in your own country? How much did it cost?	**9**
10 Which place in your country has most visitors per year?	**10**
11 Why do you think the place in question 10 is so popular?	**11**
12 Do many people in your country go abroad for a holiday? Where do most of them prefer to go?	**12**

-ness	violent	-ty	supple
-ence	coordinated	-ence	aggressive
-ness	agile	-ion	excited
-ion	polite	-ity	certain
-ment	courteous	-esy	flexible
-ment	developed	no suffix needed	calm
-ity	considerate	-ion	confident

PEARSON
Longman

SUMMARY OF NEWSPAPER REPORT

Are our kids getting the exercise they need?

A recent survey into children's sport and leisure activities has thrown up some worrying results, says Sam Brown in the *Evening Herald*. Of 100 children in the survey, only three said they did some kind of sporting activity two or three days a week. Worryingly, 85% said they prefer to play video games. Only eight kids said they didn't like video games but preferred doing something outdoors. Fifteen or sixteen kids said they had to do homework on twenty to twenty-five days in the average month, but didn't feel this was too much. They said they sleep or watch TV in the rest of the time available. 70% of them said they regularly play video games instead of doing homework (even though they know they shouldn't). 100% said they like watching sport on TV, but don't spend much time doing this with friends or family. Disturbingly, 90% of them said they'd prefer to spend an alarming amount of their time doing something alone rather than with friends or family.

SENTENCE CARD

1 _____ of the kids said they did some kind of sporting activity _____ days a week.

2 _____ said they prefer to play video games.

3 _____ said they prefer doing something outdoors to watching video games.

4 _____ said they had to do homework on _____ days in the average month.

5 They sleep or watch TV in the _____ time available when they're not doing homework.

6 _____ said they play video games instead of doing homework.

7 Watching sport on TV is very popular and _____ said they liked doing this.

8 They spend very _____ time watching sport on TV with friends or family.

9 _____ kids spend _____ time doing something alone.

QUANTIFIER CARDS

Several	Several of them	Several of them	Hardly any
Hardly any	Far too many	Far too many	Far too many
A lot of them	Many	Many	All of them
All of them	Almost none	Almost none	Little
Little	Little	Far too much	Far too much
Far too many	Little	BLANK	BLANK

PEARSON
Longman

MEDICAL WORD SEARCH

S	P	N	G	A	P	M	M	T	G	A	N	S	T	L	A	P
L	I	D	S	N	A	L	O	S	C	M	I	D	W	I	F	E
L	D	G	Y	A	I	U	R	A	W	O	N	P	E	T	H	E
E	T	H	E	E	N	N	P	D	A	M	J	V	U	O	P	A
C	A	N	C	S	K	J	H	V	R	N	E	O	D	G	N	N
L	G	A	N	T	I	B	I	O	T	I	C	I	T	W	R	K
M	O	S	D	H	L	J	N	K	H	D	T	B	R	I	U	A
O	P	I	S	E	L	T	E	N	R	C	I	L	A	W	R	B
R	S	H	C	T	E	T	H	E	I	A	O	L	N	D	Y	E
P	Y	E	A	I	R	H	E	A	T	L	N	T	S	H	L	T
H	C	A	T	S	L	I	N	S	I	P	W	I	P	E	K	H
I	H	R	H	T	C	I	D	H	S	O	D	E	L	E	U	E
S	I	L	O	S	U	R	G	E	O	N	A	D	A	T	H	K
S	A	B	G	K	M	O	U	L	G	A	D	W	N	H	P	L
A	T	M	J	D	H	S	M	D	I	A	B	E	T	E	S	P
Y	R	A	D	I	O	L	O	G	I	S	T	D	H	R	L	K
S	I	B	K	K	D	H	Y	J	K	E	V	G	T	U	N	A
F	S	G	L	P	H	Y	S	I	O	T	H	E	R	A	P	Y
K	T	O	N	A	Y	S	T	A	E	T	S	P	O	H	L	M

ANSWERS

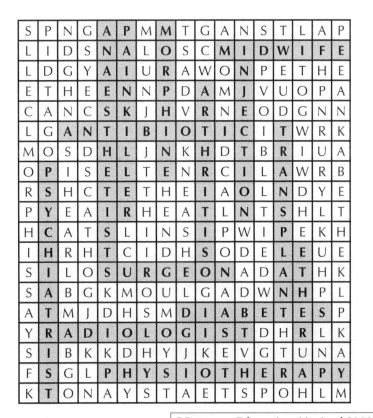

CARD ONE

When?	What you do
Now	You are a nurse working in a big city-centre hospital
This evening	Arranged to work all evening
All of next year	Work in the same hospital
Next August	Intend to travel around South America on a big trip
In five years' time	Probably in nursing management in a different hospital
By 2020	Retire, sell your flat, move to a house by the sea
For the rest of your life	Live by the sea, look after your garden and travel more

CARD TWO

When?	What you do
Now	You are a student doctor in your final year of studies
This evening	Intend to study for final medical exams
All of next year	Arranged to travel round the world with a friend and do voluntary work
Next August	Probably work in a hospital in your own country
In five years' time	Intend to become a specialist in children's medicine
By 2020	Earn a lot of money, get married, have children
For the rest of your life	Probably work as a consultant; live in a big house with your wife/husband

CARD THREE

When?	What you do
Now	You are a voluntary medical worker in a developing country
This evening	Intend to read a medical journal about new malaria treatment
All of next year	Arranged to help set up and run a malaria clinic in Sierra Leone
Next August	Probably take a short break from the clinic
In five years' time	Intend to open a second clinic if the first one is a success
By 2020	Move back to your own country
For the rest of your life	Live in your own country but do voluntary work – maybe malaria education

CARD FOUR

When?	What you do
Now	Your are a researcher into malaria and its prevention
This evening	Intend to catch up on some paperwork
All of next year	Arranged to travel to conferences all over the world presenting research findings
Next August	Probably have a break in South-east Asia (between conferences)
In five years' time	Intend to stop research and do voluntary work with malaria patients in the developing world
By 2020	Retire and buy a house in the country
For the rest of your life	Live quietly in your own country

SET ONE: PLACES

across the Sahara	over the sea to the next country	abroad	to the next town
to the next country	around the countryside	all over the world	across Lake Superior (USA)
over the Himalayan mountains	along the Mississippi River	down to the local shops	to school and back

SET TWO: TRANSPORT

SET THREE: PROBLEMS

JOURNEY A

Last year you decided to take three months off work and travel to India. You asked your boss if you could start in June. However you didn't ask your boss if you could have the time off work early enough and she said you would have to take September onwards.

The easiest way to do it was to fly directly to New Delhi. However, you decided that it would be a real adventure to travel overland to India and spend a bit of time seeing different countries (Turkey, Iran, Pakistan) on the way. Originally, you wanted to go through China too, but it meant crossing the Himalayas and this was too difficult.

You only started really thinking about the trip in the first week of August. You had no problem getting your flights to Turkey, your first stop, and you knew there would be no problem with the visas because you would get them at the airport in Istanbul. However, you didn't book your train tickets through Turkey and across the border into Iran and all the best trains were full by the time you tried to book.

Visas were necessary for Iran, Pakistan and India. The Indian one was expensive but easy to get. The other two were more of a problem. You didn't read the information on the Iranian Consulate website carefully and only sent two pictures of yourself although three were necessary. The Pakistani Consulate said it was very important to apply at least four weeks in advance, but you only left two and the visa didn't arrive in time.

It was a disaster and you had to cancel everything. Eventually, you decided to try to do a big trip next year instead.

PLAN A: You want to travel for two months next year.			
Where?	**Via?**	**How?**	**Visas necessary?**
China (maybe including Hong Kong)	Thailand, Laos, Vietnam, maybe Cambodia	Plane, train	

✂ -

JOURNEY B

Last year you took two months off work and travelled to China. You decided it would be a real adventure to go overland part of the way and spend a bit of time seeing different countries (Thailand, Laos, Vietnam). You originally wanted to go through Cambodia too, but it was too far in the wrong direction.

You were supposed to start your journey in March, but at the beginning of the year found out that you'd have some important exams to take in April. You decided to postpone your trip until May.

You had no problems getting flights to Bangkok in Thailand and were pleased to find out it wasn't necessary to have a visa. However, you didn't realise that it was impossible to buy a train ticket from Bangkok to the border with Laos, except in Bangkok itself. Furthermore, it took you a long time to find out that the only way of getting a train reservation through China was to book in Vietnam. You tried for two weeks to buy the tickets in advance in your own country but with no success.

Visas were necessary for Laos and Vietnam. The only place to buy the Laos visa was in Bangkok and this took at least five days so you'd be staying in Thailand longer than you wanted. The Vietnamese Consulate told you it wasn't possible to get your visa in advance in your own country and you could only get it at the Laos/Vietnam border because you were travelling overland. Chinese visas were, however, available before you left your country with one week's notice.

It was all very complicated but you had a great time – and decided to do another big trip next year.

PLAN B: You want to travel for three months next year.			
Where?	**Via?**	**How?**	**Visas necessary?**
India	Turkey, Iran, Pakistan, maybe China	Plane, train	

Sam's birthday present

Sam studied English at university and has read a huge variety of different literature – he loves it all. Recently, though, he's not been well and is spending a lot of time in hospital. He can't concentrate on one thing for too long and gets tired. His doctors say he mustn't get too excited but needs something to stimulate him.

Jane's birthday present

Jane loves anything to do with the future, aliens, that sort of thing, but she doesn't like a story that's too obvious. She prefers mysteries she needs to work out and hates it when she can guess the ending. She does a lot of travelling and loves to read when she's on planes and trains, but doesn't get much time to read otherwise.

Joe's birthday present

Joe hates books with imaginary stories. He likes reading about real people – doesn't matter if they're alive or dead – and the events surrounding them. He prefers if it the person is famous, but it's not always important. He's just finished a book about a real murder case and enjoyed it very much.

Mary's birthday present

Mary never gets time to read because she works too hard. So, when she goes on holiday she likes a book she can lose herself in. Anything to do with relationships and how people feel about their experiences – doesn't matter if they're real people or imaginary. She's planning a big trip next year to get away from work.

Susan's birthday present

Susan loves going to the theatre because she likes a story she can follow without spending too much time – many books take so long to read! She likes a good mystery and something about a place, a time, and people completely new to her. She's also quite keen on factual accounts of the past, but only if they are exciting!

ARCHITECTURAL COMPARISONS

VOCABULARY CARDS

ancient	dilapidated	impressive	run-down
classical	elegant	innovative	stylish
contemporary	graceful	magnificent	traditional
derelict	imposing	ornate	ugly
attractive	decorative	modern	interesting

INFORMATION CARD: BUILDING A

General facts and description	History and culture	Tourist attractions	Current developments
Built 1735 Architect: Pablo Gisera – most important architect of era Neo-classical, ornate, imposing 10,000 visitors per year	Mansion for Medici family, 1735–1905 Famous paintings Past famous visitors – the Pope, various monarchs Chapel typical of the period Government offices and apartment for President, 1905–1958 Museum, 1958–now	Art shop Permanent art exhibition Temporary art exhibitions from all over the world Café Restaurant Guided tours – qualified and experienced guides Beautiful gardens	Renovations to chapel and state rooms (finished in two years' time) Changes to opening times so building can stay open later Encouraging new exhibitions from abroad Garden shop with exotic species of plants (opening in three months' time)

✂ -

INFORMATION CARD: BUILDING B

General facts and description	History and culture	Tourist attractions	Current developments
Built 1963 Architect: Maria Sinatra – most important modern architect of era Modernist, stylish, innovative, elegant 8,000 visitors per year	House for industrialist and his family, 1963–1985 Famous modern paintings by international artists First Modernist house in the city Past famous visitors – presidents, writers, artists, politicians Modern art and architecture museum, 1985–now	Art shop Permanent art exhibition Temporary art exhibitions from all over the world Café Guided tours – experienced guides Stunning views of the city from the roof Exhibition of 1960s and 1970s household items – famous and innovative designers	Roof-top restaurant (opening in two months' time) Late night openings for access to restaurant Building additional gallery in garden to increase exhibition space (opening by end of next year) Building studio for up-and-coming artists to use and exhibit their work

8A

1 I	**3** on the way	**4** talking	**4** the dry cleaning
1 he	**2** tried	**3** to get home	**4** but the train was late
1 we	**2** stopped	**4** easy but it was really difficult	**4** to you but you didn't want to
1 she	**2** remember	**2** I'll never	**3** to get
2 must stop	**2** considered	going	**4** abroad next year
3 meeting	**1** I	**2** wasn't allowed	**3** to stay out late
3 when I was young	**1** it	**2** must remember	**3** to be
3 but decided to stay at home	**1** I	**1** he	**4** putting it in my pocket
1 I	**2** tried	**2** forgot	**3** you last year
2 appeared	**2** forgot	**3** to tell	**4** me where to meet
3 me when to meet	**2** forget	**3** talking	**4** to you at the restaurant
1 I	**3** to tell	**3** being	**3** late
1 he	**2** tried	**3** to have lunch	**1** we

QUESTION SHEET

Find someone in the class who:	Name of student and notes
… had their hair cut recently.	
… hates having their photo taken.	
… wants to have something done in their house/flat but hasn't organised it yet.	
… prefers to have something done for them even though they could do it themselves. What?	
… has had something done but they weren't happy with the results.	
… is going to have their teeth checked in the near future.	
… has had something stolen from them.	
… would like to have something changed about their appearance (face/ clothes/hair).	
… has their meals cooked for them.	

I went to an art lecture last week. It's something I don't know very much about and I learned a lot.

I failed all the exams I took last year and they were important to me.

I went to a restaurant with friends last night and there was so little food it just didn't fill me up.

I don't know what's wrong with me but I didn't get any sleep at all last night.

I went to Moscow last winter but forgot to take a thick coat.

My boss didn't turn up for our meeting yesterday. It's the third time she's done it.

That film I saw last week was so boring. I hated the story and the actors were awful.

My mother gave me a sweater for my birthday but the sleeves came down to my knees.

I looked at a new flat yesterday. It was only one room and you had to climb over the bed to get to the bathroom.

I bought this watch in an antique store yesterday. I've not seen one quite like it before.

beautiful	outstanding	lovely	impressive
enormous	tiny	huge	tiny
antique	19th-century	modern	contemporary
old	ancient	20th-century	red
Peruvian	silver	glass	beautiful
dark	multi-coloured	white	white
Japanese	Chinese	French	Spanish
silk	steel	clay	metal
Cubist	Modernist	classical	Impressionist
painting	sculpture	figurine	plate
painting	sculpture	figure	bowl
plate	figurine	bowl	plate

Write short answers to the following (no more than two to four words).
Write your answers in any circle below, but not in the same order as the questions.

- Something you like to keep an open mind about
- Something that gives you peace of mind
- Something you're always in two minds about
- A time when you went out of your mind with anger or worry
- A time when you really had to put your mind to something to solve a problem or to succeed
- The most mindless job you can think of, in your opinion

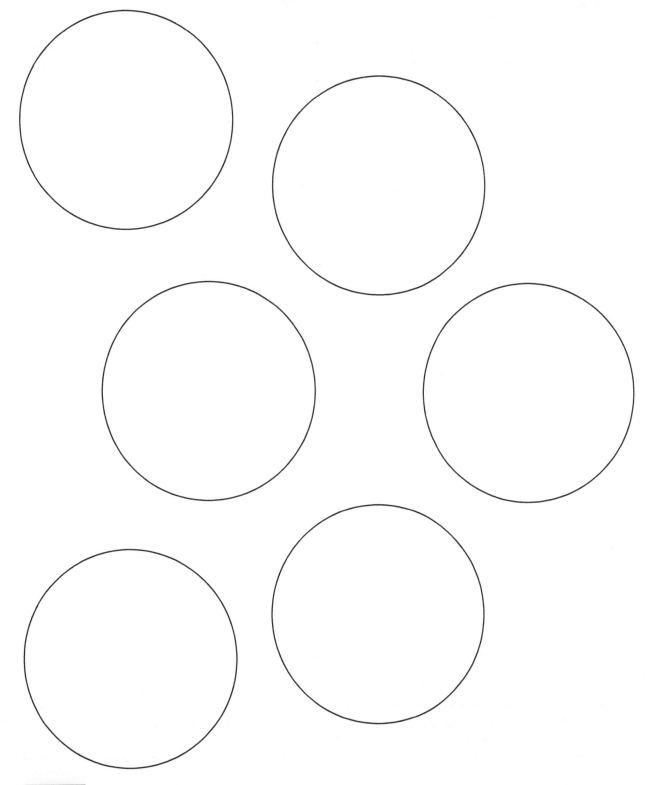

This is a true story. My wife and I had been working very hard for months and spending time away from the children. The kids had been studying really hard for weeks. We were all tired, getting on each others' nerves and generally having a pretty bad time of it.

One Sunday I was reading the paper and saw an ad for a holiday villa in Italy. The villa was fabulous – big and spacious with its own pool and stunning views over a wooded valley. It was also cheap. So, I called the number and two weeks later we were driving from the airport to the villa in a car.

When we arrived at the villa, it all looked just as it did in the ad except for one thing: there was nothing on top. We just sat in the car and stared in disbelief.

By this time it was getting dark and we couldn't all sleep in the car, so we got our bags and went inside. In the living room was a man. 'Er … hello', I said. 'Do you know what's happened to the roof?'

'Si', said the man, 'I sold it to pay for the swimming pool.'

ADDITIONAL INFORMATION CARD	
They were taking important exams.	This added to the attraction of it a lot.
He was smoking a cigarette.	The roof should have been there.
I rarely had time for this.	This situation was stressful for all of us.
My wife and I went there on our honeymoon.	A strange question to ask when you first meet someone.
He was sitting on a chair by the window.	I'd seen it in the paper.
I'd decided to hire this instead of taking a taxi or the bus.	The story happened to me and my family last year.

PEARSON
Longman

Email from Jane

Hi there

Well, only been here a few weeks but it seems like ages. It's okay in some ways. The weather's good, I guess.

Some of the local customs are interesting – in a strange way(!). But I just can't make friends, I feel all alone. Sue's just arrived and I think she's feeling the same way. Spoke to her quickly last night but she was just going out – I didn't ask where and she didn't invite me (not sure what to make of that).

Called John a few times but he's always going out to stuff, seeing people – all the things I'm not doing. And I just don't understand what people are saying. I've studied the language for years, you know that, and I really try, but I just can't understand what's going on. Listen, really sorry to whinge but …

Email from John

How're you doing?

Been here for ages but it seems like a few days. I really love it. Everything's so new and interesting. Okay, so I find quite a few of their habits strange but that just adds to the fun. Each day something different – so good! When are you coming to stay?

Saw Sue and Simon last night and we all miss you. They say Hi, by the way.

Listen, one thing that's not so good – am kind of worried about Jane. Not seen her since she got here. She's called but I'm always out and about. I heard she's been getting angry with the locals, like she hates them or something. If it's true, it worries me. I mean, she's really over-reacting. I'd like to help but just don't know what to say to her – I'm not good at giving advice (you know me!). Can you call her and …

Email from Sue

Hello You

Can't believe what's happening to me! It's all good here. Arrived about a week ago and not stopped going to museums, galleries, dance (you name it, I've done it!). Lots of problems with the money. Keep giving 10 times more than I should! Try hard but feel a bit stupid.

Listen, bit of a problem. Saw John last night and he's really angry with Jane - refusing to see her, not answering the phone. I got a bit upset about it - you know what John can be like. He says she's whinging. I don't want to get any more involved 'cos, to be honest, I'm concentrating on making <u>new</u> friends (not much luck yet - which gets me down - but it'll get better).

Sorry to do this to you, but can you call John and …

Email from Simon

Greetings!

So, what's new? I tell you what's new – this place is new. We studied this culture for years, didn't we? Was I studying somewhere else!? Feel pretty stupid thinking I'd know what was going on – and can't seem to learn. Something happens to me, I react one way and everyone gets aggressive. I'm trying, but just not doing it right. Not sure I'll stand it here if I don't settle soon.

Saw John and Sue last night – they say Hi. He's angry with Jane about something and Sue got upset about it – wouldn't talk to him most of the evening. Big mystery what the problem is but will find out and tell you.

Brighter note – went to really exciting dance thing last night. I felt really alive! But, believe me, it's the only exciting thing I've done.

Have you heard from …

Name: Pat	Company: The Teen Travel Group			
Living/working now	*Likes, dislikes and activities*	*Other places lived in*	*Likes, dislikes and activities*	*Future plans*
Paris, France – been there two years.	Love the food, people and nightlife. Can't stand the Metro, and that it's so quiet in August, there's nothing to do.	Mumbai, India Sydney, Australia	Food fantastic, but not much variety if you don't like Indian food. Hated the traffic and pollution. Loved the outdoor life. Went surfing.	Next year, going to live in Canada – hoping to be manager. Or maybe back to Sydney.

✂ -

Name: Les	Company: Explore the World			
Living/working now	*Likes, dislikes and activities*	*Other places lived in*	*Likes, dislikes and activities*	*Future plans*
London, UK – been there three years.	Really like the cosmopolitan atmosphere. Often go to the theatre. The transport system gets you down.	Hong Kong Oslo, Norway	Loved the fast pace of life. Humidity was terrible every summer. Too quiet most of the time. Good skiing.	No definite plans, might work in Mumbai, India or Cancun, Mexico.

✂ -

Name: Sam	Company: Magical Travel			
Living/working now	*Likes, dislikes and activities*	*Other places lived in*	*Likes, dislikes and activities*	*Future plans*
Cancun, Mexico – been there one summer.	It's a bit early to say what you don't like. Love the weather. Go to the beach a lot.	Vancouver, Canada Dublin, Ireland	Went skiing every winter. Hiking all year. Fantastic scenery. People very friendly, lots to do in – live music, dance. Sundays a bit quiet, though.	Considering a job in Hong Kong or Paris, France. In two minds about which.

✂ -

Name: Val	Company: Journey Fixers			
Living/working now	*Likes, dislikes and activities*	*Other places lived in*	*Likes, dislikes and activities*	*Future plans*
Oslo, Norway – just arrived one month ago	Not really sure what to make of it yet. Very interested in the culture.	Sydney, Australia Nairobi, Kenya	Not into the outdoor life. Not a good swimmer. Too hot in summer. Hated the traffic and pollution. Did a lot of safaris.	Looking into the possibility of Dublin. Never been there and like the look of it. Or maybe London.

✂ -

Name: Terry	Company: Cultural Tours			
Living/working now	*Likes, dislikes and activities*	*Other places lived in*	*Likes, dislikes and activities*	*Future plans*
Dublin, Ireland – been there two years	People very friendly. Beautiful countryside. Absolutely love it. Lots to do – walking, galleries, music.	Hong Kong Cancun, Mexico	Not a big fan of Chinese food. Weather fantastic. Culture great. Got bored with the beach very quickly. Good weather.	Company sending you to Kenya. Never been to Africa before. They might send you to Oslo, Norway.

appropriate	convenient	management	equality
like	likely	trust	able
accurate	effective	management	necessary
sensitive	appropriate	able	efficient
equality	like	likely	trust
accurate	effective	equality	efficient
sensitive	trust	effective	management

in	dis	in	un
in	in	in	in
in	dis	un	dis
in	in	mis	in
in	in	mis	un
un	dis	un	dis
in	in	mis	In

How will/would things be different if:

... you'd been born in a different country?

... you won a large sum of money on the lottery next week?

... you'd made different decisions about your studies?

... you get home earlier/later than usual tonight?

... you'd made different decisions about your career?

... you were older?

... you didn't study English?

... you hadn't met your best friend?

... you decide not to go to work/school tomorrow?

... you'd got married in younger life?